An Introduction to Geographical Economics

3330-β37-33

(Cₒ)

The need for a better understanding of the role location plays in economic life was made explicit by Bertil Ohlin in 1933. However, it is only recently, with the development of computer packages able to handle complex systems, as well as advances in economic theory (in particular, an increased understanding of returns to scale and imperfect competition), that Ohlin's vision has been met and a framework developed which explains the distribution of economic activity across space.

This book is an integrated, first-principles textbook presenting geographical economics to advanced students. Although not avoiding advanced concepts, its emphasis is on examples, diagrams, and empirical evidence.

STEVEN BRAKMAN is Associate Professor of Economics at the University of Groningen. He has published in journals including *Journal of Regional Science, Journal of Economics, Kyklos,* and *Applied Economics*. He has developed two scientific television programs (one on QWERTY and one on Keynes, together with Harry Garretsen).

HARRY GARRETSEN is Professor of Economics at the University of Nijmegen. He has published in journals including *Journal of Regional Science, Journal of Macroeconomics, Kyklos, Weltwirtschaftliches Archiv, Economics of Transition,* and *Journal of Economic Behavior and Organization*.

CHARLES VAN MARREWIJK is Associate Professor of International Economics at Erasmus University, Rotterdam. He has published in more than twenty international journals, including *Journal of International Economics, Oxford Economic Papers, Journal of Regional Science,* and *International Journal of Industrial Organization*.

Website: http://uk.cambridge.org/economics/resources/

An Introduction to Geographical Economics

Trade, Location and Growth

Steven Brakman

Harry Garretsen and

Charles van Marrewijk

CAMBRIDGE
UNIVERSITY PRESS

PUBLISHED BY THE PRESS SYNDICATE OF THE UNIVERSITY OF CAMBRIDGE
The Pitt Building, Trumpington Street, Cambridge, United Kingdom

CAMBRIDGE UNIVERSITY PRESS
The Edinburgh Building, Cambridge CB2 2RU, UK
40 West 20th Street, New York, NY 10011–4211, USA
477 Williamstown Road, Port Melbourne, VIC 3207, Australia
Ruiz de Alarcón 13, 28014 Madrid, Spain
Dock House, The Waterfront, Cape Town 8001, South Africa

http://www.cambridge.org

© Steven Brakman, Harry Garretsen, and Charles van Marrewijk 2001

First published 2001

Printed in the United Kingdom at the University Press, Cambridge

Typeface Times NR MT 10/13 pt   *System* QuarkXPress™   [SE]

A catalogue record for this book is available from the British Library

Library of Congress Cataloguing in Publication data

Brakman, Steven.
An introduction to geographical economics / Steven Brakman, Harry Garretsen, and
Charles van Marrewijk.
     p.   cm.
Includes bibliographical references and index.
ISBN 0 521 77039 4 (hb) – ISBN 0 521 77967 7 (pb)
1. Economic geography. I. Garretsen, Harry. II. Marrewijk, Charles van. III. Title.
HF1025.B68   2001
330.9 – dc21   2001025419

ISBN 0 521 77039 4 hardback
ISBN 0 521 77967 7 paperback

Contents

Figures

Tables

Technical notes

Special interest boxes

Symbols

C consumption

c_i consumption of manufacturing variety i

D_J intermediate good for sector $J = A,B$

D_{rs} distance from region r to region s

E_{rs} expenditure in region r on goods from region s

F food (representing immobile activity)

I exact price index of manufactures

i, j indices for varieties

K capital stock

L labor force

l_{ir} labor required to produce variety i in region r

M manufactures

N_r number of varieties of manufactures produced in region r

P_r locally charged price for a variety of manufactures in region r

R number of regions

r, s indices for regions

T transport costs; units to be shipped to ensure 1 unit arrives

t time index or iteration index

U utility

W_r wage in region r

w_r real wage in region r

$\bar{w}$ average real wage

x_{ir} amount of variety i produced in region r

x_r total production of manufactures of a representative producer in region r

Y income

y real income

Parameters

α fixed cost

β marginal cost

γ share of labor force in manufactures

δ share of income spent on manufactured goods

ε elasticity of substitution $= 1/(1 - \rho)$

η speed of adjustment

θ miscellaneous parameter

κ miscellaneous parameter (for Lagrangian multiplier, econometric equations and knowledge spillovers)

λ_r share of manufacturing labor force working in region r

μ capital intensity of sector A (factor abundance)

π extent of comparative advantage; profits

ρ love of variety

σ threshold value for real wage differences in simulations

τ congestion

ϕ_r fraction of food labor in region r

Preface

This book offers an introduction to an important new field in economics, entitled *Geographical Economics*, which sets out to explain the distribution of economic activity across space. In doing so, it tries to bring together and apply insights from various fields of economics. The book will therefore be of interest to students and scholars of international economics and business, as well as of economic geography, regional economics, and urban economics. The fact that we offer an "introduction" does not mean that we avoid models or shy away from difficult concepts. It indicates that we have made an effort to write a book that is accessible to readers and students who are new to the field of geographical economics.

Although we introduce and discuss various modeling approaches, we keep the required technicalities to a minimum. Whenever possible we draw attention to important concepts and applications in *special interest boxes*, making ample use of examples and diagrams to explain the workings of the models. Chapter 3, which explains the structure of the core model of geographical economics, gives background derivations in six *technical notes*. Throughout the book the level of mathematical competence required does not rise above simple optimization techniques that should be familiar to upper-level undergraduate and graduate students, both in economics and in other fields of social science. The target audience of our book is not limited to these students, but includes professionals working at government agencies, banks, international organizations, and private research firms, as well as students and scholars of international business and economic geography. The latter category may find the book of interest, if only to get to know what they disagree with when it comes to the analysis of the location of economic activity!

To help the reader in developing his or her intuition for different aspects important in determining the interaction between location decisions and economic performance, and to get a better feel for the modeling structure and empirical relevance of geographical economics, we include discussions of many real-world examples, and present and evaluate the currently available empirical evidence. In addition, we explain in detail an important but often neglected aspect of the geographical economics approach: *computer simulations*. We discuss their advantages and disadvantages, show what is needed to perform such simulations, and give the reader access to a few user-friendly simple simulations (see below). The emphasis on examples, diagrams, and empirical evidence, together with the introductory nature of the book, the limited technical requirements in our analysis, and the attention to explaining simulation exercises, sets our book clearly apart from, and makes it a suitable introduction to, *The Spatial Economy*, the seminal contribution of Masahisa Fujita, Paul Krugman and Anthony Venables which appeared in 1999 and caters to the needs of the academic world (Ph.D. students and fellow researchers).

For a number of reasons, a dedicated *website* is available for this book. First, the site gives brief general background information on the structure of the book. Second, it deals with the *exercises* to be found at the end of every chapter. The exercises not only test the reader's knowledge of the contents of the chapter but are also used to introduce some additional material. Third, the website provides some illustrations and data material on economic location, for example on the rank–size distribution for cities (see chapter 7). Fourth, it provides some simple and user-friendly simulation models, which can familiarize the reader with this aspect of the geographical economics approach. Fifth, for the interested reader the website provides some additional derivations of technical details not dealt with in the book itself, as well as some more advanced (working) papers. Sixth, the website is a source of information for links to relevant researchers and institutions. Finally, it provides some background information on the authors.

In our view, the approach in this book is best characterized as an attempt to put more geography into economics. It is the main reason for us to prefer the term *geographical economics* to alternatives, such as new regional science or the widely used term *new economic geography*. Not only does the label "new" inevitably wear off after some time, but the latter term also has the disadvantage that it suggests that the theory was developed by economic geographers. This is not the case. Instead, geographical economics has its roots firmly in international economics and modern international trade and economic growth theory. It adds the location of economic activity to these theories.

In the end a label is just a label and what really matters, of course, are the topics covered in geographical economics. In 1933 the Swedish economist Bertil Ohlin published a book called *Interregional and International Trade* in which he strongly advocated a closer collaboration between regional economics and what is now called international economics, as they share, in Ohlin's view, the same research objective. To a large extent, geographical economics can be looked upon as a (somewhat belated) reply to Ohlin's call, originating from within international economics. As Paul Krugman, the founding father of geographical economics, puts it, it is an attempt "to resurrect economic geography as a major field within economics."[1] Moreover, it is an attempt in which the modern tools of mainstream economic theory are used to explain the *who*, *why*, and *where* of the location of economic activity.

Geographical economics takes as its starting point the empirical fact that economic activity is not distributed randomly across space. A quick look at any map suffices to

---

[1] Krugman (1991b, p. 7).

make clear that the clustering of people and firms is the rule and not the exception. Geographical economics seeks to give a micro-economic foundation for this fact using a general equilibrium framework. The building-blocks in this framework use *increasing returns to scale, technological and pecuniary spillovers*, as well as *imperfect competition*. These aspects make geographical economics models difficult to solve analytically, so the approach relies to a large extent on *computer simulations* to determine the distribution of economic activity across space and to develop intuition about the strength of the forces involved. Throughout the book we will also often use computer simulations.

Given the target audience, the heart of the book, in chapters 3 and 4, explains in detail the structure and main results of the so-called core model of geographical economics. This is preceded by an introduction in chapter 1 and a discussion of the antecedents of geographical economics in chapter 2. Chapters 5–11 deal with a wide variety of extensions to, and modified empirical applications of, the core model. In our selection of these extensions we deliberately chose ones that require only relatively small modifications of the core model.

The bulk of this book was written during our visit to the School of Management, Yale University in the summer of 1999 and our stay at Trinity College, University of Cambridge in the summer of 2000. We are grateful to both institutions for their hospitality and their willingness to provide us with the facilities necessary to carry out the research for this book. In particular, we would like to thank Jeffrey Garten, Stanley Gartska, Dick Wittink, Peter Leeflang, Willem Buiter, and David Coleman for making these two visits possible. We are also grateful for the financial support we received from our respective faculties, the Department of Economics, University of Groningen (Brakman), the Nijmegen School of Management and NICE (Garretsen), and the Department of Economics of the Erasmus University and the Erasmus University Trust Fund (van Marrewijk).

A number of fellow researchers have been very helpful by commenting on (parts of) this book and by their willingness either to discuss the ideas for this book or to let us use part of their research. We are especially grateful to the following: Xavier Gabaix, Vernon Henderson, Yannis Ioannides, Peter Neary, Ron Martin, Paul Krugman (for pointing out the location of the $100 bill!), and (closer to home) Thijs Knaap, Dirk Stelder, Jolanda Peeters, Marc Schramm, Albert de Vaal, Wilfred Sleegers, Huib Ernste, Rien Wagenvoort, Richard Gigengack, Marianne van den Berg, and Jan Oosterhaven. In addition we would like to thank Stefan Schueller for excellent research assistance and students of international economics at Erasmus University for their comments on drafts of various chapters of this book. At Cambridge University Press, we would like to thank Ashwin Rattan for guidance and support during this project, the five referees whose comments helped to shape the book and Chris Doubleday who prevented us from making embarrassing mistakes. Finally, we are grateful to our respective families for continuous support and for agreeing to let us set up summer camps in New Haven and Cambridge. Without those two stays this book would not have been written.

Website: http://uk.cambridge.org/economics/resources/

Suggested course structure for *An Introduction to Geographical Economics*

An introductory course in geographical economics will have to cover all the basics of the approach and at the same time motivate students by applying their newly developed apparatus. We therefore suggest the rather flexible four-part course structure for our book illustrated in the figure below. First, an introduction into geography, trade, and development based on chapter 1. Optionally, this part may include chapter 2 on earlier theoretical developments, of which Box 2.1 and section 2.3 are recommended. Second, the analysis of the core model of geographical economics based on chapters 3 and 4 (sections 4.8 and 4.9 may be skipped on first reading). Optionally, this part may include chapter 5 on empirical evidence, of which sections 5.5 and 5.6 are recommended. Third, applying the geographical economics model to various fields of research, based on a study of chapter 6 (extensions in general) and a selection of chapters 7 to 10 (cities, multinationals, international trade, and dynamics). Section 7.2 on congestion is recommended for a better understanding of chapters 9 and 11. Fourth, and finally, a concluding part based on chapter 11, which discusses the policy implications of geographical economics and gives a critical assessment of the approach.

Course structure for *An introduction to geographical economics*

I   Introduction

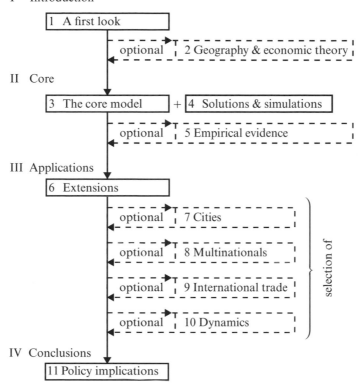

II Core

III Applications

IV Conclusions

1   A first look at geography, trade, and development

1.1   Introduction

It happened on October 12, 1999, at least according to the United Nations (UN).[1] From that day more than 6 billion people have inhabited the planet Earth. Of course, given the inaccuracy of the data, the UN could have been off by 100 million people or so. Every day some 100 million billion sperms are released[2] and 400,000 babies are born, whereas "only" 140,000 persons die. Consequently, the world population has been growing rapidly, especially over the second half of the twentieth century.

Given the average population density in the world, about 44 persons per square kilometer, if you are part of a family with two children, your family could have about 9 hectares (or 22.5 acres) at its disposal. The large majority of our readers will probably look around in amazement to conclude that they do not own an area close to this size. The reason is simple: the world population is unevenly distributed. But why?

There may be many reasons why people cluster together: sociological – you like to interact with other human beings; psychological – you are afraid to be alone; historical – your grandfather already lived where you live now; cultural – the atmosphere here is unlike anywhere else in the world; geographical – the scenery is breathtaking and the beach is wonderful. At best we will discuss the above reasons for clustering only cursorily, because our attention in this book will be focused on the *economic* rationale behind clustering or agglomeration.

In a sense, an economic motive behind population clustering might be a prerequisite for other motives. Psychological, sociological, cultural, and historical motives may have developed largely in response to an economic motive that brought people together to live in villages and cities. Before elaborating in the next chapter on how the mainstream of the economics profession until recently has dropped the ball with respect to providing a simple consistent explanation for the spatial dimensions of the economy,

---

[1] The data in the first paragraph are from http://www.popexpo.net/english.html. Unless otherwise specified, all other empirical information in chapter 1 is based on our own calculations using data from the World Bank Development Indicators CD-ROM, 1999.
[2] Apparently, the UN is familiar with our sexual habits.

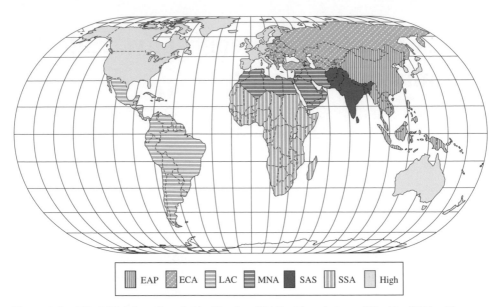

Figure 1.1.   World Bank regional classification (EAP = East Asia and Pacific; ECA = Europe and Central Asia; LAC = Latin America and Caribbean; MNA = Middle East and North Africa; SAS = South Asia; SSA = Sub-Saharan Africa; High = high-income countries).

we will first briefly describe some of the characteristics of clustering of economies in space and their interactions.

1.2   Clusters in the world economy

In describing clustering, it is useful to distinguish between various levels of aggregation at which clustering occurs:

- the global level (subsection 1.2.1, world-wide distribution of activity and resources)
- the continental level (subsection 1.2.2, population density in Europe)
- the country level (subsection 1.2.3, urban agglomeration in India)

The main reason for looking at these different levels of aggregation is that in explaining clustering, geographical economics shows that to a large extent the same basic forces apply at all levels of aggregation.

1.2.1   The global view

The World Bank collects and processes statistical information from virtually all countries in the world. To characterize various regions at a global scale the World Bank aggregates country data into the seven groups (Figure 1.1):

(i)   East Asia and Pacific (e.g. China and Indonesia),
(ii)   (East) Europe and Central Asia (e.g. Russia and Turkey),

(iii)   Latin America and Caribbean (e.g. Brazil and Mexico),

(iv)   Middle East and North Africa (e.g. Egypt),

(v)   South Asia (e.g. India),

(vi)   Sub-Saharan Africa (e.g. Nigeria and South Africa), and

(vii)   the high-income countries (e.g. the United States, the countries of the European Union, and Japan).

We will use this grouping to describe regional diversity at the global level.

Figures 1.2 and 1.3 illustrate some key economic data for the above global regional classification. These data are listed in the appendix to this chapter (Table 1A.1). There is considerable variation in land area (Figure 1.2a), from 4.8 million km² (4% of the world total) for South Asia to 31.0 million km² (25% of the world total) for the high-income countries. This can, of course, simply be an artifact of the classification method. The same holds, necessary changes being made, for the large differences in population size (Figure 1.2b), ranging from 280 million people (5%) for North Africa to 1,751 million people (30%) for East Asia. The variation becomes more striking when we investigate the ratio of these two measures, that is the population density (Figure 1.3c). The number of persons per km² varies from 20 for Europe and Central Asia to 263 for South Asia, which is more than ten times as high. There is thus an enormous difference in the distribution of the population, even at such a high level of aggregation. We return to this issue in the next section. For now, we concentrate on some of the other characteristics of the World Bank regions.

Figure 1.2c clearly shows that the distribution of economic mass, as measured by the total value of all goods and services produced in each global region, is very skewed: the gross national product (GNP) of the high-income countries accounts for 78% of world production calculated in current United States dollars, but uses only 16% of the world population. Measured similarly, Sub-Saharan Africa accounts for 1% of world production using 11% of the world population. These production levels translate into enormous differences in per capita income (Figure 1.3b), ranging from $380 per year in Sub-Saharan Africa to $25,890 per year for the high-income countries. A word of caution, however, is in order at this point. If we want to compare GNP, that is the value of production, in different countries we have to express this in a common unit of measurement, usually the US dollar. Since exchange rates tend to fluctuate widely, the World Bank calculates an average over three years for conversion (the "Atlas" method). These are the statistics reported above. However, price levels for non-tradable goods and services differ considerably between countries. Going to a movie in the United States may cost you $8, while going to the same movie in Tanzania may cost you less than $1. Getting a haircut in Amsterdam will cost you at least $10, rather than the $2 you will pay in Manila. To correct for these differences in purchasing power the United Nations devotes a lot of time and effort, gathering data on the prices of thousands of goods and services in virtually all countries, to calculating as accurately as possible "Purchasing Power Parity" (PPP) exchange rates.

A better estimate of the economic size of a region is therefore given when we use PPP

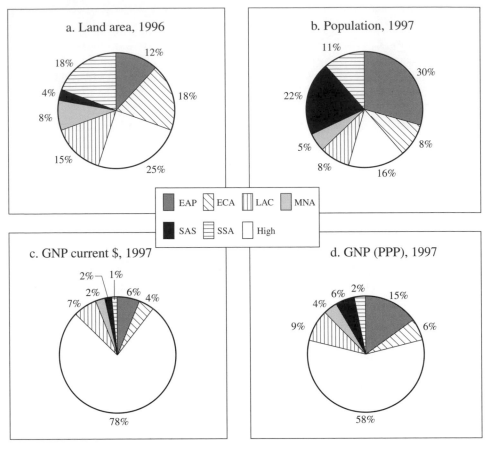

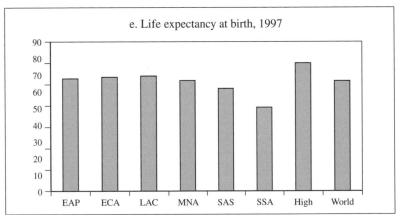

Figure 1.2. Life expectancy and regional shares of population, land, and income (EAP = East Asia and Pacific; ECA = Europe and Central Asia; LAC = Latin America and Caribbean; MNA = Middle East and North Africa; SAS = South Asia; SSA = Sub-Saharan Africa; High = high-income countries).

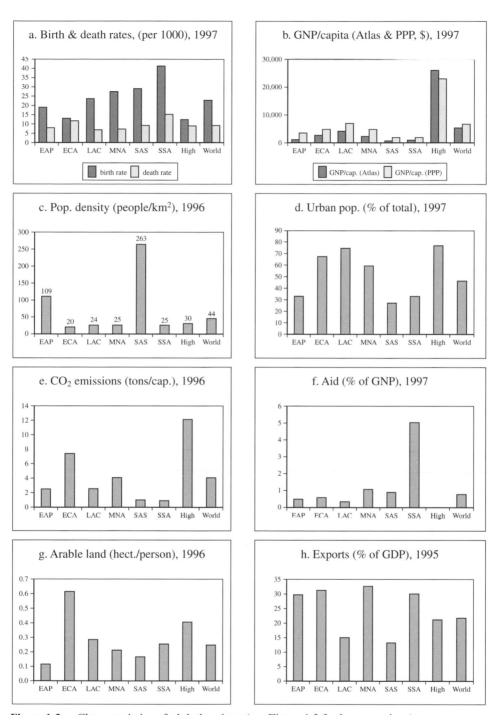

Figure 1.3. Characteristics of global regions (see Figure 1.2 for key to regions).

exchange rates rather than current dollars (or the Atlas method). It turns out that $1 in China or India will deliver you approximately the same consumption basket as $4 in the USA or more than $6 in Japan. Figure 1.2d shows that, even after correction for PPP, the high-income countries still produce most goods and services (roughly 58% of world production), leading to somewhat smaller, but still sizeable differences in per capita income (Figure 1.3b).

Most other characteristics are correlated with income per capita; see Table 1.A2 in the appendix to this chapter. People with higher incomes tend to live longer (Figure 1.2e), have more arable land at their disposal (Figure 1.3g), have fewer children (Figure 1.3a), live in cities (Figure 1.3d), receive little foreign aid (Figure 1.3f), and pollute more, especially with greenhouse gases (Figure 1.3e). Of course, there are some note-worthy exceptions. For example, (East) Europe and Central Asia has (relative to PPP income per capita) a lot of arable land available (Figure 1.3g), is highly urbanized (Figure 1.3d), and pollutes heavily (Figure 1.3e). Similarly, Latin America and North Africa and the Middle East are also highly urbanized.

Other variables are only weakly correlated with per capita income. Although death rates, for example, are particularly high in poor Sub-Saharan Africa (in part as a result of the AIDS epidemic, which may explain the high inflow of foreign aid), they are lower in Latin America and North Africa and the Middle East than in the high-income countries, which are confronted with rapidly aging populations. Remarkably, perhaps, the openness of the global regions, as measured by the percentage of GDP exported, is hardly correlated with per capita income. We will get back to this issue in chapters 8 and 9.

This subsection has shown, *inter alia*, that the world population is very unevenly dis-tributed when viewed on the large scale at which only seven regions are identified in the world. Economic activity is even more unevenly distributed than population, measured using either the Atlas method or Purchasing Power Parity. Moreover, we indicated that at this large scale there is a strong correlation between the degree of urbanization and per capita income (Table 1.A2). The next two subsections "zoom in" on the distribu-tion of activity in two stages, first to the continental level for nations and then to the national level for cities. The latter concludes by drawing attention to a remarkable empirical regularity known as the *rank–size distribution*.

1.2.2   *Population distribution in Europe*

Figure 1.4 illustrates the first "zooming in" step, where we pick the continent of Europe as an example. In terms of the regional classification of subsection 1.2.1 about half of the countries in the figure, mainly in the west, belong to the region of high-income countries (High), while the other half is part of the (East) Europe and Central Asia (ECA) region. The figure illustrates the large variation in population density at the national level for both of these global regions. Among the ECA countries the number of people per square kilometer ranges from 9 for Russia to 134 for Armenia. Among the high-income countries the variation is even larger, from a low of 3 for Iceland to a

Figure 1.4. Population density in Europe.

high of 457 for the Netherlands. The main question is, of course, why do people choose to cluster so closely together at the national level? Why do the Dutch not move *en masse* to France, which is equally wealthy but has a lot more living space available?

It is also apparent from Figure 1.4 that the clustering of activity tends to cross national boundaries. Clearly, there is a densely populated group of countries in the center of Europe, consisting of the United Kingdom, Belgium, the Netherlands, Germany, Switzerland, and Italy. This is bordered on both sides by somewhat less densely populated countries, and beyond these there are the scarcely populated countries in the north-east. This suggests some form of economic interaction among those countries which gives rise to such a coherent distribution of activity. At the same time (not shown here), we also know that within most European countries both population and economic activity are not distributed evenly. Think for instance of the differences between eastern and western Germany or between the northern and southern parts of the UK and Italy.

1.2.3 *Urban agglomeration in India*

Table 1.1 illustrates the second "zooming in" step, where we take the urban agglomerations in India as an example. The table lists just the ten largest urban agglomerations

Table 1.1. *Ten largest urban agglomerations in India*

	Population	Rank	Ln(rank)	Ln(population)
Bombay	12,596	1	0.0	16.3
Calcutta	11,022	2	0.7	16.2
Delhi	8,419	3	1.1	15.9
Madras	5,422	4	1.4	15.5
Hyderabad	4,344	5	1.6	15.3
Bangalore	4,130	6	1.8	15.2
Ahmedabad	3,312	7	1.9	15.0
Pune	2,494	8	2.1	14.7
Kanpur	2,030	9	2.2	14.5
Lucknow	1,669	10	2.3	14.3

Source: See chapter 7 (data for 1991). Population $\times$ 1,000.

in India, but Figure 1.5 is based on the 165 largest agglomerations. Even if we restrict attention to the ten largest agglomerations, we are again confronted with a considerable variation in size, and thus of population density, at the national level, ranging from about 12.5 million people in Bombay, the largest agglomeration, to about 1.7 million in Lucknow, the tenth largest.

We illustrated the large variation in density of population and economic activity at the global, continental, and national levels. It appears that the highly uneven distribution of economic activity across space has a fractal dimension, that is it repeats itself at different levels of aggregation. An important question is whether the spatial similarities between different levels of aggregation imply (at least partly) that the same clustering mechanisms are at work at the global, continental, and national levels. Another crucial question that we will address in this book is why there is clustering of economic activity at all. Finally, we will address the *regularity* of the distribution of economic activity, mainly in chapter 7. In fact, the distribution follows a remarkable pattern throughout the world. We illustrate this using the city-size distribution in India. Table 1.1 orders the ten largest urban agglomerations, first Bombay, then Calcutta, then Delhi, etc. In columns 3 and 4, we take the natural logarithms of rank and population. We do this for all 165 agglomerations in India with at least 100,000 people. Finally, we plot the log of the rank and the log of the size in Figure 1.5. The outcome is an almost perfect straight line.

Obviously, there is a negative relationship between size and rank by construction. The puzzling feature is why this is an almost perfect log-linear straight line. If, based on the data plotted in Figure 1.5, one performs a simple regression for India the estimation results yield the following rank-size distribution:

$$\ln(\text{population}) = 16.938 - 1.0482 \cdot \ln(\text{rank}) \qquad (1.1)$$

This regression explains 99.16% of the variance in city size. Based on this estimate of the rank-size distribution for India we would predict the size of the population of

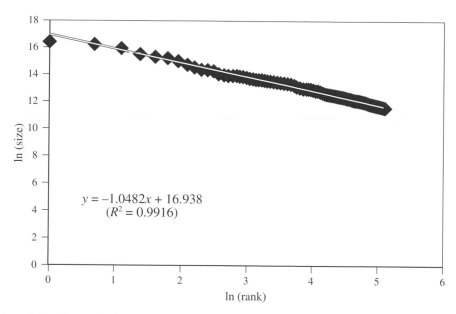

Figure 1.5. The rank–size distribution for India (urban agglomerations, 1991).

urban agglomeration number 100, for example, to be 182,000 people. This is very close to the actual size of number 100 (Tumkur), which has 180,000 people. By far the largest deviation between predicted and actual size, as evident from Figure 1.5, is for the largest urban agglomeration (Bombay). The fact that the largest agglomeration, the so-called "primate city," usually does not perform well for the rank-size distribution is a well-known problem which will be further investigated in chapter 7. All in all, the empirical success of the rank-size distribution for many countries, indicating a well-ordered pattern underlying the distribution of economic activity, poses an economic modeler the formidable task of constructing a coherent model in accordance with this empirical regularity.

1.3 Economic interaction

The uneven distribution of economic activity, and the apparent regularity in this distribution, tempts us to have a first look at the structure of the interaction between different economic centers. Clearly, such interaction takes place in many different ways, most notably in the form of trade of goods and services, but also in the shape of capital and labor flows, or via the various means of modern communication, the exchange of ideas, and the exposure to other cultural influences, etc. Again, we will give two suggestive examples to which we will return later in this book. We start with a mini-case study of the hard disk drive industry, and then move on to the structure of German trade with respect to geographic distance.

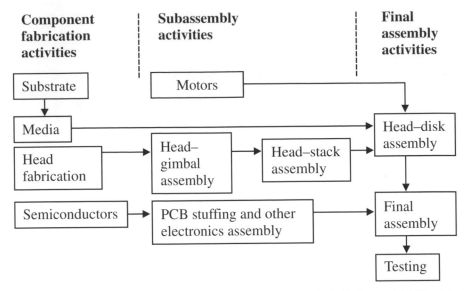

Figure 1.6. The hard disk drive value chain (based on Gourevitch, Bohn, and McKendrick 2000, Figure 1).

1.3.1 An example at the firm level: hard disk drives[3]

The manufacture of hard disk drives (HDD), essential components for the computer industry, is a very dynamic industry, with revenues of more than $30 billion, product life cycles of less than eighteen months, and prices falling at more than 40% per annum for more than a decade. Fifteen years ago not only was 80% of all production done by US firms but the same was true for the assembly activities. As we shall see, the pressure of globalization has rapidly changed the structure of doing business, as measured by the value chain, in this high-tech industry dominated by multinationals (see chapter 8).

Figure 1.6 gives a simplified picture of the main steps in the HDD value chain, the sequence and range of activities that go into making a final product. Ignoring R&D there are four major steps in the value chain: (i) electronics: this includes semiconductors, printed circuit boards (PCBs) and their assembly, (ii) heads: devices that read and write the data, which are manufactured in stages with labor-intensive subassembly activities, such as head–gimbal assembly (HGA) and head–stack assembly (HSA), (iii) media: the material on which the information is stored,[4] and (iv) motors: these spin the media with extreme precision.[5] Producers locate the the many discrete steps in the value chain around the world for various reasons. The final assembly of the disk, which gives

---

[3] This subsection is based on Gourevitch, Bohn, and McKendrick (2000).
[4] According to Gourevitch, Bohn, and McKendrick (2000, p. 304): "Typically, aluminum blank substrates are nickel-plated and polished before the platters are sputtered and finished. As with heads, media are a very high-technology aspect of HDD production."
[5] The Japanese Nippon Densan company has about a 75 percent world-wide market share in motors.

Table 1.2. *Hard disk drives: indicators of nationality of production*

Measure[a]	USA	Japan	S.E. Asia	Other Asia	Europe	Other
Nationality of firm	88.4	9.4	0	2.2	0	0
Final assembly	4.6	15.5	64.2	5.7	10.0	0
Employment	19.3	8.3	44.0	17.1	4.7	6.5
Wages paid	39.5	29.7	12.9	3.3	8.5	6.1

Note:
[a] Nationality of firm (percentage of unit output); location of final assembly; employment in value chain; and wages paid in value chain, respectively.
Source: Gourevitch, Bohn, and McKendrick (2000), Table 2 (data for 1995). All numbers as percentage of world total.

it the "Made in Singapore" or "Made in Taiwan" label, is only one, and not necessarily the most important, aspect in this process. As Gourevitch, Bohn, and McKendrick (2000), discussing the structure of Seagate, the world's largest manufacturer of HDDs, put it:

> Although Seagate has kept control over almost all production, it has globally dispersed its operations to an extraordinary degree. A single component may be worked on in five countries and cross two oceans while Seagate is building it up through its value chain. Seagate develops new products (and processes) at seven locations in the United States and Singapore. It assembles disk drives in Singapore, Malaysia, Thailand, and China. In heads, the company fabricates its wafers in the United States and Northern Ireland, and cuts them into bars and assembles them into HGAs in Thailand, Malaysia, and the Philippines. It makes media in Singapore and motors in Thailand. It manufactures printed circuit cables in Thailand and assembles the electronics onto printed circuit boards in Indonesia, Malaysia, and Singapore. It is the largest nongovernment employer in Thailand and Singapore (pp. 304–305).

Table 1.2 gives four different indicators of nationality of production for the HDD industry. The great majority (88.4% per unit of output) of HDDs are made by US firms. But in sharp contrast to fifteen years ago, only 4.6% of the final assembly of HDDs takes place in the United States. Most final assembly of disks now takes place in S.E. Asia (64.2%), which means the bulk of employment is in S.E. Asia (44%), rather than in the USA (19.3%), although the value of wages paid is much higher in the USA (39.5%) than in S.E. Asia (12.9%). Essentially, the HDD industry currently is concentrated in two clusters. The first is in Silicon Valley in the United States, with a substantial share of research, design, development, marketing, and management (with a smaller counterpart in Japan). The second is in Southeast Asia, which dominates final assembly, most labor-intensive subassemblies, and low-tech components, such as baseplates. The question why we have clustering is a central theme of this book. At the industry level this phenomenon is known as concentration; see chapters 5, 6 and 8. The hard disk drive industry discussed here is only an example. Similar concentration and

Table 1.3. *Germany: fifteen largest export markets, 1998*

	Exports	GDP	Distance to Germany
1 France	60.3	1,427	809
2 United States	51.1	8,230	7,836
3 United Kingdom	46.3	1,357	876
4 Italy	40.1	1,172	963
5 Netherlands	38.1	382	349
6 Belgium[a]	30.9	248	425
7 Austria	29.5	212	482
8 Switzerland	24.3	264	468
9 Spain	21.9	553	1,632
10 Poland	13.7	159	632
11 Sweden	12.5	226	1,259
12 Czech Republic	10.7	56	404
13 Japan	10.4	3,783	9,085
14 Denmark	9.4	175	556
15 Hungary	8.7	48	853

Note:
[a] Includes Luxembourg.
Sources: OECD (exports, 1998, in billion dollars). Data from World Bank (GDP, 1998, in billion dollars), and *Britannica Atlas* (distance in kilometers between geographic centers).

globalization results hold for other industries, such as automobiles, entertainment, and the clothing industry. Clearly, this is an aspect of modern production with a distinct geographical flavor.

1.3.2 Germany, trade, and distance

To illustrate the structure of the interaction between economic centers at the national level we focus on Germany, the largest European economy. Germany is located right in the center of the European population agglomeration (see Figure 1.4), and it is also the largest European exporter of goods and services. Table 1.3, listing the fifteen largest German export markets, gives two additional pieces of information, namely the gross domestic product (GDP) of those export markets and the "distance to Germany." The latter is explained in detail below.

A respectable $60.3 billion of German exports go to France, a neighbor of Germany and its largest export market. Remarkably, German exports to France are 20% higher than German exports to the United States, *the* economic giant in the world, with a GDP that is almost six times that of France. Similarly, German exports to France are six times higher than those to Japan, the other economic giant. In fact, Japan ranks only thirteenth on the German export market list, far behind the Netherlands, another neighbor of Germany, which ranks fifth and imports almost four times as much from Germany than Japan with an economy that is only 10% of the size of Japan's. Both the

United States and Japan are much further away from Germany than either France or the Netherlands. Apparently, there is a strong local flavor to the German top export markets: the top fifteen include all eight German neighbors,[6] the majority of which are rather small countries.

The export of goods and services from one country to another involves time, effort, and hence costs. Goods have to be physically loaded and unloaded, transported by truck, train, ship, or plane, packed, insured, traced, etc. before they reach their destination. There they have to be unpacked, checked, assembled, and displayed before they can be sold to the consumer or an intermediate firm. A distribution and maintenance network has to be established, and the exporter will have to familiarize herself with the (legal) rules and procedures in another country, usually in another language and embedded in a different culture. All of this involves costs, which tend to increase with "distance." As indicated above, this can be either physical distance, which may be aggravated or alleviated by geographical phenomena such as mountain ranges or easy access to good waterways, or political, cultural, or social distance, which also requires time and effort before one can successfully engage in international business. Throughout this book we will use the term "transport costs" as a shorthand notation for both types of distance described above. The presumption is, of course, that as transport costs increase it will become more difficult to trade goods and services between nations. The nature of transport costs is further discussed in chapters 3 and 5.

Table 1.3 gives a first impression of the relationship between transport costs and trade flows. As an initial and rather crude proxy for transport costs we calculated the "distance to Germany" for all German export markets. We took the coordinates of the geographic center of each nation as the hypothetical center of economic activity. We then act as if all German export flows are simply from the German economic center to each nation's economic center. To confirm the impression on the negative relationship between distance and trade flows given by Table 1.3 we plotted the natural logarithm of German exports against the natural logarithm of the distance to Germany for 136 German trading partners in Figure 1.7a.

To get a somewhat better idea, we performed a simple regression (t-value in parentheses):

$$\ln(\text{exports}) = 15.07 - 1.4172 \cdot \ln(\text{distance}); \qquad R^2 = 0.2534 \qquad (1.2)$$
$$(-6.74)$$

This is a first confirmation of the negative relationship between distance and trade flows. Distance is, obviously, not the only determinant of trade flows. As Table 1.3 indicates, for example, exports from Germany to Italy are larger than from Germany to Holland, even though Italy is about three times as far away using our measure of distance. Italy, however, is a much larger country (with a higher population and larger GDP) than Holland, such that the potential demand for German goods is, other things equal, larger in Italy than in Holland. Figure 1.7b corrects the German export flows

---

[6] France, the Netherlands, Belgium (which includes Luxembourg in the trade statistics), Austria, Switzerland, Poland, the Czech Republic, and Denmark.

a. German exports

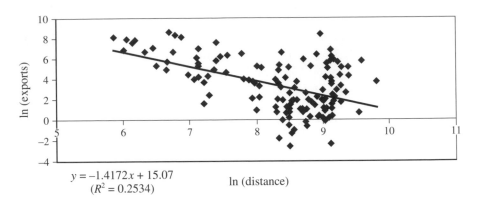

$$y = -1.4172x + 15.07$$
$$(R^2 = 0.2534)$$

ln (distance)

b. German exports, income-adjusted

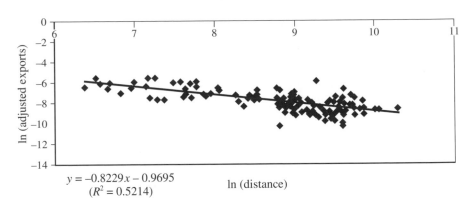

$$y = -0.8229x - 0.9695$$
$$(R^2 = 0.5214)$$

ln (distance)

Figure 1.7.   German exports and distance (monthly average, 1998). *Source*: Data from OECD (exports), *Britannica Atlas* (distance).

for this demand effect, by dividing exports by a country's GDP, and then portrays again the impact of distance on trade flows. The relationship is clearly "tighter" this way.[7] A simple regression gives (*t*-value in parentheses):

$$\text{ln(adjusted exports)} = -0.9695 - 0.8229 \cdot \text{ln(distance)}; \qquad R^2 = 0.5214$$
$$(-12.08) \tag{1.3}$$

Apparently, about 52% of the variation in German (adjusted) export flows can be explained this way. Since the estimated coefficient on distance can be interpreted as an elasticity it indicates that, other things being equal, a 10% increase in the distance to the

---

[7] Note that the range of the vertical scale is identical in the two panels of Figure 1.7.

German economic center results in an 8.2% drop in export flows from Germany. More details on this so-called "gravity" analysis will be given in chapters 2 and 9. A similar relationship, known as the "market potential" approach, has been widely used in regional economics. It will be explained in chapter 2 and applied to Germany in chapter 5.

1.4 Rapid change in the distribution of population and production

So far, we have seen several examples of the uneven distribution across space of population and economic activity, as well as the regularity in this distribution, and two examples of interaction between economic centers. As these were all rather recent examples the question may arise whether economic activity was always unevenly distributed. The answer is: "yes and no."

The answer is "yes" in the sense that cities, for example, began to emerge at the time of the Neolithic revolution as a consequence of an increase in agricultural surplus; see Huriot and Thisse (2000). Although the nature of cities has changed over time from the ancient cities of Mesopotamia, China, and India, through the city-states of Greece to the large metropolises of our time, they have, as dense concentrations of people, always represented centers of economic, political, cultural, sociological, military, and scientific power. As such, cities have to a large extent dominated the chain of events and the decisions taken in many different areas of human activity over the course of history. The balance of power between these economic centers has, of course, drastically changed over time. The cities of Egypt and Greece, for example, no longer exert the same influence they once had; nor do the cities of Britain, China, Spain, and so many other nations. However, the phenomenon "city" as such, as a representative of the uneven distribution of activity, has been with us for a long time.

The answer is "no" in the sense that the skewness or "unevenness" of the distribution of economic activity has changed over time. The clearest example in this respect is perhaps the degree of urbanization in Europe; see Bairoch (1988). Figure 1.8 shows the share of the European population in cities from 1300 to the present. The most striking feature about Figure 1.8 is how rapid such a fundamental phenomenon as the degree of urbanization can change over time when put in the proper historical perspective.[8] Until the beginning of the nineteenth century the urban share of the population increased very slowly from about 10% to 12%. Around 1800 the *urban revolution*, fueled by the Industrial Revolution (Huriot and Thisse, 2000, p. ix) drastically increased the attractiveness of the city as a place to live and work, such that the urban share of the population increased rapidly over the next 200 years to its current level of around 75%. This confronts the geographic economic modeler with yet another challenge: the model must in principle be able to explain rapid changes in the distribution of economic activity across space. This challenge does not only exist for the (changes in) the distribution of economic activity at the city level, it also exists on a global level. Figure 1.9 shows

---

[8] Chapter 7 argues that the degree of urbanization will affect the distribution of economic activity across space, as measured by the rank–size distribution, but not the regularity in this distribution.

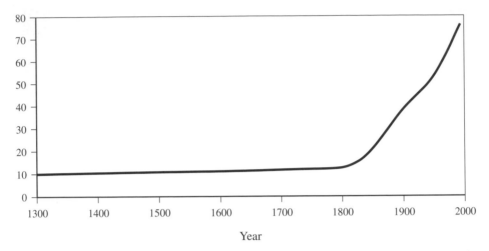

Figure 1.8.   Urban share of population in Europe. *Source*: Based on data from Huriot and Thisse 2000, p. ix.

the evolution of the share in world production, measured as a nation's GDP relative to world GDP, for four Asian countries (Japan, South Korea, Hong Kong, and Singapore) in the period 1960–99. The increase is striking for all four countries and most pronounced (as a percentage change) for South Korea. Note that these impressive increases in the share of world production indicate that output in these countries increased substantially faster than world output. Moreover, the changes occurred very rapidly and almost at the same time.

1.5   Overview of the book

The various examples and discussions presented in this chapter paint a relatively clear picture. The distribution of population and economic activity across space is very uneven, with a strong clustering or agglomeration of economic activity in various important centers. We gave illustrations of this phenomenon at the global, continental, and national levels. This suggests that there is a fractal aspect to these observations, that is they repeat themselves at various levels of aggregation. Moreover, the distribution across space is not random but follows a remarkable pattern known as the rank–size distribution. These observations suggest that similar, but not necessarily identical, economic forces may be relevant in explaining the clustering phenomenon and its regularities at different levels of aggregation.[9]

   We have also discussed the interaction between economic centers. First, using a mini-case study of the hard disk drive industry, which is dominated by multinationals trying to use the locational advantages of different nations in the production process. We found essentially two global concentrations for this industry, in Silicon Valley and in

---

[9] There have been studies of the rank–size distribution at the firm level as well.

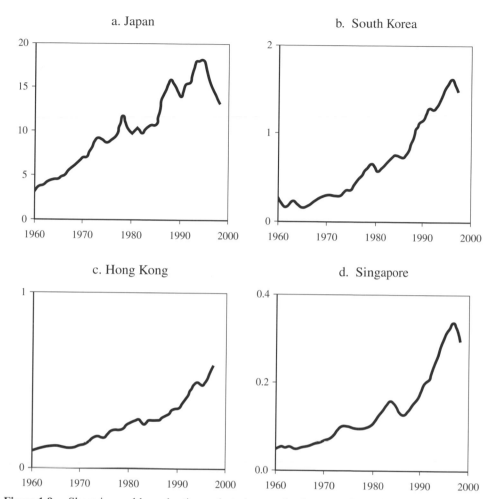

Figure 1.9.   Share in world production, selected countries (country GDP / world GDP).

Southeast Asia. Second, we briefly investigated the relationship between German exports and the distance of the export market to Germany. After correcting for the size of the destination market this relationship was clearly negative, a phenomenon known as the gravity equation. Finally, we showed that the uneven distribution of activity across space could change very rapidly over time, as demonstrated by the share of the urban population in Europe.

The remainder of this book will, of course, get back to the issues raised in this chapter in more detail. The question at this point is how to proceed. The empirical phenomena touched upon above have been studied thoroughly from many different angles, based on different theoretical frameworks, for a long time. From what is primarily a location perspective there are urban economics, economic geography, regional economics, and regional science. The interaction between economic centers is addressed by international economics, development economics, and industrial organization. One way to proceed would be to investigate each empirical phenomenon separately, using the insights of those of the above fields, inside or outside economics, which are thought to be relevant for the issue at hand. Clearly, the rest of the book would be rather fragmentary if we were to proceed in this way. Instead, we proceed differently. We have already mentioned that the fractal nature of the location phenomena described in this chapter suggests that similar economic forces might be relevant in explaining them. We therefore use throughout this book a common structural approach to help understand the phenomena that are introduced in this chapter. In fact, finding a common framework to get a better grip on a plethora of (economic) data is what makes economic models useful. That being said, the common framework should not become a straitjacket. As we shall see time and again in the chapters to come, if we want to explain a particular economic phenomenon we will have to be flexible in adapting the common framework to better suit the problem at hand. In each of those instances we will draw inspiration from the various fields of research mentioned above.[10] As explained in the preface of this book we follow the suggestions of Martin (1999, p. 67) and Fujita and Thisse (2000, p. 6) in terming this approach *geographical economics* which in our view is better suited than the often used phrase "new economic geography." The size of this book, or any other book for that matter, does not allow us to take full advantage of all insights of all contributing fields. We thus have to be eclectic in what we do and do not use, and hope that we make the right choices most of the time. We are, however, selective in our choices in the sense that we use only those insights from different fields that we can relate to the core geographical economics model.

Chapter 2 gives a brief overview of the most influential fields of economics used in the remainder of the book. Chapter 3 explains the common framework, referred to as the "core model," which is adapted to our particular needs in the subsequent chapters. Chapter 4 characterizes some important aspects of the core model and explains in detail what "simulations" are, how to use them, and what their advantages and disadvantages are. Chapter 5 gives an overview of empirical evidence to assess the relevance of geographical economics. In accordance with our modeling strategy, chapter 6 explains, using some examples, how we can adapt the core model for application purposes. As is often the case, fully appreciating the general modeling strategy is a "learning by doing" experience, as shown in chapters 7 (city distributions), 8 (multinationals), 9 (international trade), and 10 (dynamics and growth). We evaluate the geographical economics approach in chapter 11, where we also discuss in some detail avenues for further research and the policy implications of the geographical economics approach.

Appendix

Table 1.A1 summarizes the information on global regional characteristics which is illustrated graphically in section 1.2.

---

[10] *Inter alia*, urban economics, economic geography, spatial economics, regional science, international economics, development economics, and industrial organization.

Table 1.A1. *Global regional characteristics*[a]

Variable[b]	EAP	ECA	LAC	MNA	SAS	High	SSA	World
Land area	15.9	23.8	20.1	11.0	4.8	31.0	23.6	130.2
Population	1,751	474	494	280	1,281	927	612	5,820
Pop. density	109	20	24	25	263	30	25	44
GNP	1,898	1,156	1,963	706	590	22,868	323	28,908
GNP (PPP)	5,551	2,095	3,324	1,295	2,037	21,257	894	36,431
GNP/cap (Atlas)	970	2,310	3,940	2,070	380	25,890	510	5,180
GNP/cap (PPP)	3,170	4,420	6,730	4,630	1,590	22,930	1,460	6,260
Birth rate	18.9	12.8	23.2	27.0	28.6	12.2	40.8	22.5
Death rate	7.5	11.2	6.5	6.6	9.1	8.5	14.8	8.9
Arable/cap	0.11	0.61	0.28	0.21	0.16	0.40	0.25	0.24
CO_2/cap	2.5	7.4	2.5	3.9	0.9	12.1	0.8	4.0
Export %	30.1	31.4	15.1	32.9	13.3	21.2	30.2	21.6
Aid %	0.47	0.53	0.31	1.03	0.83	—	5.03	0.74
Life exp.	68.5	68.7	69.6	66.9	62.2	77.1	50.8	66.7
Urban %	33.0	67.0	74.2	58.4	27.0	76.4	32.3	46.0

Notes:

[a] EAP = East Asia and Pacific; ECA = Europe and Central Asia; LAC = Latin America and Caribbean; MNA = Middle East and North Africa; SAS = South Asia; SSA = Sub-Saharan Africa; High = high-income countries.

[b] Respectively: land area (million km², 1996); population (millions, 1997); population density (people per km², 1996); GNP at market prices (current billion US$, 1997); GNP per capita, Atlas method (current US$, 1997); GNP per capita, PPP (current international $, 1997); birth rate, crude (per 1,000 people, 1997); death rate, crude (per 1,000 people, 1997); arable land (hectares per capita, 1996); CO_2 emissions, industrial (metric tons per capita, 1996); exports of goods and services (% of GDP, 1996); aid (% of GNP, 1995); life expectancy at birth, total (years, 1997); urban population (% of total, 1997).

Table 1.A2. *Correlation coefficients*

	LA	POP	DEN	YAT	YPP	YAc	YPc	BIR	DEA	LAc	CO$_2$	EXP	AID	LIF	URB
LA	1.00														
POP	-0.25	1.00													
DEN	-0.73	0.66	1.00												
YAT	0.63	0.10	-0.21	1.00											
YPP	0.60	0.23	-0.16	0.99	1.00										
YAc	0.65	0.00	-0.27	0.99	0.97	1.00									
YPc	0.65	-0.04	-0.33	0.98	0.96	0.99	1.00								
BIR	-0.37	-0.15	0.16	-0.53	-0.58	-0.54	-0.59	1.00							
DEA	0.33	-0.14	-0.10	-0.15	-0.21	-0.17	-0.25	0.47	1.00						
LAc	0.64	-0.51	-0.51	0.29	0.22	0.34	0.36	-0.53	0.30	1.00					
CO$_2$	0.68	-0.15	-0.42	0.85	0.82	0.87	0.88	-0.78	-0.13	0.67	1.00				
EXP	0.20	-0.21	-0.53	-0.21	-0.22	-0.22	-0.21	0.02	0.29	0.18	0.09	1.00			
AID	0.36	-0.20	-0.22	-0.65	-0.55	-0.49	-0.59	0.84	0.83	-0.08	-0.45	.29	1.00		
LIF	0.28	0.09	-0.17	0.63	0.67	0.65	0.72	-0.91	-0.72	0.32	0.75	-0.19	-0.95	1.00	
URB	0.59	-0.57	-0.67	0.52	0.47	0.60	0.68	-0.63	-0.37	0.65	0.73	-0.07	-0.43	0.72	1.00

Notes:
LA = land area, POP = population, DEN = population density, YAT = GNP (Atlas), YPP = GNP (PPP), YAc = GNP/cap. (Atlas), YPc = GNP/cap. (PPP), BIR = birth rate, DEA = death rate, LAc = arable/cap., CO$_2$ = CO$_2$/cap., EXP = export %, AID = aid %, LIF = life expectancy, URB = urban%; see Table 1.A1 for further details.

Exercises

*Note: Throughout the book, exercises marked * are more advanced.*

1.1 The website for this book gives additional information on the rank–size distribution of cities for many countries, as illustrated in Figure 1.5 for India. This remarkable phenomenon will be further investigated in chapter 7. Go to the website and look up the q-value (the slope of the line in Figure 1.5) and the R^2 for the column "city proper" in the graphs of the following countries: Egypt, South Africa, France, UK, Poland, Japan, South Korea, Russia, Turkey, USA, and Brazil. Comment on your general findings.

1.2 Table 1.3 and Figure 1.7 show a negative relationship between the size of the export market and the distance to those markets for Germany. Does a similar relationship hold for your country? Do the following:

(i)   Find the ten or fifteen largest export markets for your country.
(ii)   Determine the "distance" from your country to those markets, for example using the number of kilometers between the capital cities or another, perhaps more appropriate measure.
(iii) Make a plot of your findings (in logs) and give comments on the results.
(*Note*: Do this exercise for France if "your country" is Germany.)

1.3* Finish exercise 1.2 along the lines of the analysis in section 1.4, that is:

(i)   Gather export data for as many export markets for your country as you can find.
(ii)   Determine the distance to those markets and look up the GDP of those markets.
(iii) Perform a simple regression, ln(exports) = constant + ln(distance), similar to equation (1.2).
(iv)   Correct your estimate for market size; that is perform a regression similar to equation (1.3), namely: ln(exports) = constant + ln(distance) + ln(GDP).
(v)   Comment on your findings.

For answers see the website: http://uk.cambridge.org/economics/resources/

2   Geography and economic theory

2.1   Introduction

The central message of chapter 1 is that geography is important. Economic activity is not evenly distributed across space. On the contrary, clustering of economic activities can be found at various levels of aggregation: the considerable variation in economic size of cities or regions at the national level, or the uneven distribution of wealth and production at the global level. The question arises, of course, of why location apparently is relevant for the distribution of economic activity. To answer this question, we need an analytical framework in which geography plays a part one way or another. In particular, we would like to show that the decisions of economic agents are determined by geography, and that geography itself can be derived from the behavior of economic agents. This is, in a nutshell, what the approach developed in this book tries to do. We want to make absolutely clear from the start that this approach, referred to throughout this book as geographical economics but (see the preface) perhaps better known as new economic geography, is by no means the first theory to address location issues. There is a long tradition that deals with these questions, and this will be discussed in this chapter. The novelty of geographical economics is not the research topic, but the way it tackles the relationships between economics and geography.

Before we turn to the core model of geographical economics, this chapter discusses the role of geography in economic theory. It is clearly beyond the scope of this book to try to give a complete survey of the literature. Instead, we highlight the role of geography in some important fields of economics. As we will see, although with some notable exceptions, economic theory has either not much to say on our subject matter or, when it does, it typically assumes as given what has to be explained from the underlying behavior of economic agents, namely the spatial structure of economic activity. Cities and regions vary in size and relevance (see chapter 1). This is a prime topic for regional and urban economics, which deals with the theoretical analysis of the interdependencies between cities and regions within a country. Section 2.2 discusses the main ingredients of the rather heterogeneous approaches in these fields of economics. Section 2.3 investigates the geographical components in trade theory. Data on trade flows between nations clearly indicate a local concentration in the sense that many countries predominantly trade with neighboring countries (see section 1.4). Moreover, most trade takes place within the OECD area. This suggests that geographical variables should be part of trade theory. Surprisingly, this is not the case, and this provided a strong impetus for the development of geographical economics. At a global scale, economic development is very uneven (recall Figures 1.2 and 1.3). Economic growth and wealth are certainly not evenly distributed across the world economy, but largely confined to a few parts of the map. The history of economic development makes clear that spurts in economic growth are often geographically concentrated; see section 1.4. We will argue that the relevance of geography for economic growth has long ago been recognized in development economics; see also Krugman (1995a). Section 2.4 discusses the main ingredients of neo-classical and new growth theory, focusing on the role of geography. Section 2.5 concludes and evaluates the contributions from various fields of economics. This chapter covers a lot of ground and introduces many important concepts to be discussed more thoroughly in the remainder of our book. Our approach to the overview of each field is as follows. We start with a brief summary of the main arguments involved, which then serves as background information for a discussion of the main question: what does each theory have to say about the role of geography?

2.2   Geography in regional and urban economics

According to the editors of the *Handbook of Regional and Urban Economics*, Nijkamp (1986) and Mills (1986), regional economics analyzes the "spatial dispersion and coherence of economic activity." When you compare this to the definition of economic geography, used in the textbook of Dicken and Lloyd (1990), as the study of "the spatial organization of economic systems" one would be inclined to think that regional economics and economic geography are two different labels for the same field of research. This is, however, not the case. Or, more accurately, it is no longer the case. Although both fields have their roots in the German-based tradition of Von Thünen, Christaller, Weber, and Lösch (see below) and still basically address the same research question, regional economics and economic geography now differ quite considerably.

   Regional economics is based on neo-classical economic theory and is, in effect, "the formalized successor to the German 'location economics' tradition" (Martin, 1999, p. 61).[1] Economic geography, on the other hand, is more eclectic and empirically oriented. It gets its inspiration from heterodox economic theories and increasingly from outside of economics, from areas such as sociology, political science, or regulation theory (Storper, 1997; Scott, 2000; Peck, 2000). We will get back to this division in chapter 11. Despite their differences, our main observations in subsection 2.2.2 apply to both fields. We start, however, in subsection 2.2.1 with an overview of a younger field of study, namely urban economics, which studies the spatial structure of urban areas. Like regional economics, urban economics is based heavily on the tools of neo-classical

---

[1]   According to this view regional economics is also known as regional science.

analysis, such that the division between regional and urban economics is not always clear. Our objective is more limited than striving for complete coverage of the literature. We want to show that concepts and ideas used in geographical economics do not come out of the blue but have been studied before. In addition, we want to suggest that geographical economics has something to add to these analyses. The "proof" of this suggestion starts in chapter 3.

2.2.1 Urban economics

The fact that within every country economic activity is not evenly distributed across space is the starting point for urban economics. The modern analysis of the agglomeration of firms and people in cities or metropolitan areas relies strongly on "the economics of agglomeration, a term which refers to the decline in average costs as more production occurs within a specified geographical area" (Anas, Arnott, and Small, 1998, p. 1427). In other words, it relies strongly on increasing returns to scale.[2] Before we go into the relevance of scale economies for cities and other forms of agglomeration, we first discuss a model in which there are no increasing returns to scale whatsoever. This model, the *monocentric city model*, originates with Von Thünen (1826) and remains a benchmark model for urban (and regional) economics to this day. A brief discussion is justified if only to be able to note the differences from the geographical economics approach and to make clear that in the end the analysis of cities will remain rather limited as long as there are no increasing returns to scale.

The monocentric city model.

The monocentric city model assumes the existence of a featureless plain, perfectly flat and homogeneous in all respects. In the midst of this plain there is a single city. Outside the city, farmers grow crops which they must sell in the city. There are positive transportation costs associated with getting the farming products to the city, which differ for the various crops, as do the prices for these crops. Von Thünen analyzes how the farmers locate themselves across the plain. Each farmer wants to be as close to the city as possible to minimize transport costs. This incentive to be close to the city results in higher land rents near the city than at the edge of the plain. Each farmer thus faces a trade-off between land rents and transport costs. Von Thünen shows that competition for locations ensures that the resulting equilibrium allocation of land among the farmers will be efficient. For every type of crop there is a bid-rent curve which indicates, according to the distance to the city, how much the farmers are willing to pay for the land (see Figure 2.1a). Since the bid-rent curves differ by crop as a result of different prices for those crops in the city and different transport costs, the farmers of a particular type of crop are able to outbid their competitors, that is they are willing to pay more, for any given distance to the city. As we move away from the city center in Figure

---

[2] This formulation of increasing returns to scale does not say how the decline in a firm's average costs comes about. This might be at the firm level or the industry level; see Box 2.1 for a discussion of internal and external economies of scale.

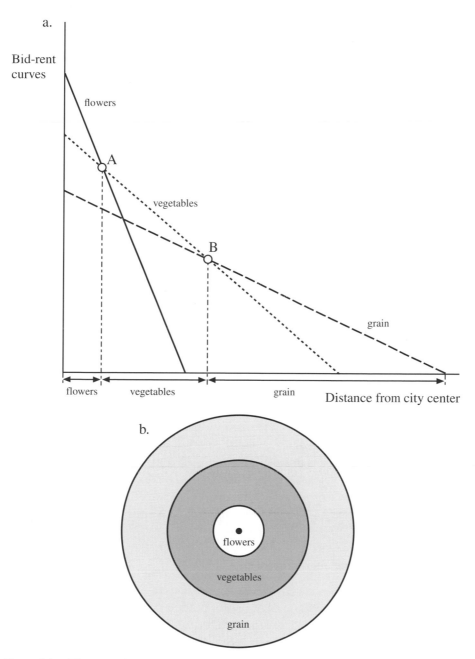

Figure 2.1. The Von Thünen model.

2.1a, we see that first the flower producers outbid the other two groups of farmers, that between points A and B the vegetable producers are willing to pay the highest rents, and that to the right of point B (and thus the farthest removed from the city) grain producers will pay the highest rent. This results in a concentric circle pattern of land use around the city, every ring consisting of farms that grow the same crop; in sequence: flowers, vegetables, and grain (Figure 2.1b).

Urban economics probably started as a separate discipline with Alonso (1964), who essentially took the Von Thünen model and replaced the city by a central business area and the farmers by commuters. The commuters travel back and forth to their work at the center and each commuter derives utility from living space but also faces transportation costs. Again, land rents are highest near the city and fall with distance. The bid-rent approach can thus be applied and competition for land among the commuters implies an efficient allocation of land. The efficiency of land allocation in the mono-centric model hinges on the assumption that there are no externalities of location (see below).[3]

As Anas, Arnott, and Small (1998, p. 1435) point out, a number a stylized facts about urban spatial structure are in accordance with the monocentric model. First, the population density declines with distance from central business areas. Second, almost every major city in the Western world decentralized in the twentieth century (people have started to locate further away from the city center), which can be linked to a fall in transport costs. The monocentric model also has some serious limitations. We mention just two. First, the model does not account for the interaction between cities; it cannot deal with urban systems. Second, the model takes the existence and location of the city as given and focuses on the location of farmers/commuters outside the city. The question why there is a city to begin with is left unanswered. To deal with these limitations, urban economists have long recognized that theories of clustering cannot do without some type of increasing returns to scale. These can occur at the firm level or at a more aggregated level (the industry level or the national level). We will see in this book that the type of increasing returns may matter a great deal. Box 2.1 therefore elaborates upon the terminology used for various forms of scale economies.

Box 2.1.   External and internal economies of scale

The term "economies of scale," or "increasing returns to scale," refers to a situation in which an increase in the level of output produced implies a decrease in the average costs per unit of output for the firm. It translates itself to a downward-sloping average cost curve; see Figure 2.2. To identify the source of the fall in average costs Scitovsky (1954) distinguished between *internal* and *external* economies of scale. With internal economies of scale the decrease in average costs is

---

[3] If there are externalities there will not be a Pareto-efficient allocation of land; see Fujita (1989, part II).

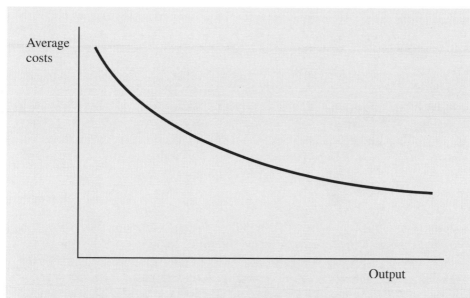

Figure 2.2.   Average costs under increasing returns to scale.

brought about by an increase in the production level of the firm itself. The more the firm produces, the better it can profit from scale economies, and the higher its cost advantage over smaller firms. The market structure underlying internal scale economies, typically used in the geographical economics literature, must necessarily be one of *im*perfect competition, as internal economies of scale imply market power. With external economies of scale the decrease in average costs comes about through an output increase at the level of the industry as a whole, making average costs per unit a function of industry-wide output. Furthermore, Scitovsky distinguishes between *pure* and *pecuniary* external economies.

With *pure* (or *technological*) external economies, an increase in industry-wide output alters the technological relationship between inputs and output for each individual firm. It therefore has an impact on the firm's production function. A frequently used example (dating back to Alfred Marshall) concerns information spillovers. An increase in industry output increases the stock of knowledge through positive information spillovers for each firm, leading to an increase in output at the firm level. In urban economics, but also in new growth theory (section 2.4) and new trade theory (box 2.4), pure external economies are assumed to exist. The market structure can then be perfectly competitive since the size of the *individual* firm does not matter.

Pecuniary external economies are transmitted by the market through price effects for the individual firm, which may alter its output decision. Two examples, again based on Marshall, are the existence of a large local market for specialized inputs and labor market pooling. A large industry can support a market for specialized intermediate inputs and a pool of industry-specific skilled workers, which benefits the individual firm. Contrary to pure external economies these spillovers do not affect the technological relationship between inputs and output (the production function). Pecuniary externalities exist in the geographical economics literature through a love-of-variety effect in a large local market. Each consumer's utility depends positively on the number of varieties that she can buy of a manufactured good. The price effects crucial to pecuniary externalities can only come about with imperfect competition. This is consistent with the imperfect competition requirement for internal economies of scale also used in the geographical economics literature.

Some final remarks are in order. First, spillovers or externalities are crucial for external economies. The concept of spillovers is sometimes used only for pure external economies, pecuniary external economies being referred to as a case of market interdependence. We stick to the use of spillovers or externalities when we refer to external economies of scale in general. Similarly, the term "increasing returns" is sometimes used for internal economies of scale only. We also use the term when discussing external economies. From the context it will be clear if we are referring to the firm or the industry level.

Second, external economies can apply at a higher level of aggregation than the firm. This is often the industry level, but in modern trade theory and modern growth theory it can also be the economy as a whole. Third, the external economies in the models are static, whereas the literature also considers dynamic external economies. In that case the average costs per unit of output are a negative function of the *cumulative* output of the industry. Again, if this is relevant, it will be clear whether we are referring to static or dynamic external economies. Fourth, the external economies discussed above are positive. They can, as we shall see in chapter 7, also be negative, that is an increase in a firm's production leads to an increase in per unit costs for other firms.

Urban economics and increasing returns

We now turn to a prime example of modern urban economics where, in contrast to the monocentric city model, increasing returns to scale are included. Specifically *external* economies to scale are crucial in the important strand of work in urban economics initiated by Henderson (1974, 1977, 1988), following the writings of Mills (1967), on cities or, more precisely, a *system of cities*. The starting point is quite different from the monocentric model. There are no transport costs and the hinterland of a city is no longer part of the analysis. In a sense it is an analysis of cities in which space, certainly space outside the city, has no role to play. The justification for this geographical neglect of non-city space is that in modern industrialized countries a large part of the overall economic activity and population is situated in urban areas (see chapters 1 and 7), such that the relevance of urban versus non-urban transactions is assumed to be limited. Instead, the analysis focuses on the forces determining the size of cities and the inter-actions between them. The agglomerating forces in the Henderson model are positive external economies of scale which are industry-specific. The latter means that there are positive spillovers when a firm of a particular industry locates in a city where other firms in the same industry are located. These may be due to the sharing of informa-tion, the existence of a large pool of labor, or the existence of specialized suppliers (see Box 2.1). The external economies may therefore in principle involve either pure exter-nal economies (as in the original Henderson approach) or pecuniary external econo-mies.[4] The spreading forces are negative external economies of scale within the city, like congestion, which are a function of the overall size of the city. A large city implies rel-atively high commuting costs and land rents. The diseconomies of scale do not depend on the type of production taking place in the city; they depend only on the overall size of a city. Together with the industry-specific external economies this has two impor-tant implications. First, it can rationalize systems of cities, i.e. the existence of cities with different sizes catering to the needs of different industries, a result that depends on the assumption that the positive spillovers of location are industry-specific, each industry having its own optimum size.[5] Second, it provides cities with an incentive to specialize in the production of those goods for which the economies of scale are rela-tively strong, and can thus rationalize an urban system in which cities of different sizes trade with each other.

Which type of external economies to scale?
There is ample empirical support for the idea that industry-specific spillovers are important for cities (Henderson, Kuncoro, and Turner, 1995; Beardsell and Henderson, 1999; Black and Henderson, 1999a). These industry-specific external economies are known as *localization* economies as opposed to *urbanization* economies. The latter are external economies that apply to firms across industries and capture the notion of positive spillovers for a firm as a result of total economic activity in a city. Both types of external economies often relate to the location of cities in a static sense, but they are also applied in a dynamic context (how do cities develop over time?). With respect to the growth of cities in the USA, Glaeser *et al.* (1992) find no support for the hypothesis that cities specializing in certain industries grow faster on average. Instead, they conclude that if external economies are important it is probably more important

[4] Recently, research in urban economics increasingly uses pecuniary externalities and hence also imperfect competition; see Henderson (2000) for a survey. See Tabuchi (1998) for an attempt to synthesize urban economics à la Alonso/Henderson with geographical economics.
[5] As a consequence, in equilibrium each city is also of an optimal size, maximizing the utility of the inhab-itants. The reasoning is as follows. Suppose a city is not of an optimal size. This creates a profit opportu-nity. If the city is too large, moving people out of the city would be welfare-improving, and vice versa if it is too small. Henderson introduces the city entrepreneur who, in view of this profit opportunity, orga-nizes enough people to move into a city that is too small, or out of a city that is too large. These entre-preneurs are necessary because an individual in a city of non-optimal size has no incentive to move on her own; see also Becker and Henderson (2000). Section 6.4 argues that city entrepreneurs or large agents could be incorporated in the models of geographical economics.

to have a variety of diversified industries in a city.[6] If the latter is the case, the question arises why so many cities are specialized in particular industries. Glaeser *et al.* (1992, pp. 1148–1150) suggest that both localization and urbanization economies are relevant (though they favor urbanization economies in the end), while Black and Henderson (1999a) argue, also in a dynamic context, that localization economies are more relevant.[7] We return to these empirical concerns in chapters 5 and 7. From a theoretical point of view it should be stressed that Henderson's urban systems approach does not take the existence of the city for granted like the monocentric model. It also provides for a theory of the interactions between cities. The problem with the approach is that the space outside the cities is (deliberately) not part of the analysis. This is troublesome if one wants to be able to say where cities are located relative to one another and to the "non-city" part of the geography: "the systems of cities literature has emphasized urban space but neglected national space" (Dobkins and Ioannides, 1999).[8] As we will see, the location of manufacturing activity and the relationship between these locations and the rest of space is a key issue in geographical economics. To analyze this relationship, transportation costs have to be part of the analysis since they are crucial in determining the balance between agglomeration and spreading forces (Fujita, Krugman, and Venables, 1999, p. 23). Chapter 7 returns to the topic of urban economics and discusses, using the city-size distribution as an example, how geographical economics may add to our theoretical and empirical understanding of urban systems and their evolution over time.[9]

In their excellent survey of theories of agglomeration, which includes urban economics, Fujita and Thisse (1996, 2000) discuss three basic approaches: increasing returns, externalities, and spatial competition. In the terminology of Box 2.1 their use of increasing returns and externalities corresponds to our definitions of pure external economies and pecuniary external economies, respectively. Both types of external economies will be important in our book. This leaves spatial competition which is meant to refer to the fact that competition among firms is almost by definition of an oligopolistic nature when space is taken into consideration. Competition is restricted by distance; a firm typically is thought to compete only with its neighboring firms.

---

[6] Using the terminology of Glaeser *et al.* (1992), their study is an attempt to test for the relevance of three externalities: (i) the Marshall–Arrow–Romer (MAR) externality where knowledge spillovers occur between firms that belong to the same industry and where local monopoly is better suited than local competition to foster these spillovers; (ii) the Porter externality (based on Porter, 1990; see chapter 8) where knowledge spillovers are also industry-specific but where the preferred market structure is local competition; (iii) Jacobs externality (based on Jacobs, 1969) where the knowledge spillovers are not industry-specific but between firms of different industries and where local competition stimulates these spillovers. The empirical evidence in Glaeser *et al.* (1992) is relatively favorable for the Jacobs externality. Henderson, Kuncoro, and Turner (1995) and Black and Henderson (1999a) are two examples of empirical studies which conclude that localization economies and hence, in a dynamic context, MAR externalities are far more important than for instance the Glaeser study suggests. We return to this issue in chapter 7.

[7] When applied to cities, external economies are typically urbanization economies in the geographical economics approach; see chapter 7.

[8] In contrast to central place theory; see section 2.2.2.

[9] We will also briefly discuss recent attempts in urban economics (Eaton and Eckstein, 1997; Black and Henderson, 1998, 1999b) to model urban growth to learn about the evolution of city-size distributions.

Spatial competition is therefore intrinsically linked with strategic behavior by firms. In the remainder of the book we will not deal with spatial competition. The reason is simply that in geographical economics, and in particular in the Dixit and Stiglitz (1977) version of monopolistic competition (see section 2.3 and chapter 3), which invariably characterizes the market structure in the geographical economics models, strategic behavior is not taken into account. Firms take each other's (pricing) behavior as given. In addition to the three approaches mentioned by Fujita and Thisse (1996), Anas, Arnott, and Small (1998) give two additional reasons for (urban) agglomeration: the existence of non-homogeneous space and internal economies of scale in a production process (with no external economies). With the former, one can rationalize agglomeration without any form of increasing returns to scale (think about the differences in the actual physical geography giving rise, for example, to a natural harbor and the corresponding agglomeration). Non-homogeneous space or non-neutral space will be discussed at various instances in the remainder of this chapter and more extensively in section 6.2.

2.2.2 Regional economics

Regional economics analyzes the spatial organization of economic systems and must somehow also account for the uneven distribution across space. It has its roots in a research tradition going back to Von Thünen (1826), Launhardt (1885), Weber (1909), Christaller (1933), and Lösch (1940). All these German contributions take the national or economy-wide space into consideration, in contrast to modern urban economics, to analyze where economic activities are located. This is a relevant question as the movement of goods or people is not costless and production is typically subject to some form of increasing returns. The founding fathers of regional economics focus, however, on different aspects of the location of economic activity. Von Thünen, for example, emphasized the location decisions made by farmers, while Weber analyzed the optimal location and plant size for manufacturing firms. This subsection focuses on the ideas first put forward (and tested) by Christaller and Lösch, who not only tried to explain the location of cities, but also differentiate cities by the various functions they perform. This approach is known as *central place theory* and shows "that different points or locations on the economic landscape have different levels of *centrality* and that goods and services are efficiently provided on a *hierarchical* basis" (Mulligan, 1984, p. 4).[10]

Central place theory

Given an even distribution of identical consumers across a homogeneous plane, the central place theory argues that locations differ in centrality, and that this centrality determines the type of goods the location provides. The provision of these goods is

---

[10] Note the difference from the analysis of urban systems mentioned in the subsection 2.2.1. Central place theory analyzes not only the connections between cities, but also the hierarchy of cities, and the interaction between cities and the rural area. This is also true for very recent models of urban growth (see Black and Henderson, 1999b, and chapter 7).

determined by internal increasing returns to scale, while location is relevant because consumers incur transport costs. To minimize these costs consumers want access to nearby suppliers of goods. For some types of goods, such as bread, this is easier than for others, such as television sets, because the increasing returns to scale are relatively limited. Thus, the economy can support many relatively small locations (villages) where bakers are active to supply bread. In contrast, there can only be relatively few locations (small cities, the central places) where electronics firms sell television sets, which people buy less frequently. To minimize transport costs both these types of locations are rather evenly distributed across space. Moreover, we get a hierarchy of locations in which the city performs all functions (sells bread and television sets), but the village performs only some functions (sells only bread). This is illustrated in Figure 2.3 where the equidistant central place is surrounded by six equidistant smaller cities, which together form a hexagon. Each small city in turn is surrounded by six equidistant villages.

The fact that it deals explicitly with the location of economic activity is an important advantage of central place theory. The main problem with the approach is that the economic rationale behind consumers' and firms' decisions remains unclear. What kind of behavior of individual agents leads to a central place outcome? Increasing returns at the firm level requires some form of imperfect competition, which is lacking. Consequently, central place theory, especially the graphical version still found in most introductory textbooks on economic geography, is indeed more a descriptive story, or an exercise in geometry as Figure 2.3 depicts, than a causal model (Fujita, Krugman, and Venables, 1999, p. 27).

Regional scientists and economic geographers have, of course, also been aware of the limitations of this version of central place theory, which during the last thirty years has received less interest, particularly within economic geography (Martin, 1999). For a theoretical foundation, economic geographers have started to look elsewhere (see below). Regional scientists have, however, tried to build on the basic ideas of the central place theory. Regional science has developed models, following Isard (1956, 1960), to give a theoretical (often highly formalized) economic foundation for central place theory; see Mulligan (1984). It is fair to say that these models are mostly of a partial equilibrium nature, explaining some aspects of the central place system while ignoring others. A typical model in this tradition does not deal with individual firms or consumers, but essentially formalizes the geometric pattern of a central place system as illustrated in Figure 2.3; see Nijkamp (1986).[11] The central place outcome is merely rationalized and not explained from the underlying behavior of consumers and producers, nor from their decisions and (market) interactions. For example, the demand curve facing a firm at a particular location is not derived from first principles but simply assumed. Geographical economics has attempted to fill this gap in the literature by

---

[11] It is beyond the scope of this chapter to survey the modern contributions to regional science/regional economics and we therefore pay no attention to important earlier building blocks of this approach, for instance, the work by Perroux (1955); see however the contributions in Nijkamp (1986).

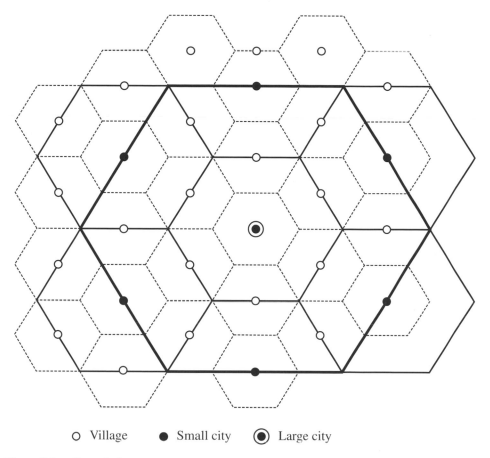

○ Village   ● Small city   ◉ Large city

Figure 2.3. Central place system.

giving a microeconomic foundation to the hierarchy of central places (Fujita, Krugman, and Mori, 1999; Fujita, Krugman, and Venables, 1999, ch. 9; and chapter 7 of this book).

Box 2.2. Central place theory in a Dutch polder

Between 1937 and 1942 an area of 48,000 hectares (120,000 acres) was reclaimed from the sea and turned into a polder in the center of the Netherlands. The new polder, called the *Noord-Oost Polder* (Northeast Polder), was, and still is, mainly used for agriculture. The Dutch authorities also planned the establishment of a number of (small) towns and villages in this polder, and their planning was explicitly influenced by the work of Christaller and Lösch on central places. The polder clearly met some of the assumptions of central place theory: the land is

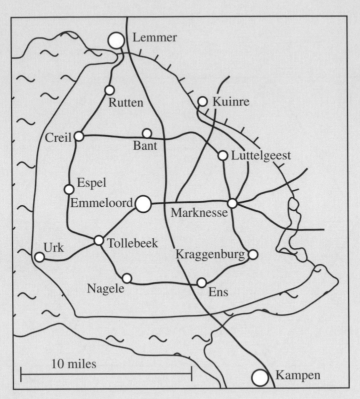

Figure 2.4.   Central places in a Dutch polder.

extremely flat and almost perfectly homogeneous in all other respects. The initial settlers in the polder (the farmers) were also evenly distributed across the polder, and it was not too far-fetched to assume that these farmers had identical preferences.

The layout of the new locations in the polder, mapped in Figure 2.4 therefore looked very much like the central place layout shown in Figure 2.3. There was one central place (the city of Emmeloord) which became surrounded over a period of ten years by a number of smaller (almost) equidistant locations. These smaller locations were explicitly devised to supply only lower-order goods, whereas Emmeloord was designed to supply the higher-order goods.[12] Based on this core idea from central place theory, the authorities made projections about the size of each location. As Table 2.1 shows, these projections were far removed

---

[12] The layout of the various villages and towns was such that it took each farmer at most ten minutes' travel time (by bike!) to reach a lower-order goods store. Also, in their planning frenzy, the Dutch authorities decided that locations should be equal with respect to the religion of their inhabitants. So they tried to make sure that every location had proportional shares of Catholic and Protestant people.

Table 2.1. *Population of locations in the Noord-Oost Polder*

	Start	Planned population	Population in 1985
Emmeloord	1946	10,000	18,976
Marknesse	1946	2,000	2,194
Ens	1948	2,000	1,618
Kraggenburg	1948	2,000	655
Luttelgeest	1950	2,000	666
Bant	1951	2,000	651
Rutten	1952	2,000	620
Creil	1953	2,000	687
Nagele	1954	2,000	1,014
Espel	1956	2,000	714
Tollebeek	1956	2,000	579

Source: "Dorpen in de IJsselmeerpolders," Rijksdienst voor de IJsselmeerpolders, 1986.

from reality after 30–40 years. The central place had become much larger than predicted and, with one exception, the other locations had become smaller than expected. Exercise 2.2 at the end of this chapter addresses the possible explanations for this result.

Market potential

The above remarks about the foundation of central place theory apply more generally. There are more examples of theories, like central place theory, trying to come to grips with a spatial regularity. In contrast to (neo-classical) economic theory, there is a tendency merely to give a representation, using, for example, simple equations, of the regularity without a connection to a model of rational individual behavior by economic agents. Other examples of "models," (Krugman, 1995a), used to describe or mimic particular empirical spatial regularities are (i) the equations underlying the rank–size distribution (chapter 7), (ii) the gravity model of trade (chapter 9), and (iii) the market potential analysis (chapter 5). The latter, due to Harris (1954), is widely used in regional economics. For the USA, and using the value of retail sales per US county, Harris found that the market potential of any location could be described by:

$$MP_i = \sum_{j=1}^{R} \left(\frac{M_j}{D_{ij}} \right) \tag{2.1}$$

in which MP_i is the market potential of location i, M_j is the demand by location j for goods from location i, and D_{ij} is the distance between locations i and j.

The market potential equation thus provides an indication of the general proximity of a location (in his study, a US county) to total demand. Harris (1954), and many regional economists since then, found that the market potential (and hence demand) is typically high in those areas where production is also located. This gives support to the notion of clustering of economic activity, and indicates that the agglomeration and location decisions on which it is based are not only a supply-side issue, but that demand also plays its part. In fact, the idea that production takes place where demand is high can also be reversed. Demand is high where production is located as a result of the purchasing power of the workers making production at that location possible. Though convincing from an empirical point of view, the market potential analysis lacks a theoretical foundation (and thereby it also lacks content: what does MP_i represent?). This is, as we shall see in sections 2.3 and 2.4, not very surprising because economic trade theory and growth theory have great difficulties in explaining any phenomenon in which geography plays a part. In particular the distance variable D is difficult to reconcile with economic theory (in Box 2.5 we will argue that the same is true for the gravity model of international trade). The ideas behind the market potential analysis, however, play a prominent role in geographical economics. As argued in chapter 3, the core model of geographical economics can be interpreted as an attempt to provide a theoretical foundation for equation (2.1). Empirical work in geographical economics also uses the market potential approach, as we will see in sections 5.5 and 5.6 of chapter 5.

Both examples (central place theory and the market potential approach) illustrate some points that apply to regional economics in general.[13] The theoretical approaches, like central place theory, and the more empirically inspired approaches, like the market potential analysis, deal with important aspects of the spatial organization of economic activity. However, the framework of analysis does not, by and large, meet the standards of mainstream economic theory, which requires the conclusions to be based on the actions and interactions of individual economic agents in the market-place. This calls for the analysis of individual consumer and producer behavior, market structure, and the resulting equilibria. Such a microeconomic foundation of geography does not exist in regional economics (Fujita and Thisse, 1996, 2000).[14] Different strands of economic

---

[13] Another early approach influential in regional economics and relevant here is the so-called *export base multiplier approach*. The main idea is a restatement of the Keynesian income multiplier. Suppose that total regional income I consists of income earned in the non-tradable sector I_n and income earned by the tradable sector with exports I_e. Also assume that the income earned locally (I_n) is a constant fraction a of the (exogenous) income earned with exports (with $0 < a < 1$). Then, an increase in exports will set in motion a more than proportional increase in total regional income using the income multiplier, leading to a total increase $I = I_e / (1 - a)$. The conclusion is that the economic development of a region depends on the expansion of its tradable sector and the size of the income multiplier. Further developments in this approach focused on the role of the non-tradable sector, emphasizing that the share of income earned locally was not a simple function of export income but related to the characteristics of the regional economy, thus endogenizing regional economic development. As Fujita, Krugman, and Venables (1999, p. 28) argue, this means that a is no longer fixed but increases if, through a process of endogenous growth, the non-tradable sector expands. The main proponent of this approach, Pred (1966), envisaged a growth process for the regional economy similar to the process of circular and cumulative growth discussed in section 2.4.

[14] In modern economic geography (Martin, 1999; Scott, 2000; Peck, 2000), the search for such a microeconomic foundation provided by geographical economics is rejected. Instead an alternative foundation of economic geography is preferred, not based on neo-classical economics. We return to this matter and the relationship between geographical economics and economic geography in chapter 11.

theory may provide such a microeconomic foundation, but, as we shall see in the remainder of this chapter, are lacking in geographical content. In our view, geographical economics can be seen as *new* economic geography to the extent that it combines well-established spatial insights from regional and urban economics with the general equilibrium framework of mainstream economic theory. It thus tries to put more economic theory into geography but, above all, more geography into economics. Whether this attempt yields new insights into the relationships between geography and economics or only grounds existing (and for some economic geographers outdated) work on a different analytical framework is a different question. This question can be addressed only in chapter 11, after the reader has gained a thorough knowledge of geographical economics in chapters 3–10.

2.3   Trade theory

This section discusses the role of geography in the theory of international trade. We are more specific here than in sections 2.2 and 2.4 because the core model of geographical economics has its roots firmly in international trade theory. In many ways it is an extension of the so-called *new trade theory*, specifically that of Krugman (1979, 1980). Subsection 2.3.2 will therefore focus on the geographical content of these two seminal papers by Paul Krugman, rather than giving a survey of new trade theory.[15] Subsection 2.3.1 briefly discusses its "predecessor," *neo-classical trade theory*. We want to point out that the discussion of trade theory in this section only touches upon issues like the (Dixit–Stiglitz) modeling of imperfect competition, transportation costs, and the determination of different equilibria. These issues (and the technicalities that go along with them) are addressed in more detail in chapter 3.

2.3.1   Neo-classical trade theory

The label neo-classical trade theory refers to theories in which the trade flows between nations are based on comparative advantage, resulting from technological differences (Ricardo) or from factor abundance. In the *factor abundance model*, developed by Eli Heckscher, Bertil Ohlin, and Paul Samuelson, comparative advantage is determined, as the name suggests, by cross-country differences in the relative abundance of factor endowments. It suffices to think of the simple $2 \times 2 \times 2$ (2 goods, 2 countries, and 2 factors of production) factor abundance model which is still the backbone of any introductory course in international trade. It was widely used, for example, in the recent debate on the effects of globalization on the OECD labor markets; see Box 2.3. Assume that there are two countries, North and South, two tradable goods, apparel and machinery, and two factors of production, high-skilled labor and low-skilled

---

[15] In the new trade theory, trade is analyzed in models in a world of increasing returns to scale and monopolistic competition. Bhagwati, Panagariya, and Srinivasan (1998, ch. 11) give a very good survey of the basic models of which Krugman (1979, 1980) are prime (but not the only) examples.

labor. Suppose that North is relatively well endowed with high-skilled labor, and South with low-skilled labor. Production of both goods requires both inputs, but the production of machinery is relatively high-skilled intensive. Consumers in North and South have identical preferences and consume both goods. In the absence of trade North, which is abundant in high-skilled labor, can more easily make machinery than South, because machinery production is high-skilled intensive. In autarky this results in relatively low prices for machinery in North and apparel in South. Once North and South start to trade, prices will be equalized, resulting in a higher price for machinery in North and a higher price for apparel in South. As a consequence, North will have an incentive to (partially) specialize in the production of machinery. A similar reasoning holds for South with respect to apparel. The resulting trade flows are of the inter-industry type (trade of machinery for apparel). Furthermore, factor prices will be equalized between North and South as a result of trade.

The factor abundance model uses some additional specific assumptions, such as perfect competition, homogeneous goods, production with constant returns to scale, no transport costs associated with the trade of goods, and mobility of factors of production between industries, but not between countries. It is clear (see section 2.2) that a number of these assumptions are at odds with key assumptions in regional and urban economics, where we have external and/or internal increasing returns to scale, imperfect competition, positive transport costs, and mobility of factors of production (and firms). We concluded that these ingredients are required to account for spatial economic patterns. Does this mean that geography or the location of economic activity is a non-issue in neo-classical trade theory? Well, yes and no.

To explain this answer, it is useful to distinguish between the first nature and the second nature of the economics of location; see Krugman (1993a). The location of economic activity is relevant in the factor abundance model as far as the uneven distribution of factor endowments is concerned. This distribution is given, and thus a first-nature determinant of location in Krugman's terminology. In our example, North specializes in machinery and South in apparel as a result of the geographic distribution of endowments, which translates itself to uneven distribution of economic activity across global space. In this restricted sense, geography matters. We would like to reach this conclusion, however, in another way, namely by showing how the relevance of location follows from the decisions made by economic agents and their interactions. In other words, the location of production should be an endogenous variable, a second-nature determinant of location in Krugman's terminology. This second nature is clearly lacking in factor abundance theory. As argued in chapter 3, endogenization of location decisions is needed to have agglomeration of economic activity. Differences in endowments cannot imply a core–periphery pattern of production; they just lead to specialization (as opposed to agglomeration). Trade between countries cannot lead to inequality, in the sense that machinery and apparel cannot both agglomerate in North.

The factor abundance model leads to factor price equalization of high-skilled wages between North and South (similarly for low-skilled wages). This has been used to analyze a phenomenon with an obvious geographical component: globalization and its alleged impact on the allocation of production and income in the Western industrialized economies (North); see Venables (1998) and Box 2.3. Globalization can be defined as the growing interdependence between countries through increased trade and/or increased factor mobility.

Box 2.3.   Globalization, factor abundance, and clustering

Suppose the world can be characterized with a factor abundance model with two countries (North and South), two manufactured goods (machinery and apparel) and one non-tradable, non-manufactured good. North is relatively well endowed with high-skilled labor, and South with low-skilled labor. Both factors of production are needed for the production of all goods, but machine production is relatively intensive in high-skilled labor. North thus has a comparative advantage in the production of machines. Both countries produce both tradable goods, there is perfect competition, technology is fixed, and there is no cross-border labor mobility. Suppose that initially, due to very high transaction costs, both countries do not trade at all. Subsequently, the transaction costs decrease, and trade opens up. The fall in transaction costs (which serves as proxy for globalization) can be policy-driven (lowering of tariffs and the like) or technology-driven (improved transport- and communication technologies). What are the main effects of trade for North? It will specialize in the production of machinery and start to import apparel, that is the machinery sector expands and the apparel sector contracts. This has the following implications for North:

(i) There will be one high-skilled wage and one low-skilled wage (the factor price equalization theorem). Since wages are determined on the world market, changes in national factor supplies no longer have any impact on wages.

(ii) North is confronted with an increase in the world production of apparel, which results in a fall in the relative price of apparel. This will hurt low-skilled labor in North, used intensively in the production of apparel, by lowering their real wage (Stolper–Samuelson theorem).

(iii) The expansion of the machinery sector in North increases the relative demand for high-skilled labor, thus raising high-skilled wages relative to low-skilled wages in North. This induces firms in North to substitute away from high-skilled labor, and *de*creases the skill intensity of manufacturing production in North.

(iv) The contraction of the apparel sector in North does not only change the mix of manufacturing production in North, it also implies a contraction of the manufacturing sector as a whole because some of the labor released from the apparel sector will be employed in the non-tradable services sector. Consequently, the non-manufacturing sector expands and North is confronted with a *deindustrialization*.

The factor abundance model can thus be used to give a theoretical foundation for the idea that globalization (increased imports by North of low-skilled intensive goods from South) may hurt low-skilled workers, by lowering their relative wages, and may lead to de-industrialization. The main geographical dimension of this analysis of globalization is the implication that North (the OECD countries) specializes in production which is intensive high-skilled labor, while South (Southeast Asia, Latin America, and the transition economies in eastern Europe) specializes in production which is intensive in low-skilled labor.

An important question for this version of the globalization debate is, of course, whether there is any empirical evidence to support the factor abundance model so as to validate implications (i)–(iv) above. Recently, they have been the subject of an impressive amount of empirical research (Lawrence and Slaughter, 1993; Wood, 1994; and Collins, 1998; for surveys see Wood, 1995, 1998). Although there is some disagreement, the general consensus is that the four implications of the factor abundance model are not convincingly substantiated by the empirical evidence. It is therefore doubtful whether globalization is the main determinant of the changes in production structures or of the worsening of the position of the low-skilled labor in North.

Relative differences in factor endowments can thus be used to give a theoretical justification for the differences in specialization patterns between countries. Other versions of neo-classical trade theory have similar implications as far as the relevance of geography is concerned. In the Ricardian model, comparative advantage, and hence the trade pattern, is determined by exogenous cross-country differences in technology. Countries specialize in the production of those goods in which they have a comparatively high productivity, and this determines the location of production. Our main objection to the factor abundance model also holds for the Ricardian model: to the limited extent that geography matters, this relevance is given exogenously. Naturally, differences in factor endowment or technology can be the result of differences in geography. Consider, for example, land as a factor of production, as in the Von Thünen tradition in urban economics. The availability of (fertile) land shapes comparative advantage. Similarly, the physical geography of a country (access to the sea, altitude, climate, etc.) can also be an underlying determinant of comparative advantage, which certainly holds for the stock of natural resources. Gallup, *et al.* (1998) show that such cross-country differences in geography indeed help to explain differences in economic development. We return to this issue in section 2.4, see Box 2.6, and section 6.2.

The limited role for geography in neo-classical trade theory is probably best illustrated by the so-called specific-factors model. Part of a country's factor endowments (for example, labor) are then internationally mobile, whereas other parts (for example, land and capital) are not. Production of a certain good requires inputs from the mobile factor as well as one particular, or *specific*, immobile factor (usually land or sector-specific capital). Differences in endowment of the specific factors thus influence the production and trade pattern, with a country specializing, *ceteris paribus*, in the production of the good requiring the input of the specific factor with which the country is relatively well endowed. There is a geographic link to the extent that the distribution of the immobile endowments (notably land) is determined by geographical conditions. Again, such a connection is indirect at best, and the impact of geography is determined outside the trade model.

To summarize, Anas, Arnott, and Small (1998, p. 1445) correctly state that inhomogeneous space, also known as non-neutral space, has traditionally been invoked to explain the uneven distribution of economic activity. Non-neutral space gives rise to different sources of comparative advantage, which make spreading of economic activity impossible. The location relevance therefore only exists by assumption, and there is no interdependence between geography and economics. In particular, the equilibrium location of economic activity is not the result of the underlying behavior of economic agents. The (trade) equilibrium, which in contrast to geographical economics (see section 3.2) is usually unique, is fully determined by exogenous forces. More importantly, neo-classical trade theory does not allow for the establishment of a core–periphery equilibrium, which presents a problem in view of the many examples given in chapter 1. To enable agglomeration of economic activity some of the assumptions underlying neo-classical trade theory have to be changed. An obvious candidate is the introduction of internal increasing returns to scale, and hence of imperfect competition; see subsection 2.3.2.

A final remark on the relationship between geography and neo-classical trade theory: without an uneven distribution of resources, and thus without comparative advantage, there is, *ceteris paribus*, no longer a rationale for trade, and geography ceases to be an issue.[16] On introducing positive transportation costs, a similar conclusion can be reached even if comparative advantages exist. If these costs are high enough, the production of goods will be perfectly dispersed across space (Ottaviano and Puga, 1997). The economy will then consist of many small firms, producing for their own consumption, a situation referred to as *backyard capitalism* in the literature.

2.3.2   New trade theory

From the late 1970s neo-classical trade theory has been challenged by the development of new trade theory, which is now complementary to neo-classical trade theory and part of almost every textbook on international trade. The reason for trade between countries in new trade theory does not depend on comparative advantage. In fact, Paul Krugman (1979, 1980) has developed a (by now standard) model in which countries engage in welfare-enhancing trade even when there is no comparative advantage whatsoever. The starting point for new trade theory was the stylized fact that a very large

---

[16] We reach a similar conclusion for the relevance of geography in neo-classical growth theory (section 2.4).

part of international trade takes place between countries with very similar factor endowments; see the German example in section 1.4. This trade is not, as the neo-classical trade theory would predict, inter-industry trade (exporting cereal in exchange for cars) but intra-industry trade (exporting cars in exchange for cars). The empirical relevance of intra-industry trade was, of course, well known but the theoretical foundation of this type of trade called for a class of models in which some of the building blocks of the neo-classical trade theory had to be overturned.

Krugman 1979

The basic insights from Krugman (1979) can be illustrated as follows. Suppose there are two countries of equal market size, West and East, which have the same endowments, use the same technology, and both have one (immobile) car-producing firm. In the factor abundance model these countries would not trade. Both firms make various types of cars under increasing returns to scale for each type. In autarky, the firms produce three types of cars, namely types X, Y, and Z in West and types A, B, and C in East. There is thus one industry that produces six types, or *varieties*, of cars. The consumers (workers) in West and East are immobile, evenly distributed, and have identical preferences. The varieties are imperfect substitutes and preferences are such that consumers always prefer more varieties of a car to fewer (this is the "love-of-variety" effect; see also chapter 3). The key to understanding the rationale for trade in this model is the combination of increasing returns to scale at the firm level (*internal* economies of scale; see Box 2.1) and the love-of-variety effect in consumers' preferences, which is an externality not taken into account by firms. Moving from autarky to free trade these two assumptions ensure that trade will take place and is welfare-improving.

The extent to which each firm can exploit the increasing returns to scale is determined by the size of the market. The opening up of trade enlarges the market size for each type of car. Since each variety is produced under increasing returns to scale, this larger market enables the firms to better exploit the increasing returns.[17] The opening up of trade means that the car production *per variety* can increase as the larger market makes it profitable to expand the scale of production. In doing so, the prices per variety will decrease. To make this possible in the integrated market of West and East the total number of varieties produced must decrease. To see this, note that the total (West + East) endowments and the total market size are fixed, such that it is not possible simultaneously to increase the production of all six varieties. In free trade the two countries together produce fewer than six varieties, say four (X, Y, A, and B). There are then two positive welfare effects. First, the decrease in prices brought about by the increased scale of production implies that workers/consumers end up with a higher real wage. Second, consumers are able to consume four rather than three varieties,[18] which increases welfare through the love-of-variety effect.

---

[17] "The effect [of trade] will be the same as if *each* country had experienced an increase in its labor force" (Krugman, 1979, p. 474).

[18] Note that in autarky the world as a whole produces six varieties, but each country produces and consumes only three varieties.

Although the basic insights of Krugman (1979) are easy to understand, the introduction of increasing returns to scale implies a market structure of imperfect competition. The theoretical challenge was therefore to provide a trade model with imperfect competition, a difficult challenge in view of the discussion on regional and urban economics (section 2.2). Fortunately, Krugman could build on a model of monopolistic competition which had just been published (Dixit and Stiglitz, 1977). The Dixit–Stiglitz approach is now widely used in many fields, including geographical economics. In chapter 3 (see also Box 3.1) we discuss and explain the main features of the Dixit–Stiglitz model. In view of the difficulty of dealing with imperfect competition it is not surprising that the new trade theory also includes models with pure external, instead of internal, economies of scale (Helpman, 1984b; Helpman and Krugman, 1985), as it allows one to remain with a market structure of perfect competition; see Box 2.4.

Box 2.4.   New trade theory and external economies

Suppose an industry, say the personal computer (PC) industry, is characterized by pure external economies of scale, arising for example from information spill-overs when the increase in the production of a single firm increases the production knowledge for all firms in the PC industry. This implies not only that average costs per PC for each firm are a decreasing function of the *industry* output, but also that we can still use perfect competition (Box 2.1). There is no advantage to a firm in being large (in view of the external economies of scale), so typically the economy now consists of many small firms. Under perfect competition, price equals average cost for each firm. Finally, suppose there are two countries, *A* and *B*, and that consumers in both countries have identical preferences.

As in the case of internal economies of scale, intra-industry trade may develop between the two countries with both countries producing and exporting PC varieties. With external economies, however, we can also have an equilibrium in which one country produces the total world demand for PCs. If, for some historical reason, the PC industry initially establishes itself in country *A*, the external economies may turn this initial distribution of production into a lasting equilibrium ("lock in") even if the PC industry in country *B* would be more efficient. Two issues, also part of geographical economics, are relevant in this case. First, initial conditions can determine the (stable) equilibrium outcome. Depending on who enters the market first, either country could end up being the world producer of PCs. Second, the resulting trade equilibrium may be inefficient.

A simple example illustrates the possibility of a "bad" equilibrium. Suppose country A is the first to set up a PC industry and produces 500,000 PCs. At this level of *industry* output a price (equal to average cost) of $1,000 per PC can be charged to meet world demand, which is fixed at 500,000 units for simplicity. Suppose that the PC industry in country *B* could produce 500,000 PCs more

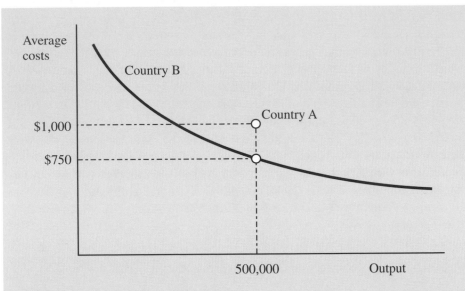

Figure 2.5.   Lock-in effect: example.

efficiently, say for $750 per unit. This does not imply that country *B* will start pro-
ducing PCs since these costs apply for the whole *industry*. In the absence of a PC
industry in country *B*, and thus in the absence of positive external economies, a
single firm in country *B* may only be able to produce 500 PCs at a price above
$1,000, that is at a higher cost than in country *A*, thus not making it worthwhile
to set up shop in country *B*. This is illustrated in Figure 2.5.

External economies of scale are important in this example. Given that world
demand is met by the industry in country *A* at an average cost of $1,000, the indi-
vidual firm in country *B* can only produce at a higher average cost. This is true
for all firms in country *B*. It is only when all firms in *B jointly* decide to start producing PCs that they can take over the PC market as this brings average cost
down below $1,000 as a result of external economies of scale. But there's nothing
that induces firms in *B* to make such a decision because the individual firm is only
confronted with the fact that its average costs exceed the prevailing market price.
This problem would not occur with *internal* economies of scale, where average
costs for a firm fall as the firm produces more output.[19]

The question is now whether new trade theory has something to say on the role of
geography. In the Krugman (1979) model the answer is simple. The location of economic activity is not really an issue. Trade costs are zero, so firms are indifferent about

---

[19] For further reading on external economies and trade, see Helpman and Krugman (1985, ch. 2), and the
surveys in the *Handbook of International Economics* (Helpman, 1984b; Krugman, 1995b). For a similar
example, see Krugman and Obstfeld (1994, pp. 150–151).

the location of their production sites. Even if there were positive trade costs the (exogenous) market size is evenly distributed between the two countries, which precludes any agglomeration of economic activity. It is indeterminate which country ends up producing which varieties. All one can say is that countries produce different varieties and the pattern of trade is indeterminate. Nevertheless, this model is important as the basis of the core model of geographical economics, for example with respect to the analysis of producer and consumer behavior. With external economies of scale the location of economic activity is also not addressed. One could argue that the lock-in effects in some of these models allow initial conditions to play a role in determining the allocation of production. As with neo-classical trade theory, this role for geography is determined outside the model.

Krugman 1980

Krugman (1980) is a crucial step from the initial new trade model in Krugman (1979) to the core model of geographical economics. The rationale for intra-industry trade is the same as in the 1979 model, with a few notable differences. First, in the 1980 model the opening up of trade, and hence the increase of the market size, does *not* lead to an increase in the scale of production, despite increasing returns to scale at the firm level. Instead, the volume of production of each variety (at the firm level) is the same under autarky and trade, and prices do not change.[20] The gains from trade are now completely due to the love-of-variety effect as consumers can choose among more varieties under trade than under autarky. The core model of geographical economics coincides with Krugman (1980) on this important issue. Second, in the 1980 model, trade between nations incurs transport costs, which is obviously relevant from a geographical point of view. Third, in the 1980 model, demand per variety is no longer symmetric as countries differ in market size. This uneven distribution of market size becomes important when combined with positive transportation costs because a country will produce those varieties for which the demand in the country is relatively high. In this sense the location of production matters and concentration of economic activity can be an outcome of the model. The reasoning is simple: given the uneven distribution of demand, firms, which are still immobile, minimize transport costs if they produce those varieties for which home demand is relatively strong. Moreover, and in contrast to the model without transport costs, the direction of trade is no longer indeterminate because the concentration of production implies that countries will be net exporters of those varieties for which home demand is relatively high. As Krugman (1980, p. 955) puts it: "Countries will tend to export those kinds of products for which they have relatively large domestic demand. Notice that this argument is wholly dependent on increasing returns; in a world of diminishing returns, strong domestic demand for a

---

[20] If the number of firms (and hence the number of varieties) is large the elasticity of demand will be constant (Dixit and Norman, 1980). In chapter 3 we will see that this feature, which follows from the Dixit–Stiglitz (1977) formulation of monopolistic competition, is also a crucial element of the geographical economics models. This assumption is not undisputed; Holmes (1999) criticizes new trade theory and geographical economics for this assumption.

good will tend to make it an import rather than an export." This phenomenon is known as the home-market effect.[21]

In an attempt to test for the home-market effect, Davis and Weinstein (1999) refer to Krugman (1980) as a model of economic geography. This suggests that there is no fundamental difference between this model and the core model in chapter 3. We do not agree with that view for three reasons. First, neither firms nor workers decide anything about location in Krugman (1980). There is no mobility of firms or the factors of production. Given their (exogenous) location, firms only make a decision about the varieties they want to produce. Second, the concentration of production of varieties (and by assumption of demand) does not allow for the agglomeration of economic activity. Core–periphery equilibria are not possible because the concentration of demand in the first country, say for X varieties, is mirrored by a similar concentration of demand for the $(1 - X)$ varieties in the other country. In this sense both countries are characterized by a geographic concentration of industry. Third, the allocation of the market size for the varieties is not an outcome of the model but is simply given (income is therefore also given). This is closely linked to the immobility of workers (who demand the goods produced) and firms. In these respects, location in Krugman (1980) is still determined outside the model.

Compared to neo-classical trade theory, where almost everything of geographical interest is of the first-nature type, the analysis in this version of new trade theory comes closer to a setting in which the role of geography is founded on the decisions of individual agents, and is thus of the second-nature type. However, it still does not offer a theory of geographical economics. This is not surprising because the new trade theory was not developed for that purpose, but to provide a foundation for intra-industry trade. Interestingly, however, and although not offering a theory of location, new trade theory can be used to give a theoretical foundation for the empirical relationships among trade, income, and distance as provided by the gravity model; see Box 2.5.

Box 2.5.   New trade theory and the gravity model

We used a variant of the gravity model in chapter 1 to show that German trade flows are geographically concentrated. Despite its empirical success the gravity model, which states that (economic) proximity and trade flows are positively correlated, has been criticized for not having a sound theoretical foundation. The model has gained more acceptance from a trade-theoretical point of view

---

[21] Davis (1998) shows that the home-market effect is not robust; see also section 6.2. The home market effect occurs in Krugman (1980) because a larger market for a good in a country (and thus higher demand for this good) implies a more than proportional change in employment and production of that good, which in turn means that the country must be a net exporter of the good. In general, the extent to which relatively large home demand leads to exports depends on the elasticity of the labor supply. If this is not perfectly elastic, as in the core model of chapter 3, the relatively high demand will also result in higher wages.

because its basic equation can partly be derived from new trade theory. Helpman (1987), for example, derives a gravity equation from a new trade model with economies of scale at the firm level, product differentiation, and imperfect markets. Suppose there are two countries, Home and Foreign, and two sectors in the economy, X and Y (the numéraire). Both sectors produce under internal economies of scale using monopolistic competition. Free entry ensures the absence of equilibrium profits, which determines the number of varieties produced. Let X be the total production of X at home and x the amount of X per variety. Foreign variables are indicated by an asterisk (*). The number of varieties equals:

$$n = X/x \qquad \text{(similarly for Foreign)}$$

Using Dixit–Stiglitz identical homothetic preferences (see chapter 3) in both countries, each variety will be consumed in the ratio (GNP = gross national product):

$$s = GNP/(GNP + GNP^*) \qquad \text{(thus } s^* = 1 - s)$$

The value of exports of X for Home equals:

$$s^* nxp = s^* Xp \qquad (sn^* xp = sX^* p \text{ for Foreign})$$

where p is the price of x (for Y the equations are analogous). The total volume of trade V can now be derived as follows:

$$V = s(pX^* + Y^*) + s^*(pX + Y) = sGNP^* + s^* GNP = 2sGNP^*$$

Finally, if the current account is in equilibrium the expression for V can be rewritten as:

$$V = 2sGNP^* = 2ss^*(GNP + GNP^*)$$

The last expression is a basic variant of the gravity model as it indicates that the volume of trade depends positively on the (economic) size of the trading partners. A similar expression can be derived if more countries are incorporated. What is missing from this foundation of the gravity model is the fact that the volume of trade also depends significantly on distance, which is not accounted for in Helpman (1987). This is not surprising since new trade theory does not offer a theory of location. As with other well-established empirical relationships including "distance" as a variable, like the market potential index (see section 2.2.2), the approach must be founded on a theory in which location really matters to start with.[22]

---

[22] The similarity between the gravity model and the market potential index is obvious (Krugman, 1995a, pp. 44–45). In both cases the economic interaction between locations is a function of the "size" of those locations weighted by the distance between locations. See Deardorff (1998) on the compatibility of the gravity approach and neo-classical trade models.

Krugman and Venables 1990

The consequences of Krugman (1980) are analyzed in Krugman and Venables (1990). They allow *countries* to differ in size, thereby developing a model which looks very similar to the core model of geographical economics one year before this core model was published by Paul Krugman in 1991. It is a two-country model, where country 1 is large: it has more factor endowments (capital and labor) and a larger market than country 2.[23] In the main part of their paper the relative endowments are the same for the two countries, so there is no comparative advantage and trade is of the intra-industry type. In both countries, there are two sectors, both producing tradable goods, one perfectly competitive and the other, producing manufactures, imperfectly competitive. Country 1 also has a larger number of firms in the manufacturing sector. This sector produces differentiated products under increasing returns to scale and monopolistic competition. Entry and exit of firms is allowed, but firms cannot move between countries. The latter also holds for the factors of production. Both for firms and for the factors of production there is only inter-sectoral mobility. The central question is how an increase in the degree of economic integration (using a fall in transport costs as a proxy) affects the core (country 1) and periphery (country 2).

In autarky (when high transportation costs prohibit trade) both countries have a share in the manufacturing sector equal to their share in world endowments. The difference in endowments is given by segments A and B in Figure 2.6. It turns out that for an intermediate range of transport costs, economic integration strengthens the core (see Figure 2.6): the core's share of world industry S_1 gets larger than its share of world endowments (the latter is 0.6) and vice versa for the periphery ($S_2 < 0.4$). New firms enter the manufacturing sector in country 1, while some firms exit this sector in country 2. Given the larger market in country 1 and the minimization of transport costs, new firms prefer country 1 even though wages are higher. As transport costs continue to fall the core's share of world industry eventually starts to decrease again. At very low transport costs the advantage of producing in the country with the larger market becomes small, which combined with the stiffer labor market competition in country 1 (more firms compete for the country's production factors, which raises factor prices) implies that new firms find it profitable to start production in country 2 where wages are lower. At the extreme case of zero transport costs, wages will be equal and each country's share of manufactures will return to its share in world endowments. There is thus a non-linear relationship between a country's share in world industry and transport costs (Figure 2.6) in which the shares always sum to one.

Why is the analysis underlying Figure 2.6 interesting? First of all, it deals with the agglomeration of economic activity, because it allows for an uneven overall distribution of manufacturing activity. Recall that this is not the case in the Krugman (1980) model, where there is a geographic concentration of a single industry but there is no concentration of manufacturing production as a whole. Second, as will become clear

---

[23] Our discussion of Krugman and Venables (1990), including Figure 2.6, is based on Ottaviano and Puga (1997).

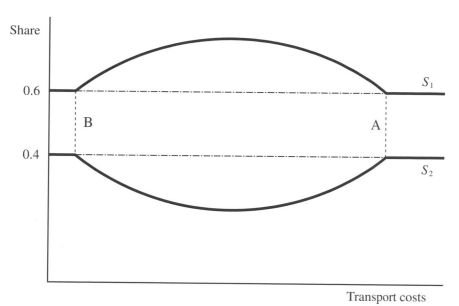

Figure 2.6. Shares of world production in manufactures.

in chapters 3–5, the U-shaped pattern in Figure 2.6 foreshadows important theoretical and empirical results in the geographical economics literature. Third, Figure 2.6 is based on numerical examples and they are used to analyze the effects of economic integration on the core and periphery. This resembles the strategy in geographical economics to use computer simulations to analyze the agglomeration of economic activity. So, is this a fully fledged geographical economics model? Well, it goes a long way, but in the end it is not.[24] The main reason is that the existence of core and periphery is not derived from the model itself. The assumption that the market size differs begs the question why there should be a core and periphery to start with. Along with fixing the market size goes the assumption that workers are immobile. Mobility of workers (and hence of demand) would run counter to the idea that one could *a priori* fix the relative market size of the two countries. The core model of chapters 3 and 4 adds endogenization of market size (and mobility of consumer/workers who determine the market size) to the Krugman and Venables (1990) model. In the introduction to their book, Fujita, Krugman, and Venables (1999) list four main features of geographical economics. Two of these features (Dixit–Stiglitz monopolistic competition and transportation costs of the iceberg type) are also at home in Krugman (1980). The Krugman and Venables (1990) model adds a (crude) attempt to use simulations. In our view, the real novelty of geographical economics is to be found in the fourth feature, dynamics, which tackles the question of how to deal with the mobility of economic agents (notably firms and

---

[24] See also Bhagwati, Panagariya, and Srinivasan (1998, pp. 188–189) for the observation that geographical economics can to a considerable extent be looked upon as an extension of the new trade theory of Krugman (1979, 1980).

workers) and which thereby endogenizes the size of the market. Before we turn to the core model in which the four features come together, we conclude chapter 2 with a discussion of the role of geography in theories of economic growth and development. This serves as an introduction to chapter 10.

2.4 Economic growth and development

Trade theory deals, above all, with the question of how international trade determines the allocation of economic activity among countries. As such it does not deal with the dynamic issue of economic growth and development over time. A geographical neglect of economic growth would not be a problem in the context of our study if countries experienced a more or less similar process of economic growth and converged to roughly the same levels of economic well-being. A quick look at the data (see Figures 1.2 and 1.3) makes clear that this is not the case. Growth rates of GDP per capita vary considerably between countries, and so does the level of GDP per capita. Moreover, the data suggest that there may be a geographical component involved. High and low growth countries are often geographically concentrated; think of Southeast Asia and Sub-Saharan Africa, respectively. High and low levels of GDP per capita are also clearly not randomly distributed across space: one observes clusters of rich and poor countries. In this section we ask whether theories on economic growth and development have something to say on the relationship between geography and economic growth. We do not give a survey but focus only on basic (and well-known) insights to assess the geographical relevance of growth theory.[25]

Economic growth theory
Geography is not really relevant in neo-classical growth theory. In the short run a positive growth rate of output per capita is possible by means of capital accumulation or technological progress. Since capital accumulation is subject to the law of diminishing returns, it is only through technological progress that a positive growth rate of output per capita can be sustained in the long run. Technological progress is exogenous, such that in the end it leaves the growth of output per head unexplained. Cross-country differences in the level of output per capita are thought to be temporary. Assuming that countries have access to the same technology and are equal in all other (structural or institutional) respects, neo-classical growth theory predicts that countries will converge to the same level of output per capita in the long run. The capital stock (per capita) will be low for *initially* poor countries, which implies a high return on investment (capital accumulation), and this fosters the convergence process. There will be absolute convergence: countries end up with the same equilibrium level of output (and capital) per capita. Even though convergence may be slow, the neo-classical growth model predicts that poor countries will catch up and that actual differences in growth rates are best thought of as reflecting this process of convergence. In such a world the spatial

---

[25] Good textbooks on growth are Jones (1998), Romer (1996), and Barro and Sala-i-Martin (1995).

agglomeration of high or low (growth rates of) GDP per capita does not warrant much attention. The basic version of the neo-classical growth model has a hard time explaining the stylized facts of growth; see also chapter 10. Either convergence is extremely slow, or the theory's main prediction, absolute convergence, is flawed. There are two options for improving upon this state of affairs: (i) adapt the neo-classical growth model to allow for persistent differences, or (ii) provide an alternative theory of economic growth.

Option (i) might include the introduction of a third factor of production, human capital, besides labor and physical capital, or the use of conditional instead of absolute convergence. This second possibility requires some explanation. Under conditional convergence, countries no longer have access to the same technology or may have different institutional characteristics. Consequently, countries need not converge to the same long-run equilibrium level of output per head. Instead, convergence is conditioned on the characteristics of a country. This allows for a (weak) link between geography and neo-classical growth theory: to the extent that the cross-country differences in technology or institutions are location-specific, geography matters. Empirical support is given by Gallup, Sachs, and Mellinger (1998), in a cross-country setting, and Black and Henderson (1998), for the growth of US cities, by showing that physical geographical differences, like climate or access to the sea, have a strong impact on economic growth (see Box 2.6). As with neo-classical trade theory, the role of geography in neo-classical growth theory is limited and indirect. Its impact is determined outside the model and there is no feedback from the growth variables to the location variables.

Option (ii) requires the development of an alternative theoretical model to neo-classical growth theory. Since the seminal work of Romer (1986, 1990) and Lucas (1988), this avenue of research has become known as *new growth theory*. Although the models may vary considerably, two crucial (intertwined) differences from the neo-classical growth model are the attempts to endogenize economic growth and to dispense with the assumption of diminishing returns to accumulable factors (Van Marrewijk, 1999). With respect to the use of scale economies, various options exist in the new growth theory literature. Initially, most models used pure external economies at the national or industry level, rather than internal economies at the firm level (see Box 2.1). Subsequent research also used positive internal economies under imperfect competition, similar to new trade theory. Positive external economies may give rise to positive spillovers, strategic complementarity, and hence to multiple equilibria.[26] Other possibilities also exist, like the celebrated AK-model with constant returns to capital at the economy-wide level, which implies that countries do not converge to the same long-run equilibrium. Endogenization of the growth process focuses on technological progress, a positive function of the overall stock of capital or labor, or of R&D expenditures. Let Y be output, K the stock of capital, L labor, and $A(.)$ the technology function. Consider the following production function:

---

[26] Spillovers are not the same as strategic complementarity. Positive spillovers arise if an increase in the effort of one agent positively affects the payoff of other agents. Strategic complementarity arises if an increase in the effort of one agent increases the optimal efforts of other agents.

$$Y = A(.)K^{1-b}L^b, \quad 0 < b < 1 \tag{2.2}$$

This production function is very similar to the well-known Cobb–Douglas production function typically underlying the neo-classical growth model. In fact, if we assume that A is a constant we do have the Cobb–Douglas production function and it can readily be seen that output per capita Y/L is determined by the stock of capital per worker K/L. Growth of the latter is subject to diminishing returns (as long as $0 < b < 1$). Returning to equation (2.2), non-decreasing scale economies can be incorporated by specifying $A(.)$ as a function of the aggregate capital stock, human capital, or some dynamic "innovation" function, which captures the accumulation of aggregate knowledge in the economy. The crux of all these attempts is to ensure there are no longer diminishing returns to accumulable factors of production.

Whether the new growth theory is really different from the neo-classical growth theory, and whether it is possible to differentiate empirically between the two theories, is not undisputed (Solow, 1994). Our main interest here is in the possible role for geography in the new growth theory. In many versions of the new growth theory there is no such role. To allow for location to be relevant, countries must differ in some respect. Take, for example, external economies to scale. If these are the same for all countries, the economy can be described by one uniform "global" production function with increasing returns to scale. Location is not irrelevant if the spillovers associated with the external economies are somehow localized. Grossman and Helpman (1991) analyze localized spillovers where the positive externalities associated with R&D, or, more generally, with knowledge, only exist within a certain group of countries. This model is in a number of respects very close to the core model of geographical economics; see Brakman and Garretsen (1993, p. 179). The existence of localized externalities, and hence the limited geographical range of knowledge spillovers, may be due to cultural, political, and institutional differences that can all contribute to the localization of these external economies. They can help explain not only why some (group of) countries have a higher growth rate and level of output per capita than others, but also why this difference might not diminish over time, making core–periphery equilibria possible. The new growth models can thus account for the agglomeration of economic activity. The problem is how location itself is analyzed. The introduction of location in the new growth theory bears a great resemblance to the relevance of location in the neo-classical growth models that allow for conditional convergence. In both cases the role of location does not follow from the model itself, and in both cases it is stipulated either theoretically or empirically that a country's rate of technological progress depends on the location of that country. The conclusion must be that location is still not part of the analysis and that the endogenization of economic growth does not extend to the role of geography. Even though some versions of the new growth theory are in a number of respects rather similar to the geographical economics models (increasing returns to scale, imperfect competition, differentiated products, and multiple equilibria), the new growth theory does not offer a theory of location.

Box 2.6.   The relevance of physical geography

In their work on the geographic concentration of US industries, Ellison and Glaeser (1997, 1999) argue that this concentration may arise for two reasons. The first reason is the existence of increasing-returns technologies and other economies of scale. We might call this the role of *economics* in geography. This is what the geographical economics models are first and foremost about. The second reason for concentration is the existence of *natural* cost advantages that are due to differences in the actual physical geography. Ellison and Glaeser (1999, p. 315) conclude that about 20% of the observed agglomeration of US industries can be explained by variables that measure natural advantages. Similarly, Haaland *et al.* (1999) conclude in a different context that industry concentration in Europe is significantly determined by differences in endowments across Europe. Although home-market effects are even more important in explaining the geographical concentration of industry, the relevance of endowments also (indirectly) implies that physical geography may be important since differences in endowments can be due to differences in physical geography (section 2.3.1).

In their study of the evolution of US cities, Black and Henderson (1998) state that the growth performance of cities may differ for two reasons: differences in physical geography and differences due to the concentration effects emphasized by geographical economics. They measure the latter by means of the market potential for each city. With respect to physical geography, they find that "cities in warm (less heating degree days) and drier (less precipitation) climates on the coast indeed grow faster" (pp. 27–28). At any rate, these studies point to the relevance of physical geography in explaining the agglomeration of economic activity.

In a large cross-country study, Gallup, Sachs, and Mellinger (1998) investigate the impact of physical geography on economic growth. The starting point for their analysis is the observation that virtually all countries in the tropics are relatively poor, whereas countries situated outside the tropics are almost invariably relatively rich (in GDP per capita). Moreover, coastal countries generally have higher incomes than countries without good access to the sea. In a number of cross-section estimations they regress economic growth on various indicators of physical geography (controlling for the standard determinants of growth). They too find that physical geography matters, although not necessarily in a direct manner (the location in the tropics is not significant but the presence of malaria very significantly lowers growth). However, the location of a country relative to the sea (either by being a coastal country or a country with navigable waterways leading to the sea) gives a straightforward direct (positive) impact of physical geography on economic growth. Additional evidence by Mellinger, Gallup, and Sachs (2000) lends support to the idea that physical geography is important in explaining growth and income differences across the world.

The point we want to emphasize is that physical geography matters for the location of economic activity. In the terminology used in this chapter, the first-nature aspects of location choices are important. This should be stressed because geographical economics, and thus much of the remainder of this book, focuses on the second-nature of location choice, thereby often assuming that space (physical geography) is homogeneous (although we discuss non-neutral space in chapter 6). These approaches are not in conflict with each other, as Gallup, Sachs, and Mellinger (1998, p. 132) also recognize: "the two approaches can of course be complementary: a city might emerge because of cost advantages arising from differentiated geography but continue to thrive because of agglomeration economies even when the cost advantages have disappeared. Empirical work should aim to disentangle the forces of differentiated geography and self-organizing agglomeration economies." In chapter 9 we show how the first-nature and second-nature determinants of location can be combined in one model.

Economic development

So far, we have used the words economic growth and economic development interchangeably. However, within economic theory the analysis of economic development usually refers to the conditions under which developing countries can achieve economic growth. This is a somewhat narrower scope than the analysis of economic growth, which should apply to all countries, and which deals more with ongoing growth and less with preconditions for growth. Nowadays, studies of economic development make extensive use of (old and new) economic growth theory. In this respect development economics is to a large extent an application of mainstream economics to developing countries.[27] This has not always been the case. Especially in the 1950s and 1960s, development economists like Myrdal (1957) and Hirschman (1958) and others like Perroux (1955), following Rosenstein-Rodan (1943), used an analytical framework which was very different from the neo-classical approach that is now dominant in development economics. This framework came under attack for its (alleged) lack of analytical coherence, which was not very surprising because these authors, sometimes explicitly but more often implicitly, relied on external economies and imperfect competition, concepts that were not at home in mainstream economics in those days. The theories used by these development economists are interesting because they tried not only to explain the (lacking) conditions for economic growth in developing countries, but also to have a keen eye for the geographical dimension of economic development, both within developing countries and between rich and poor countries. This explains why economic geographers to this

---

[27] A good example is the textbook by Agenor and Montiel (1996).

day, when discussing economic development, still refer to the work of these "older" development economists.[28]

Again, it is not our aim to survey this field. We therefore restrict ourselves to a brief discussion of the main concepts. In the influential *big push* analysis of Rosenstein-Rodan (1943) an insufficient local market size is seen as the main cause of the under-development of a region or a country. The solution to underdevelopment is to be found in a coordinated (that is, government-led) expansion of investment which enables firms to reap the benefits of (external and internal) scale economies, thus fostering industri-alization of the backward region or country. An individual firm has no incentive to expand its production level because of the absence of increasing returns to scale at the firm level. The expansion of production only becomes profitable, and here the external economies enter the story, if a sufficient number of other firms also expand their pro-duction (hence the term "big push"). Industrialization in the backward region or country also requires the manufacturing labor force to expand. If labor is immobile between countries, the expansion of the manufacturing labor force has to come about by drawing labor from other sectors of the economy (typically the agricultural sector), which requires a sufficiently elastic labor supply. Without a big push in investment the periphery cannot catch up with the core, so to speak.

Myrdal (1957) also describes the sustainability of core–periphery patterns of eco-nomic development (see also Thirlwall, 1991). He does not so much emphasize the con-ditions under which the backward country or region may start a process of economic development. Instead, he argues that if, for whatever reason, a region or country gets a head-start in terms of economic development, this lead will very likely be self-reinforcing. Myrdal introduced the concept of *circular* or *cumulative causation* to describe this process. Once a country or region takes the lead in economic develop-ment, positive external economies in this country or region will ensure that it will become to firms a more attractive place (not, as the neo-classical growth model pre-dicts, a less attractive one) in which to invest, and a more attractive location for labor. The existence of strong *localized* spillovers leads to the establishment of a core (with the relatively larger market) and a periphery.[29]

Hirschman (1958) also focuses on the self-reinforcing nature of (differences in) eco-nomic development. His use of *backward* and *forward linkages* can be thought of as illustrating how firms, by locating production in a particular region, increase the prof-itability for other firms doing so too. In modern terminology, the ideas put forward by Hirschman have a clear flavor of increasing returns to scale. It should be noted that the use of increasing returns to scale in the writings of Rosenstein-Rodan, Myrdal, or Hirschman is (at best) indirect in the sense that they do not analyze the relevance of scale economies for economic development themselves. This relevance is distilled from

---

[28] See for example chapter 6 of the widely used textbook on economic geography by Dicken and Lloyd (1990) and the discussion of the export-based multiplier in section 2.2.2.

[29] The terminology suggests a resemblance to endogenous growth theory. This is no coincidence because the main ideas of this "older" literature on development economics are the same as in modern growth theory, even though these ideas are expressed in different ways.

their works from the perspective of modern economic theory.[30] In fact, the difficulties of analyzing the role of increasing returns and imperfect competition ensured that the heyday of this branch of development economics was rather short-lived. The neo-classical theory of economic development with its emphasis on perfect competition and decreasing returns remained far more influential.

Nowadays, this last statement no longer holds. With the rise of the new trade theory, the new growth theory and, of course, geographical economics, increasing returns and imperfect competition have become more of a rule than an exception in economic theorizing. When it comes to economic development these "new" theories formalize the insights of Rosenstein-Rodan *cum suis* and give these insights a micro-economic foundation.[31] We arrived at a similar conclusion at the end of our discussion of urban and regional economics in section 2.2. In the next chapter our in-depth discussion of the core model of geographical economics will make clear how increasing returns, imperfect competition and, most notably, the role of location are handled. In chapter 10 we will pick up the topic of growth and development from the perspective of geographical economics.

2.5   Conclusions

What is the main message of this chapter? It is that all the theoretical approaches discussed in the previous sections have something useful to say on the relationship between geography and economics, but that each approach also has its limitations. Without too much exaggeration one can argue that in regional and urban economics there is ample room for geography (or space) in the analysis, but less for economic theory. That is, these approaches lack the micro-economic foundation of individual behavior, and the general equilibrium structure that constitutes the backbone of mainstream economic theory nowadays. Conversely, both for the old as well as the new trade and growth theories, such a micro-economic foundation and general equilibrium structure exists, but the problem is that geography is sometimes next to irrelevant or, when it matters, its role is not (sufficiently) linked to the underlying behavior of economic agents. In our view, geographical economics can be looked upon as an attempt to further break down the fence between geography and economics. In doing so, it has its roots firmly in mainstream economic

---

[30] This might be true in general, but consider for example the following quotation from Myrdal (1957):
the power of attraction today of a center has its origin mainly in the historical accident that something was once started there, and not in a number of other places where it could equally well or better have been started, and the start met with success. Thereafter the ever-increasing internal and external economies – interpreted in the widest sense of the word to include, for instance, a working population trained in various crafts, easy communications, the feeling of growth and elbow room and the spirit of new enterprise – fortified and sustained their continuous growth at the expense of other localities and regions where instead relative stagnation or regression became the pattern (pp. 26–27).

[31] In the case of Rosenstein-Rodan's big push theory the best example is Murphy, Shleifer, and Vishny (1989). They develop a model in which pecuniary external economies are generated by increasing returns to scale on the level of the firm. Krugman (1995a, pp. 8–14) uses one of the models developed by Murphy, Shleifer, and Vishny (the version in which there is a wage premium in the manufacturing sector compared to the traditional sector of the economy) to show how it captures the main insights from the aforementioned development economists.

theory, so it is, in particular, an attempt to bring more geography into economics. For that reason, we prefer the term geographical economics to new economic geography.

How do we proceed from here? In chapters 3 and 4, the core model of geographical economics will be developed and discussed at length. The empirical evidence with respect to geographical economics will be the topic of chapter 5. The stylized facts are subsequently used as input for chapters 6–10, in which various extensions of the core model will be analyzed. In the final chapter of the book, chapter 11, we will return to the question whether geographical economics delivers what it promises to do, namely a better understanding of the relationships between geography and economics. Finally, given that Von Thünen's *Isolated State* was published in 1826, it is quite puzzling why, until very recently, mainstream economics neglected the issue of the location of economic activity. Part of the answer must surely be (see Krugman, 1995a) that the analysis of the location of economic activity must be grounded on increasing returns to scale and imperfect competition, and that economists have long struggled to incorporate both these elements into their models. Still, this cannot fully explain the neglect. Maybe Mark Blaug (1984, p. 630) had a point when he stated that

> in the final analysis, all the attempts to account for the curious disdain of location theory on the part of mainstream economists end up by invoking conservatism and blinkered thinking, which restates the puzzle instead of solving it. Perhaps, the solution of the mystery is simpler than anyone has imagined. If Ricardo had based his rent theory on locational advantages instead of fertility differences, if [Von] Thünen had been a lucid instead of an obscure writer . . . is there any reason to doubt that the whole of classical locational theory would have found a place in Marshall's *Principles* and, thereby, in the corpus of received economic doctrine?

Exercises

2.1* Assume a trade model with transportation costs but without increasing returns to scale. In fact, think of this model as a neo-classical trade model with transportation costs associated with the trade of goods. Discuss the location of economic activity in such a model.

2.2* See Box 2.2 about the central place theory in a Dutch polder. Why do you think it might be the case that the predictions of the Dutch authorities about the relative size of settlements in this polder have not materialized?

2.3 We know from chapter 1 (see Figures 1.2 and 1.3) that economic activity is clearly not distributed randomly across the world. How would you explain this, assuming that you can only use the neo-classical trade or growth theory for your answer?

2.4* Increasing returns to scale are an important topic in chapter 2 (see Box 2.1). Below are three examples of a production structure. Explain for each example what kind of returns to scale is relevant.

(i)   Assume a firm i faces the following cost function (which summarizes its production structure): $l_i = \alpha + \beta x_i$ where l_i is the amount of labor necessary to produce output x_i and where α and β describe respectively the fixed and marginal labor input requirement.

(ii) Assume an economy has the following production function (see section 2.4): $Y = AK$. Additional question: is it to be expected that the same degree of returns to scale hold for the production function of the individual firm i? If not, how can these two production functions be reconciled?

(iii) Assume the individual firm has the following production function: $y = ak^{0.3}$ with $a = K$, where K is the economy-wide capital stock.

2.5 Consider the following two quotations from the *Oxford Handbook of Economic Geography*. Explain in each instance how in your view these quotations relate to the location theories discussed in chapter 2:

(i)   "So the tradition of international trade theory has sidestepped geographical questions – most modeling imagines a world without transport costs, let alone cities! – while that of geography has sometimes been based on what trade theorists would consider half-worked-out models, and often rejected formalism altogether."

(ii) "the analytical machinery of microeconomics [plays a strong role] in Krugman's geography and his work, despite its originality, can perhaps best be seen as a continuation of the tradition of . . . regional science. Better yet, we might call it a 'new' regional science."

3   The core model of geographical economics

3.1   Introduction

As has already been mentioned in the preface, Bertil Ohlin (1933) observed long ago that the fields of trade theory on the one hand and regional and urban economics on the other had in principle the same research objectives. Both areas want to answers the questions: who produces what, where, and why. Despite Ohlin's observation, each field has continued to go its own way since the nineteenth century. Chapter 2 showed that trade theory assumes that countries are dimensionless points in space. Trade theorists are mostly interested in how market structure, production techniques, and consumer behavior interact. The resulting factor and commodity prices determine the pattern of international trade flows. Location is at best an exogenous factor and usually does not play a role of any significance.[1] Regional and urban economics, instead, take market structure and prices as given and try to find out which allocation of space is most efficient. The underlying behavior of consumers and producers, central in trade theory, is less important (Fujita and Thisse, 1996). Although both strands of literature produce valuable insights in their own right, trade theory and regional and urban economics are productively combined in geographical economics.

This chapter discusses and explains the core model of geographical economics, a small general equilibrium model developed by Krugman (1991). As we shall see, the equilibrium equations of this model are non-linear. This means that small changes in parameters do not always produce the same effects; sometimes the effects are small, sometimes they are large. Translated into regional and urban economics, this means, for example, that the location decision of a single producer might not change the spatial pattern of production, but it *could* have dramatic or "catastrophic" (to borrow

[1] Gravity models, discussed in section 1.4, Box 2.5, and in chapter 9, are the exception to the rule. These models are easily extended to include all kinds of transport costs. Limao and Venables (2000), for example, include trading costs related to within-country infrastructure and trading costs related to international trade in a gravity equation. However, gravity models are notoriously difficult to derive from micro-economic principles. Deardorff (1998) shows that the gravity equation is consistent with many models. Note, that Deardorff, using the difference between cif and fob measures of trade (see Box 3.3), derives a gravity equation *including* transport costs, which in standard derivations is usually missing.

a term from the chaos literature) consequences. It is possible that the location decision of a single producer could trigger a process of cumulative causation and that the spatial pattern of production could change dramatically. Also, the model has multiple equilibria, and this characteristic is, as we have explained in chapter 2, one of the major differences from regional science or urban economics. There is no presumption on which location might become the center of production, but once a location gets a head start the process of cumulative causation starts working. Initially small differences between locations can evolve over time to large differences in the long-run equilibrium. These and other features make models of geographical economics analytically complicated.

We therefore explain the model in three steps. First, we give a simple example in section 3.2 to illustrate some important features of the core model, to which we return in the rest of this chapter. It is important to realize that it is indeed only an example and not a model; that is, many aspects are assumed rather than derived. Second, we explain the basic structure of the core *model* of geographical economics in non-technical terms in section 3.3. Third, we focus on the modeling details of the core model in sections 3.4–3.7, and explain some of its interactions in sections 3.8 and 3.9. After the explanation of the model we return to our example in section 3.10.

3.2 An example of geographical economics

It is possible to construct a simple example to illustrate some of the main findings of the geographical economics approach.[2] Suppose there are two regions (or countries), North and South, and two sectors of production, manufacturing and agriculture. The manufacturing industry produces varieties, that is differentiated products, under internal economies of scale. The cost per unit of output therefore falls as a firm expands its production level. As a result, each firm produces only one variety. A firm can reside either in North or South, that is a firm has to decide where to produce. This location decision essentially differentiates the example from new trade theory.

Total demand for each variety of manufactures in this example is exogenous. We assume that each firm sells 4 units to workers in the manufacturing industry and 6 units to farmers. Total demand for each variety is therefore 10 (6+4). The production of agriculture, and hence the demand it generates, is location-specific. Its spatial distribution is exogenously given; we assume that 4 units are sold in North and 2 units in South. The location of the workers in the manufacturing sector, and hence the 4 units they demand at that location, are not exogenous. The role of the immobile workers is important as they ensure that there is always positive demand in *both* regions. Finally, transport costs between North and South are 1 euro per unit. The firms choose locations to minimize transport costs.

We are now able to determine the location decision of each firm. First, we can calculate the regional sales of each firm, given the location of the other firms. In Table 3.1,

---

[2] A simpler version of this example can be found in Krugman and Obstfeld (1994, p. 185).

Table 3.1. *Geography of sales*

	Sales in North	Sales in South	Total sales
All firms in North	4+4=8	0+2=2	10
All firms in South	0+4=4	4+2=6	10
25% firms in North, 75% firms in South	1+4=5	3+2=5	10

Table 3.2. *Transport costs*

	If location in North	If location in South
All firms in North	0+2=**2** (to farmers in South)	4+4=8 (to workers and farmers in North)
All firms in South	4+2=6 (to workers and farmers in South)	0+4=**4** (to farmers in North)
25% firms in North, 75% firms in South	3+2=5 (to workers and farmers in South)	1+4=5 (to workers and farmers in North)

three (non-exhaustive) possibilities are given: all firms in North, all firms in South, or 25% of all firms in North and 75% of firms in South. Sales in each region are equal to sales to workers in manufacturing plus sales to farmers. Take, for example, the last row in Table 3.1. The firm sells 5 units in North, namely 4 to the farmers located in North plus 1 ($=25\%\times4$) unit to the manufacturing workers located in North. Similarly, the firm sells 5 units in South, namely 2 units to the farmers located in South plus 3 ($=75\% \times 4$) units to the manufacturing workers located in South.

Second, using Table 3.1 we can construct a decision table, by calculating transport costs as a function of the firm's location decision, given the location of the other firms. Suppose, for example, that all firms are located in North. Table 3.2 indicates that transport costs for a firm locating in South will then be 8 euro, namely 4 for sales to the farmers in North and 4 for sales to all workers in manufacturing located in North (abstracting from sales to its own workers). Similarly, if the firm locates in North, transport costs would be only 2 for the sales to the farmers in South. Since transport costs are minimized by locating in the North if all other firms are located in North, the firm also decides to locate production in North. As Table 3.2 shows (second row) a firm will locate in South if all other firms are also located there, whereas (last row) the firm is indifferent between locating in North or South (since transport costs are the same if the firm locates in either region) if 25% of the firms are located in North and 75% in South.

On the basis of this example, we can illustrate a few distinctive characteristics of the geographical economics approach. We return to each of these observations later in this chapter.

First, there is the concept of *cumulative causation*. If, for some reason, one location has attracted more firms than the other, a new firm has an incentive to locate where the other firms are. Take the first row in Table 3.2. If all firms are located in North, a firm, minimizing transport costs, should also locate there to minimize transport costs. Similarly, for the second row in Table 3.2 the firm will locate in South.

Second, Table 3.2 illustrates the existence of *multiple equilibria*. Agglomeration of all firms in either North or South is an equilibrium. However, we cannot determine beforehand where agglomeration will occur. This depends critically on initial conditions, that is the previous location decisions of other firms.

Third, an equilibrium might be *stable* or *unstable*. The bold entries in Table 3.2 are both stable equilibria; if a single firm decides to relocate, this decision would not influence the location decisions of the other firms. The last row in Table 3.2 describes an unstable equilibrium. If a single firm decides to relocate, the new location will immediately become more attractive for all other firms. This will trigger a snowball effect: all firms will follow the pioneer. In this example, only agglomeration is a stable equilibrium.

Fourth, we note that a stable equilibrium can be *non-optimal*. If all firms are located in North transport costs are only 2; if all firms are located in South transport costs are 4 (see the bold entries in Table 3.2). Thus, transport costs for the economy as a whole are minimized if all firms agglomerate in North, whereas agglomeration in South is a stable equilibrium.

Fifth, the tables illustrate the *interaction of agglomeration and trade flows*. With complete agglomeration, that is all manufactures are produced in a single region, trade between regions will be of the inter-industry type (food for manufactures). In fact, this equilibrium also reflects the *home-market* effect; the combination of economies-of-scale and transport costs is responsible for the clustering of all footloose activity in a single location. Because of this combination, transport costs can be minimized. The large region ends up with a large market for manufacturing goods, which can be sold without incurring transport costs. The consequence is that this region becomes the exporter of manufactured goods; large regions tend to become exporters of those goods for which they have a large local market, hence the term home-market effect. If the manufacturing industry is located in both regions, as described by the last row in the tables, trade will also be of the intra-industry type. Besides trading manufactured goods for agricultural products, different varieties of the differentiated manufactured products will be traded between both regions.

The example is useful as it illustrates important aspects of geographical economics. But an example is just an example and it is not a substitute for a well-specified model. What is missing in the example? First of all, the interaction of transport costs, price-setting behavior, and location choice is missing. We simply assume that the demand each firm faces is given and independent of price-setting behavior and transport costs. In fact, prices are completely lacking in the example. There is no analysis of the market structure. In reality, prices, wages, and transport costs will determine the purchasing power of consumers. One might guess that this interaction drives the location decisions of consumers and producers. Furthermore, it is a partial equilibrium model in the sense that firms do not worry about the necessary labor; wherever they decide to locate,

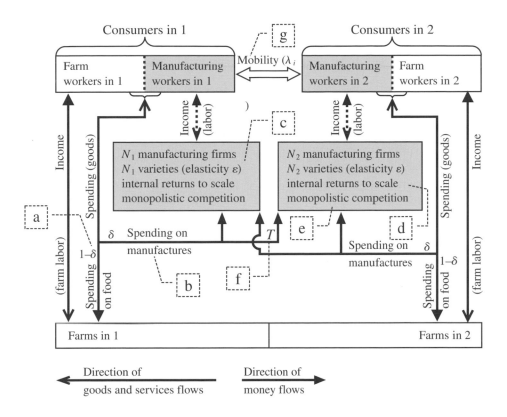

Figure 3.1.   Structure of the core model of geographical economics.

labor is not the problem. It will turn out that assumptions about the functioning of the labor market are important. The reader might also notice the similarity of the example and Krugman's (1980) new trade model discussed in chapter 2. In both models, scale economies and transport costs are important forces. The most important difference is that in our example firms can locate in either region. Consequently, the example gives rise to both agglomeration and multiple equilibria. It is now time to move from the example to the core model.

3.3   The structure of the model

This section gives a non-technical overview of the general structure of the core model of geographical economics. The nuts and bolts of the core model are laid out in Dixit and Stiglitz (1977) and Krugman (1979, 1980). This work stimulated a large body of work on the new trade theory (see section 2.3.2). Krugman (1991) extended the latter by incorporating cross-border factor mobility, and this has become the core model of geographical economics.

This structure is illustrated in Figure 3.1, which serves as a frame of reference throughout the remainder of this chapter. *We urge the reader to have a regular look at this picture to understand the main arguments in the text more easily.* The details of the structure of the model will be explained in the sections to follow.

The core model identifies two regions, labeled 1 and 2. There are two sectors in the economy, the manufacturing sector and the food sector. Consumers in region 1 consist of farm workers and manufacturing workers; similarly, for region 2. The farm workers earn their income by working for the farmers in their region. If they own the farm it is as if they hire themselves. They then play a dual role, both as farmers and as farm workers. The income stream of the farm workers is part of a bilateral transfer: they receive an income from the farmer (the farm wage rate) and in return have to supply labor services to the farmer. All such bilateral transfers are indicated with bidirectional arrows in Figure 3.1. The solid-headed arrows indicate the direction of money or income flows, that is, indicate the direction of income and spending (see, however, Box 3.1 on the numéraire, wages, and real wages). What the flow represents is indicated along the line connecting the arrow points. The open-headed arrows indicate the direction of goods or services flows. These are indicated *in parentheses* along the line connecting the arrow points. The farmers in region 1 use the labor services of the farm workers from region 1 to produce food under constant returns to scale and perfect competition. They sell this food to the consumers, either in region 1 or in region 2. By assumption, there are no transport costs for food, an issue addressed in chapter 6.

The manufacturing sector consists of N_1 firms in region 1 and N_2 firms in region 2. Each manufacturing firm produces a differentiated product, that is it produces a unique product, using only labor under internal economies of scale. This implies that the firms have monopolistic power, which they use in determining the price of their product. There are transport costs involved in selling a manufactured good in another region. These costs do not arise if the manufactured good is sold in the region in which it is produced. As a result of the transport costs involved in exporting manufactured goods to another region, firms will charge a higher price in the other region than at home. The manufacturing workers earn their income (the manufacturing wage rate) by supplying labor to the firms in the manufacturing sector of their region.

The consumers spend their income on food and manufactures. Since food is a homogeneous good they do not care whether it is produced in region 1 or in region 2. As there are no transport costs for food, it fetches the same price in both regions (implying that farmers earn the same wage in both regions). Spending by consumers on manufactures has to be allocated over the many varieties produced in regions 1 and 2. Other things being equal, consuming imported varieties is more expensive than consuming domestic varieties as a result of the transport costs of manufactured goods. However, since the varieties are differentiated products and the consumers have a liking for variety, they will always consume at least some units of all varieties produced, whether at home or abroad.

A few final remarks on Figure 3.1 are in order. First, the figure mentions the most important parameters to be used throughout the remainder of this book, namely ε, δ,

λ_i, and T. At this point it is not important to know what these parameters are. They, and others, will be discussed in the rest of this chapter. Second, Figure 3.1 shows seven "callouts," labeled a–g. These callouts refer to important construction details of the core model. They will be used as a reference and a reminder in section 3.4 on the demand structure of the model (callouts a, b, and c), section 3.5 on the supply structure of the model (callouts d and e), section 3.6 on the role of transport costs (callout f), and section 3.8 on the dynamics of the model (callout g). Third, and most importantly, there are shaded boxes in Figure 3.1. These draw attention to the distinguishing feature of geographical economics: mobility of factors of production (see chapter 2). The core model applies mobility only to the manufacturing sector; thus manufacturing workers can relocate from region 1 to region 2, or vice versa. The relocation of manufacturing firms from one region to another is the other side of the same coin, as an expansion of the manufacturing workforce in a region implies expansion of production in the manufacturing sector. It is important to note that in principle the shaded boxes can disappear in a region, for example if all manufacturing workers (and thus the entire manufacturing sector) move to region 2. The non-shaded boxes, labeled farm workers and farmers, cannot disappear from a region. The farmers need the land for cultivation and are thus not mobile. The region therefore can always spend income generated by this sector. Actually, the distinction between mobile activity and immobile activity is important. For ease of reference we labeled these sectors "manufactures" and "food," respectively. Obviously, the immobile sector could also produce iron ore, or paper, etc.

Box 3.1.   Terminology

The terminology used in economic analysis can be confusing to the reader for various reasons. Sometimes the same term has different meanings in different fields of economics. Sometimes a term can be interpreted in various ways. Sometimes the same area of research is known under a range of names. Although the terminology used in our book will, inevitably, occasionally also puzzle the reader, we would like to limit this puzzlement to a minimum. This box will therefore briefly describe and explain our main terminology.

Agglomeration and spreading
We are interested in explaining various forms of clustering of (economic) activity, which we refer to as "agglomeration." We use the term "spreading" to refer to the opposite of "agglomeration." Other terms used in the literature, such as "centripetal," "centrifugal," "convergent," and "divergent," will not be used in this book because they can be confusing. For example, "converging" may indicate either that all industry "converges," that is tends to locate in one region, or that all regions "converge," that is all industries are spread across regions.

Numéraire
The economic agents in the general equilibrium models of geographical economics do not suffer from money illusion, that is their decisions are based on relative prices and do not depend on the absolute price level. This allows us to set the price of one of the goods in the model equal to 1, and express all other prices in the model relative to the price of the numéraire good. The remainder of the book chooses food as the numéraire good, such that the price of food is always equal to 1.

Wages and real wages
The core general equilibrium modeling approach used in this book chooses a numéraire good to pin down relative prices. Wages in different regions expressed in the numéraire should be referred to as "numéraire wages." Although better than the frequently used term "nominal wages" (since the monetary sector is not explicitly modeled) it is a cumbersome term. We therefore use the shorter term "wages" whenever we refer to "numéraire wages" and will explicitly use the term "real wages" when the numéraire wages are corrected for the price level to determine purchasing power.

3.4   Demand

The rest of this chapter describes and explains many details of the structure of the core model of geographical economics, as graphically summarized in Figure 3.1. Whenever appropriate we will refer to the callouts *a–g* of Figure 3.1. This chapter serves a dual purpose, namely (i) giving a description and explanation of the core model that is as clear and accessible as possible, and (ii) being complete in this description, in particular by deriving all technical details. To strike a balance between these two objectives we have placed all derivations in Technical Notes. We advice the reader to *skip all Technical Notes on first reading* in order to follow the flow of the arguments more easily. The mathematically inclined reader can then return to the technical details in the notes at a later stage.

3.4.1   *Spending on food and manufactures (callout a)*

As explained in section 3.3 the economy has two goods sectors, manufactures M and food F. Although "manufactures" consist of many different varieties, we can define an exact price index to represent them as a group, as will be explained below. We call this price index of manufactures I. If a consumer earns an income Y (from working either in the food sector or the manufacturing sector) she has to decide how much of this income to spend on food and how much on manufactures. The solution to this problem depends on the preferences of the consumer, assumed to be of the Cobb–Douglas specification given in equation (3.1) for all consumers, where U represents utility, F represents food consumption and M represents consumption of manufactures.

$$U = F^{1-\delta} M^{\delta}, \quad 0 < \delta < 1 \tag{3.1}$$

Obviously, any income spent on food cannot simultaneously be spent on manufactures, that is the consumer must satisfy the budget constraint in equation (3.2).

$$F + I \cdot M = Y \tag{3.2}$$

Note the absence of the price of food in this equation. This is a result of choosing food as the numéraire (see Box 3.1), which implies that income Y is measured in terms of food. Thus, only the price index of manufactures I occurs in equation (3.2). To decide on the optimal allocation of income over food and manufactures the consumer now has to solve a simple optimization problem, namely maximize utility, given in equation (3.1), subject to the budget constraint of equation (3.2). The solution to this problem is given in equation (3.3), and derived in Technical Note 3.1.

$$F = (1 - \delta) Y; \quad IM = \delta Y \tag{3.3}$$

As equation (3.3) shows, it is optimal for the consumer to spend a fraction $(1 - \delta)$ of income on food, and a fraction δ of income on manufactures. This explains callout a in Figure 3.1. We will henceforth refer to the parameter δ given in equation (3.1) as the fraction of income spent on manufactures.

Technical Note 3.1.   Derivation of equation (3.3)

To maximize equation (3.1) subject to the budget constraint (3.2) we define the Lagrangean Γ, using the multiplier κ:

$$\Gamma = F^{1-\delta} M^{\delta} + \kappa[Y - (F + IM)]$$

Differentiating Γ with respect to F and M gives the first-order conditions:

$$(1 - \delta) F^{-\delta} M^{\delta} = \kappa; \quad \delta F^{1-\delta} M^{\delta-1} = \kappa I$$

Taking the ratio of the first-order conditions gives:

$$\frac{\delta F^{1-\delta} M^{\delta-1}}{(1 - \delta) F^{-\delta} M^{\delta}} = \frac{\kappa I}{\kappa}; \quad \text{or} \quad IM = \frac{\delta}{1 - \delta} F$$

Substituting the latter in budget equation (3.2) gives:

$$Y = F + IM = F + \frac{\delta}{1 - \delta} F; \quad \text{or} \quad F = (1 - \delta) Y$$

which indicates that the share $(1 - \delta)$ of income is spent on food, and thus the share δ on manufactures, as given in equation (3.3).

3.4.2   Spending on manufacturing varieties (callout b)

Now that we have determined in subsection 3.4.1 the share δ of income which is spent on manufactured goods, we still have to decide how this spending is allocated among the different varieties of manufactures. In essence, this is a similar problem as in subsection 3.4.1, that is we have to allocate spending optimally over a number of goods which can be consumed. This problem can only be solved if we specify how the preferences for the aggregate consumption of manufactures M depend on the consumption of particular varieties of manufactures. In this respect the core model of geographical economics fruitfully applies a model of monopolistic competition developed in the industrial organization literature by Dixit and Stiglitz; see Box 3.2. Let c_i be the level of consumption of a particular variety i of manufactures, and let N be the number of available varieties. The Dixit–Stiglitz approach uses a constant elasticity of substitution (CES) function to construct the aggregate consumption of manufactures M as a function of the consumption c_i of the N varieties:[3]

$$M = \left(\sum_{i=1}^{N} c_i^\rho \right)^{1/\rho}, \quad 0 < \rho < 1 \tag{3.4}$$

Note that the consumption of all varieties enters equation (3.4) symmetrically. This greatly simplifies the analysis in what follows. The parameter ρ, discussed further below, represents the love-of-variety effect of consumers. If $\rho = 1$, equation (3.4) simplifies to $M = \sum_i c_i$ and variety as such does not matter for utility (100 units of one variety give the same utility as one unit of 100 varieties). Products are then perfect substitutes (one unit less of one variety can exactly be compensated by one unit more of another variety). We therefore need $\rho < 1$ to ensure that the product varieties are imperfect substitutes. In addition, we need $\rho > 0$ to ensure that the individual varieties are substitutes (and not complements) for each other, which enables price-setting behavior based on monopoly power; see section 3.5.

It is worthwhile to dwell a little longer on the specification of (3.4). Suppose all varieties are consumed in equal quantities, that is $c_i = c$ for all i. We can then rewrite equation (3.4) as:

$$M = \left(\sum_{i=1}^{N} c^\rho \right)^{1/\rho} = (Nc^\rho)^{1/\rho} = N^{1/\rho}c = N^{(1/\rho)-1}(Nc) \tag{3.4'}$$

In many models, including many new growth models and geographical economics models, the term Nc in equation (3.4') corresponds to a claim on real resources, because Nc has to be produced in the first place, while the number of available varieties N represents an externality or the extent of the market. Since $0 < \rho < 1$, the term $(1/\rho) - 1$ is larger than 0. This implies that an increase in the extent of the market N, which requires a proportional increase in the claim on real resources Nc, increases utility M derived from the consumption of manufactures (consumption of N varieties) by more than the

---

[3] Many textbooks discuss the properties of the CES function. See also Brakman and Van Marrewijk (1998), who compare its properties with those of other utility functions.

increase in the claim on real resources (since the term $N^{(1/\rho)-1}$ rises it represents a bonus for large markets). In this sense an increase in the extent of the market, which increases the number of varieties N from which the consumer can choose, more than proportionally increases utility; hence the term "love-of-variety effect."

Box 3.2.   Dixit–Stiglitz monopolistic competition

It has often been said that there is only one way for competition to be perfect, but many ways for it to be imperfect. Consequently, many competing models exist to describe imperfect competition, investigating many different cases and assumptions with respect to market behavior, the type of good, the strategic interaction between firms, preferences of consumers, etc. That was also the case with monopolistic competition (see, for example, Tirole, 1988), until in 1977 Avinash Dixit and Joseph Stiglitz published an article, entitled "Monopolistic competition, and the optimum product diversity," in the *American Economic Review* that would revolutionize model-building in at least four fields of economics: trade theory, industrial organization, growth theory, and geographical economics.[4]

The big step forward was to make some heroic assumptions concerning the symmetry of new varieties and the structural form. This allowed for an elegant and consistent way to model production at the firm level benefiting from internal economies of scale in conjunction with a market structure of monopolistic competition, without getting bogged down in a taxonomy of oligopoly models. These factors are responsible for the present popularity of the Dixit–Stiglitz model. In all fields that now use the Dixit–Stiglitz formulation intensely, researchers were aware that imperfect competition was relevant as an essential feature of many empirically observed phenomena. This meant that the model was immediately accepted as the new standard for modeling monopolistic competition; its development was certainly very timely. In international trade theory, the introduction of the monopolistic competition model enabled international economists to explain and understand intra-industry trade, which until then was empirically observed but never satisfactorily explained (Krugman, 1979, 1980). In industrial organization it helped to get rid of many *ad hoc* assumptions which had hampered the development of industrial organization models (Tirole, 1988). The Dixit–Stiglitz model was also used to explore the role of intermediate differentiated goods in international trade models. This re-formulation of the standard Dixit–Stiglitz model plays an important role in the link between international trade and economic growth (see, for example, Grossman and Helpman, 1991). Finally, the model is intensively used in geographical economics, the topic of this book.

---

[4] The paper by Spence (1976) on a similar topic slightly predates Dixit and Stiglitz (1977), but had considerably less influence. For an excellent discussion of Dixit–Stiglitz monopolistic competition, see Neary (2001) and Baldwin *et al.* (2000b).

Following the brief digression on the love-of-variety effect it is time to go back to the problem at hand: how does the consumer allocate spending on manufactures over the various varieties? Let p_i be the price of variety i for $i=1,...,N$. Naturally, funds $p_i c_i$ spent on variety i cannot be spent simultaneously on variety j; this is represented in the budget constraint for manufactures in equation (3.5):

$$\sum_{i=1}^{N} p_i c_i = \delta Y \tag{3.5}$$

In order to derive a consumer's demand, we must now solve a somewhat more complicated optimization problem, namely maximize utility derived from the consumption of manufactures given in equation (3.4), subject to the budget constraint of equation (3.5). The solution to this problem is given in equations (3.6) and (3.7), and derived in Technical Note 3.2.

$$c_j = p_j^{-\varepsilon}(I^{\varepsilon-1}\delta Y), \quad \text{where} \quad I \equiv \left(\sum_{i=1}^{N} p_i^{1-\varepsilon}\right)^{1/(1-\varepsilon)} \quad \text{for} \quad j=1,...,N \tag{3.6}$$

$$M = \delta Y/I, \quad \text{and} \quad \varepsilon \equiv \frac{1}{1-\rho} \tag{3.7}$$

A discussion and explanation of the meaning of equations (3.6) and (3.7) is certainly warranted. We do this in the next subsection. *At this point, we want to emphasize that equation (3.6) gives the demand curve.* We conclude this subsection simply by noting that we have derived the demand for each variety of manufactures, which explains callout b in Figure 3.1.

Technical Note 3.2.   Derivation of equations (3.6) and (3.7)

We proceed as in Technical Note 3.1. To maximize equation (3.4) subject to the budget constraint (3.5) we define the Lagrangean Γ, using the multiplier κ:

$$\Gamma = \left(\sum_{i=1}^{N} c_i^{\rho}\right)^{(1/\rho)} + \kappa\left(\delta Y - \sum_{i=1}^{N} p_i c_i\right)$$

Differentiating Γ with respect to c_j and equating to 0 gives the first-order conditions:

$$\left(\sum_{i=1}^{N} c_i^{\rho}\right)^{(1/\rho)-1} c_j^{\rho-1} = \kappa p_j, \quad \text{for} \quad j=1,...,N$$

Take the ratio of these first-order conditions with respect to variety 1, note that the first term on the left-hand side cancels (as does the term κ on the right-hand side), and define $\varepsilon \equiv 1/(1-\rho)$ as discussed in the main text. Then:

$$\frac{c_j^{\rho-1}}{c_1^{\rho-1}} = \frac{p_j}{p_1} \quad \text{or} \quad c_j = p_j^{-\varepsilon} p_1^{\varepsilon} c_1 \quad \text{for} \quad j=1,...,N \tag{*}$$

Substituting these relations in the budget equation (3.5) gives:

$$\sum_{j=1}^{N} p_j c_j = \sum_{j=1}^{N} p_j (p_j^{-\varepsilon} p_1^{\varepsilon} c_1) = p_1^{\varepsilon} c_1 \sum_{j=1}^{N} p_j^{1-\varepsilon} = p_1^{\varepsilon} c_1 I^{1-\varepsilon} = \delta Y, \quad \text{or} \quad c_1 = p_1^{-\varepsilon} I^{\varepsilon-1} \delta Y$$

where use has been made of the definition of I in equation (3.6) of the main text. This explains the demand for variety 1 as given in equation (3.6). The demand for the other varieties is derived analogously. The question remains why the price index I was defined as given in equation (3.6). To answer this question we have to substitute the derived demand for all varieties in equation (3.4), and note along the way that $-\varepsilon\rho = 1 - \varepsilon$ and $1/\rho = -\varepsilon/(1 - \varepsilon)$:

$$M = \left(\sum_{i=1}^{N} c_i^{\rho}\right)^{1/\rho} = \left(\sum_{i=1}^{N} (p_i^{-\varepsilon} I^{-1} \delta Y)^{\rho}\right)^{1/\rho} = \delta Y I^{\varepsilon-1} \left(\sum_{i=1}^{N} p_i^{-\varepsilon\rho}\right)^{1/\rho}$$

$$= \delta Y I^{\varepsilon-1} \left(\sum_{i=1}^{N} p_i^{1-\varepsilon}\right)^{-\varepsilon/(1-\varepsilon)}$$

Using the definition of the price index I from equation (3.7) this simplifies to:

$$M = \delta Y I^{\varepsilon-1} \left(\sum_{i=1}^{N} p_i^{1-\varepsilon}\right)^{-\varepsilon/(1-\varepsilon)} = \delta Y I^{\varepsilon-1} I^{-\varepsilon} = \delta Y / I$$

This is discussed further in the main text.

3.4.3   Demand effects; income, price, elasticity ε (callout c), and the price index I

Subsection 3.4.2 derived the demand for varieties of manufactures. The demand for variety 1, for example, is given by $c_1 = p_1^{-\varepsilon}(I^{\varepsilon-1}\delta Y)$; see equation (3.6). Apparently, this demand is influenced by four things, namely (i) the income δY spent on manufactures in general, (ii) the price p_1 of good 1, (iii) some parameter ε, and (iv) the price index I. Let's go over these points in detail.

Point (i) is straightforward. The more the consumer spends on manufactures in general, the more she spends on variety 1. In fact, this relationship is equiproportional: other things being equal, a 10% rise in spending on manufactures results in a 10% increase in the demand for all varieties of manufactures.

Point (ii) is also straightforward, but very important. It is straightforward in the sense that we obviously expect that the demand for variety 1 is a function of the price charged by the firm producing variety 1. It is very important in view of *how* demand for variety 1 depends on the price p_1. Note that the last part of equation (3.6) is written within brackets. This expression depends on the price index for manufactures I and the income δY spent by consumers on manufactures in general. Both are macro-economic entities which the firm producing variety 1 will take as given, that is it will assume it has no control over these variables (see below for a further discussion). In that case, we can

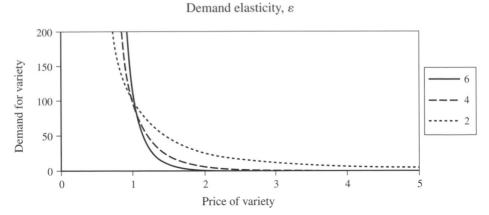

Figure 3.2. Dependence of demand for a variety of manufactures on price and ε (demand given by $c_1 = 100p_1^{-\varepsilon}$).

simplify the demand for variety 1, by defining constant$_1 \equiv (I^{\varepsilon-1}\delta Y)$, as $c_1 = $ constant$_1 p_1^{-\varepsilon}$. This in turn implies that the price elasticity of demand for variety 1 is constant and equal to the parameter $\varepsilon > 1$ (that is $-(\partial c_1/\partial p_1)(p_1/c_1) = \varepsilon$; see also note 5). This simple price elasticity of demand is the main advantage of the Dixit–Stiglitz approach (see Box 3.2) as it greatly simplifies the price-setting behavior of monopolistically competitive firms (see section 3.5). Figure 3.2 illustrates the demand for a variety of manufactures as a function of its own price for different values of ε. Note that the demand for a particular variety falls much faster as a result of a small price increase, say from 1 to 1.5, if the price elasticity of demand is high.

Point (iii) becomes clear after the discussion in point (ii). We have defined the parameter ε not only to simplify the notation of equation (3.6) as much as possible, but also because it is an important economic parameter as it measures the price elasticity of demand for a variety of manufactured goods. In addition, as we discussed in the previous subsection, this parameter measures the elasticity of substitution between two different varieties, that is how difficult it is to substitute one variety of manufactures for another variety of manufactures.[5] Evidently, the price elasticity of demand and the elasticity of substitution are related in the Dixit–Stiglitz approach, a point which has been criticized in the literature.[6] Be that as it may, our intuitive explanations of some phenomena in the remainder of this book will sometimes be based on the price elasticity of demand interpretation of ε, and sometimes on the elasticity of substitution

---

[5] To prove this you can use equation (*) in Technical Note 3.2, where the equation on the left can be written e.g. as $c_2/c_1 = (p_2/p_1)^{-\varepsilon}$ from which it follows immediately that

$$-[d(c_2/c_1)/d(p_2/p_1)][(p_2/p_1)/(c_2/c_1)] = \varepsilon.$$

[6] To make things even more complicated, when combined with a simple production function of internal returns to scale, also used in geographical economics, the parameter ε can be interpreted as a measure of returns to scale. This is discussed in section 3.5. In view of the drawbacks of this interpretation we will not use it in the rest of the book (for a discussion of this issue, see Neary, 2001).

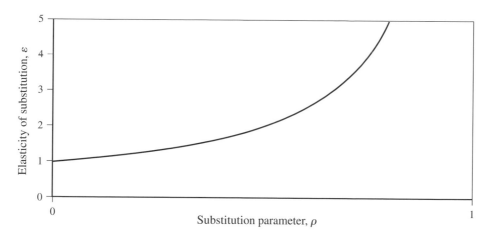

Figure 3.3. Relationship between ρ and ε.

interpretation, using that which we feel is easiest for the problem at hand. Another, final remark can be made on the parameter ε. It was defined using the parameter ρ in the preference for manufacturing varieties equation (3.4) as $\varepsilon \equiv 1/(1 - \rho)$. Does this mean we will not use the parameter ρ anymore in the rest of the book? No. The reason is that we want to keep the notation as simple as possible, which sometimes requires the use of ε and sometimes requires the use of ρ. These are the only two parameters for which we will do this, referring to ε as the "elasticity of substitution," and to ρ as the "substitution parameter." It is useful to keep their relationship, illustrated in Figure 3.3, in mind. This sufficiently explains callout c in Figure 3.1.

Point (iv), finally, indicates that the demand for variety 1 depends on the price index I. If the price index I increases, implying that "on average" the prices of the manufacturing varieties competing with variety 1 are rising, then the demand for variety 1 is increasing (recall that $\varepsilon - 1 > 0$). The varieties are therefore economic substitutes for one another (if the price of a particular variety increases, its own demand falls and the demand for all other varieties rises).

Note that, although it may appear a bit cumbersome at first sight, the price index I in equation (3.7) is defined analogously to the function in equation (3.4) specifying the preference for varieties, with $1 - \varepsilon$ in (3.7) playing the role of ρ in (3.4). In fact, if we use this information to calculate the elasticity of substitution for prices in equation (3.7) we would get $1/[1 - (1 - \varepsilon)] = 1/\varepsilon$, the inverse of the elasticity of substitution for varieties. This is no coincidence, as it indicates that if the elasticity of substitution for varieties is high a small price change can have large effects, and vice versa if it is small.[7] Most importantly, however, note that the definition of the price

---

[7] Properties like this are known under the label duality; see the appendix in Brakman and Van Marrewijk (1998) for an overview.

index I implies that $M = \delta Y/I$; see equation (3.7). The price index I gives an exact representation of the utility derived from the consumption of manufactures; this utility increases if, and only if, spending on manufactures δY increases faster than the price index I. Such a price index is called an exact price index; see Diewert (1981) for further details. Also note that $IM = \delta Y$ is required to justify our actions in subsection 3.4.1, where we used the price index I to derive the division of income over food consumption and labor consumption. Otherwise, our calculations there would not have been consistent.

We will frequently use the price index I to derive real wages in the model. It is therefore worthwhile to take a closer look at the definition of consumption-based price indices; see also Obstfeld and Rogoff (1996, p. 226). One can ask the question: "What is the minimum amount of expenditure required to buy 1 unit of utility?" Let I be this minimum expenditure on manufactures, such that $M = 1$. Then we call I the consumption-based price index. From this definition it follows directly from equations (3.5) and (3.7) that I is indeed such an index.[8] It is obvious that an increase in the number of varieties decreases I. We already explained that an increase in the number of varieties more than proportionally increases the sub-utility for manufactures. This effect has a mirror image in the price index I; more varieties lower I, because it takes less expenditure for $M = 1$. Furthermore, the term I enabled us to write the demand equations more efficiently as $c_j = p_j^{-\varepsilon}(I^{\varepsilon-1}\delta Y)$.

To finish our discussion of the demand structure of the core model we want to make two remarks. The first is relatively short. We could use the same procedure applied in subsection 3.4.2 to derive the exact price index for the allocation over varieties also to derive such a price index for the problem in subsection 3.4.1, allocating income over food and manufactures. As the reader may wish to verify, the result would be: $1^{1-\delta}I^\delta = I^\delta$, where the "1" on the left-hand side represents the price of food, which is set equal to 1 as it is the numéraire. Thus, the consumer's utility increases if, and only if, Y/I^δ rises, that is if the income level rises faster than the exact price index I^δ. We can thus define *real income y* (equation (3.8)) as an exact representation of a consumer's preferences (see Box 3.1 and section 3.8). Similarly, if the wage rate is W, we can define the *real wage w* also using the exact price index; again, see equation (3.8). Moreover, if an individual consumer only has wage income, that is if $Y = W$, then the individual real income y is equivalent to the real wage w.

$$\text{real income: } y = YI^{-\delta}; \quad \text{real wage: } w = WI^{-\delta} \tag{3.8}$$

The second remark concerns point (ii) above, where we argued that the (own) price elasticity of demand for the producer of variety 1 is equal to ε. Recall the specification of the demand function: $c_1 = p_1^{-\varepsilon}(I^{\varepsilon-1}\delta Y)$. We argued that the term in brackets is

---

[8] One might wonder why this index looks so different from the familiar Paasche or Laspeyres price indices. The reason is that for practical reasons the weights in these indices are fixed, but in reality they are not. Consumers switch from more expensive goods to less expensive ones if relative prices change. How this substitution takes place is determined by consumer preferences. If we know these preferences, as in the model in the text, we can calculate the exact price index.

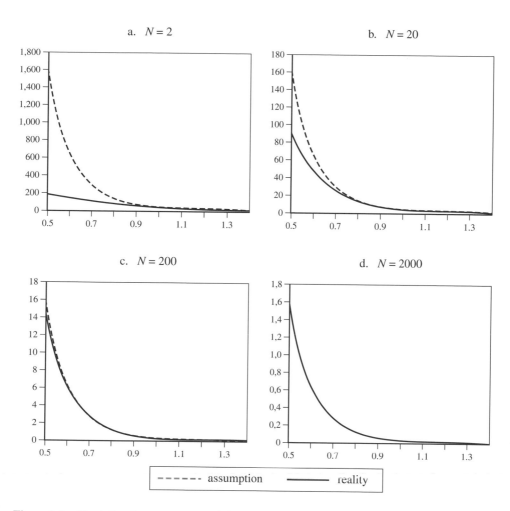

Figure 3.4. Deviation between assumed demand and reality (spending on manufactures = 100, prices of other firms = 1, $\varepsilon = 5$).

treated as a constant by the producer because these are macro-economic entities. Although this is true it overlooks a tiny detail: one of the terms in the specification of the price index of manufactures I is the price p_1. Thus, a truly rational producer would also take this minuscule effect on the aggregate price index into consideration.[9] For that reason it is often assumed that the number of varieties N produced is "large," that is if our producer is one of 80,000 firms we can safely ignore this effect. This is illustrated in Figure 3.4 where we have plotted the demand curve facing the producer of a variety

---

[9] In fact, using equation (3.6) the price elasticity of demand for a specific variety can be derived. Illuminating in this respect is the analysis in the neighborhood of p if $p_i = p$ for all other varieties, in which case $-(\partial c/\partial p)(p/c) = \varepsilon(1 - 1/N)$. The second term on the right-hand side is inversely related to the number of varieties N, approaching 1 if N becomes large.

if she assumes she cannot influence the price index of manufactures, and the true demand taking this effect on the price index into consideration (details below Figure 3.4). Clearly, the assumption is a bad approximation if there are just two firms (panel *a*), but then nobody would suggest that you should use monopolistic competition in a duopoly. If there are twenty firms the approximation is already much better (panel *b*), if there are 200 firms the deviation is virtually undetectable (panel *c*), while it is unobservable if there are 2,000 firms (panel *d*). This suggests we can safely ignore this detail for a reasonably large number of varieties.

3.5 Supply

3.5.1 Production structure (callout d)

We start the analysis of the supply side of the core model with a description of the production structure for food and manufactures; see also Figure 3.1. Food production is characterized by constant returns to scale and occurs under conditions of perfect competition. Workers in this industry are assumed to be immobile. As mentioned in section 3.3 the food sector is therefore the natural candidate to be used as the numéraire. Given the total labor force L, a fraction $(1 - \gamma)$ is assumed to work in the food sector. The labor force in the manufacturing industry is therefore γL. Production in the food sector, F, equals, by choice of units, food employment:

$$F = (1 - \gamma)L, \qquad 0 < \gamma < 1 \tag{3.9}$$

Since farm workers are paid the value of marginal product this choice of units implies that the wage for the farm workers is 1, because food is the numéraire.

Production in the manufacturing sector is characterized by internal economies of scale, which means that there is imperfect competition in this sector (see Box 2.1). The varieties in the manufacturing industry are symmetric and are produced with the same technology. Note that at this point we are already introducing an element of location. Internal economies of scale mean that each variety is produced by a single firm; the firm with the largest sales can always outbid a potential competitor. Once we introduce more locations each firm has to decide where to produce. The economies of scale are modeled in the simplest way possible:

$$l_i = \alpha + \beta x_i \tag{3.10}$$

where l_i is the amount of labor necessary to produce x_i of variety i. The coefficients α and β describe, respectively, the fixed and marginal labor input requirement. The fixed labor input α in (3.10) ensures that as production expands less labor is needed to produce a unit of i, which means that there are internal economies of scale. This is illustrated in Figure 3.5, showing the total labor required to produce a certain amount of output, and the average amount of labor required to produce that amount of output. This explains callout *d* in Figure 3.1.

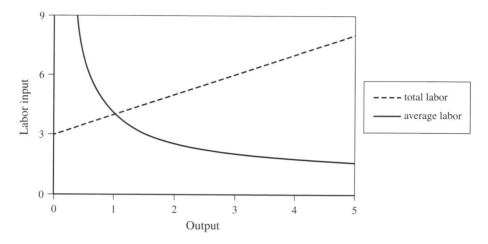

Figure 3.5. Production function for a variety of manufactures (fixed labor requirement $\alpha = 3$, marginal labor requirement $\beta = 1$).

3.5.2 Price-setting and zero profits (callout e)

Each manufacturing firm produces a unique variety under internal returns to scale. This implies that the firm has monopoly power, which it will use to maximize its profits. We will therefore have to determine the price-setting behavior of each firm. The Dixit–Stiglitz monopolistic competition model makes two assumptions in this respect. First, it is assumed that each firm takes the price-setting behavior of other firms as given, that is if firm 1 changes its price it will assume that the prices of the other $N-1$ varieties will remain the same. Second, it is assumed that the firm ignores the effect of changing its own price on the price index I of manufactures. Both assumptions seem reasonable if the number of varieties N is large, as also discussed in subsection 3.4.3. For ease of notation we will drop the subscript index for the firm in this section. Note that a firm which produces x units of output using the production function in equation (3.10) will earn profits π given in equation (3.11) if the wage rate it has to pay is W.

$$\pi = px - W(\alpha + \beta x) \tag{3.11}$$

Naturally, the firm will have to sell the units of output x it is producing, that is these sales must be consistent with the demand for a variety of manufactures derived in section 3.4. Although this demand was derived for an arbitrary consumer, the most important feature of the demand for a variety, namely the constant price elasticity of demand ε, also holds when we combine the demand from many consumers with the same preference structure (see also Exercise 3.4). If the demand x for a variety has a constant price elasticity of demand ε, maximization of the profits given in equation (3.11) leads to a very simple optimal pricing rule, known as mark-up pricing, as given in equation (3.12) and derived in Technical Note 3.3.

$$p(1-1/\varepsilon) = \beta W \qquad (\text{or} \quad p = \beta W/p) \tag{3.12}$$

The term "mark-up pricing" is obvious. The marginal cost of producing an extra unit of output is equal to βW, while the price p the firm charges is higher than this marginal cost. How much higher depends crucially on the price elasticity of demand. If demand is rather inelastic, say $\varepsilon = 2$, the mark-up is high (in this case 100%). If demand is rather elastic, say $\varepsilon = 5$, the mark-up is lower (in this case 25%). Note that the firm must charge a higher price than marginal cost in order to recuperate the fixed costs of labor αW. Because the price elasticity of demand ε is constant, the mark-up of price over marginal cost is also constant, and therefore invariant with the scale of production. Note that the price is fixed if the wage rate is fixed.

Technical Note 3.3.   Derivation of equation (3.12)

The demand x for a variety can be written as $x = \text{con} \cdot p^{-\varepsilon}$, where "con" is some constant. Substituting this in the profit function gives:

$$\pi = \text{con} \cdot p^{1-\varepsilon} - W(\alpha + \beta \text{con} \cdot p^{-\varepsilon})$$

Profits are now a function of the firm's price only. Differentiating with respect to the price p and equating to 0 gives the first-order condition:

$$(1 - \varepsilon)\text{con} \cdot p^{-\varepsilon} + \varepsilon W \beta \text{con} \cdot p^{-\varepsilon-1} = 0$$

Canceling the term $\text{con} \cdot p^{-\varepsilon}$ and rearranging gives equation (3.12).

Now that we have determined the optimal price a firm will charge to maximize profits we can actually calculate those profits (if we know the constant in Technical Note 3.3). This is where another important feature of monopolistic competition comes in. If profits are positive (sometimes referred to as excess profits) it is apparently very attractive to set up shop in the manufacturing sector. One would then expect that new firms enter the market and start to produce a different variety. This implies, of course, that the consumer will allocate her spending over more varieties of manufactures. Since all varieties are substitutes for one another, the entry of new firms in the manufacturing sector implies that profits for the existing firms will fall. This process of entry of new firms will continue until profits in the manufacturing sector are driven to zero. A reverse process, with firms leaving the manufacturing sector, would operate if profits were negative. Monopolistic competition in the manufacturing sector therefore imposes as an equilibrium condition that profits are zero. If we do that in equation (3.11) we can calculate the scale at which a firm producing a variety in the manufacturing sector will operate, equation (3.13), how much labor is needed to produce this amount of output, equation (3.14), and how many varieties N are produced in the economy as a function of the available labor in the manufacturing sector, equation (3.15). See Technical Note 3.4.

Technical Note 3.4.   Derivation of equations (3.13)–(3.15)

Put profits in equation (3.11) equal to zero and use the pricing rule $p(1-1/\varepsilon) = \beta W$ from equation (3.12):

$$px - W(\alpha + \beta x) = 0; \qquad px = \alpha W + \beta Wx; \qquad \left[\frac{\varepsilon}{\varepsilon - 1}\beta W\right]x = \alpha W + \beta Wx$$

$$\left[\frac{\varepsilon}{\varepsilon - 1} - 1\right]\beta Wx = \alpha W; \qquad x = \frac{\alpha(\varepsilon - 1)}{\beta}$$

This explains equation (3.13). Now use the production function (3.10) to calculate the amount of labor required to produce this much output:

$$l = \alpha + \beta x = \alpha + \beta \frac{\alpha(\varepsilon-1)}{\beta} = \alpha + \alpha(\varepsilon-1) = \alpha\varepsilon$$

This explains equation (3.14). Finally, equation (3.15), determining the number of varieties N produced, simply follows by dividing the total number of manufacturing workers by the number of workers needed to produce one variety.

$$x = \frac{\alpha(\varepsilon-1)}{\beta} \tag{3.13}$$

$$l = \alpha\varepsilon \tag{3.14}$$

$$N = \gamma L/l = \gamma L/\alpha\varepsilon \tag{3.15}$$

Equation (3.13), giving the scale of output for an individual firm, may seem strange at first sight. No matter what happens, the output per firm is fixed in equilibrium. The constant price elasticity of demand in conjunction with the production function is responsible for this result. It implies that the manufacturing sector as a whole only expands and contracts by producing more or fewer varieties, as the output level per variety does not change. From (3.15) we see that a larger market caused, for example, by the opening of the borders, or increased international trade only affects the number of varieties. As a result of economies of scale it is not profitable to have the same variety produced by more than one firm; each firm will produce only one variety.

The question may arise of where the economies of scale are; do they not matter anymore? There is another way of looking at the parameter ε. In equilibrium, it is also used as a measure of economies of scale. Scale economies can be measured in various ways, but one specific measure of economies of scale is average costs divided by marginal costs; if marginal costs are lower than average costs an increase in production will reduce the cost per unit. For the core model we can calculate this measure for the equilibrium level of production. The labor requirement is $\alpha\varepsilon$, see equation (3.14), the production level is $\alpha(\varepsilon-1)/\beta$, see equation (3.13), so the average costs are $\alpha\varepsilon/(\alpha(\varepsilon-1)/\beta) = \beta\varepsilon/(\varepsilon-1)$. The marginal labor costs are simply β, so this measure of economies of scale reduces to average costs / marginal costs $= \varepsilon/(\varepsilon-1)$, which in equilibrium only depends on the elasticity of substitution parameter ε (note, in particular, that the parameters α and β of the production function do not enter). For low values of ε this measure of scale economies is high, while for high values this measure is low. The latter means that varieties are becoming more and more perfect substitutes. In the limit, only a single variety survives. Production of this single variety takes place at the largest possible scale (all manufacturing labor is employed in producing the single variety) leaving less room for economies of scale than if ε is low, and many different varieties are produced by many different firms. Recall, finally, that this measure only indicates the level of economies of scale in equilibrium. So the internal economies of scale are not absent, but only show up in a rather special way in the Dixit–Stiglitz model of monopolistic competition.

3.6   Transport costs: icebergs in geography

The aim of the core model of geographical economics is to introduce geography in a non-trivial way. That is to say, the model must show how geography affects the decisions of individual consumers and producers and how these decisions in turn shape the spatial distribution of economic activity. To be able to do so, transport costs have to be introduced. Only if it is costly to move products and people over space does geography make sense in the core model.

The transport costs we introduce are special. In principle, one could model a transport sector and add this to the model, but this would be very cumbersome. Every cost is also a gain for someone else, and transport costs are income for the transport sector so one must deal with spending from this sector. Also the location decision of the transport sector might be different from the location decisions of the other sectors. It is for these reasons that Samuelson (1952) introduced the concept of *iceberg* transport costs. In the context of the core model of geographical economics, iceberg transport costs imply that a fraction of the manufactured goods does not arrive at the destination when goods are shipped between regions. The fraction that does not arrive represents the cost of transportation. The core model uses T as a parameter to represent these costs, where T is defined as the number of goods that need to be shipped to ensure that one unit arrives per unit of distance. Suppose, for example, that the unit of distance is equal to the distance from Naaldwijk, in the center of the Dutch horticultural agglomeration, to Paris, and that 107 flowers are sent from Holland to France, while only 100 arrive unharmed in Paris and can be sold. Then $T=1.07$. It is as if some goods have melted away in transit, hence the name iceberg costs. This way of modeling the transport costs without introducing a transport sector is very attractive in combination with the price-setting behavior of producers. This explains callout f in Figure 3.1. Box 3.3 discusses the relevance of transport costs.

Box 3.3. The relevance of transport costs

Transport costs are essential throughout this book. Without transport costs there is no geography, and the whole exercise of transforming economic models into geographical economics models becomes pointless or very academic. Adam Smith noted the importance of locations near the coast, which reduce transport costs: ". . . so, it is upon the sea-coast, and along the banks of navigable rivers, that industry of every kind naturally begins to sub-divide and improve itself, and it is frequently not till a long time after that those improvements extend themselves to the inland part of the country" (cited in Radelet and Sachs, 1998).

Many measures have been constructed to measure transport cost, ranging from direct measures to travel time (see the example on Germany in chapter 5). The most straightforward measure in international trade is the difference between the so-called cif (cost, insurance, freight) and fob (free on board) quotations of trade. Cif measures the value of imports from the point of entry, inclusive of cost, insurance and freight. Fob measures the value of imports "free on board," that is, the cost of the imports inclusive of all charges incurred in placing the merchandise on a carrier in the exporting "port." The difference between these two values is a measure of the cost of getting an item from the exporting country to the importing country, but clearly underestimates the actual transport costs of international trade. Often one finds the formula of $[(cif/fob) - 1] \times 100\%$, which represents the unit transport cost (percentage) to the fob price and provides a measure of the transport cost *rate* on imports. Different goods have different transport costs. One might expect that goods with high value-added will have relatively low cif/fob ratios, and perishable goods, higher ones. Hummels (1999b), for example, finds for the United States, that the *ad valorem* freight rate is 7.6% for food and live animals, but only 2.25% for machinery and transport equipment. Table 3.3 gives some indication of this transport cost measure for various countries.

The differences in shipping costs can be explained by noting that countries located further away from major markets face higher shipping costs (for example, New Zealand), and by observing whether or not countries are landlocked. For example, the landlocked developing countries (not shown in the table) have on average 50% higher transport costs than coastal developing economies (Radelet and Sachs, 1998). These authors also find that for developing countries a doubling of trading cost reduces economic growth by 0.5%. As argued above, these

Table 3.3. *Cif/fob ratios, 1965–1990 (%)*

Country	cif/fob ratio	Country	cif/fob ratio
Australia	10.3	New Zealand	11.5
Austria	4.1	Norway	2.7
Canada	2.7	Philippines	7.6
Denmark	4.5	Portugal	10.3
France	4.2	Singapore	6.1
West Germany	3.0	Spain	6.4
Greece	13.0	Sweden	3.5
Ireland	5.0	Switzerland	1.8
Italy	7.1	Thailand	11.0
Japan	9.0	United Kingdom	6.0
Netherlands	5.6	United States	4.9

Source: Radelet and Sachs (1998).

figures probably underestimate true trade costs. Hummels (1999a, p. 27) finds that freight rates differ substantially over exporters. However, *expenditures* on freight are at "the low end of the range." This suggests that these costs are substantial and that import choices are made to minimize transport costs. Note that products with very high transport costs are not even traded at all. Hummels (1999b) also shows that, in contrast to popular opinion, transport costs have *not* declined uniformly. His general conclusions are that in the post World War II period, the costs of ocean travel have increased and the costs of air transport have fallen, and that the costs of distant travel have fallen relative to proximate transport.

For a final indication of the importance of transport costs we can compare freight costs with other trade costs, like tariffs. For the USA, Davis (1998) finds that industry-level transport costs as a percentage of imports range between 1.9% and 8.5 % of import values, with a mean of 4.8%. Industry-level tariffs ranged from 0.5% to 15.4 %, with a mean of 4.1%. Transport costs, therefore, seem to be at least as important as policy-induced trade barriers. Note, however, that the transport costs variable T used in the main text is inclusive of such policy-induced trade barriers (as are cultural, sociological, etc. barriers; see also chapter 1). Although data are always subject to measurement error, the impression remains that trade costs are substantial and cannot be ignored.

Now that we have seen that transport costs between and within countries are substantial, one might ask whether or not they matter. The answer is: they do. Limao and Venables (2000) find that transport costs are very important in the ability of countries to participate in the global economy. The tendency towards trade liberalization makes transport costs as such relatively more important than the official trade barriers, like tariffs. Using various econometric techniques they find that the elasticity of trade with respect to transport costs is high, approximately equal to -2.5. This implies, for example, that a median land-locked country has only about 30% of the trade flows that a coastal country has. Being land-locked raises transport cost by around 50%. Moreover, Limao and Venables find that the relatively poor quality of Sub-Saharan African infrastructure is to a large extent responsible for the relatively low level of African trade with the rest of the world. Finally, it must be noted that distance not only has a physical representation, but also a mental element. McCallum (1995) finds that Canadian provinces traded more than twenty times the volume of trade with each other than they traded with similar counterparts in the USA. In chapter 5 (section 5.6) we will look into the role of mental distance for the case of post-reunification Germany.

Throughout the rest of the book the parameter T denotes the number of goods that need to be shipped to ensure that one unit of a variety of manufactures arrives per unit of distance, while T_{rs} is defined as the number of goods that need to be shipped from region r to ensure that one unit arrives in region s. We will assume that this is proportional to the distance between regions r and s. If we let D_{rs} denote the distance between region r and region s (which is 0 if $r=s$), we therefore assume that:

$$T_{rs} = T^{D_{rs}}, \quad \text{for} \quad r,s = 1,2; \qquad \text{note:} \quad T_{rs} = T_{sr}, \quad \text{and} \quad T_{rr} = T^0 = 1 \quad (3.16)$$

These definitions ease notation in the equations below and allow us to distinguish between changes in the parameter T, that is a general change in (transport) technology applying to all regions, and changes in the "distance" D_{rs} between regions, which may result from a policy change, such as tariff changes, a cultural treaty, new infrastructure, etc. For the two-region core model discussed here we will always assume that the distance between the two regions is 1. Equation (3.16) and the equations below do not yet use this fact in order to develop a general model of multiple regions at the same time.

3.7   Multiple locations

Now that we have introduced two regions and transport costs it becomes important to know where the economic agents are located. We therefore have to (i) specify a notation to show how labor is distributed over the two regions, and (ii) investigate what the consequences are for some of the demand and supply equations discussed in sections 3.4 and 3.5. To start with point (i), we have already introduced the parameter γ to denote the fraction of the labor force in the manufacturing sector (see section 3.5) such that $1 - \gamma$ is the fraction of labor in the food sector. We now assume that of the laborers in the food sector a fraction ϕ_i is located in region i, and of the laborers in the manufacturing sector a fraction λ_i is located in region i. Figure 3.6 illustrates the division

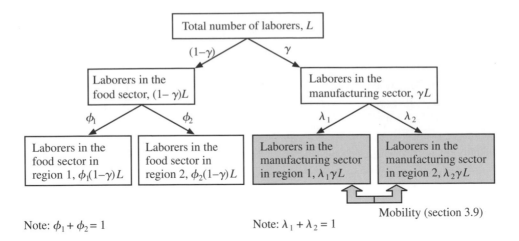

Figure 3.6. Division of labor over the regions.

of labor. The boxes for the manufacturing sector are shaded, as in Figure 3.1, to indicate that the size of the working population can increase or decrease, depending on the mobility of the manufacturing workforce.

Point (ii) involves more work. We will concentrate on region 1. Similar remarks hold for region 2. It is easiest to start with the producers. Since there are $\phi_1(1-\gamma)L$ farm workers in region 1 and production is proportional to the labor input (see equation 3.9), food production in region 1 equals $\phi_1(1-\gamma)L$, which is equal to the income generated by the food sector in region 1 and the wage income paid to farm workers there. Since we have introduced transport costs into the model, the wage rate paid to manufacturing workers in region 1 will in general differ from the wage rate paid to manufacturing workers in region 2. We will identify these with a sub-index, so W_1 is the manufacturing wage in region 1. From now on, and throughout the remainder of the book, whenever we speak of "the wage rate" we refer to the manufacturing wage rate. If we know the wage rate W_1 in region 1, we can see from equation (3.12) that the price charged in region 1 by a firm located in region 1 is equal to $\beta W_1/\rho$. The price this firm located in region 1 will charge in region 2 will be T_{12} times higher than in region 1 (in this case: $T_{12} = T^{D_{12}} = T$) as a result of the transport costs; see also exercise 3.4. Note that this holds for all N_1 firms located in region 1. Finally, since there are $\lambda_1\gamma L$ manufacturing workers in region 1, we can deduce from equation (3.15) the number of firms N_1 located in region 1: $N_1 = \lambda_1\gamma L/\alpha\varepsilon$. Note in particular, that the number of firms located in region 1 is directly proportional to the number of manufacturing workers located in region 1.

We now turn to the demand side of the economy. As discussed above, the price a firm charges to a consumer for one unit of the variety it produces depends both on the location of the firm (which determines the wage rate the firm will have to pay to its workers) and on the location of the consumer (which determines whether or not the consumer will have to pay for the transport costs of the good). As a result, the price index of manufactures will differ between the two regions. Again, we will identify these with a sub-index, so I_1 is the price index in region 1. We can now, however, be more specific since we have just derived the price a firm will charge in each region, and how many firms there are in each region. All we have to do is substitute this information in equation (3.6); see Technical Note 3.5:

$$I_1 = \left(\frac{\beta}{\rho}\right)\left(\frac{\gamma L}{\alpha \varepsilon}\right)^{1/(1-\varepsilon)} (\lambda_1 W_1^{1-\varepsilon} + \lambda_2 T^{1-\varepsilon} W_2^{1-\varepsilon})^{1/(1-\varepsilon)} \tag{3.17}$$

Technical Note 3.5.   Derivation of equation (3.17)

The number of firms in region s equals: $\left(\dfrac{\lambda_s \gamma L}{\alpha \varepsilon}\right)$

The price a firm located in region s charges in region r equals: $\left(\dfrac{\beta}{\rho} W_s T_{rs}\right)$

Substituting these two results in the price index for manufactures equation (3.6), assuming that there are $R\,(\geq 2)$ regions, gives the price index for region r:

$$I_r = \left[\sum_{s=1}^{R} \left(\frac{\lambda_s \gamma L}{\alpha \varepsilon}\right)\left(\frac{\beta}{\rho} W_s T_{rs}\right)^{1-\varepsilon}\right]^{1/(1-\varepsilon)}$$

$$= \left(\frac{\beta}{\rho}\right)\left(\frac{\gamma L}{\alpha \varepsilon}\right)^{1/(1-\varepsilon)} \left[\sum_{s=1}^{R} \lambda_s W_s^{1-\varepsilon} T_{rs}^{1-\varepsilon}\right]^{1/(1-\varepsilon)} \tag{*}$$

Equation (3.17) in the text is a special case for $R=2$ and $r=1$.

The impact of location on the consumption decisions of consumers in different locations on the basis of equation (3.6) requires us to know the income level of region 1. This brings us to the determination of equilibrium in the next section.

3.8   Equilibrium

Given the details of the core model of geographical economics as laid out in the previous sections, we have already explained a significant part of the structure of this model as shown by Figure 3.1. What needs to be done is to establish the equilibrium relationships, which effectively will tie up all loose ends. In particular, we have to determine the way in which the equilibrium relationships together with the shaded boxes in Figure 3.1 ultimately determine the spatial distribution of economic activity. These shaded boxes (callout g in Figure 3.1) refer to the mobility of manufacturing workers and firms between the two regions. As has already been explained at length in chapter 2 this mobility really sets geographical economics apart from new trade theory, upon which so much of the core model is based.

To understand the determination of equilibrium and the role of factor and firm mobility therein, we proceed in three steps. First, in this section, we focus on the *short-run* equilibrium relationships, that is we give the equilibrium analysis for an exogenously given distribution of the manufacturing labor force. It is thus assumed that the manufacturing labor force is not mobile between regions in the short run. The spatial distribution of the manufacturing workers and firms is not yet determined by the model itself, but simply imposed upon the model. Second, in section 3.9, we briefly address the issue of dynamics, that is, how we move through a sequence of short-run equilibria (no factor mobility) over time to a *long-run equilibrium* (with factor mobility). This is crucial for the geographical economics approach. Third, the *analysis* of both short-run and long-run equilibria turns out to be so involved that we deal with it separately in the next chapter.

3.8.1   Short-run equilibrium

The next subsection summarizes the economy-wide short-run equilibrium relationships, that is the equations for both regions in a two-region setting. This subsection will pull together and briefly discuss the three short-run equilibrium equations for region 1. So what are the short-run equilibrium relationships? Well, we have already used a few of these without explicitly stating it. For example, we have already assumed that the labor markets clear, that is (i) all farm workers have a job, and (ii) all manufacturing workers have a job. Point (i) has determined the production level of food in each region, in conjunction with the production function for food and perfect competition in the food sector. Point (ii) has determined the number of manufacturing varieties produced in each region, in conjunction with the production function for manufactures, the price-setting behavior of firms, and entry or exit of firms in the manufacturing sector until profits are zero. Evidently, there are no profits for firms in the manufacturing sector (because of entry and exit), nor for the farmers (because of constant returns to scale and perfect competition). This implies that all income earned in the economy for consumers to spend derives from the wages they earn in their respective sectors. This brings us to the next equilibrium relationship, that is how to determine income in each region. In view of the above, this is simple. There are $\phi_1(1 - \gamma)L$ farm workers in region 1, each earning a farm wage rate of 1 (food is the numéraire), and there are $\lambda_1 \gamma L$ manufacturing workers in region 1, each earning a wage rate W_1. As there are no profits or other factors of production, this is the only income generated in region 1. If we let Y_i denote income generated in region i this implies:

$$Y_1 = \lambda_1 W_1 \gamma L + \phi_1(1 - \gamma)L \tag{3.18}$$

where the first term on the right-hand side represents income for the manufacturing workers, and the second term reflects income for the farm workers.

As discussed in sections 3.6 and 3.7, the actual amount of transport costs between regions for the manufacturing sector is given by $T-1$. Since all firms in a region face identical marginal production costs and the same constant elasticity of demand (see also below), they all charge the same price to local producers, say p_1 for region 1 producers and p_2 for region 2 producers (see also exercise 3.4). This mill price, or free on board (fob) price, of a variety produced in region 1 charged to consumers in region 1, is related to the marginal production costs in region 1 through the optimal pricing condition (3.12): $p_1 = \beta W_1/\rho$. This indicates that the fob price is directly proportional to the wage rate. The price of a variety produced in region 1 after being delivered in region 2 is Tp_1, which is the cost, insurance, and freight (cif) price of this variety (see Box 3.3 on fob and cif prices). Also recall from section 3.7 that, since there are $\lambda_1 \gamma L$ manufacturing workers in region 1, it follows from equation (3.15) that the number of firms N_1 located in region 1 equals $N_1 = \lambda_1 \gamma L/\alpha\varepsilon$. That is, the number of firms located in region 1 is directly proportional to λ_1, the number of manufacturing workers located in region 1. All three aspects discussed above, namely (i) prices of locally produced goods are directly proportional to the local wage rate, (ii) prices charged in the other region are higher by the transport costs between regions, and (iii) the number of varieties produced in a region is directly proportional to the number of manufacturing workers in a region, are important for understanding why the price index I can have a different value in the two regions. For region 1 the price index I_1 is (see Technical Note 3.5 for further details):

$$I_1 = \left(\frac{\beta}{\rho}\right)\left(\frac{\gamma L}{\alpha\varepsilon}\right)^{1/(1-\varepsilon)} (\lambda_1 W_1^{1-\varepsilon} + \lambda_2 T^{1-\varepsilon} W_2^{1-\varepsilon})^{1/(1-\varepsilon)} \tag{3.19}$$

Thus, the price index in region 1 is essentially a weighted average of the price of locally produced goods and imported goods from region 2.

Demand in region 1 for products from region 1 is based on individual demand derived in equation (3.6), by summing the demand for all consumers in region 1. It is thus dependent on the aggregate income Y_1 in region 1, as given in equation (3.18), the price index I_1 in region 1, as given in equation (3.19), and the price $p_1 = \beta W_1/\rho$ charged by a producer from region 1 for a locally sold variety in region 1. We simply have to substitute these three terms for individual income, price index, and price as given in equation (3.6) to obtain $(\delta\beta^{-\varepsilon}\rho^{\varepsilon}) Y_1 W_1^{-\varepsilon} I_1^{\varepsilon-1}$, that is total demand in region 1 for a variety produced in region 1.

We can derive demand in region 2 for products from region 1 in a similar way, by substituting aggregate income Y_2, price index I_2, and the price $Tp_1 = T\beta W_1/\rho$ charged by a producer from region 1 for a good sold in region 2 in equation (3.6) to get $(\delta\beta^{-\varepsilon}\rho^{\varepsilon}) Y_2 W_1^{-\varepsilon} T^{-\varepsilon} I_2^{\varepsilon-1}$. If there are positive transport costs, that is $T>1$, demand in region 2 for products from region 1 is lower than without transport costs, because transport costs make them more expensive.

Total demand x_1 for a producer in region 1 is the sum of the demands discussed in the previous two paragraphs, that is the sum of demand from region 1 and demand from region 2:

$$x_1 = (\delta\beta^{-\varepsilon}\rho^\varepsilon)\,(Y_1 W_1^{-\varepsilon} I_1^{\varepsilon-1} + Y_2 W_1^{-\varepsilon} T^{-\varepsilon} I_2^{\varepsilon-1}) \tag{3.20}$$

This equation simply states that total demand for a particular variety depends on income in *both* regions, transport costs, and the price (proportional to the wage rate) relative to the price index. We can now immediately see another advantage of modeling transport costs as melting icebergs, namely that the price elasticity of demand with respect to the fob price is constant (equal to ε).

We already derived the breakeven level of production $x = \alpha(\varepsilon-1)/\beta$ for a producer of manufactures in equation (3.13). Equating this breakeven production level to the total demand derived in equation (3.20) allows us to determine what the price (and thus the wage rate) of a variety should be in order to sell exactly this amount. For a producer in region 1 this implies $\alpha(\varepsilon-1)/\beta = (\delta\beta^{-\varepsilon}\rho^\varepsilon)\,(Y_1 W_1^{-\varepsilon} I_1^{\varepsilon-1} + Y_2 W_1^{-\varepsilon} T^{1-\varepsilon} I_2^{\varepsilon-1})$. Note the important difference from equation (3.20) for the term T on the right-hand side, namely $1 - \varepsilon$ instead of $-\varepsilon$. This follows from the fact that the producer includes the amount which melts away *en route* from region 1 to region 2; in order to supply one unit of a variety in region 2, T units have to be shipped. Solving the above equation for the wage rate in region 1 gives:

$$W_1 = \rho\beta^{-\rho}\left(\frac{\delta}{(\varepsilon-1)\alpha}\right)^{1/\varepsilon} (Y_1 I_1^{\varepsilon-1} + Y_2 T^{1-\varepsilon} I_2^{\varepsilon-1})^{1/\varepsilon} \tag{3.21}$$

Intuitively the equation makes perfect sense; wages in region 1 can be higher if this region is located close to large markets (Y_1 in region 1 with $T = 1$ and Y_2 in region 2 with $T > 1$) and the less competition a firm in region 1 faces (recall point (iv) in section 3.4.3). Thus the larger region 2 is and the smaller T, the higher W_1. As we shall see in chapter 5, this important consequence of the core model is used in empirical research.

Technical Note 3.6.   Derivation of equation (3.21)

Equation (3.6) gives the demand for an individual consumer in a region. If we replace in that equation the income level Y with the income level Y_r of region r, the price index I with the price index I_r of region r, and the price p_j of the manufactured good with the price $\beta W_s T_{rs}/\rho$ which a producer from region s will charge in region r (see section 3.7), we obtain the demand in region r for a product from region s:

$$\delta Y_r(\beta W_s T_{rs}/\rho)^{-\varepsilon} I_r^{\varepsilon-1} = \delta(\beta/\rho)^{-\varepsilon} Y_r W_s^{-\varepsilon} T_{rs}^{-\varepsilon} I_r^{\varepsilon-1}$$

To fulfill this consumption demand in region r, note that T_{rs} units have to be shipped and produced. To derive the total demand in all R (≥ 2) regions for a manufactured good produced in region s, we must sum production demand over all regions (that is, sum over the index r in the above equation and multiply each entry by T_{rs}):

$$\delta(\beta/\rho)^{-\varepsilon} \sum_{r=1}^{R} Y_r W_s^{-\varepsilon} T_{rs}^{1-\varepsilon} I_r^{\varepsilon-1} = \delta(\beta/\rho)^{-\varepsilon} W_s^{-\varepsilon} \sum_{r=1}^{R} Y_r T_{rs}^{1-\varepsilon} I_r^{\varepsilon-1}$$

In equilibrium this total demand for a manufactured good from region s must be equal to its supply $(\varepsilon - 1)\alpha/\beta$; see equation (3.13). Equating these two gives

$$(\varepsilon-1)\alpha/\beta = \delta(\beta/\rho)^{-\varepsilon}W_s^{-\varepsilon} \sum_{r=1}^{R} Y_r T_{rs}^{1-\varepsilon}I_r^{\varepsilon-1}$$

which can be solved for the wage rate W_s in region s:

$$W_s = \rho\beta^{-\rho}\left(\frac{\delta}{(\varepsilon-1)\alpha}\right)^{1/\varepsilon}\left(\sum_{r=1}^{R} Y_r T_{rs}^{1-\varepsilon}I_r^{\varepsilon-1}\right)^{1/\varepsilon} \qquad (*)$$

Equation (3.21) in the text is a special case for $R=2$ and $s=1$.

Note that there is a close resemblance between this equation and the market potential approach, or the gravity approach discussed in chapter 2. Similarly to those approaches, the attractiveness of a region is related to the purchasing power of all regions, directed at a specific market and distance. The advantage of using a general equilibrium approach, as we do here, is that price indices play a crucial role and the income levels are endogenously determined, which is now made explicit.

Given the distribution of the manufacturing work force λ_i, we have now derived the short-run equilibrium equations for region 1. They are equation (3.18), determining income level Y_1, equation (3.19), determining price index I_1, and equation (3.21), determining the wage rate W_1. Similar equations hold for region 2, giving a total of six non-linear equations, as discussed in more detail in the next subsection, and analyzed in detail in the next chapter.

3.8.2 Discussion of symmetric example

This subsection discusses three possible short-run equilibria in a two-region version of the model. The two regions are identical in all respects, except possibly with respect to the distribution of the manufacturing labor force. In particular, we now also assume that the farm workers are equally divided over the two regions, that is $\phi_1 = \phi_2 = \frac{1}{2}$. Moreover, the reader will have noted that there are two awkward constants at the beginning of the right-hand side of equations (3.19) and (3.21). We will put those constants equal to 1 for the moment. We also put $L=1$ and $\gamma=\delta$ in equation (3.18). Both assumptions will be discussed in more detail in the next chapter. We thus get the following equations for the short-run equilibrium:

$$Y_1 = \lambda_1\delta W_1 + (1/2)(1 - \delta) \qquad (3.22)$$

$$Y_2 = \lambda_2\delta W_2 + (1/2)(1 - \delta) \qquad (3.22')$$

$$I_1 = (\lambda_1 W_1^{1-\varepsilon} + \lambda_2 T^{1-\varepsilon}W_2^{1-\varepsilon})^{1/(1-\varepsilon)} \qquad (3.23)$$

a. Spreading

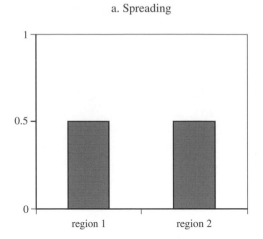

b. Agglomerate in region 1   c. Agglomerate in region 2

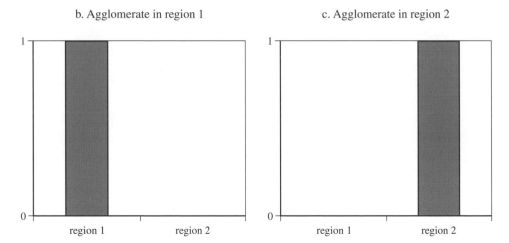

Figure 3.7.   Distribution of manufacturing labor force: three examples.

$$I_2 = (\lambda_1 T^{1-\varepsilon} W_1^{1-\varepsilon} + \lambda_2 W_2^{1-\varepsilon})^{1/(1-\varepsilon)} \tag{3.23'}$$

$$W_1 = (Y_1 I_1^{\varepsilon-1} + Y_2 T^{1-\varepsilon} I_2^{\varepsilon-1})^{1/\varepsilon} \tag{3.24}$$

$$W_2 = (Y_1 T^{1-\varepsilon} I_1^{\varepsilon-1} + Y_2 I_2^{\varepsilon-1})^{1/\varepsilon} \tag{3.24'}$$

Although we have now stripped down the short-run equilibrium of the core model of geographical economics to its bare essentials in its simplest version (two regions, identical in all respects except for the manufacturing labor force, and with a suitable choice of parameters), it still does not yield easily to analysis, except in three special cases for the distribution of the manufacturing labor force. Each is discussed in turn below.

First, even *spreading* (Figure 3.7a): suppose the two regions are identical in *all* respects, that is the manufacturing workforce is also evenly distributed ($\lambda_1 = \lambda_2 = \frac{1}{2}$). Naturally, we then expect the wage rates of the short-run equilibrium also to be the same for the two regions. Can we explicitly calculate this wage rate? Yes, if we are clever enough. One way to proceed is to guess an equilibrium wage rate, and then verify if we have guessed right (a procedure which we will also use in the next chapter). So, let's guess (for no particular reason, except that we turn out to be right in the end) that the equilibrium wage rates are $W_1 = W_2 = 1$. It follows from equation (3.23) that $I_1 = (1/2)^{1/(1-\varepsilon)}(1 + T^{1-\varepsilon})^{1/(1-\varepsilon)}$ (and similarly for I_2), while from equation (3.22) it follows that $Y_1 = \frac{1}{2}$ (and $Y_2 = \frac{1}{2}$). Using these results in equation (3.24) shows indeed that $W_1 = W_2 = 1$, so we guessed right. Thus, we can determine analytically the short-run equilibrium in this case. Note that in the spreading equilibrium, all variables are the same for the two regions, and therefore the real wages must be the same as well.

Box 3.4. Agglomeration and spreading forces: a simple diagram

It is instructive to take a closer look at this specific example, because it can be used to illustrate the economic forces which work in the model (this example is taken from Neary, 2001). Figure 3.8 illustrates profit maximization for a single firm in the market.

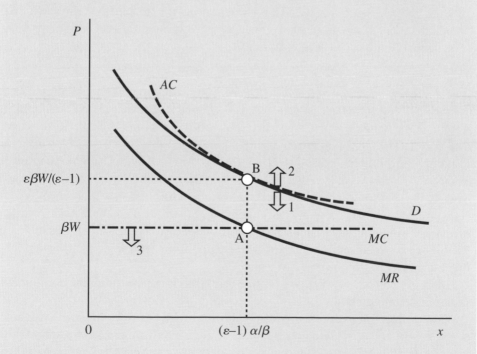

Figure 3.8. Monopolistic competition.

The volume of sales is depicted along the horizontal axis, and the price along the vertical axis. The D, AC, MC, and MR lines are the demand curve, the average cost curve, the marginal cost curve, and the marginal revenue curve, respectively. As always the intersection of the MR and MC lines gives the profit-maximizing volume of sales (point A), $x = \dfrac{\alpha(\varepsilon-1)}{\beta}$, and the corresponding price $p = \varepsilon\beta W/(\varepsilon-1)$ (point B). At B the AC and D curve are tangent, because of the zero profit condition. In this partial equilibrium setting it is simple to see what happens, *starting from the spreading equilibrium*, if one firm decides to move from region 2 to region 1. If this raises profits in region 1 the initial equilibrium was unstable and more firms will follow; if it lowers profits the initial equilibrium was stable and the firm has an incentive to return. We can distinguish two immediate effects. The first is the price index effect, which shifts the demand curve (indicated by arrow 1 in the figure) and the corresponding MR curve down. It follows immediately from equation (3.6) and given that an increase in the number of firms (varieties) lowers the price index, that this price index effect reduces the demand for each individual firm. This effect stimulates spreading. The second effect is that the new firm (and the corresponding labor force) increases demand for labor, and thus increases wages. The subsequent income increase shifts the demand curve upward; the combination of (3.22) and (3.24) makes this clear (indicated by arrow 2 in the figure). This effect stimulates agglomeration. Neary (2001) shows that it is likely that the latter shift is stronger than the first, if the share spent on manufactures is larger and transport costs are lower (the symmetric equilibrium is unstable). Arrow 3 will be discussed below.

Second, *agglomeration in region 1* (Figure 3.7b): suppose now that all manufacturing activity is agglomerated in region 1 ($\lambda_1 = 1$), such that there are no manufacturing laborers in region 2 ($\lambda_2 = 0$). Can we determine the equilibrium? Yes. Let's guess again that $W_1 = 1$. Then, it follows from equation (3.23) that $I_1 = 1$ (and $I_2 = T$), while from equation (3.22) it follows that $Y_1 = (1 + \gamma)/2$ (and $Y_2 = (1 - \gamma)/2$). Using these results in equation (3.24) shows indeed that $W_1 = 1$, so we guessed right. Thus, we can derive analytically the solutions to the short-run equilibrium in this case. Note that the wage rate W_2 is not mentioned in the above discussion. Since there are no manufacturing workers in region 2 we cannot say what their wage rate is. See also chapter 4. In terms of Figure 3.8, the arrows are reversed when we have an equilibrium with agglomeration in region 1 (if a firm moves from region 1 to region 2).

Third, *agglomeration in region 2* (Figure 3.7c): this is the mirror image of the second situation described above.

We were able to derive the short-run equilibrium analytically for three separate cases: $\lambda_1 = 0$, $\lambda_1 = \frac{1}{2}$, and $\lambda_1 = 1$. Unfortunately, these are the only three cases for which this is possible. In all other circumstances (and recall that λ_1 can vary all the way from 0 to 1 so there are infinitely many other cases), one cannot derive the short-run equilibrium analytically. So we have to find another way to determine these equilibria, and to determine what they mean in economic terms. We shall do that numerically rather than analytically, as shown in the next chapter. As it turns out, the numerical results will guide us to new analytical results.

3.9   A few remarks on dynamics

We have argued repeatedly that the introduction of a small general equilibrium model, which incorporates location, increasing returns to scale, imperfect competition, and transport costs, in conjunction with mobility of factors of production is essentially the defining characteristic of the geographical economics approach. It implies that the shaded boxes in Figures 3.1 and 3.6, illustrating the structure of the core model, can change in size over time as a result of factor mobility, which in turn implies that the short-run equilibrium can change. Since labor is the only factor of production in the core model we must therefore address labor mobility. Some information in this respect is given in chapter 9. At this point it is sufficient to note that one would expect the mobile workers to react to differences in the real wage w, which adequately measures the utility level achieved, rather than the (numéraire) wage rate W. We have already determined the real wage in section 3.4; see equation (3.8). All we have to do now is note that these real wages may differ between regions, that is

$$w_r = W_r I_r^{-\delta} \qquad (3.8')$$

The adjustment of the short-run equilibrium over time is very simple. If the real wage for manufacturing workers is higher in region 1 than in region 2 we expect that manufacturing workers will leave region 2 and settle in region 1. If the real wage is higher in region 2 than in region 1, we expect the reverse to hold. We let the parameter η denote the speed with which manufacturing workers react to differences in the real wage, and use the simple dynamic system:

$$\frac{d\lambda_1}{\lambda_1} = \eta(w_1 - \overline{w}); \qquad \text{where} \quad \overline{w} = \lambda_1 w_1 + \lambda_2 w_2 \qquad (3.25)$$

Note that $\overline{w}$ denotes the average real wage in the economy. A similar equation holds for region 2. Although this is essentially an *ad hoc* dynamic specification, it can be grounded in evolutionary game theory (see Weibull, 1995), or otherwise justified (see chapters 6 and 10). Now that we have specified how the manufacturing workforce reacts to differences in the real wage between regions we can also note when a long-run equilibrium is reached. This occurs when one of three possibilities arises, as summarized in Table 3.4, namely (i) the distribution of the manufacturing workforce between regions 1 and 2 is such that the real wage is equal in the two regions, not necessarily the symmetric equilibrium, (ii) all manufacturing workers are located in region 1, or (iii) all manufacturing workers are located in region 2.

Returning to Figure 3.8, we can show that once we introduce labor mobility there is a third (agglomerating) force in that example (indicated in Figure 3.8 by arrow 3). In

Table 3.4. *When is a long-run equilibrium reached?*

Possibility 1	Possibility 2	Possibility 3
If the real wage for manufacturing workers in region 1 is the same as the real wage for manufacturing workers in region 2.	All manufacturing workers are located in region 1 (agglomeration in region 1)	All manufacturing workers are located in region 2 (agglomeration in region 2)

that example we analyze what happens, starting from the symmetric equilibrium, if one firm decides to move to region 1. Migration only stops when a long-run equilibrium is reached and real wages are equalized (for an interior stable equilibrium). Now, because the cost of living has fallen in the larger region, the wages must fall, and vice versa in region 2. As β is constant this implies that in Figure 3.8 the MC and AC curves shift downward, raising profitability and thus providing an extra agglomerating force (see, for a combined and complete analysis of all the effects in Figure 3.8, Neary, 2001). In chapter 4 we will discuss under what circumstances we can find such long-run equilibria in which real wages are equalized.

3.10   The simple example and the core model

Sections 3.3–3.9 above gave a general overview, and explained many details, of the modeling structure of the core model of geographical economics. Section 3.2 above, on the other hand, gave a simple partial equilibrium example to illustrate five characteristics of the geographical economics approach. It is time to see to what extent we can already identify the five characteristics mentioned in the example of section 3.2 in the workings of the core model as laid out in sections 3.3–3.9.

First, *cumulative causation*: in the example of section 3.2 it was argued that if, for some reason, one region has attracted more manufacturing firms than the other region, a new firm has an incentive to locate where the majority of other firms are. In the core model this is clearly visible in equation (3.20) by the fact that, other things being equal, an increase in local income leads to a higher increase in demand than the same income increase in the other region.

Second, *multiple equilibria*: it was pointed out in the example of section 3.2 that there may be multiple long-run equilibria; in particular, agglomeration of all firms in North, agglomeration of all firms in South, and a 1:3 distribution of firms between North and South. Similarly, in the discussion of the core model in section 3.8.2 three short-run equilibria were discussed, namely, agglomeration in region 1, agglomeration in region 2, and spreading of manufacturing activity over the two regions. The remarks on dynamics in section 3.9, as summarized in Table 3.4, show that all three of these short-run equilibria are also long-run equilibria (see the next point).

Third, *stable and unstable equilibria*: it was argued in the example of section 3.2,

Table 3.5. *Total welfare and distribution of food production*
a. Even distribution of food production (50% in region 1)

	Agglomeration in region 1				Agglomeration in region 2		
	# labor	Welf./cap.	Total		# labor	Welf./cap.	Total
Farm 1	5	10	50	Farm 1	5	5	25
Man. 1	8	12	96	Man. 1	0	—	—
Farm 2	5	5	25	Farm 2	5	10	50
Man. 2	0	—	—	Man. 2	8	12	96
Total welfare			171	Total welfare			171

b. Uneven distribution of food production (60% in region 1)

	Agglomeration in region 1				Agglomeration in region 2		
	# labor	Welf./cap.	Total		# labor	Welf./cap.	Total
Farm 1	6	10	60	Farm 1	6	5	30
Man. 1	8	12	96	Man. 1	0	—	—
Farm 2	4	5	20	Farm 2	4	10	40
Man. 2	0	—	—	Man. 2	8	12	96
Total welfare			176	Total welfare			166

Note: The numbers in the table are for illustrative purposes only; man. = manufacturing workers; farm = farm workers; # labor = number of workers in that region; welf./cap. = welfare per capita.

although we never analyzed a dynamic system, that there can be stable and unstable equilibria. In particular, agglomeration of firms in either North or South is a stable equilibrium, while the 1:3 distribution of firms between North and South is an unstable equilibrium. A similar observation holds for the core model. There are, however, three important qualifications, namely (i) we specifically introduce a dynamic system in section 3.9, (ii) the analysis of this system is not easy, and therefore postponed until chapter 4, and (iii) as we shall demonstrate in chapter 4, both agglomeration and/or spreading of manufacturing activity can be stable equilibria.

Fourth, *non-optimal equilibria*: in the example of section 3.2 we saw that one long-run equilibrium might be better than another long-run equilibrium from a welfare point of view. Note that we have four different economic agents in the core model of sections 3.3–3.9, namely the manufacturing workers in both regions and the farmers in both regions. This reduces to three economic agents in the long-run equilibrium, where the real wage is the same for all manufacturing workers. Suppose we take a closer look at the agglomeration equilibria described in subsection 3.8.2. Assume for the moment that the agglomeration equilibria are stable (remember that this is analyzed in chapter 4). Some possibilities are illustrated in Table 3.5, and discussed below.

In subsection 3.8.2 the farmers are equally divided over the two regions. From a welfare point of view, it then does not matter whether manufacturing is agglomerated in region 1 or in region 2. This is illustrated in Table 3.5a, but this observation requires some explanation. Suppose that manufacturing is agglomerated in region 1. This is good news for the farmers in region 1 (their welfare is 10 in Table 3.5), because they have easy access to a large number of locally produced varieties. It is bad news for the farmers in region 2 (their welfare is 5 in Table 3.5), because they have to import all manufacturing varieties from region 1. Now suppose instead that all manufacturing is agglomerated in region 2. This time it is good news for the farmers in region 2, and bad news for the farmers in region 1. To the manufacturing workers it does not matter where they are agglomerated, their real wage is the same (12 in Table 3.5). Since total welfare is essentially the sum of the real wages of all economic agents, and the number of farmers is exactly evenly distributed over the two regions, it does not matter from a total welfare point of view whether manufacturing is agglomerated in region 1 or in region 2 (it clearly does matter for individual economic agents, notably the farmers; the total welfare is 171 in either case in Table 3.5).

A similar argument does not hold if the immobile activity, that is food production, is unevenly distributed, as it is in the example in section 3.2. This is illustrated in Table 3.5b, where 60% of the farmers are located in region 1, and 40% in region 2. Again, agglomeration of manufacturing in region 1 is good news for the farmers in region 1, and bad news for the farmers in region 2. And again, these roles are reversed if manufacturing agglomerates in region 2. This time, however, agglomeration of manufacturing in region 1 is better from a total welfare point of view, simply because more farmers can then benefit, through the love-of-variety effect, from the local production of manufactures. This is analyzed in greater detail in chapter 4.

Fifth, *interaction of agglomeration and trade flows*: in the example in section 3.2, we noted that the so-called home-market effect was a crucial aspect of geographical economics. According to Helpman and Krugman (1985, p.197), one can observe "the tendency of increasing returns industries, other things equal, to concentrate near their larger markets and to export to smaller markets." This effect is caused by the interaction of external and internal economies of scale. Firms want to locate near demand, where they can benefit from a larger market and possible spillovers (see arrow 2 in Figure 3.8). These scale economies mean that increasing-returns activities are pulled towards large markets, and the more so if these locations have good access to other markets. Because activities are attracted toward the preferred locations, (real) wages increase and labor has an incentive to migrate toward these locations, increasing the attractiveness even further. In the end, a disproportionately large share of activity ends up in these preferred locations, and this region becomes a net exporter of manufactures. Hence the name "home-market effect."

It is important to see that the introduction of transport costs is the determining factor for this effect. Comparison of Krugman (1980) with his 1979 article makes this point clear. What happens if trade is allowed between a large and a small country in the absence of transport costs? One might expect a home-market effect, with the larger country exporting manufactures and importing the homogeneous product. This is not the case, however. Free trade ensures that prices of all varieties are equalized between countries, and in the absence of transport costs this also equalizes wages. Furthermore, production costs are not affected by the presence of other firms in the same location. The trade structure is therefore indeterminate; production of manufactures can take place anywhere; neither location has a natural cost advantage over the other. With free trade, however, the total number of varieties available to consumers in each country increases. This in essence generates the gains from trade in the model.

The introduction of transport costs changes this dramatically, as has already been shown by Krugman (1980). This seemingly innocuous extension of the model creates the home-market effect. By concentrating production of manufactures in the larger market it is possible to benefit from scale economies, and at the same time economize on transport costs. This increases the real wage of manufacturing workers in the larger market, which makes this region the more attractive place to live.

Finally, we can already say something about the structure of trade between the regions by comparing the spreading equilibrium and the agglomeration equilibria with each other. Suppose, for example, that manufacturing production is agglomerated in region 1. In that case, the farmers in region 2 have to import all manufacturing varieties from region 1. Region 2 thus exports food in exchange for manufacturing varieties, an example of pure inter-industry trade, that is trade between regions of different types of goods.

In contrast, suppose that manufacturing production is evenly spread over the two regions, as is food production (the symmetric equilibrium), using the specification of sub-section 3.8.2. There it is shown that $Y_1 = Y_2 = \frac{1}{2}$ in this case, which implies that the demand for food in either region is equal to $(1 - \delta) Y_1 = (1 - \delta)/2$. Since the production level of food in, for example, region 1 is equal to $\phi_1(1 - \gamma)L = (1/2)(1 - \delta)1 = (1 - \delta)/2$ (see subsection 3.8.2) it follows that the total demand for food in region 1 is equal to the total production of food in region 1. In the spreading equilibrium, there is thus no trade of food between the two regions. Since all consumers will spend money on all manufacturing varieties, including those produced in the other region, there will be trade in manufacturing varieties between the two regions. This is thus an example of pure intra-industry trade, that is trade between regions of similar types of goods (importing manufacturing varieties in exchange for other manufacturing varieties).

It is now time to analyze the main implications of the core model of geographical economics more formally and completely. This is considered in the next chapter.

Exercises

3.1 From introductory micro-economics we know that the condition for profit maximization for a firm is $MC = MR$, that is marginal cost equals marginal revenue. Under perfect competition this condition implies that $MC = p$, that is marginal cost is equal to the price of a good (marginal cost pricing). Now use Figure 3.8 to show that with the average cost curve in the core model (use equation (3.10)), marginal cost pricing always results in a loss for the firm (implying that imperfect competition is the dominant market form).

3.2 Start again from the example in section 3.2, but now assume that each firm has the possibility of opening a second plant in the other region. Each firm minimizes the combined costs of setting up a second plant and transport costs. Suppose setting up a plant costs 2 units. Decide where to locate given the location of the other firms.

(i)   If all other firms have a single plant in South, what is optimal for our firm?
(ii) If all other firms have two plants, one in each location, what is optimal for our firm?

3.3* Suppose we start with a situation of complete agglomeration of manufacturing production in region 1, that is $\lambda_1 = 1$. Without calculating the equilibrium values explicitly one might suspect that $W_1 = 1$ is the equilibrium value in this case. Substituting this in the income and price equations we find:

$$Y_1 = \frac{(1+\delta)}{2}; \qquad Y_2 = \frac{(1-\delta)}{2}; \qquad I_1 = 1; \qquad I_2 = T$$

Using these values, $W_1 = 1$ is indeed an equilibrium value for wages in region 1, as can be verified from (3.24). Real wages also equal 1 in region 1. Calculate the potential real wage in region 2 by using equations (3.24′) and (3.8′). Under what condition for ε and δ is $w_2 < w_1 = 1$ if T becomes arbitrarily large?

3.4* Suppose a monopolistic producer located in region 1 can sell either in region 1 or in region 2. Let p_{11} (p_{12}) be the price charged in region 1 (respectively in region 2), and let x_{11} (x_{12}) be the demand in region 1 (respectively in region 2). Obviously, the demand functions depend on the price charged in either region. Production requires only labor as an input, which is paid wage rate W_1, and benefits from internal returns to scale, using α fixed labor and β variable labor. Finally, there are (iceberg) transport costs: the firm must produce Tx_{12} units to ensure x_{12} can be sold in region 2, with $T > 1$. The firm's profit function π and demand functions x_{11} and x_{12} ($\varepsilon > 1$, and Y_1 and Y_2 are constants) are given below:

$$\pi = p_{11}x_{11} + p_{12}x_{12} - W_1(\alpha + \beta x_{11} + \beta T x_{12})$$

$$x_{11} = p_{11}^{-\varepsilon} Y_1; \qquad x_{12} = p_{12}^{-\varepsilon} Y_2$$

First, comment on the profit function above. Second, substitute the demand functions in the profit function. Third, determine what the optimal prices p_{11} and p_{12} are, that is solve the profit maximization problem. Fourth, show that $p_{12} = Tp_{11}$, that is the optimal price charged in region 2 is exactly T times higher than the optimal price charged in region 1.

3.5* In the example of section 3.2 we showed that some equilibria are better from a welfare perspective than other equilibria. Can you show this using equations

(3.22)–(3.24) and (3.22′)–(3.24′)? Assume that the farmers are not symmetrically distributed over both regions. Suppose region 1 has one-third of all farmers and region 2, two-thirds of all farmers. Can you show that from a welfare point of view, agglomeration in region 2 is better than agglomeration in region 1, as might be expected because region 2 potentially has the largest market. *Hint*: Make sure that complete agglomeration in region 1 and complete agglomeration in region 2 are both equilibria. Use the resulting equations to show that (U indicates utility)

$$\text{For } \lambda_1 = 1: U_{\lambda=1} = 1 + \frac{(1-\delta)}{3} + \frac{2}{3}(1-\delta)T^{-\delta}$$

$$\text{and for } \lambda_1 = 0: U_{\lambda=0} = 1 + \frac{2}{3}(1-\delta) + \frac{(1-\delta)}{3}T^{-\delta}$$

A more in-depth analysis of welfare is given in chapter 4.

4   Solutions and simulations

4.1   Introduction

Chapter 3 has carefully developed and discussed the main features of the core model of geographical economics. Most importantly, perhaps, the model is coherent: it is a miniature world in which the demand in one region for the manufactures of another region is not imposed beforehand but derived from the income generated in the region by its production and exports to other regions. Despite the care taken in setting up the different aspects of the model as simply and tractably as possible it turns out to be quite complex to study analytically.

This chapter focuses on the possibilities and the advantages and disadvantages of computer simulations to better understand the workings of the core model of geographical economics. In doing so, we will be able to say more on the determination of the long-run equilibrium in the core model. We start by explaining in some detail what computer simulations are, what they can and cannot do, and the specification issues involved in getting them to work. Subsequently, we show how computer simulations can be useful in three ways. First, we demonstrate that simulations allow us to do things one cannot do analytically. In general this is indispensable in more complicated models to get a "feel" for the model. The most important goal of these simulations is to see how certain crucial aspects of the model react to changes in important parameters of the core model. Second, analytical solutions are sometimes possible and simulations can give rise to ideas which can be proven analytically. Of the latter we give two examples, in sections 4.6 and 4.7 below. Third, as we show at the end of this chapter, simulations can be useful in demonstrating that certain ideas or suggestions do not always hold, simply by producing a counter-example.

4.2   Short-run equilibrium

The analytical framework of the previous chapter, combining economies of scale, imperfect competition, location, external economies, and immobile workers, is summarized for the case of R regions in equations (4.1)–(4.3):[1]

---

[1] See the (*) equations in Technical Notes 3.5 and 3.6 of chapter 3.

$$Y_r = \lambda_r W_r \gamma L + \phi_r (1 - \gamma) L \qquad (4.1)$$

$$I_r = \left(\frac{\beta}{\rho}\right)\left(\frac{\gamma L}{\alpha \varepsilon}\right)^{1/(1-\varepsilon)} \left(\sum_{s=1}^{R} \lambda_s T_{rs}^{1-\varepsilon} W_s^{1-\varepsilon}\right)^{1/(1-\varepsilon)} \qquad (4.2)$$

$$W_r = \rho \beta^{-\rho} \left(\frac{\delta}{(\varepsilon-1)\alpha}\right)^{1/\varepsilon} \left(\sum_{s=1}^{R} Y_s T_{rs}^{1-\varepsilon} I_s^{\varepsilon-1}\right)^{1/\varepsilon} \qquad (4.3)$$

These determine income Y_r, the price index I_r, and the wage rate W_r, respectively, for region r. If these three equations hold for each region we have found a short-run equilibrium in which world demand for food and each variety of manufactures is equal to world supply and no producer is earning excess profits. To be of any geographic interest at all we need at least two locations, which implies, since the above three equations must hold for each location, that we have to investigate at least six simultaneous non-linear equations. That is very difficult. In fact it is so difficult that the model can only be solved analytically in some special cases; see the website. How should one proceed in general?

This is the point where we come to hail and glorify the benefits of the computer era, which allows us to tackle models like the core geographical economics model by means of computer *simulations*. Five requirements must be met for these simulations to work for the core model. First, we must be clear for what it is we are solving. The short-run equilibrium determines the *endogenous* variables income Y_r, price index I_r, and wage rate W_r for each region r (and in doing so also gives us the real wages; see below). So we must find solutions to the equations above for these variables, that is determine numeric values of Y_r, I_r, and W_r for which equations (4.1)–(4.3) hold.

Second, it must be realized that the solutions for the endogenous variables depend on the values of λ_r (the distribution of the mobile labor force which is fixed in the short run) and the values of all the *parameters* (L, α, β, γ, δ, ϕ_r, ρ, ε, and T, where we recall that $T_{rs} = T^{D_{rs}}$ and D_{rs} is the economic distance between regions r and s). This implies in particular that we cannot start to find solutions for the endogenous variables before specifying values for the exogenous variables and parameters. To start with the latter, Table 4.1 specifies parameter values for the two-region "base scenario." As will become clear later in this chapter (see Proposition 4.1) the first column contains the most important information. In this base scenario the share of income spent on manufactures (δ) is chosen fairly low at 0.4, while the substitution parameter (ρ) and the transport costs (T) are chosen fairly high, at 0.8 and 1.7, respectively. Note that the elasticity of substitution parameter ε, clearly present in equations (4.1)–(4.3), is absent from Table 4.1, because it can be determined using the formula $\varepsilon = 1/(1 - \rho) = 5$. The rest of Table 4.1 shows that the share of the labor force in manufacturing (γ) is 0.4, the marginal labor required to produce a variety of manufactures (β) is 0.8, the fixed labor requirement (α) is 0.08, the total number of laborers (L) is 1, while immobile (i.e. agricultural) production is equal in the two regions ($\phi_1 = \phi_2 = 0.5$). The latter is an important assumption, because it implies that the two regions are identical with respect to all

Table 4.1. *Base scenario parameter configuration, two regions*

$\delta = 0.4$	$\gamma = 0.4$	$L = 1$
$\rho = 0.8$	$\beta = 0.8$	$\phi_1 = \phi_2 = 0.5$
$T = 1.7$	$\alpha = 0.08$	$\sigma = 0.0001$

parameters listed in Table 4.1. The final parameter in Table 4.1 (σ) will be discussed below.

Why have we chosen this set of base scenario parameters? To some degree, the choice is arbitrary. This holds in particular for the share of income spent on manufactures, δ, and the elasticity of substitution between varieties, $\varepsilon = 1/(1 - \rho)$. Both have been based on reasonable empirical estimates, to be further discussed later. Given the choice of δ and ρ, the value of the transport costs T is chosen to demonstrate an important aspect of the core model of geographical economics, as illustrated in Figure 4.1 and discussed below. The justification for all other parameter values will become clear after the analysis in section 4.6.

Third, we must specify a *solution method*, that is a well-specified procedure that will lead us to solving equations (4.1)–(4.3) for numeric values of the endogenous variables, given the chosen levels of the exogenous variables and parameters. Several options are available at this point, and we will use some of them in this book, but the order of equations (4.1)–(4.3) readily suggests a method, termed *sequential iterations*, to be used in this chapter. It works as follows:

(i)   Guess an initial solution for the wage rate in the two regions, say ($W_{1,0}$, $W_{2,0}$), where 0 indicates the number of the iteration (we will use $W_{1,0} = W_{2,0} = 1$).
(ii) Using ($W_{1,0}$, $W_{2,0}$) calculate the income levels ($Y_{1,0}$, $Y_{2,0}$) and price index ($I_{1,0}$, $I_{2,0}$) as implied by equations (4.1) and (4.2), respectively.
(iii) Using ($Y_{1,0}$, $Y_{2,0}$) and ($I_{1,0}$, $I_{2,0}$) as calculated in step (ii) determine a new possible solution for the wage rate ($W_{1,1}$, $W_{2,1}$) as implied by equation (4.3).
(iv) Repeat steps (ii) and (iii) until a solution is found.

Note that equations (4.1)–(4.3) are used repeatedly in sequence to find a solution, hence the name of the method.

Fourth, a *stopping criterion* must be specified. The above description of the solution method casually directed us in step (iv) to "repeat steps (ii) and (iii) until a solution is found," but when is a solution found? How close should we get to be satisfied that the numeric values we find are indeed a solution to equations (4.1)–(4.3)? We can use as a stopping criterion the condition that the relative change in the wage rate should not exceed some small value σ from one iteration to the next for all regions r, that is

$$\left| \frac{W_{r,iteration} - W_{r,iteration-1}}{W_{r,iteration-1}} \right| < \sigma, \quad \text{for all } r.$$

Table 4.1 indicates that we chose the value $\sigma = 0.0001$ for our simulations.

Fifth, and finally, we must choose a *programming language* and write a small program to perform the above calculations. Again, several options are available, but we used Gauss™, a widely used and versatile mathematical programming language, for all our simulations. Examples of these programs can be found on the website.

4.3   Some first results

After explaining in some detail in section 4.2 how to perform simulations in principle it is time to show and discuss the results of some actual simulations. It was, deliberately, *not* specified in section 4.2 what the values of the short-run exogenous variables λ_r (the share of the mobile work force in region r) were in the two-region base scenario, although it was mentioned that such a specification is needed to perform simulations. The reason for this omission is quite simply that we do not only want to use simulations to find just *a* solution for *a* given parameter setting of the model, but also want to use them to learn something about the structure of our model; notably, by investigating how the short-run equilibrium (Y_r, I_r, W_r) changes if the short-run exogenous variables λ_r change, as we will do in this section.

Assuming that there are just two regions is particularly useful for illustrative purposes. After all, specifying λ_1 automatically implies λ_2 using $\lambda_1 + \lambda_2 = 1$. Varying λ_1 between 0 and 1 therefore gives a complete description of all possible distributions of the mobile workforce in a two-region setting. If we find another variable that interests us we can simply depict its dependence on the distribution of the mobile workforce in a graph. Although we are interested in various aspects of the model we first focus attention on the real wage in region 1 relative to the real wage in region 2, as it will give us an indication of the dynamic forces operating in the model. Recall that the real wage in region s is given by

$$w_s = W_s I_s^{-\delta} \tag{4.4}$$

which implies that once we find a short-run equilibrium for a particular distribution of the mobile labor force, that is a solution to equations (4.1)–(4.3), it is trivial to calculate the real wage in all regions using equation (4.4), and thus the relative real wage w_1/w_2.

Figure 4.1 illustrates how the relative real wage in region 1 (w_1/w_2) varies as the share of the mobile workforce in region 1 (λ_1) varies. The figure is the result of fifty-nine separate simulations in which the value of λ_1 is gradually increased from 0 to 1. Each time, the short-run equilibrium, the solution to equations (4.1)–(4.3), is calculated using the procedure described in section 4.2. Then the real wage in the two regions is calculated using equation (4.4), which determines w_1/w_2, and therefore one observation in Figure 4.1. What can we learn from this graph?

First, recall that we argued in chapter 3 that the mobile workforce has an incentive to move to regions with a higher real wage, such that a short-run equilibrium is also a long-run equilibrium if, and only if, the real wage for the mobile workforce is the same in all regions. That is to say, a long-run equilibrium requires that the relative real wage

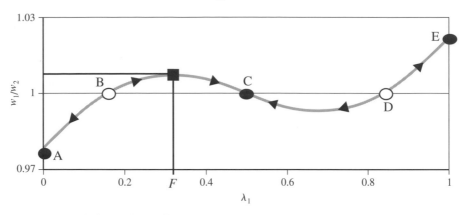

Figure 4.1.   The relative real wage in region 1.

is 1 as long as there are mobile laborers in both regions. It is only when a long-run equilibrium implies complete agglomeration (one region ends up with all mobile laborers: either $\lambda_1 = 1$ or $\lambda_2 = 1$) that the relative real wage is not equal to one (see points A and E).[2] In Figure 4.1 the long-run equilibria B, C, and D are reached for $w_1/w_2 = 1$. Chapter 3 heuristically found two types of long-run equilibria: (i) spreading of manufacturing production over the two regions (point C in Figure 4.1), and (ii) complete agglomeration of manufacturing production in either region 1 or region 2 (points A and E, respectively). Figure 4.1 clearly illustrates that there is a third type of long-run equilibrium in which manufacturing production is partially agglomerated in one of the two regions (points B and D), leading to a total of five long-run equilibria. It would have been virtually impossible to find equilibria B and D analytically.

Second, we get a clear feel for the dynamics of the system, allowing us to distinguish between stable and unstable equilibria. Suppose, for example, that $\lambda_1 = F$ in Figure 4.1. Note that the mobile workforce is larger in region 2 than in region 1. As illustrated, the associated short-run equilibrium implies $w_1/w_2 > 1$. The higher real wage in region 1 gives the mobile laborers an incentive to move from region 2 to region 1. This migration into region 1 represents an increase of λ_1 in Figure 4.1. This process will continue until the spreading equilibrium at point C is reached, where the real wages are equalized. Similar reasoning, leading to the spreading equilibrium at point C, would hold for any arbitrary initial distribution of the mobile labor force strictly in between points B and D, which could therefore be called the "basin of attraction" for the spreading equilibrium. Thus, the spreading equilibrium is a stable equilibrium, in the sense that any deviation of the mobile labor force from point C within its basin of attraction will activate economic forces to bring us back to the spreading equilibrium. Similar reasoning holds for the two complete agglomeration equilibria, points A and E, each with its

---

[2] If there is complete agglomeration the relative real wage cannot actually be calculated since there are no manufacturing workers in one of the regions. Points A and E in Figure 4.1 are therefore limit values.

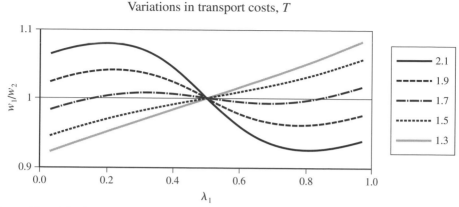

Figure 4.2.   The impact of transport costs.

own basin of attraction (from point A to point B, and from point D to point E, respectively). These stable equilibria are illustrated with closed circles in Figure 4.1. In contrast, the partial agglomeration long-run equilibria, points B and D, are *un*stable, illustrated with open circles. If, for whatever reason, we are initially at point B or D, a long-run equilibrium is reached in the sense that the real wages are equal for regions 1 and 2. However, any arbitrarily small perturbation of this equilibrium will set in motion a process of adjustment leading to a different (stable) long-run equilibrium. For example, a small negative disturbance of λ_1 at point B leads to complete agglomeration of manufacturing activity in region 2, while a small positive disturbance of λ_1 at point B leads to spreading of manufacturing activity.

4.4 Structural change I: transport costs

The main identifying characteristic of regions in the core model of geographical economics are the transport costs, assumed to be zero within a region, but positive between two different regions. The term "transport costs" is a shorthand notation for many different types of obstacles to trade between locations, such as tariffs, language and culture barriers, and indeed the costs of actually getting goods or services at another location (see also Box 3.3). A natural question is thus what the effect of changes in transport costs are in the core model. This question must be answered by repeating the simulation procedure of section 4.3 for different levels of transport costs. Figure 4.2 depicts the result of such simulations for five values of transport costs, namely $T=1.3$, 1.5, 1.7, 1.9, and 2.1.

As Figure 4.2 shows, if transport costs are large, say $T=2.1$ or $T=1.9$, and given the other parameters of the model (see Table 4.1), the spreading equilibrium is the globally stable equilibrium. It makes intuitive sense that if manufactures are difficult to transport from one region to another the dynamics of the model lead to spreading of manufacturing activity; distant provision of manufactures is too costly so they need to be provided locally. On the other hand, if transport costs are smaller, say $T=1.3$ or $T=1.5$, the spreading equilibrium is unstable while the agglomerating equilibria are stable, with an initial λ_1 between 0 and 0.5 as the basin of attraction for complete agglomeration in region 2, and an initial λ_1 between 0.5 and 1 as the basin of attraction for complete agglomeration in region 1. Again this makes sense intuitively. With very low transport costs, the immobile market can be provided effectively from a distance, which therefore does not pose a strong enough force to counter the advantages of agglomeration (home-market effect). One may now start to get the feeling that the intermediate transport cost case, $T=1.7$, in which the relative real wage crosses 1 in the interior three times, is special. In particular after reading Paul Krugman's original paper on the core model of geographical economics, where he concludes with respect to his version of Figure 4.2 that (Krugman, 1991, p. 492, our notation):[3] "it implicitly assumes that w_1/w_2 is a monotonic function . . . or at least that it crosses one only once. In principle this need not be the case . . . I have not been able to rule this out analytically."

This immediately reveals another advantage of simulations: after only one counter-example produced by a simulation we can stop trying to rule something out analytically that cannot be ruled out. This brings us back to the question whether the situation with intermediate transport costs, $T=1.7$, as depicted in Figure 4.1, is special or not? Well, yes and no, as decisively shown by Fujita, Krugman, and Venables (1999). "Yes" in the sense that it only holds for a fairly limited range of transport costs. "No" in the sense that for any arbitrary parameter configuration as given in Table 4.1 there is always a range of transport costs for which the relative real wage crosses 1 in the interior three times. We return to this issue in section 4.7.

4.5   Structural change II: other parameters

Analogously to the example of transport costs in section 4.4 we can analyze the impact of the other parameters on the short-run equilibrium using simulations. Figure 4.3a illustrates the impact of ρ, the substitution parameter. For low values of ρ the elasticity of substitution between manufactures is low, indicating that it is hard to substitute one type of manufacture for another. That makes locally produced manufactures more attractive and valuable, hence the tendency for manufacturing production to agglomerate in one region if the elasticity of substitution is low. The reverse reasoning holds if the elasticity of substitution is high, implying that spreading of manufacturing production is a stable equilibrium. Figure 4.3b illustrates the impact of δ, the share of income spent on manufactures. As this share decreases the impact of the mobile sector on income decreases, implying that the income of the mobile workforce is increasingly determined by the immobile sector. Thus low shares of income spent on manufactures lead to weaker linkages, such that, other things equal, the spreading equilibrium is globally stable. Finally, Figure 4.3c illustrates the impact of γ, the share of the labor force in the manufacturing sector. As clearly shown, this parameter has virtually no impact

---

[3] The analysis is, however, performed in Fujita, Krugman, and Venables (1999).

a. Variations in ρ (substitution parameter)

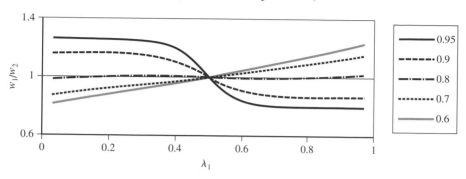

b. Variations in δ (share of income spent on manufactures)

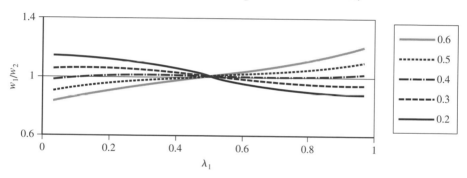

c. Variations in γ (share of labor force in manufacturing)

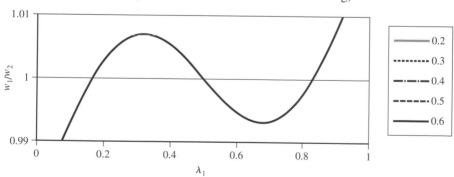

Figure 4.3.   The impact of some parameters.

on the relative real wage. If, for example, the share of the manufacturing workforce in region 1 is 35%, a tripling of γ from 20% to 60% increases w_1/w_2 only from 1.006866 to 1.006782. In terms of the dynamic properties of the model, therefore, little generality is lost in suitably "normalizing" this parameter.

Figure 4.3 does not, for good reasons, show the impact of the other parameters in Table 4.1. The stopping criterion σ must be chosen in such a manner that it is small enough to yield reliable results. Indeed, lowering it further by a factor of ten to 0.00001 has no noticeable impact on Figure 4.1. Also, at least for the moment, we want to investigate only regions which are identical in all respects, except for the distribution of the mobile labor force, so we are not interested in changing ϕ. Most importantly, we could also have included graphs analyzing the effect of changes in the size of the labor force L, the fixed cost of production α, or the marginal cost of production β, but they all would look *exactly* like Figure 4.1. This can be verified on the website. Evidently, changes in these parameters do not influence the relative real wage, and thus essentially do not affect the underlying dynamics and stability analysis of the system. Note that this does *not* mean that changes in these parameters do not have a real impact on the prosperity of nations, a question which we will address in section 4.8; it just means that they affect the real wages of the two regions equiproportionally. This fact will simplify our analysis later, once we have established it analytically, an issue addressed in the next section.

4.6   Normalization analysis

In this section our claim about the small impacts on the short-run equilibrium and the real wage of changes in the parameters L, α, and β will be analyzed. For ease of reference we repeat equations (4.1)–(4.4).

$$Y_r = \lambda_r W_r \gamma L + \phi_r (1 - \gamma) L \tag{4.1}$$

$$I_r = \left(\frac{\beta}{\rho}\right)\left(\frac{\gamma L}{\alpha \varepsilon}\right)^{1/(1-\varepsilon)}\left(\sum_{s=1}^{R} \lambda_s T_{rs}^{1-\varepsilon} W_s^{1-\varepsilon}\right)^{1/(1-\varepsilon)} \tag{4.2}$$

$$W_s = \rho \beta^{-\rho}\left(\frac{\delta}{(\varepsilon-1)\alpha}\right)^{1/\varepsilon}\left(\sum_{r=1}^{R} Y_r T_{rs}^{1-\varepsilon} I_r^{\varepsilon-1}\right)^{1/\varepsilon} \tag{4.3}$$

$$w_s = W_s I_s^{-\delta} \tag{4.4}$$

First, suppose the labor force L increases by some multiplicative factor, say θ, taking the distribution of the labor force as given. Assume that the wage W does not change. From equation (4.1) it then follows that income in each region changes by the same factor θ, while equation (4.2) shows that the price index in each region increases by the factor $\theta^{1/(1-\varepsilon)}$. Using these two results in equation (4.3) shows indeed that the wage in each region does not change. The real wages in each region therefore changes equiproportionally by the factor $\theta^{-\delta/(1-\varepsilon)}$ (see equation (4.4)), such that the distribution of relative real wages is not affected.[4] Recalling the one-to-one relationship between the size of the manufacturing workforce in a region and the number of varieties produced in that region (see equation (3.15)), it is obvious that an equiproportional increase in the manufacturing workforce in all regions allows for a larger range of varieties to be produced in each region. This drives down the price index in all regions equiproportionally, which in turn increases the real wages equiproportionally through a love-of-variety effect.

Second, suppose the fixed cost of production α increases by a multiplicative factor θ for all regions. Assume, for the sake of argument, that the wage does not change. From equation (4.1) it follows that income does not change, and from equation (4.2) that the price index increases by the factor $\theta^{-1/(1-\varepsilon)}$. Using these two results in equation (4.3) shows that the wage in each region indeed does not change. The real wage in each region therefore changes equiproportionally by the factor $\theta^{\delta/(1-\varepsilon)}$ (see equation (4.4)), such that the distribution of relative real wages is not affected. The intuitive reasoning is very similar to the first case described above. Just like a rise in the labor force, a fall in the fixed costs of production in a region allows for an increase in the number of varieties produced in that region (see equation (3.15)). If this holds for all regions it drives the price index down in all regions equiproportionally, thus increasing the real wages equiproportionally through a love-of-variety effect.

Third, suppose the marginal cost of production β increases by a multiplicative factor θ for all regions. Assume, for the sake of argument, that the wage W does not change. From equation (4.1) it follows that income in each region does not change, and from equation (4.2) that the price index increases by the factor θ. Using these two results in equation (4.3) shows again that the wage in each region indeed does not change. The real wage in each region therefore changes equiproportionally by the factor $\theta^{-\delta}$ (see equation (4.4)), such that the distribution of relative real wages is not affected. Quite similarly to the above two cases, the real wage rises if the marginal labor cost of production falls by lowering prices and the price index; see equations (3.12) and (3.17). The above reasoning proves Proposition 4.1.[5]

Proposition 4.1.

Suppose that (Y_r, I_r, W_r, w_r) solves equations (4.1)–(4.4). Then a change in the size of the population L or the manufacturing cost function parameters α and β by a factor θ changes this solution to $(\theta Y_r, \theta^{1/(1-\varepsilon)} I_r, W_r, \theta^{-\delta/(1-\varepsilon)} w_r)$, $(Y_r, \theta^{-1/(1-\varepsilon)} I_r, W_r, \theta^{\delta/(1-\varepsilon)} w_r)$, and $(Y_r, \theta I_r, W_r, \theta^{-\delta} w_r)$, respectively. The equiproportional change in the real wage implies that the parameters L, α, and β essentially do not influence the dynamics and stability of the model. These parameters do, however, influence the real wage (=welfare) level.

Now that it has been established how the short-run equilibrium reacts to changes in the parameters α, β, and L, and that these parameters affect the real wage in all

---

[4] The term "distribution of relative real wages" is more appropriate in a multi-region setting than in a two-region setting. Proposition 4.1 below, however, applies for an arbitrary number of regions.
[5] See Neary (2001) for a discussion.

Table 4.2. *Parameter normalization*

$\gamma = \delta$	$L = 1$
$\beta = \rho$	$\alpha = \gamma L / \varepsilon$

regions equiproportionally, thus essentially not influencing the dynamics of our model, we are in a position to "suitably" choose these parameters to simplify nota-tion, following Fujita, Krugman, and Venables (1999); see Table 4.2. Note that we have taken the liberty of "normalizing" γ by setting it equal to δ (see also exercise 4.1). There are two justifications for this. First, as demonstrated in Figure 4.3c, this parameter has virtually no impact on the relative real wage. Second, as the reader may wish to verify, by setting $\gamma = \delta$ the real wage for the mobile workforce is the same as the real wage of the immobile workforce in the spreading equilibrium. Obviously, that argument only has some weight if the spreading equilibrium is established in the long run. To the extent that γ has some impact on the relative real wage, and thus the dynamics of the system, its normalization is questionable. Note, finally, that with this normalization, using $\varepsilon = 1/(1 - \rho)$, equations (4.1)–(4.3) simplify to (4.1')–(4.3').

$$Y_r = \delta \lambda_r W_r + (1 - \delta)\phi_r \tag{4.1'}$$

$$I_r = \left(\sum_{s=1}^{R} \lambda_s T_{rs}^{1-\varepsilon} W_s^{1-\varepsilon} \right)^{1/(1-\varepsilon)} \tag{4.2'}$$

$$W_s = \left(\sum_{r=1}^{R} Y_r T_{rs}^{1-\varepsilon} I_r^{\varepsilon-1} \right)^{1/\varepsilon} \tag{4.3'}$$

4.7   Sustain and break analysis

We have analyzed the impact of a number of parameters analytically and explained what we can and cannot do with the normalization. Our task has now become consid-erably easier because we can focus attention on the parameters δ, ρ, and T, the first column of Table 4.1. As promised in section 4.5 we now analyze how "special" the sit-uation depicted in Figure 4.1 (for $T = 1.7$), in which the relative real wage crosses 1 in the interior three times, really is. The simulation results shown in Figure 4.2 are sug-gestive in this respect. It looks like complete agglomeration is a stable equilibrium for small transport costs, while the spreading equilibrium is stable for large transport costs. We analyze these two suggestions in this section. In doing so, we make use of and build on the analysis and terminology developed in chapters 4 and 5 of Fujita, Krugman, and Venables (1999).

4.7.1 *Sustain, break, and transport costs*

Suppose that all manufacturing activity is located in region 1. Given the normalization $\phi_1 = \phi_2 = 0.5$ and the analysis in chapter 3, it is easy to verify that the solution to equations (4.1′)–(4.3′) if $\lambda_1 = 1$ is given by $W_1 = 1$, $Y_1 = (1 + \delta)/2$, $Y_2 = (1 - \delta)/2$, $I_1 = 1$, and $I_2 = T$. There are no manufacturing workers in region 2, so it is not really appropriate to talk of their wage W_2, but we can calculate what this wage would have been by using equation (4.3′). Similarly, we can calculate the implied real wage w_2 by using equation (4.4). Noting that the real wage in region 1 (w_1) is equal to 1, we see that it will be attractive for mobile workers located in region 1 to move to region 2 if the implied real wage in region 2 (w_2) is larger than 1. If that occurs complete agglomeration of manufacturing activity in region 1 is not "sustainable." The appendix to this chapter shows that $w_2 > 1$, and therefore agglomeration is not sustainable, if, and only if, equation (4.5) holds.

$$f(T) \equiv [(1 + \delta)/2]T^{-(\rho + \delta)\varepsilon} + [(1 - \delta)/2]T^{(\rho - \delta)\varepsilon} > 1 \qquad (4.5)$$

The function $f(T)$ is illustrated in Figures 4.4 and 4.A1. Note that $f(1) = 1$, while the appendix shows that $f'(1) = -\varepsilon\delta(1 + \rho) < 0$. Thus, for small transport costs (T close to 1) the function $f(T)$ will be smaller than 1, that is $w_2 < 1$. This implies that complete agglomeration of manufacturing in one region is always a sustainable equilibrium for sufficiently small transport costs, since the real wage in the periphery will be smaller than in the center. As transport costs increase, however, the first term in equation (4.5) becomes arbitrarily small, while the second term becomes arbitrarily large if, and only if, $\rho > \delta$. We can conclude therefore that complete agglomeration of manufacturing in one region is not sustainable for sufficiently large transport costs if $\rho > \delta$. Fujita, Krugman, and Venables (1999, p. 58) label this the "no-black-hole" condition because if this condition is not fulfilled "the forces working toward agglomeration would always prevail, and the economy would tend to collapse into a point." Stated differently, if the no-black-hole condition is not met, full agglomeration occurs irrespective of the level of transport costs. In chapter 5 (sections 5.5 and 5.6) we will discuss some empirical evidence about the no-black-hole condition. Figure 4.4 illustrates the above discussion if the no-black-hole condition is met. For sufficiently small transport costs, the function $f(T) < 1$, and complete agglomeration in one region is sustainable. If the transport costs exceed a critical level, labeled "sustain-point" in Figure 4.4, the function $f(T) > 1$, and complete agglomeration is not sustainable.

The second suggestion mentioned at the beginning of this section was that the spreading equilibrium is stable for large transport costs. So, suppose manufacturing activity is evenly spread over the two regions. It is easy to verify from equations (4.1′)–(4.3′) that if $\lambda_1 = \lambda_2 = 0.5$, the solution is given by $W_1 = W_2 = 1$, $Y_1 = Y_2 = 0.5$, $I_1 = I_2 = [0.5(1 + T^{1-\varepsilon})]^{1/(1-\varepsilon)}$. We want to investigate changes in this spreading equilibrium if a small (infinitesimal) number of workers are relocating from region 1 to region 2. In particular, we want to establish under what conditions this small movement results in a higher real wage for the moving workers, thus setting in motion further

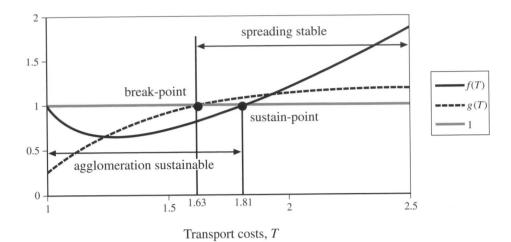

Transport costs, T

Figure 4.4. Sustain-point and break-point I. (For the parameters δ and ρ, see Table 4.1; other parameters normalized, see Table 4.2. Note that the agglomeration equilibrium is sustainable if $f(T)<1$ [see equation (4.5)] while the spreading equilibrium is stable if $g(T)>1$ [see equation (4.6)].)

movements of labor and a process of agglomeration. If so, the spreading equilibrium is unstable. The point where the spreading equilibrium switches from stable to unstable is labeled the "break-point" by Fujita, Krugman, and Venables (1999). The technical details of this analysis are cumbersome and delegated to the appendix to this chapter. At this point it suffices to note that the spreading equilibrium is unstable if, and only if, the inequality in (4.6) holds.

$$g(T) \equiv \frac{1 - T^{1-\varepsilon}}{1 + T^{1-\varepsilon}} + \left[1 - \frac{\delta(1+\rho)}{\delta^2 + \rho}\right] < 1 \tag{4.6}$$

Note that the first term on the left-hand side of equation (4.6) is monotonically rising (from 0 to 1) as transport costs T rise (from 1 to ∞), while the second term is a constant fraction strictly in between 0 and 1 if, and only if, $\rho > \delta$, that is if the no-black-hole condition is fulfilled. In that case, the function $g(T)$ is smaller than 1 (the spreading equilibrium is unstable) for sufficiently small transport costs (T close to 1). Once transport costs exceed a certain threshold level, labeled "break-point" in Figure 4.4, the function $g(T)>1$ and the spreading equilibrium is stable. If the no-black-hole condition is not fulfilled the spreading equilibrium is unstable for *all* transport costs. The break-point can be derived explicitly using equation (4.6); see exercise 4.4.

Proposition 4.2 (Fujita, Krugman, and Venables, 1999).

Suppose the no-black-hole condition ($\rho > \delta$) holds in a symmetric two-region setting of the geographical economics model, then (i) complete agglomeration of manufacturing activity is not sustainable for sufficiently large transport costs T, and (ii) spreading is a stable equilibrium for sufficiently large transport costs T.

Note that the transport cost level chosen in Table 4.1 ($T = 1.7$) lies in between the break-point and the sustain-point of Figure 4.4, such that (i) the spreading equilibrium is stable, and (ii) the agglomeration equilibria are sustainable, as illustrated in Figure 4.1. How "special" is this situation depicted in Figure 4.1, in which the relative real wage crosses 1 in the interior three times? Assuming that the no-black-hole condition holds, it is *not* special in the sense that, independently of the other parameters of the model, there is always a range of transport costs for which it occurs. But it is special in the sense that this range is relatively small.

To conclude this subsection, it is useful to point out the *hysteresis* or path-dependency aspect of the model, that is, history matters. Suppose that transport costs are initially high, say $T = 2.5$ in Figure 4.4. Then spreading of manufacturing activity is the only stable long-run equilibrium. Now suppose that transport costs start to fall, given that the spreading equilibrium is established, say to $T = 1.7$. This will have no impact on the equilibrium allocation of manufacturing production since spreading remains a stable equilibrium. Only after the transport costs have fallen even further, below $T = 1.63$ in Figure 4.4, will the spreading equilibrium become unstable. Any small disturbance will then result in complete agglomeration of manufacturing production in one region. It is not possible to predict beforehand which region this will be, but suppose that agglomeration takes place in region 1. Given that region 1 contains all manufacturing activity assume now that the transport costs start to rise again, perhaps because of the imposition of trade barriers, say back to $T = 1.7$. What will happen? The answer is: nothing! Agglomeration of manufacturing activity remains a stable equilibrium. So for the same level of transport costs ($T = 1.7$) the equilibrium that becomes established depends on the way this level of transport costs is reached, on history. This phenomenon is called hysteresis or path-dependency. Obviously, predictions of what will happen if certain parameters change are considerably harder in models characterized by path-dependency.

4.7.2 *Sustain, break, and other parameters*

Now that equations (4.5) and (4.6) have determined for what levels of transport costs agglomeration is sustainable and spreading is stable, respectively, the impact of other parameter changes can easily be investigated. This is done in Figure 4.5. The impact of the substitution parameter ρ is depicted in Figure 4.5a. The range of ρ varies from δ to 1, to comply with the no-black-hole condition ($\rho > \delta$). For a given share δ of income spent on manufactures and given transport costs T, Figure 4.5a indicates that agglomeration is sustainable for low values of ρ, that is when it is hard to substitute one variety of manufactures for another. This is intuitively obvious. If it is difficult to substitute one variety for another, distant provision of a variety leads to a high price not only to recover the transport costs, but also because producers take advantage of their monopolistic position by charging a high mark-up over marginal costs. The periphery is thus less attractive for mobile workers if the elasticity of substitution is low, making agglomeration a sustainable equilibrium for all values of ρ below a critical level.

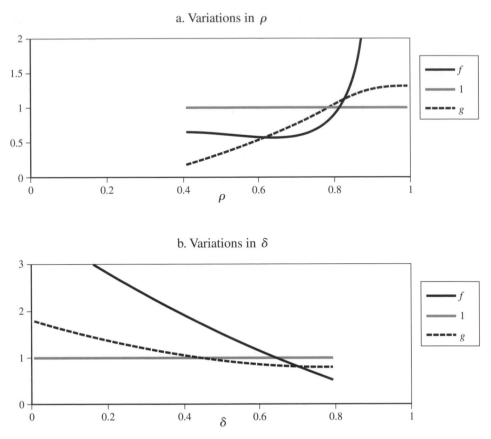

Figure 4.5.   Sustain-point and break-point II. (For the parameters δ, ρ, and T, see Table 4.1; other parameters normalized, see Table 4.2. Note that the agglomeration equilibrium is sustainable if $f < 1$ [see equation (4.5)], while the spreading equilibrium is stable if $g > 1$ [see equation (4.6)].)

Similarly, the spreading equilibrium is not stable for low values of ρ. As is the case for transport costs T investigated in subsection 4.7.1, there is a region of overlap where spreading is a stable equilibrium and agglomeration is sustainable at the same time.

The impact of the share of income δ spent on manufactures is illustrated in Figure 4.5b, where δ varies between 0 and ρ to comply with the no-black-hole condition ($\rho > \delta$). Given the elasticity of substitution and the transport costs, it is apparent that agglomeration is not sustainable if δ, the share of income spent on manufactures, is small. Again, this makes sense. If only a small fraction of income is spent on manufactures the impact of the manufacturing sector on the real wage is small and the economic forces active in the model are dominated by the immobile sector. Only if the share of income spent on manufactures exceeds a critical level are the demand linkages created by this sector strong enough to sustain an agglomeration equilibrium. Similarly, for small fractions of income spent on manufactures the spreading equilibrium is a stable equilibrium. Again, there is a range of overlap where spreading is a stable equilibrium and agglomeration is sustainable at the same time. It is instructive to see how the curves in Figures 4.4 and 4.5 change if other parameters, not depicted in the respective figure, are changing. This can be done with the "sustainbreak" Excel file on the website; see exercise 4.5.

4.8   Welfare

So far there has been very little attention to the welfare implications of the distribution of manufacturing activity in the geographical economics literature. In their book, Fujita, Krugman, and Venables (1999) (deliberately) shy away from welfare analysis, but nevertheless (pp. 348–349) consider it an important topic for further research for geographical economics. We will now pay some attention to this topic in order to get some idea how the normative implications of the core model might be addressed.

It is clear that different allocations of manufacturing activity will have different welfare implications for different sets of people; see, Table 3.5. Given transport costs T, for example, it is clear that the mobile workforce will generate a higher welfare level in the complete agglomeration equilibrium than in the spreading equilibrium, since in the latter they have to import part of their consumption of manufactures from the other region. It is also obvious that the immobile workforce in region 2, given complete agglomeration in region 1, is worse off compared to the spreading equilibrium as they will have to import all their manufactures from the other region. It is impossible to argue *ex ante* which effect is more important, so we will have to weigh the importance of various groups, using their sizes as weights.

Recall that there are two types of agents, manufacturing workers and farmworkers, within each region. The share of all manufacturing workers in region r is λ_r, and the share of all farm workers is ϕ_r. Since there are γL manufacturing workers in total and $(1 - \gamma)L$ farm workers, we concluded in equation (3.18) that total income in region r is equal to $Y_r = \lambda_r W_r \gamma L + \phi_r (1 - \gamma) L$, because manufacturing workers in region r earn wage W_r and farm workers earn wage 1. To determine the welfare level for both types of workers we will have to correct for the price level I_r in region r. In this chapter, we will focus attention on total welfare. To determine this, let $y_r \equiv Y_r I_r^{-\delta}$ be the real income in region r, and note that total welfare is given simply by:

$$\text{welfare} = \sum_{r=1}^{R} y_r \tag{4.7}$$

Based on the parameters of Table 4.1, Figure 4.6 gives a clear picture of the welfare level attained for different allocations of manufacturing activity for a large range of transport costs. Apparently, for low transport costs, agglomeration of manufacturing activity is welfare maximizing, while for high transport costs, spreading of manufacturing activity is welfare-maximizing. Obviously, total welfare in general declines if transport costs increase as more units of produced manufactures melt away in transit to the other region. The shape of the welfare surface shown in Figure 4.6 and the results

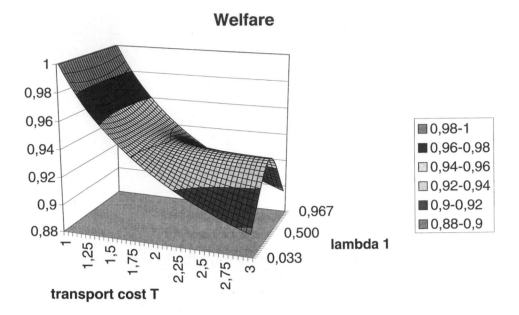

Figure 4.6. Allocation of manufacturing production and total welfare.

on stability in the previous section clearly suggest that there is a relationship between welfare maximization and stability. After all, complete agglomeration is welfare-maximizing and stable if transport costs are low, while spreading is welfare-maximizing and stable if transport costs are high. This suggestion is strongly supported by Figure 4.7, in which panel *a* depicts "stability" (namely w_1/w_2 for $0 < \lambda_1 < 0.5$ and w_2/w_1 for higher λ_1), while panel *b* depicts a very similar picture of inverse welfare (normalized to 1 at the spreading equilibrium for all values of T). It looks like welfare reaches a local maximum at a stable long-run equilibrium (see, however, the analysis below for a reminder that appearances may be deceptive).

On the basis of this last impression there are essentially two ways to continue. First, we can try to prove analytically that there is a relationship between stability and welfare maximization, like the analytical results derived in sections 4.6 and 4.7. This is not the route we pursue here because analytical results are hard to come by. Second, we can try to verify in detail if the suggested relationship exists for other parameter settings or transport costs. Although this second approach can never be used to prove anything, it may build our confidence or, if we can find just one counter-example, may reveal that it is futile to try to prove the suggested relationship analytically. Here we give one example.

In this example the second approach leads to results almost directly. If there is a relationship between stability and (local) welfare maximization it would have to hold in particular close to the break-point. Figure 4.8a, however, shows that close to the break-point ($T = 1.63$) welfare is locally maximized at the spreading equilibrium even if the

Panel a: Stability

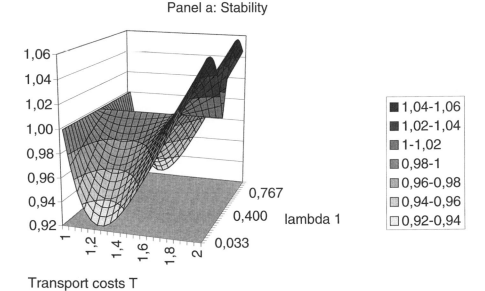

Transport costs T

Panel b: 1/normalized welfare

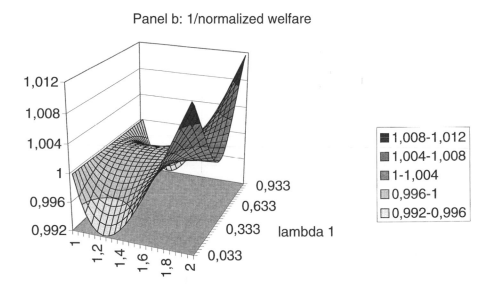

Figure 4.7. Stability and inverse welfare (normalized). (Panel *a* depicts w_1/w_2 for $0 < \lambda_1 < 0.5$ and w_2/w_1 for larger λ_1; welfare is normalized to 1 at the spreading equilibrium in panel *b*.)

spreading equilibrium is unstable; see $T = 1.62$ in Figure 4.8b. A similar example holds close to the sustain-point.

To conclude this section we note that it is not appropriate to analyze the impact of changes in the parameters ρ or δ on welfare since these affect the utility function itself. The impact of the other parameters is summarized in Proposition 4.1.

a. Close to the break-point: welfare

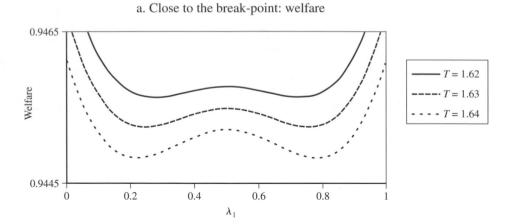

b. Close to the break-point: relative real wage

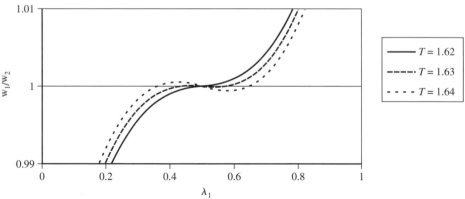

Figure 4.8.   Welfare and stability close to the break-point.

4.9   Stability and welfare in the limit

Before concluding this chapter there is one more issue we wish to address. As stated in Proposition 4.2, the spreading equilibrium is stable for sufficiently large transport costs T, provided the no-black-hole condition ($\rho > \delta$) holds. Similarly, the spreading equilibrium seems to be welfare-maximizing for sufficiently large transport costs T; see Figure 4.6. Section 4.8 showed that the apparent link between welfare and stability is elusive. The question arises whether this elusiveness also holds in the limit, for arbitrarily large transport costs. As we shall see shortly, the answer is more positive in the limiting case: for almost all parameter settings the spreading equilibrium is both stable and welfare-

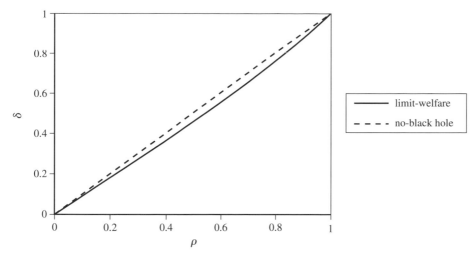

Figure 4.9.   Relationship between no-black-hole and limit-welfare conditions.

maximizing for sufficiently large transport costs. Recalling the solutions for spreading and agglomeration as given in section 4.7 and using equation (4.7) reveals:

$$\text{welfare}_{spreading} = \left(\frac{1 + T^{1-\varepsilon}}{2}\right)^{-\delta/(1-\varepsilon)} \quad ; \quad \text{welfare}_{agglomeration} = \frac{1+\delta}{2} + \frac{1-\delta}{2}T^{-\delta}, \quad \text{so} \qquad (4.8)$$

$$\lim_{T\to\infty}\text{welfare}_{spreading} = \left(\frac{1}{2}\right)^{-\delta/(1-\varepsilon)} \quad ; \quad \lim_{T\to\infty}\text{welfare}_{agglomeration} = \frac{1+\delta}{2} \qquad (4.9)$$

Thus, for large transport costs, spreading of manufacturing activity leads to higher welfare than complete agglomeration, and the relationship between allocation and welfare resembles the "blanket" depicted in Figure 4.6 if, and only if, $2^{\delta/(1-\varepsilon)} > (1+\delta)/2$, which we will label the limit-welfare condition.

   The limit-welfare condition and the no-black-hole condition are illustrated for the complete parameter space of (ρ,δ) in Figure 4.9. In each case the condition is satisfied for all parameter values below the relevant curve. The limit-welfare condition is slightly more stringent than the no-black-hole condition, which means therefore that the latter is a necessary but not a sufficient condition for the limit-welfare condition to hold. For the small parameter space between the two curves, where the no-black-hole condition is satisfied but the limit-welfare condition is not, spreading of manufacturing activity is a stable equilibrium for sufficiently large transport costs, but it is not welfare-maximizing.

4.10   The racetrack economy: many locations in neutral space

The greater part of the analysis in this chapter, and all the illustrative examples up to now, have focused on the two-region core model of geographical economics. Nonetheless, the short-run equilibrium equations (4.1)–(4.3) hold generally if we identify an arbitrary number R of locations, as long as we specify the distances D_{rs} between all locations r and s, such that we can calculate $T_{rs} = T^{D_{rs}}$, and know the production level ϕ_r of the immobile activity, food, in each location r. In general, it is virtually impossible to derive analytic results for a setting with an arbitrary number of locations. The normalization analysis of section 4.6 is a fortunate exception, as it allows us to keep on focusing in what follows on the three most important structural parameters: the transport costs T, the elasticity of substitution ε, and the share of income spent on manufactures δ.

4.10.1   Many locations in neutral space

The main advantage of the two-region core model as presented in chapter 3, is that "space" is inherently neutral. Neither location is preferred by construction over the other location. Any endogenous location results, such as agglomeration or spreading, that arise in the two-region core model are therefore consequences of the structure of the economic interactions among agents within the model, and do not arise from some pre-imposed geographic structure favoring economic activity in a particular location.

To preserve the neutrality of space in a many-location setting it is useful to analyze a simple configuration, in which the locations are evenly distributed in a circle with transportation only possible along the rim of that circle. This setting has been used before, for example in economic geography or in industrial organization. In Brakman et al. (1996) we refer to this setting as the "equidistant circle," but Fujita, Krugman, and Venables (1999, pp. 82–85) more aptly call it "the racetrack economy." The structure of the racetrack economy is quite simple, as illustrated in Figure 4.10. The R locations are equally and sequentially spaced around the circumference of a circle, with location R next to location 1, as in a clock. The distance between any two adjacent locations is 1, thus the transport cost between adjacent locations is T. The distance between any two arbitrary locations is the length of the shortest route along the circumference of the circle. We assume the production of the immobile food activity is evenly distributed among all locations.

Figure 4.10a illustrates a racetrack economy with three locations. The distance between all locations is 1, since they are all adjacent to one another. Figure 4.10b shows a racetrack economy with five locations. The distance from location 1 to locations 2 and 5 is 1, because these are adjacent locations, and the distance from location 1 to locations 3 and 4 is 2, because it requires 2 steps from location 1 to reach either location. Similarly, Figure 4.10c illustrates a racetrack economy with twelve locations, where, for example, the distance from location 1 to locations 5 and 9 is 4, as both locations require 4 steps to be reached from location 1.

Figures 4.10d and 4.10e show a typical simulation run for a racetrack economy with twelve locations.[6] The simulation procedure is as follows.

---

[6] The parameters for Figures 4.10d and 4.10e are: $\delta = 0.4$; $\varepsilon = 5$; $T = 1.25$.

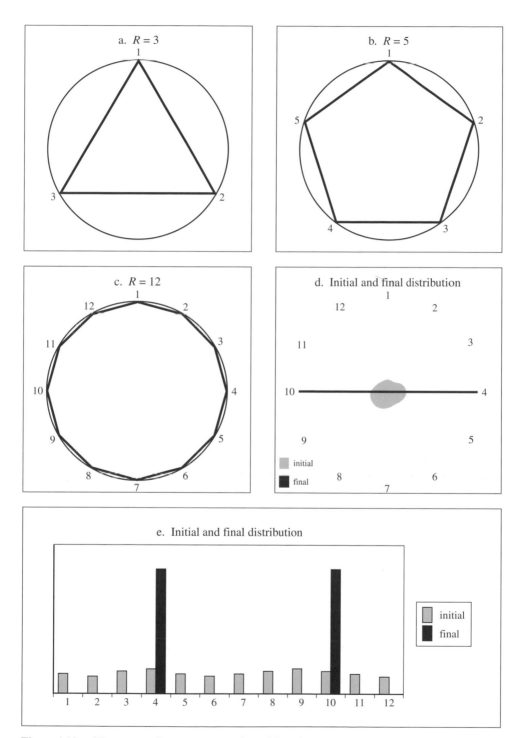

Figure 4.10.   The racetrack economy, number of locations = R.

(1) As in the core model we start with an initial distribution of the manufacturing labor force across the twelve locations. This distribution is chosen randomly.
(2) We determine the short-run equilibrium, given this initial distribution, using the iterative procedure described in section 4.2.
(3) We calculate the real wage in the short-run equilibrium for all twelve locations.
(4) We redistribute the manufacturing workforce across the locations, moving laborers towards locations with high real wages and away from locations with low real wages; it is possible at this stage that a location stops producing manufacturing goods because there are no manufacturing workers anymore.
(5) We repeat steps 2–4 until a long-run equilibrium is reached in step 3; that is, until the real wage is equal in all locations with a positive manufacturing labor force, or until all manufacturing labor is agglomerated in only one location.

Figure 4.10d illustrates the simulation run using the same graphical approach as panels *a–c*. Apparently, all manufacturing production eventually ends up in only two cities, namely locations 4 and 10, exactly opposite to one another. Both locations produce exactly half of the manufacturing varieties. Figure 4.10e shows the same simulation run using a column chart of the initial and final distributions of manufacturing production. The locations 4 and 10 which eventually emerge from the simulation as the only locations with manufacturing production were already large initially, which allowed them to grow. Initial size is, however, not the only determining force for the long-run equilibrium. This is demonstrated by location 9, which initially is slightly larger than location 10, but eventually disappears as it is too close to location 4. A more detailed example is given in chapter 7.

If we repeat the simulation with the twelve-location racetrack economy for a different randomly chosen initial distribution of the manufacturing workforce, and for different parameter values, it turns out that the outcome depicted in Figure 4.10 panels *d* and *e* is quite typical. Usually, all manufacturing production is eventually agglomerated in only one or two locations. If there are two locations, they are equal in size and opposite to one another (but these are, of course, not always in locations 4 and 10). All other locations eventually do not produce any manufactured goods. The next subsection discusses this phenomenon and two problems associated with it.

4.10.2   Preferred frequency

Using an ingenious analysis, that is beyond the scope of this book, Fujita, Krugman, and Venables (1999, pp. 85–94) assume that there are infinitely many locations on the racetrack economy to show that there tends to be a "preferred frequency" number of long-run equilibrium locations, dependent on the structural parameters. For a large range of parameter values the preferred frequency is 1, indicating that eventually all manufacturing production is produced in only one location; the monocentric equilibrium. For other parameter values the preferred frequency is 2; half the manufacturing production is eventually produced in one location, the other half in another location at the opposite side of the racetrack economy. Similarly, if the preferred frequency is 3, one-third of the manufacturing varieties are eventually produced in each of three locations, evenly spread across the racetrack economy, etc.

The preferred frequency tends to increase if (i) the transport costs increase, (ii) the share of income spent on manufactures decreases, and (iii) the elasticity of substitution increases. All three results are intuitively plausible. In the case of (i): if transport costs increase, one would expect production to locate close to the market, increasing the number of long-run equilibrium locations. For (ii): if the share of income spent on manufactures decreases the immobile food sector becomes economically more important, thus increasing the spreading force in the model, such that manufacturing firms locate more closely to their consumers and the number of long-run equilibrium locations increases. For (iii): if the elasticity of substitution decreases the market power of firms increases as it becomes harder to substitute one variety for another, such that the firms can get away with producing manufacturing varieties at only a few locations.

The preferred-frequency analysis convincingly shows two fundamental shortcomings of the core model as generalized by the racetrack economy. First, the powers of agglomeration tend to be too strong. For a large range of parameter settings, only one location emerges, particularly if the share of income spent on manufactures, the mobile activity, is not too small. In this respect we are already glad when we find two locations in the long-run equilibrium of our simulations (with twelve locations), and delighted when we find three locations in the final equilibrium. Most locations end up with no manufacturing activity whatsoever. The second problem is the uniform size of locations in the long-run equilibrium. This, of course, vacuously holds if we have only one location, but even if we have more than one location in the long-run equilibrium, say two or three, then those locations are exactly equal in size, and evenly distributed across the racetrack economy. This poses a problem, of course, for empirical applications, say if we want to explain the rank–size distribution for India as described in chapter 1, which requires the existence of many locations of unequal size. This phenomenon is further addressed in chapter 7.

4.11   Conclusions

This chapter discussed the use of computer simulations in geographical economics: what they are, how to perform them, their advantages, and their limitations. As regards the latter, even an infinite number of computer simulations cannot replace an analytical result. Nonetheless, the advantages of these simulations are enormous as they (i) allow us to do things we cannot do analytically, (ii) give a general "feel" for the model, (iii) suggest results that can be proved analytically, or (iv) disprove alleged results by producing a counter-example. We have given examples of each of these advantages in the symmetric two-region core model of geographical economics. Chapters 3 and 4 belong together and cover the basic theory of the geographical economics approach. With the material of these two chapters in mind, we can now return to the empirical examples brought forward in chapter 1 and specifically look into the empirical relevance of geographical economics. This is the topic of chapter 5.

Appendix

4.A.1   The function f(T)

Following the procedure described in section 4.7 the implied wage in region 2, given complete agglomeration of manufacturing in region 1, is given by:

$$W_2 = \left(\frac{1+\delta}{2} T^{1-\varepsilon} + \frac{1-\delta}{2} T^{\varepsilon-1} \right)^{1/\varepsilon} \tag{4.A1}$$

Using this to determine the implied real wage in region 2 it is convenient to note that

$$w_2^\varepsilon = \frac{1+\delta}{2} T^{1-\varepsilon-\varepsilon\delta} + \frac{1-\delta}{2} T^{\varepsilon-1-\varepsilon\delta} = \frac{1+\delta}{2} T^{-(\rho+\delta)\varepsilon} + \frac{1-\delta}{2} T^{(\rho-\delta)\varepsilon} \equiv f(T) \tag{4.A2}$$

$$f'(T) = \varepsilon \left(-\frac{1+\delta}{2} (\rho+\delta) T^{-(\rho+\delta)\varepsilon-1} + \frac{1-\delta}{2} (\rho-\delta) T^{(\rho-\delta)\varepsilon-1} \right) \tag{4.A3}$$

$$f(1)=1; \quad f'(1) = -\varepsilon\delta(1+\rho)<0; \lim_{T\to\infty} f(T)=\infty \text{ iff } \rho>\delta \tag{4.A4}$$

Using equation (4.A4) the graph of the function $f(T)$ is sketched in Figure 4.A1. In panel a, the no-black-hole condition is met $(\rho>\delta)$; in panel b, it is not $(\rho<\delta)$. These results are used in section 4.7.

4.A.2   Stability of the spreading equilibrium

The spreading equilibrium is given by $W_1=W_2=1$, $Y_1=Y_2=0.5$, $I_1=I_2=[0.5(1+T^{1-\varepsilon})]^{1/(1-\varepsilon)}$. We want to investigate changes in the equilibrium if an infinitesimal number of workers relocates from region 1 to region 2, where we will ignore all second-order effects of induced changes for the other regions. Thus we can write $dY=dY_1=-dY_2$ and similarly for other variables, differentiate (4.1′) and evaluate at the spreading equilibrium to get (4.A5). Doing the same with (4.2′) gives (4.A6).

$$dY = \delta d\lambda + \frac{\delta}{2} dW \tag{4.A5}$$

$$(1-\varepsilon)\frac{dI}{I} = I^{\varepsilon-1}(1-T^{1-\varepsilon}) \left(\frac{1-\varepsilon}{2} dW + d\lambda \right) \tag{4.A6}$$

Define $Z \equiv (1-T^{1-\varepsilon})/(1+T^{1-\varepsilon})$, and note that Z is an index of trade barriers which ranges from 0 when there are no transport costs $(T=1)$ to 1 when transport costs are prohibitive $(T\to\infty)$. With this notation we can rewrite (4.A6) as (4.A7).

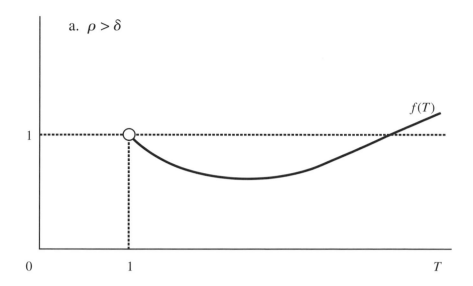

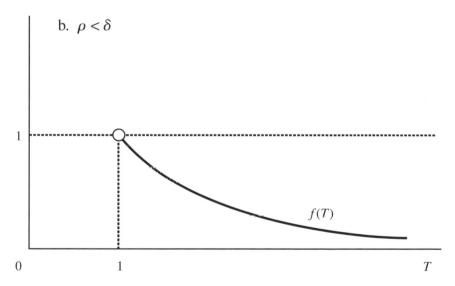

Figure 4.A1. Sketch of the function $f(T)$.

$$\frac{dI}{I} = \frac{2Z}{1-\varepsilon}\, d\lambda + ZdW \tag{4.A7}$$

Differentiating (4.3′) and (4.4) and evaluating at the spreading equilibrium gives (4.A8) and (4.A9), respectively:

$$\varepsilon\, dW = 2ZdY + (\varepsilon - 1)Z\frac{dI}{I} \tag{4.A8}$$

$$I^\delta dw = dW - \delta \frac{dI}{I} \tag{4.A9}$$

Equations (4.A5) and (4.A7)–(4.A9) can be solved to determine the effect of a small disturbance on the real wage. Substituting (4.A5) in (4.A8) and combining with (4.A7) gives system (4.A10). Solving (4.A10) gives (4.A11).

$$\begin{bmatrix} 1 & -Z \\ Z & \dfrac{\varepsilon - \delta Z}{1 - \varepsilon} \end{bmatrix} \begin{bmatrix} \dfrac{dI}{I} \\ dW \end{bmatrix} = \begin{bmatrix} \dfrac{2Z}{1-\varepsilon} d\lambda \\ \dfrac{2Z\delta}{1-\varepsilon} d\lambda \end{bmatrix} \tag{4.A10}$$

$$\begin{bmatrix} \dfrac{dI}{I} \\ dW \end{bmatrix} = \dfrac{1}{\Delta} \begin{bmatrix} \dfrac{\varepsilon - \delta Z}{1 - \varepsilon} & Z \\ -Z & 1 \end{bmatrix} \begin{bmatrix} \dfrac{2Z}{1-\varepsilon} d\lambda \\ \dfrac{2Z\delta}{1-\varepsilon} d\lambda \end{bmatrix} \tag{4.A11}$$

where $\Delta \equiv [(1 - \varepsilon)Z^2 - \delta Z + \varepsilon]/(1 - \varepsilon)$. Thus:

$$\frac{dI}{I} = \frac{d\lambda}{\Delta} \frac{2Z\varepsilon}{(1-\varepsilon)^2}(1 - \delta Z) \text{ and } dW = \frac{d\lambda}{\Delta} \frac{2Z\varepsilon}{(1-\varepsilon)}(\delta - Z)$$

Finally, substituting these results in (4.A9) gives the change in the real wage:

$$\frac{dw}{d\lambda} = \frac{2ZI^{-\delta}}{(\varepsilon - 1)} \left[\frac{\delta(2\varepsilon - 1) - Z[\varepsilon(1 + \delta^2) - 1]}{\varepsilon - \delta Z - (\varepsilon - 1)Z^2} \right] = \frac{2ZI^{-\delta}(1 - \rho)}{\rho} \left[\frac{\delta(1 + \rho) - Z[\delta^2 + \rho]}{1 - \delta Z(1 - \rho) - \rho Z^2} \right]$$

The spreading equilibrium is unstable if $dw/d\lambda$ is positive. The sign depends on the numerator of the expression since the denominator is always positive. Thus, $dw/d\lambda = 0$ if, and only if, $Z = \delta(1 + \rho)/(\delta^2 + \rho)$. A necessary and sufficient condition for the break-point to be reached is that the right-hand side of the last equality is smaller than 1, that is the no-black-hole condition, $\rho > \delta$, must be satisfied. Otherwise, the spreading equilibrium is unstable for all transport costs.

Exercises

4.1 Apply the same procedure as used to prove Proposition 4.1 to analyze the impact of the parameter γ and explain where and why the procedure fails in this case.

4.2 Go to the website of the book, where you will find Excel files containing the data and some of the figures used in this book. Look up the file for Figure 4.2, where you will find additional information on the relationship between the relative real wage and transport costs. Make XY-scatter plots (using smoothed lines) for the transport cost range $T = 1.50$; 1.55; 1.60; 1.65; 1.70 and for the range $T = 1.75$; 1.80; 1.85; 1.90. Comment on your findings (in terms of stability).

4.3 The text in this chapter has not proved that the break-point arises for a lower value of transport costs T than the sustain-point. Convince yourself that it does by calculating these values for a grid of admissible (ρ, δ)-parameter combinations, as in Figure 4.9.

4.4 Explicitly calculate the break-point as a function of the transport costs T, using equation (4.6). Your answer should be: $T = \left[\dfrac{(\rho - \delta)(1 - \delta)}{(\rho + \delta)(1 + \delta)} \right]^{1/(1-\varepsilon)}$.

4.5 Analyze the impact of other parameters on the sustain- and break-points of Figures 4.4 and 4.5 by using the "sustainbreak" Excel file on the website. In particular, how do these points move in Figure 4.4 if ρ or δ is increased. Can you intuitively explain this movement? Similarly for Figure 4.5, panels a and b.

4.6 Go to the website of the book, where you will find Excel files containing the data and some of the figures used in this book. Look up the file for Figures 4.3b and 4.3c, where you will find additional information on the relationship between the relative real wage, welfare, and the parameters δ and γ. What is the impact of these parameters on welfare? Can you explain?

5 Geographical economics and empirical evidence

5.1 Introduction

In the first chapter of this book a number of stylized facts about the clustering of economic activity were presented to justify our inquiry into the relationship between economics and geography.[1] Chapters 2–4 have mainly looked at this relationship from a theoretical point of view. In this chapter we start with the reminder that in reality there is a considerable degree of clustering, that is location matters. Our main objective in this chapter is to assess the empirical relevance of geographical economics and to see whether and how the theoretical model of chapters 3 and 4 can be tested.

In the next section we briefly review the main facts about the concentration and agglomeration of economic activity at different levels of aggregation. This continues, and partly restates, our discussion of stylized facts of location in chapter 1. Against this background, section 5.3 deals with the question of whether these facts can be reconciled with the various economic theories of location presented in Chapters 2–4. To answer this question, we summarize the main predictions about clustering (if any) that follow from the various theories, and conclude that the stylized facts are in accordance with several theories (and not only with geographical economics). This does not come as a big surprise since many empirical studies about the concentration or the agglomeration of economic activity are simply not primarily concerned with the testing of specific theories.

In sections 5.4 and 5.5 we analyze two recent attempts which explicitly try to test (part of) the implications of the geographical economics models. The bulk of this chapter consists of an in-depth discussion of these two attempts, such that we will not offer a fully-fledged survey of the empirical aspects of trade, growth, and location. For recent surveys, see Hanson (2000). In section 5.4 the first attempt to test for the relevance of geographical economics is discussed. Here the so-called home-market effect is used to discriminate between trade theories. The second attempt is based on the idea of the existence of a spatial wage structure: the further one moves away from centers of economic activity the lower wages will be. Such a spatial wage structure sets geo-

---

[1] In section 5.2 we will elaborate upon the distinctions among specialization, concentration, and agglomeration of economic activity.

graphical economics apart from other trade theories. We discuss its empirical relevance in section 5.5. Section 5.6 presents a case study of geographical economics, focusing on post-reunification Germany, which applies the idea of a spatial wage structure. Section 5.7 concludes this chapter.

5.2 The spatial distribution of economic activity

5.2.1 Distinguishing among concentration, specialization, and agglomeration

Before we return to the empirical features of the location of economic activity it is necessary to clarify the distinctions among concentration, specialization, and agglomeration from an empirical point of view. We start with the distinction between concentration and agglomeration. As opposed to specialization (see below), both concentration and agglomeration refer to the question how (some part of) economic activity, like a specific industry or the manufacturing sector as a whole, is distributed across space. Concentration and agglomeration are both concerned with the question whether or not a specific part of economic activity can be found at a few locations, be it a city, a region, or a country. Even though concentration and agglomeration both deal with the location of economic activity their foci are quite different. Following Brülhart (1998a, p. 776), concentration analyzes the location across space of a few well-defined sectors (notably industries), whereas agglomeration analyzes the location across space of a much larger part of economic activity, such as the manufacturing sector as a whole; compare, for instance, Figures 5.1b and 5.1d. In the former there is concentration of the two industries (I in country A and II in country B) whereas in the latter there is agglomeration of industrial activity (nearly all of industries I and II are located in country A).

The empirical analysis of the geographical concentration of industries tries to show whether or not particular industries are geographically clustered. As such the concentration of industries does thus not need to tell us anything about the distribution of the overall manufacturing activity across space, that is to say it does not necessarily provide information on the degree of agglomeration. On the contrary, there may be geographical concentration without agglomeration. Again, to see the difference but now for regions within a single country (see Figure 5.1c), suppose country A consists of four regions and there are still two industries of equal size, I and II. Geographical concentration could imply that industry I is mainly located in region 1 of country A (whereas industry II ends up in country B). Despite the fact that, as opposed to Figure 5.1b, there is now clearly also concentration at the regional level in country A, the overall distribution of manufacturing activity between the two *countries* is even. Agglomeration within this country would mean that the bulk of both industries would locate in the same country or perhaps even within a single region of that country as is the case in Figure 5.1d. Hence, concentration and agglomeration can be two rather different things. Of course, when in reality the majority of industries are geographically concentrated at the same *location* this also implies a high degree of agglomeration of

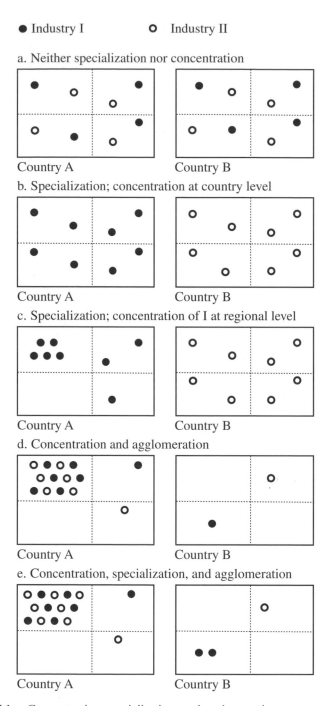

Figure 5.1.   Concentration, specialization, and agglomeration.

manufacturing activity as a whole (Figure 5.1d). As a rule of thumb, it is useful to keep in mind that studies of agglomeration analyze how aggregate economic activity, often manufacturing production, is distributed across space. The empirical analysis of concentration does the same but only for a particular type of economic activity, say the production of aircraft, and then tries to show at this lower level of aggregation how the production of aircraft is located across space.

Concentration and agglomeration can be distinguished from specialization; see Hallet (2000).[2] Specialization deals with the question of whether or not a location's share in, say, the production of cars or apparel is relatively large compared to the share of other locations in the production of cars or apparel. Ever since Adam Smith (1776) and his writings about the fruits of the international division of labor, the emphasis in trade theory has been on specialization. Studies of specialization are attempts to reveal a country's or region's economic structure. In Figure 5.1a, countries A and B are not specialized whereas in Figure 5.1b they obviously are. In Figure 5.1b, specialization coincides with concentration; this is because both countries are assumed to be of equal size. Actual data on specialization as such are, however, not very useful from the perspective of geographical economics since they do not need to tell us anything about the relative distribution of economic activity across space. Figure 5.1e illustrates that concentration and specialization need not coincide. For instance, the fact that in the EU the Netherlands and Germany are, compared to the EU average, specialized in chemical products and machinery, respectively, is not conclusive evidence about either the concentration of chemical products or machinery production across the EU countries or the degree of economic agglomeration in the EU. The Dutch specialization in chemical products might, for instance, be consistent with France being home to a larger part of the production of chemical products (in absolute terms), which, as far as the concentration of the chemical industry is concerned, makes France more important than the Netherlands. Similarly, taken together the specialization patterns of the individual EU countries do not tell us how large each country's share is in total manufacturing production and hence provide no conclusive information about the degree of agglomeration of manufacturing activity.

To distinguish agglomeration from concentration (a matter of degree) and specialization (a fundamental difference) is also important from a theoretical point of view. It has become clear from the previous two chapters that the agglomeration of economic activity is a key issue in geographical economics. As with many trade models, geographical economics also deals with specialization and concentration, but the emphasis on agglomeration sets geographical economics apart from the neo-classical and the

---

[2] Though we think such a distinction can be made, this is not always deemed relevant. Brülhart (1998a), for instance, treats concentration and specialization as similar terms. Also, the term concentration is sometimes not used in geographical economics because it would give the false impression that one is dealing with some index measuring the share of individual firms in the production of certain goods. Statements like the European car industry is concentrated because the top five automobile firms have a market share exceeding $x\%$ are not relevant in this book, where concentration applies to geographical concentration. Also, in contrast to Fujita and Thisse (2000), we think it is useful *not* to use agglomeration and concentration interchangeably.

new trade theories where, see section 2.3, the concern is with specialization or concentration but not with agglomeration.[3] Ideally, therefore, we would like to discuss empirical studies that allow for specialization, concentration, and agglomeration simultaneously. Unfortunately, the vast majority of empirical studies on trade are first and foremost about specialization; see Leamer and Levinsohn (1995). Stimulated by the new trade theory and geographical economics there is by now also a large number of studies dealing with geographical concentration, but there are very few studies which explicitly try to test for the only theory which strongly emphasizes the possibility of agglomeration, geographical economics. As we will see in the next section, this state of the art in empirical research is one reason why it is rather difficult to discriminate between alternative theories of location. The specialization/concentration/agglomeration distinction is important but it should not cloud the fundamental issue that location, whether because of specialization, concentration, or agglomeration, matters empirically.

Chapter 1 of this book discussed a number of stylized facts about the location of economic activity. We showed that at various levels of aggregation economic activity is clearly *not* randomly distributed across space, and also that geography, using the actual distance between locations as a proxy, is an important determinant of economic transactions, giving rise to the observed location patterns. The conclusion that irrespective of the level of aggregation, similar spatial distributions of economic activity can be observed even led us to conclude (see section 1.4) that there is a fractal dimension to the location of economic activity. In the next subsection two of these dimensions, namely the geographical unit of analysis and the type of economic activity, are used to remind us of the basic empirical fact of the non-randomness of the spatial distribution of economic activity. Box 5.1 at the end of section 5.2 gives some data and background information on the actual degree of specialization, concentration, and agglomeration for the EU countries.

5.2.2   *Location matters: a reminder*

At the highest level of aggregation, the supranational level, estimations of, for instance, the gravity model (see equations (1.2) and (1.3)) invariably lead to the conclusion that trade is a decreasing function of the economic distance between countries and that countries predominantly trade with neighboring countries. As far as the trade pattern, and hence the degree of specialization, is concerned, the empirical evidence shows that intra-industry trade has become increasingly important in the post-war era (chapter 9). This is not only true for OECD countries but also increasingly for non OECD countries. Within the EU, for instance, intra-industry trade accounts for more than 60% of all trade. Apart from the gravity model, chapter 1 also illustrated agglomeration at the

---

[3] Brülhart (1998a, p. 776) argues that concentration can be used when factors of production are immobile, whereas agglomeration can be used when these factors are mobile. We agree, and argued in chapter 2 that it is one of the defining differences between the old and new trade theory on the one hand and geographical economics on the other.

level of the world economy as a whole; see Figure 1.3. The findings point to the high-income countries as the main centers of the world economy and *within* these high-income countries three core centers are clearly discernible. These data are related to a large number of empirical studies on the (lack of) convergence of GDP per capita between countries. In general, these studies (see, for instance, Barro and Sala-i-Martin, 1995) lead to two conclusions. First, for the world economy as a whole there is no or at best a very limited tendency towards convergence of individual countries' GDP per capita. This means that the differences between the cores and peripheries do not appear to narrow, and they may very well increase even further, thereby strengthening agglomeration. Within groups of countries, like the EU, a different picture emerges. Here, convergence is taking place. For the EU countries this indicates that, say, the difference between Germany and Portugal in GDP per capita has decreased over time, hence reducing the degree of agglomeration somewhat (see below).

Switching from the supranational level to the regional level, it is also obvious that location matters. The equivalent of the open-economy gravity model for a closed economy is the market potential approach (see section 2.2). Estimations of the market potential function show that firms tend to locate in or near regions where demand is relatively high, thus fostering and reinforcing a process of agglomeration. In sections 5.5 and 5.6 we apply the market potential function to regions in the USA and Germany. More information on agglomeration at the regional level can be found in economic growth literature with the growth process being analyzed for regions instead of countries. These studies look at regions within a single country as well as at regions within a group of countries. Neven and Gouyette (1995), for instance, find evidence for convergence for a large group of EU regions in the 1960s and 1970s. This convergence process now seems to have come to a halt. The main message from these *regional* convergence studies is that there are considerable differences between regions in terms of GDP per capita, supporting the idea of agglomeration of economic activity across space. Moreover, and in accordance with the idea of agglomeration, regions with a relatively high GDP per capita tend to be located near each other, as do regions with low levels of GDP per capita.

Empirical research in urban economics is also concerned with the *regional* level in the sense that the urban areas or cities are regions in a national space. This national space as such is not considered to be very interesting, since it is taken for granted that agglomeration exists within this space. The analysis focuses on the cities themselves as the centers of economic activity (see section 2.2), without interaction between the cities and the rest of the country. The empirical question is not only how cities interact and develop over time (the rise and fall of individual cities) but also whether or not industries are geographically concentrated in certain cities. The development of the urban system provides information on the agglomeration of cities. The main issue is (the change in) the city-size distribution, which appears to be rather stable for the industrialized countries; see, for instance, Gabaix (1999b) or Black and Henderson (1998, 1999b) for the USA. The city-size distribution in some Western countries displays a regularity known as the rank–size distribution, illustrated for India in chapter 1. A special case of the rank–size distribution is Zipf's Law, stating that the largest city is twice as large as the second largest city, five times as large as the fifth largest city, etc. We return to Zipf's Law in chapter 7.

The empirical evidence with respect to the geographical concentration of industries across cities leads to the conclusion that positive externalities stimulate the concentration of firms in cities. There is, however, a lively discussion in the literature about which type of positive externality is more relevant for the geographical concentration of industries across the urban landscape. Section 2.2 distinguished between economies of localization and of urbanization. The former applies to industry-specific external economies of scale, whereas the latter refers to inter-industry external economies of scale. Applied to cities, both types of economies of scale have recently been the topic of a considerable amount of empirical research. Depending, among other things, on the static or dynamic nature of these two economies of scale, there are studies in which localization economies are found to be more relevant (for example, Beardsell and Henderson, 1999), as well as studies in which urbanization economies are more relevant (for example, Glaeser *et al.*, 1992, for the growth of US cities). For us it is only important that external economies of scale lead firms to locate in cities because other firms do the same. Whether or not firms in a city belong to the same industry is of secondary importance here (yes, in the case of localization economies; no, in the case of urbanization economies).

Studies about the geographical concentration of economic activity are not confined to the mix of industrial activity in cities. On the contrary, when it comes to the empirical analysis of the location of economic and industrial activity, the majority of empirical research deals with this issue and not, or at best only indirectly, with agglomeration. It is beyond the scope of this chapter to give a complete overview of the results, so we only briefly discuss the influential study by Ellison and Glaeser (1997). They develop an index of the geographic concentration of industries and study this index for the USA. The index, which (surprise!) has become known as the Ellison–Glaeser index, measures the degree to which industry i is geographically concentrated (in terms of employment) in location s at time t. It corrects for the fact that in industries consisting of a few relatively large plants, industry concentration will be higher. The index takes on the value zero if industry employment is not concentrated; Ellison and Glaeser (1997, p. 890) argue that in this case it is *as if* "the plants in the industry [had] chosen locations by throwing darts on a map."[4] The main empirical

---

[4] The index γ_i (see Ellison and Glaeser, 1997, p. 899, or Dumais, Ellison, and Glaeser, 1997, p. 7) measures the degree to which industry i is geographically concentrated at time t: $\gamma_i = [G_{it}/(1 - \Sigma_s s^2_{it}) - H_{it}]/(1 - H_{it})$; where G_{it} is defined as $\Sigma_s (s_{ist} - s_{st})^2$ with s_{ist} being the share of industry's i employment at time t located in state s, and with s_{st} being the state s's share of aggregate employment at time t. H_{it} is a Herfindahl index measuring the plant-level concentration of employment in a industry. When for an industry i it turns out that $\gamma_i = 0$ there are no agglomeration forces, and the location of that industry across the USA can be looked upon as being "generated by the simple dartboard model of random location choices with no natural [location] advantages or industry specific spillovers" (Ellison and Glaeser, 1997, p. 900). Note, that γ_i has no upper limit as $0 \leq H_{it} \leq 1$. For their sample of 459 four-digit industries the mean (median) value for $\gamma_i = 0.051$ (0.026) which indicates a very skewed distribution. For 43% of the industries $\gamma_i < 0.02$ which is the category of not very concentrated industries and 59 industries have $\gamma_i > 0.1$ which means that these are the most geographically concentrated industries in the USA.

finding is that at the four-digit industry level, industrial employment is indeed geographically concentrated, so the "dartboard approach" is rejected, even though for many industries the degree of concentration is rather small. Using this index, it appears that the geographical concentration is fairly stable (at the industry level, not at the plant level), and that the degree of concentration decreases slightly over time; see Dumais, Ellison, and Glaeser (1997, p. 7). In our view, the results found in this and other studies using the Ellison–Glaeser index clearly indicate that geographical concentration of industries is the rule, and not the exception. This conclusion holds not only for the USA but also for the countries of the EU; see Brülhart (1998b), Brülhart and Torstensson (1996), and Box 5.1 with its references.[5]

To summarize: this brief recap of the facts illustrates (nothing more, but certainly nothing less) that agglomeration can be observed at various levels of aggregation, and that the geographical concentration of firms and industries is widespread. Two further questions arise. First, can these facts be reconciled with economic theory at large? Second, if the answer to the first question is affirmative, how can we discriminate between different theories in general, and with respect to geographical economics in particular?

Box 5.1. Specialization, concentration, and agglomeration in the European Union

A recent empirical study by Midelfart-Knarvik *et al.* (2000) provides useful information on the degree of specialization, concentration, and agglomeration for the EU countries. The study analyzes production data for fourteen EU countries and thirty-six industries from 1970 to 1997. Specialization is measured using the Krugman specialization index, that is for each individual EU country the index is defined as the absolute value of a country's share in the production of industry k minus the share of the other EU countries in the production of industry k, summed over all industries. If the Krugman specialization index is zero the country has an industrial structure that is identical to the rest of the EU: a case of non-specialization. The larger the value of the Krugman index, the more this country is specialized. Figure 5.2 illustrates the Krugman specialization index for three four-year periods in the 1970s, 1980s, and 1990s. The figure clearly indicates that the EU countries are specialized (the indices are not zero), with France and the UK displaying an industrial production structure most similar to the EU average. As is also evident, and easy to understand, the small EU countries tend to be more specialized in their production pattern than the large EU countries.

It is apparent from Figure 5.2, that the degree of specialization fell for ten and rose for four countries between the 1970s and the 1980s, leading to a fall of specialization for the EU on average in that period. From the 1980s to the 1990s,

---

[5] A related topic is the clustering of firms that engage in foreign direct investment, that is to say the geographical concentration of this investment. We will deal with this phenomenon in chapter 8 in our analysis of multinationals.

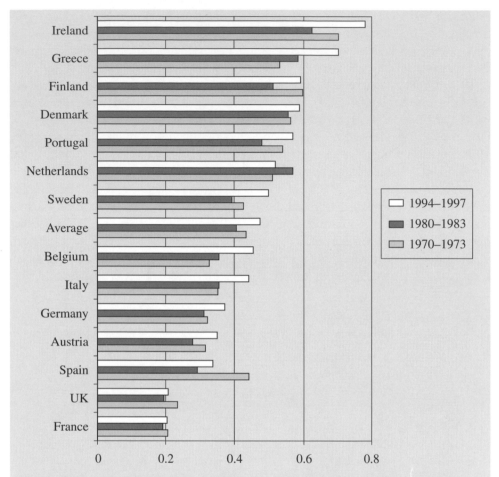

Figure 5.2.   Krugman specialization index. *Source*: Midelfart-Knarvik *et al.*, 2000, p. 6.

however, there has been a strong *increase* in the degree of specialization for nearly all EU countries, particularly for Greece, Ireland, and Sweden, but with the exception of the Netherlands. This conclusion is confirmed by Amiti (1999). These calculations, however, do not give any information on the location of industries across the EU countries. As we saw in Figure 5.1, high as well as low specialization indices may be associated either with geographic concentration of industries, or with the absence thereof.

The degree of industry concentration is measured as the relative production share across countries for a given industry: for example, the degree of concentration of the shipbuilding industry is measured by the relative share each EU country has in shipbuilding; a skewed distribution of these shares implies that shipbuilding is concentrated. In this manner one gets to know for each of the industries how its production is distributed across the EU countries. It turns out

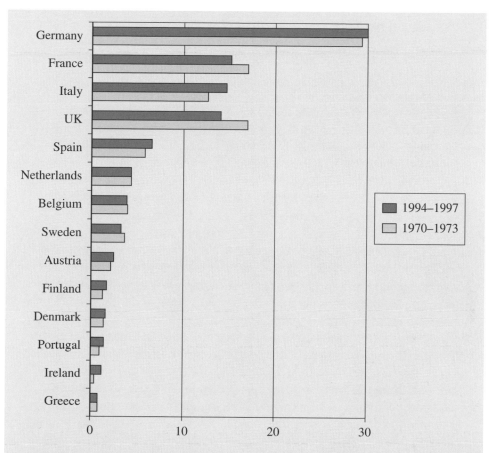

Figure 5.3. Agglomeration of manufacturing in the EU. *Source*: Midelfart-Knarvik *et al.*, 2000, p. 18; production data, four-year averages (% of total).

that when all industry concentration results are grouped together, there is no clear discernible upward or downward trend in concentration in the period 1970–1997. So, overall, the degree of industry concentration in the EU only showed a moderate increase during this period. For individual industries the results are different. Some initially concentrated industries (textiles, furniture) have become even more concentrated over time, whereas the reverse is true for some other initially concentrated industries (beverages, tobacco, radio and television, and communications). A similar mixed picture emerges for initially geographically dispersed industries. Notwithstanding these industrial differences, it is clear that the majority of industries are geographically concentrated in the EU, as they are in the USA.

But again we have to be careful as concentration is not necessarily the same as agglomeration (see Figure 5.1). We can measure the degree of agglomeration by using a country's share in the total EU manufacturing activity as a proxy. This is illustrated in Figure 5.3. Some spreading of manufacturing activity has occurred in the period 1970–1997, that is the three core countries, the UK, France, and Germany, have lost some of their share in manufacturing activity (a fall from 63.2% to 59.0%) to the periphery of the EU, that is the southern EU countries, Finland, and Ireland.

To summarize: based on production data for the last three decades the following trends arise for the manufacturing sectors of the EU countries: (i) increased specialization, (ii) fairly constant (overall) degree of industry concentration with large differences between individual industries, and (iii) a small decrease in the degree of agglomeration. These conclusions are subject to a number of caveats. First, in a related study, Hallet (2000) looks at EU specialization and concentration using *regional* rather than country data. He also finds that industry concentration is fairly constant but, in contrast to the Midelfart-Knarvik *et al.* (2000) study, concludes that the EU regions have become *less* specialized during the sample period 1980–1995. Apparently, it can matter a great deal at which level of spatial aggregation the analysis takes place. This points to a fundamental issue. Economic geographers, for instance Cheshire and Carbonaro (1995) and Martin (2001), emphasize that it is necessary for measuring specialization or concentration to define the geographical unit of analysis according to its economic functionality. It is by no means obvious that the EU regions or the EU countries, which are administratively, politically, and historically defined, meet this requirement.

Second, the use of manufacturing production data, rather than employment data or data on other economic activities, is important for arriving at the above conclusions, as related studies have shown. As Hallet (2000) points out, it is becoming increasingly important for the EU to include the services sector in the analysis. After all, the majority of employment and value-added is now in the services sector, rather than the manufacturing sector. The consequences of this inclusion are not clear beforehand, given the difficulties with which many services are tradable.

5.3   The facts and economic theory

Several aspects of the stylized facts of concentration, specialization, and agglomeration can be accounted for by various economic theories. We have already noted the presence of agglomeration on a supranational or regional level, and the relevance of economic distance (the gravity model) and intra-industry trade for the underlying specialization pattern. The relevance of agglomeration at this level was also linked to studies of economic growth pointing to persistent differences in GDP per capita between (groups of) countries. To start with the latter, both neo-classical and new growth theory can account for this state of affairs. From our discussion in section 2.4, this will be obvious for new growth theory. If the speed of convergence is very slow, and/or one looks at conditional convergence instead of absolute convergence, the existence of agglomeration need not be at odds with neo-classical growth theory either. Similarly, the relevance of new trade theory as well as geographical economics in accounting for intra-industry trade is obvious, but the existence of intra-industry trade can also be explained in modern versions of the neo-classical trade model, where technology differs between countries; see, for example, Davis (1995).[6] Trade theory can be called upon to give a foundation not only for specialization patterns across space, but also for agglomeration. This is true not only for the geographical economics model, but also for neo-classical trade theory in which endowments are geographically concentrated. The basic new trade model has not much to offer here because it has nothing to say on the issue of *where* production will take place.

If we look at the stylized facts on agglomeration and specialization for cities, a similar conclusion emerges. Various theories can be used to explain the facts. Glaeser *et al.* (1992) try to establish empirically which types of externalities are more relevant in explaining the growth of US cities, assuming that new trade and new growth theory provide a relevant explanation. In the end, however, they conclude (p. 1151) that the "evidence on externalities is indirect, and many of our findings can be explained by a neo-classical model in which industries grow where labor is cheap and demand is high." As for the finding that industries are geographically concentrated, Ellison and Glaeser (1997) show that their empirical results can be substantiated by either the neo-classical or the modern theory of trade and location. In their theoretical model, concentration of industries can result because of either natural advantages of a location (first-nature) or location spillovers (second-nature). In fact, it turns out that the relationship between levels of concentration and industry characteristics is the same whether concentration is the result of first-nature or second-nature causes. This implies that both neo-classical and modern theories based on increasing returns can be used as explanations for the actually observed geographic concentration of industries in the United States. Ellison and Glaeser (1997, p. 891) conclude that "geographic concentration by itself does not imply the existence of spillovers; natural advantages have similar effects and may be important empirically."[7]

The overall conclusion must be that the same empirical facts about specialization or agglomeration can be explained using different theoretical approaches. On the one hand, this is good news, because it means that these are not facts in search of a theory. On the other, this conclusion is not satisfactory for our present purposes, because it leaves unanswered the question as to the (relative) empirical relevance of individual theories like geographical economics. This point has, of course, not gone unnoticed in the literature. Several studies mentioned in the previous section try to test for the relevance of one or more theories of location by investigating how much of the observed specialization or agglomeration can be explained by each theory. A good example is the study of the US city-size distribution by Black and Henderson (1998, 1999a), which tests for the importance of actual geography and characteristics of city neighbors as

---

[6] The same is true for the gravity model; see Deardorff (1998).
[7] Ellison and Glaeser (1999) show that natural advantages can indeed explain a considerable part of the geographic concentration of industries for the USA.

determinants of (changes in) city-size. Both forces turn out to be relevant. Following up on the development of the Ellison–Glaeser index, Dumais, Ellison, and Glaeser (1997) try to show how much of the observed concentration is due to each of the three well-known Marshallian externalities (see Box 2.1). They find evidence lending support to one of these externalities, labor-market pooling, and thus also indirectly find evidence for theories that rely on pecuniary external economies, like geographical economics. This does not mean that a neo-classical explanation of the observed geographic concentration in the US is irrelevant. On the contrary, Ellison and Glaeser (1999, p. 315) estimate that approximately 20% of this concentration can be explained by geographical advantages (endowments).

These and other first-nature or second-nature investigations do not offer direct and conclusive tests for or against a particular theory. They test for the significance of particular variables, like endowments or economies of scale, for the location of economic activity, and do not discriminate between theories. The significance of some of these explanatory variables is consistent with geographical economics, and with other approaches. In many studies, the variables underlying the neo-classical approach as well as those that serve as proxies for the modern trade or growth theories are all empirically relevant. Such studies, therefore, do not try to test the relevance of the underlying individual theoretical approaches.[8] To elaborate upon this last important point, take the study of Haaland *et al.* (1999), which for a group of thirteen European countries and thirty-five industries regresses the concentration of each industry upon variables capturing up to four trade-theoretical approaches. Two variables, namely labor intensity and human capital intensity of industrial production, are used as proxies for the factor abundance model, whereas technological differences between industries represent the Ricardian technology model. The new trade model and geographical economics are represented using the relative concentration of expenditures (market size), and a variable measuring economies of scale. A measure of intra-industry, input–output linkages is included for the geographical economics model only. The set of seven independent variables is completed by a variable measuring trade costs. Both neo-classical variables, such as human capital intensity, and new variables, such as market size, were found in this study to be important determinants of industry concentration in Europe.[9] These conclusions are important if one wants to explain industry concentration in Europe on the assumption that various determinants (and hence theories) might be relevant. It is only if one wants to discriminate among theories that the usefulness of such an approach is limited.

The problem is aptly summarized by Brülhart (1998a, p. 792) who argues that such a "regression analysis of industry concentration suggests that all major theoretical approaches are relevant. However they have not been used so far to assess relative

---

[8] This need not be an issue if one is merely trying to explain the variable of interest (here, industry concentration) and wants to take all potentially relevant factors into account (see Midelfart-Knarvik *et al.*, 2000, p. 33 for a similar observation). For our present purposes it is troublesome, because we want to learn more about the empirical relevance of a particular theory, geographical economics.

[9] Other examples include Van den Berg and Sturm (1997) and Kim (1995).

merits of competing models across industries or countries." For geographical economics there are two other important problems. First, allegedly independent variables in some studies, notably proxies for market size, are *not* independent variables, but endogenous variables determined by the location of industries, workers, and firms in the geographical economics approach.[10] Second, the geographical economics model is characterized by multiple equilibria. Which equilibrium becomes established depends on the initial conditions. Without knowledge of the initial conditions it is difficult to test the model. The core model of chapters 3 and 4 allows for both full agglomeration and spreading of economic activity to be long-run equilibria. At the end of section 5.5 we will return to this problem. As we argued in this section, it is necessary to discriminate between the geographical economics model and competing theories to learn more about the empirical relevance of these approaches. This is precisely what section 5.4 (home-market effect) and section 5.5 (spatial wage structure) will do. There are many models that predict the spatial agglomeration or concentration of economic activity. Also, both internal and external economies of scale and the various externalities to which they give rise can be called upon to rationalize such a spatial clustering. In the core model of geographical economics there is, however, a very specific reason for positive externalities, namely the existence of regional demand linkages across space (recall the wage equation (3.21) in chapter 3). The studies on both the home-market effect and as the spatial wage structure are attempts to test for these regional demand linkages (Hanson, 2000).

5.4   The relevance of geographical economics I: the home-market effect

In his survey of geographical economics, Paul Krugman (1998, p. 172) concludes that empirical work has "failed to offer much direct testing of the specifics of the models." According to Krugman, recent empirical work by Donald Davis and David Weinstein on the home-market effect is an exception. We agree, and discuss their approach at some length in this section and show how difficult it remains in the end to reach clear-cut conclusions on the relevance of geographical economics.

5.4.1   The home-market effect

In a series of recent papers, Davis and Weinstein (1996, 1997, 1998a, 1998b, 1999) have developed an empirical methodology that enables them "to distinguish a world in which trade arises due to increasing returns as opposed to comparative advantage" (Davis and Weinstein, 1998a, p. 8). Following Krugman (1980) (see section 2.3), Davis and Weinstein note that new trade models without transport costs imply that trade leads to specialization, which is also the main implication of neo-classical trade models. With positive transport costs, however, the new trade theory allows for an empirical hypothesis that differentiates trade models based on increasing returns,

---

[10] See also Haaland *et al.* (1999, p. 9) and Midelfart-Knarvik *et al.* (2000).

including geographical economics, from their neo-classical counterpart, because it gives rise to the so-called home-market effect. In chapter 2 we explained that this effect implies that if a country has a relatively high demand for a good, say cars, it will be a net exporter of cars. More precisely, it implies that an increase in a country's demand for cars will lead to a *more than proportional* increase in that country's production of cars. In a neo-classical trade model such an increase in home demand will be at least partly met by an increase in foreign production of cars. The home-market effect translates in Davis and Weinstein's work into the following question: are idiosyncratic changes in demand associated with greater than proportional changes in output? If the answer is affirmative, this is taken as a confirmation of the geographical economics model. A negative answer would imply that either the neo-classical trade model or the new trade model with zero trade costs is empirically more relevant.

The central empirical equation used by Davis and Weinstein is derived from a theoretical model where it is assumed that comparative advantage determines trade and production at the industry level, whereas increasing returns drive within-industry specialization. In fact, they thus acknowledge that in practice more than one theory explains the structure of trade flows. The geographical unit of analysis is either a country or, as in Davis and Weinstein (1999), a region within a country. In all cases the following equation is estimated:[11]

$$X_{gnr} = \kappa_{gnr} + \kappa_1 \cdot SHARE_{gnr} + \kappa_2 \cdot IDIODEM_{gnr} + END + err_{gnr} \qquad (5.1)$$

where:

$X_{gnr} =$	output of good g in industry n in country r
$SHARE_{gnr} =$	share of output of good g in industry n for country r in the total output of good g in industry n
$IDIODEM_{gnr} =$	difference between the demand for good g of industry n in country r and the demand for good g of industry n in other countries
$END =$	(factor endowments for country r)·(input coefficients for good g in industry n)
$err_{gnr} =$	error term
$\kappa_{gnr} =$	constant

The crucial variable is $IDIODEM_{gnr}$, a mnemonic for IDIOsyncratic DEMand, and this variable represents the home-market effect. If every country demanded the same share of good g in industry n this variable would be zero. A coefficient for $IDIODEM_{gnr}$ exceeding 1 implies that an increase in demand for good g of industry n in country r leads to a more than proportional increase in output X_{gnr}. The inclusion of the variable $SHARE_{gnr}$ captures the tendency that, in the absence of idiosyncratic demand, each country r produces good g in industry n in the same proportion as other countries do. The fact that endowments can also determine the output X_{gnr} is the reason for the inclu-

---

[11] In the following, r is referred to as a country, but it could denote a region.

sion of *END*, ensuring that the role of neo-classical trade theory is not neglected. The home-market effect is therefore verified if $\kappa_2 > 1$.[12]

5.4.2 Estimation results

Equation (5.1) is estimated for a sample of OECD countries by Davis and Weinstein (1996, 1997). In the construction of the variables, the aim is to stay as close as possible to the theoretical model of Krugman (1980). As far as *IDIODEM* is concerned, this means that the variable lacks some real geographical content, since it is assumed that the relative location of countries does not matter, implying that demand linkages between neighboring countries are *a priori* no stronger than the linkages between countries on opposite sides of our planet. This is not very realistic (recall our discussion of the gravity model in chapter 1), and it is partly for this neglect of geography that the evidence in Davis and Weinstein (1996, 1997) with respect to the home-market effect is mixed at best. For example, in Davis and Weinstein (1997) the parameter κ_2 exceeds 1 for only nine industries in their sample of twenty-two OECD countries and twenty-six industries.

To improve upon these results, two strategies are followed in their subsequent work on the home-market effect. In Davis and Weinstein (1998a) the same data-set of OECD countries is analyzed, but *IDIODEM* is measured differently. They note that "the structure of demand in Germany and France affects the incentives for producers locating in Belgium more strongly than the demand in Japan and Australia. We must introduce these aspects of real world geography" (Davis and Weinstein, 1998a, p. 20). The latter is achieved by introducing different transport costs for each industry, which is taken into consideration in deriving the demand a producer in every country faces. This modification of *IDIODEM* is important because the support for the home-market effect is now much more conclusive.[13]

The second strategy to improve upon their earlier results, pursued in Davis and Weinstein (1999), is to stick to the initial measurement of *IDIODEM* (without transport costs), but to apply equation (5.1) to *regions within a single country*, rather than between countries. A sample consisting of forty regions *r*, nineteen goods *g*, and six industry aggregates *n*, is analyzed for Japan. The main results are given in Table 5.1.

The first column of Table 5.1 shows the results of the pooled regression when factor endowments *END* are not included. In this case, κ_2 is not only significant but also larger than 1, thus supporting the home-market effect. Davis and Weinstein

---

[12] If only factor endowments mattered for the determination of output, given the technology matrix, equation (5.1) would reduce to $X_{gnr} = END$. If $\kappa_2 < 1$ this is taken as evidence that neo-classical trade theory or new trade models are more relevant.

[13] Brülhart and Trionfetti (1999) try to discriminate between new trade theory and neo-classical trade theory by testing whether or not demand for goods is *home-biased* (yes in the new trade theory, no in the neo-classical trade theory). This test (which does not require positive transport costs) concludes (for the period 1970–1985) that demand is indeed home-biased. In other words, foreign goods and home goods are not perfect substitutes. Their approach closely follows Davis and Weinstein (1998a). The empirical estimates of home bias in demand are found after first estimating a gravity equation. These estimates are then added to what is basically equation (5.1) as an additional explanatory variable. Interestingly, *IDIODEM* does not have much explanatory power and the hypothesis that $\kappa_2 = 1$ cannot be rejected.

Table 5.1. *Home-market effect for Japanese regions*

IDIODEM	1.416	0.888
	(0.025)	(0.070)
SHARE	1.033	−1.7441
	(0.007)	(0.211)
END included?	No	Yes
# observations	760	760

Source: Davis and Weinstein (1999). Standard errors in parentheses; estimation method: Seemingly Unrelated Regressions.

(1999, p. 396) interpret this result as "clearly in the range of economic geography." Things are, however, different when factor endowments *END* are included; see the second column of Table 5.1. The coefficient for *IDIODEM* is still significant, but now smaller than 1. The second specification, therefore, does not provide support for the home-market effect in the aggregate. A breakdown of the data to the goods level, however, indicates that for eight of the nineteen goods, κ_2 is larger than 1 (at a 5% level of significance).

5.4.3   The home-market effect and geographical economics: an assessment

The empirical work of Davis and Weinstein on the home-market effect is obviously important from the perspective of geographical economics since the home-market effect is a crucial element of the core geographical economics model. From the model in chapter 3 (see, in particular, section 3.10), it can be discerned that an increase in demand for manufactures in a region, which enlarges the home-market for these goods, implies a more-than-proportional increase in manufacturing production in that region. There are two main problems that limit the usefulness of the home-market effect as a test of the empirical relevance of the geographical economics model.

First, the home-market effect is at home not only in geographical economics but also in other trade models with positive transport costs. In the discussion of new trade theory in section 2.3, it was argued that the main innovation of Krugman (1980) was to show how the introduction of transport costs together with increasing returns to scale lead to the home-market effect.[14] Davis and Weinstein do not consider this to be a problem because they refer to Krugman (1980) as their economic geography model. We do not agree. The main difference between Krugman (1980) and the geographical economics model of chapters 3 and 4 is that in the former the market size and thus demand in each region is exogenous, whereas in the latter the market size and demand

---

[14] Fujita, Krugman, and Venables (1999, p. 59) reach a similar conclusion: "the home market effect should apply whether or not a cumulative process of agglomeration is at work. Indeed, Krugman (1980) . . . did so in the context of a model in which relative market sizes were purely exogenous." See also Neary (2001) on this issue.

are endogenous. This endogenization arises because in the long run manufacturing labor (and firms) can move between regions.

This issue of endogenization goes beyond the mere use of the labels "new trade theory" or "geographical economics." Davis and Weinstein (1999, p. 389) say that their aim is to see whether the existence of the home-market effect "can improve our understanding of production patterns of trade at the goods level relative to the hypothesis that all production is determined by endowments." The determination of trade by endowments, that is the inclusion of *END* in equation (5.1), captures the relevance of neo-classical trade theory. However, in the geographical economics approach the distribution of mobile endowments is not fixed in the long run, but determined by the spreading and agglomerating forces characterizing this approach.[15] This effect may be partially captured by *END* in the last column of Table 5.1. This does not hold for new trade theory, for which the distribution of endowments is fixed. The studies of the home-market effect by Davis and Weinstein therefore do not offer a convincing test for the relevance of the geographical economics literature.

A second problem with the use of the home-market effect is the fact that it is not very robust, that is it ceases to exist if the assumptions underlying the Krugman (1980) model are slightly changed; see also Brülhart (1998, p. 795). As Davis (1998) shows (see section 6.2), the home-market effect does not necessarily arise if not only differentiated goods but *all* goods are subject to (equal) transport costs. Notwithstanding the special nature of the home-market effect, it does point to another, more promising method to test for the empirical relevance of geographical economics. The extent to which an increase in a region's demand for a manufactured good translates into a (more than proportional) increase in that region's production of the good depends on the elasticity of labor supply. If labor supply is not perfectly elastic, the increased demand will lead not only to increased production but also to higher nominal wages in that region (see equation (4.42) of Fujita, Krugman, and Venables, 1999, p. 57). Hence, given the (reasonable) assumption that labor supply is not perfectly elastic, it is interesting to see whether regions with a relatively high demand for manufactures also pay higher wages. That is, do wages fall the further one moves away from industrial centers? This topic is addressed in the next section.

5.5 The relevance of geographical economics II: a spatial wage structure

The negative relationship between manufacturing wages in a location and the distance of that location from the center(s) of production sets geographical economics apart

---

[15] More specifically, in their estimation of the determinants of the production of Japanese manufacturing sectors, Davis and Weinstein (1999, pp. 396–397) include factor endowments along with the region's demand for manufactured goods. In terms of the geographical economics model this is not without problems since both the regional demand for manufactured goods (market size) and the region's share of factor endowments (labor) are determined simultaneously. Hanson (1998; see section 5.5) therefore argues that only truly immobile endowments (such as land) should be taken into account. In fact, this means that only first-nature determinants of location should be considered exogenous.

from the two alternative trade theories. In neo-classical trade theory, there is no foundation for such a spatial wage structure. The existence of economic centers can be rationalized by location-specific endowments but this does not imply a spatial wage structure. Even with (endowment-driven) agglomeration, the main prediction of the neo-classical trade theory is that trade will lead to factor price equalization. In the new trade models it is true that in autarky wages are higher for the country with the larger labor force, but when trade opens up wages are equalized. This follows from the specialization in production of varieties of the manufactured good, such that some varieties are produced in one country and the other varieties in the other country. This rules out a spatial wage structure in new trade models because there is no endogenous agglomeration of manufacturing production across space, and thus no possibility of a center of manufacturing production.[16]

5.5.1   Regional wages and the distance from the center

Gordon Hanson (1997, 1998, 1999) investigates whether there is empirical evidence supporting the idea of a spatial wage structure. Hanson (1997) analyzes what he calls regional wage gradients for Mexico, and this study serves as a good starting point for a discussion of the more encompassing, but also more complicated, analysis of regional wages in Hanson (1998, 1999).[17] In the Mexico paper Hanson starts with the observation that the agglomeration of economic activity can also be explained by theories other than geographical economics, but that this is not true for the spatial structure of regional wages that goes along with agglomeration in the geographical economics model. Mexico provides an interesting case because of the clear-cut changes in Mexican trade policy in the post-war period. Initially, high trade barriers and a policy of import substitution stimulated the establishment of Mexico City as the center of manufacturing production. Subsequently, a policy of trade liberalization culminating in the North America Free Trade Agreement (NAFTA) has led to a gradual shift of manufacturing production from Mexico City to the US–Mexican border regions.[18] This shift has reinforced the considerable differences in GDP per capita between northern and southern Mexico; GDP per capita in the Chihuahua region in the north is, for instance, about three times as high as in the Veracruz region in the south. Hanson looks at regional wages in Mexico before and after the trade liberalization, and tests the following two hypotheses, conditional on the fact that Mexico City is the industrial center.

---

[16] This point also holds for the Davis and Weinstein studies of the home-market effect, which deal essentially with what we have defined in section 5.2 as the concentration of industries across regions/countries.

[17] Hanson (1999) is a revised version of Hanson (1998). See below for the differences.

[18] See also Hanson (1996) for a discussion of the effects of US–Mexican trade on manufacturing employment in US regions near the US–Mexican border. Krugman and Livas Elizondo (1996) develop a geographical economics model in which increased trade reduces the sustainability of existing centers of production. Similarly, Ades and Glaeser (1995) present empirical evidence which shows that countries with a low degree of openness typically have a relatively high degree of agglomeration of economic activity. In chapter 7, where we discuss the dominance of the largest, or primate, city in many national urban systems, we will return to the case of Mexico and Mexico City.

Figure 5.4.   Mexico.

(i)   Relative regional wages, that is a region's wage relative to Mexico City, are lower when transport costs (distances from Mexico City and the United States) are higher.

(ii)   Trade liberalization has led to a compression of regional wage differentials.

Hanson finds strong empirical support for hypothesis (i), but only weak support for hypothesis (ii). The confirmation of hypothesis (i) is in line with one of the main building blocks of geographical economics, namely that regional wages are a positive function of market access (Mexico City being the main market, see Figure 5.4). The opening up of trade with the United States obviously increased market access (in terms of forward and backward linkages) for Mexican regions like Mexicali or Ciudad Juarez that are close to the US border, but also decreased the centrality of Mexico City in general. With respect to the latter, this should lead to an overall convergence of regional wages with the wages in Mexico City; however, with the exception of the US border regions in Mexico, the evidence is not very strong. The empirical specification is simple; the following equation is estimated:[19]

---

[19] When estimating equation (5.2) a trade policy dummy is added to distinguish between the periods before and after trade liberalization. Other region-specific effects (various amenities) are also included. Equation (5.2) is then estimated for the period 1965–1988 on the two-digit industry level as well as on the state level. t_{it} is measured as distance in kilometers to Mexico City and tf_{it} is measured as distance in kilometers to the nearest US border crossing.

$$\ln(W_{it}/W_{ct}) = \kappa_0 + \kappa_1 \ln(t_{it}) + \kappa_2 \ln(tf_{it}) + err_{it} \qquad (5.2)$$

where:

W_{it} = nominal wage in Mexican region i at time t
W_{ct} = nominal wage in Mexico City at time t
t_{it} = unit transport costs from region i to Mexico City at time t
tf_{it} = unit transport costs from region i to the US market
err_{it} = error term

Equation (5.2) specifies that relative regional wages fall when the distance between a region and the center increases. It is a simple reduced form of the wage equation in the core model of geographical economics, ignoring the impact of various structural parameters and focusing on the transport costs. Hypothesis (i) implies that both parameters, κ_1 and κ_2, are negative. Hypothesis (ii) implies that the parameter κ_1 decreased significantly after trade liberalization. In chapter 9 we use equation (5.2) to test hypothesis (i) at the global level (see Box 9.3). If market size and thus demand are thought to be a determinant of regional wage gradients, it is better to test directly for the relevance of demand for regional wages.[20] Thus, Hanson (1998, 1999) tries to establish the relevance of demand linkages for the spatial distribution of wages across US counties. Taking into account that real wages matter, Hanson (1998, p. 14) specifies an empirical wage equation including the three central structural parameters of the core model of geographical economics, namely the elasticity of substitution between manufactured goods, the expenditure share on manufactured goods, and the transport costs for manufactured goods.

5.5.2   Theoretical foundation and empirical specification

Before we turn to the empirical results, we briefly discuss the theoretical approach in Hanson (1998).[21] Following Helpman (1998) and Thomas (1996), the agricultural sector of the core model of geographical economics is replaced by a housing sector (see section 6.2 for a discussion of the Helpman model). The reason is that the core model of chapters 3 and 4 displays a bias toward monocentric equilibria: all manufactures end up being produced at one location. This is clearly not in accordance with the facts about the spatial distribution of manufacturing activity for the United States, or any other industrialized country. Moreover, in industrialized countries agriculture provides only a weak spreading force in contrast to the prices of non-tradables, like housing. The perfectly competitive housing sector serves now as the spreading force, because housing can be relatively expensive in large agglomerations where demand for housing

---

[20] In Hanson (1997) the changes in the Mexican regional wages and industry concentration are at least to some extent exogenous (due to government policy). In the geographical economics approach, however, these changes are, in principle, endogenous.

[21] We also deal extensively with Hanson (1998) to build upon his approach when investigating, in section 5.6, the spatial wage structure in Germany.

is high. This geographical economics model with a housing sector typically results in a more even distribution of manufacturing activity than the core model of chapters 3 and 4. The equilibrium conditions are very similar to the core model; in particular, the wage equation, which is central to the empirical analysis, is identical to the normalized equation (4.3′):[22]

$$W_j = \left(\sum_k Y_k I_k^{\varepsilon-1} T^{D_{jk}(1-\varepsilon)} \right)^{1/\varepsilon} \tag{5.3}$$

Recall that W is the wage rate, Y is income, I is the price index, ε is the elasticity of substitution, T is the transport cost parameter, and $T_{jk} = T^{D_{jk}}$, where D_{jk} is the distance between locations j and k. Also remember that T is defined as the number of goods that have to be shipped in order to ensure that one unit arrives over one unit of distance. Given the elasticity of substitution ε, it can be seen directly from equation (5.3) that for every region wages are higher when demand in surrounding markets (Y_k) is higher, when access to those markets is better (lower transport costs T), and when there is less competition for the varieties the region wants to sell in those markets (competition effect, measured by the price index I_k).

Two empirical specifications of equation (5.3) are estimated. In the first version, equation (5.3) is simplified by assuming that wages in region j depend only on a constant and income Y_k, with the impact of the latter on wages in j being larger the shorter the distance between regions k and j.[23] Distance is measured relative to the economic center of a state; see Hanson (1998, p. 32) for details. The resulting specification is:

$$\log(W_j) = \kappa_0 + \kappa_1 \log\left(\sum_k Y_k e^{-\kappa_2 D_{jk}} \right) + err_j \tag{5.4}$$

where κ_0, κ_1, and κ_2 are parameters to be estimated. This specification is an example of a market potential function, with one major difference compared to standard market potential functions, that W instead of sales is the explanatory variable (see also section 2.2). The advantage is that it is easy to estimate and shows whether there is a spatial wage structure or not. The disadvantage is that there is no clear-cut connection with the theoretical model and its structural parameters. In this sense the first specification still suffers from the same drawbacks as the empirical specification of the wage equation in Hanson (1997). The second specification of equation (5.3) therefore bases the estimation results upon the theoretical model. To do this, Hanson rewrites equation (5.3) by assuming that the equilibrium real wages are equal across regions and by imposing the equilibrium condition for the housing market:[24]

---

[22] In the housing model of geographical economics, Hanson assumes that real wages are equal across regions, which means that the economy is by definition in its long-run equilibrium. The condition that housing payments in each region equal the share of expenditures allocated to housing is added as an equilibrium condition (Hanson, 1998, p. 12).

[23] We also use this as a first specification in the case study of Germany.

[24] Lack of reliable data on the regional price index of manufactures I_k and on the regional price of housing P_k makes this rewriting necessary. In section 5.6 we use (5.4′) as a second specification in our estimations for Germany. To get from equation (5.3) to equation (5.4′) use (i) the equilibrium for the housing market: $P_j H_j = (1 - \delta)Y_j$, and (ii) real wage equalization between regions: $W_j / P_j^{1-\delta} I_j^{\delta} = W_k / P_k^{1-\delta} I_k^{\delta}$.

$$\log(W_j) = k_0 + \varepsilon^{-1}\log\left(\sum_k Y_k^{\varepsilon+(1-\varepsilon)/\delta} H_k^{(1-\delta)(\varepsilon-1)/\delta} W_k^{(\varepsilon-1)/\delta} T^{(1-\varepsilon)D_{jk}}\right) + err_j \quad (5.4')$$

where k_0 is a parameter and H_k is the housing stock in region k. Note that equation (5.4′) includes the three structural parameters of the core model: δ, ε, and T. Given the availability of US data on wages, income, the housing stock, and a proxy for distance, equation (5.4′) can be estimated. In both empirical specifications of the theoretical wage equation (5.3), the dependent variable is the wage rate measured at the US county level.[25]

5.5.3   Estimation results

Table 5.2 gives a summary of Hanson's estimates. The first (market potential) specification of equation (5.3), as given by equation (5.4), confirms the basic ideas of the geographical economics model. Both the income coefficient and the distance coefficient have the expected sign, with a significant impact on US county wages. As Hanson (1998, p. 19) puts it: "spatial labor demand is conditioned by access to consumer markets." The relevance of the income variable Y_k increases over time. These results are consistent with the geographical economics model but do not constitute direct evidence in favor of the model, because the estimated market potential equation is at best a reduced-form equation of the theoretical model.

The second specification of equation (5.3), as given in equation (5.4′), deals with this problem by providing estimates for the structural parameters of the model. The results are summarized in Table 5.2 for the full sample of 3,075 US counties, with the first column giving the estimates for the period 1970–1980, and the second column, those for 1980–1990. Note that all three structural parameters are highly significant in both estimation periods.

Comparing the two periods for the estimation of equation (5.4′) in Table 5.2, a first surprising conclusion is that transport costs have increased over time (see also below), which leads Hanson to conclude that the benefits of spatial agglomeration have increased over time. Similarly, the elasticity of substitution ε has decreased, implying that imperfect competition has become more important and mark-ups over marginal costs have increased during the period 1970–1990. The estimate for δ, the share of income spent on manufactures, is fairly high and constant over time (about 0.9). It implies that only 10% of US personal income is spent on housing, which is clearly too low an estimate.

It can also be shown, based on the values for δ and ε shown in Table 5.2, that the degree of agglomeration of US manufacturing production depends on the level of transport costs. To understand this, we must return to the no-black-hole condition, discussed in chapter 4 for the core model, where the condition was stated as $\rho > \delta$.[26] It was

---

[25] An alternative version uses US county employment as the dependent variable. To control for correlation of the error term with the regression function, Hanson uses three checks (measuring independent variables at the state level, using time differences, and excluding the high-population counties).

[26] The no-black-hole condition had already been described by Krugman (1991a, p. 496) although not with this name.

Table 5.2. *Estimation of the market potential equation and the structural wage equation*

Market potential equation (5.4)	1980–1990	Structural wage equation (5.4′)	1970–1980	1980–1990
κ_0	Not reported	δ	0.927	0.913
			(0.017)	(0.018)
κ_1	0.378	ε	10.414	5.770
	(0.027)		(2.007)	(0.821)
κ_2	12.696	$\log(T)$	1.580	4.133
	(1.065)		(0.234)	(0.502)
		Adjusted R^2	0.203	0.308
		# observations	3075	3075
		$\varepsilon/(\varepsilon-1)$	1.106	1.210
		ρ	0.904	0.826

Source: Hanson (1998), p. 39 and Hanson (1999), p. 36; standard errors in parentheses; κ_0=constant, κ_1=parameter for distance-weighted income, κ_2=distance parameter, ε = substitution elasticity, δ=share of income spent on manufactures, T=transport costs; $\varepsilon/(\varepsilon-1)$=mark-up; $\varepsilon = 1/(1-\rho)$.

argued in chapter 4 that if the condition $\rho > \delta$ is fulfilled, the equilibrium regional distribution of economic activity depends on the level of transport costs, whereas if this condition is not fulfilled full agglomeration (a monocentric equilibrium) is the only feasible equilibrium in the long run, and the equilibrium spatial distribution of manufacturing activity would not depend at all on the level of transport costs. On the basis of the estimated value of δ and the implied value of ρ in both periods in Table 5.2 it *appears* that the no-black-hole condition is violated, suggesting that the location of US manufacturing activity does not depend on the level of transportation costs. This conclusion is *not* correct, as Hanson (1999, p. 24) notes, because the interpretation of the condition is reversed in the housing model of geographical economics estimated in equation (5.4′). Why does this switching of the interpretation of the no-black-hole condition take place? The reason is that Hanson builds on the model developed by Helpman (1998), where the agricultural sector of the core model is replaced by a housing sector. Since the agricultural good is freely traded between regions, whereas housing is a non-tradable good, the interpretation of the no-black-hole condition is reversed; see Helpman (1998, pp. 50–51). Therefore, the results in Table 5.2 imply that (Hanson, 1999, p. 24): "for the US economy, it appears that spatial agglomeration is increasing in transport costs. This finding suggests that spatial agglomeration in the United States is associated with pecuniary externalities created by transport cost and firm-level scale economies."

To verify the strength of demand linkages across space, Hanson analyzes the demand effects of a negative income shock in a particular location (the center of the state of Illinois) and shows the extent to which other locations are affected by this shock. It turns out that the effects of such a shock are relatively small in a geographical sense, but that the demand linkages between neighboring locations are quite strong and increasing over time (Hanson, 1998, p. 26). We address the geographical strength of demand linkages for Germany in section 5.6.

5.5.4   Some critical remarks

The fact that we discuss the empirical studies of Hanson in detail reflects our view that these studies constitute the most structural attempt to date to arrive at an empirical validation of the geographical economics approach. Still, there are number of objections that can be raised against these studies, some of which are mentioned by Hanson (1998, p. 31) and remedied in Hanson (1999).

First, there is no role for fixed region-specific endowments determined by actual geography and hence there is no role for neo-classical trade theory in Hanson (1998). Access to the sea, the location of mountain ranges, and other physical features of the United States are also relevant in explaining regional wages and the concentration of economic activity across space (see section 5.2; Ellison and Glaeser, 1999; and Black and Henderson, 1998, 1999a). Given the discussion of Davis and Weinstein (1998a, 1999) in section 5.4, one should only look at immobile endowments, since mobile endowments (such as labor) are already an ingredient of the geographical economics model.[27]

Second, Hanson (1998) assumes that the United States is a closed economy. Only national demand matters for regional wages. This is not an unreasonable assumption as a first approximation, but even there it is clear that the concentration of economic activity (and hence of regional wages) is also determined by the degree of openness of the US economy. Hanson (1996) himself shows, for example, that manufacturing labor demand in the US part of six US–Mexican twin cities/regions depends positively on employment in the export assembly plants of the Mexican twin city. For more open economies the closed economy assumption is obviously more problematic. We return to this issue in section 5.6.

Third, the theoretical model used by Hanson is taken from Thomas (1996), who builds on Helpman (1998). A central issue in Thomas (1996) is the non-linear relationship between transport costs on the one hand and industrial agglomeration and relative wages on the other. This non-linearity is not a novel feature; see our discussion of Krugman and Venables (1990) in section 2.3. It implies that as transport costs decrease from very high to intermediate levels, the agglomeration of economic activity is strengthened and the relative wage of large regions increases. However, if transport costs fall even further, from intermediate to low levels, firms and workers relocate to the smaller regions, the share of large regions in manufacturing production decreases, and the wage differential between large and small regions narrows. For an intermediate range of transport costs, the advantages of market proximity outweigh the disad-

---

[27] To deal with this point Hanson (1999, p. 5) adjusts for exogenous amenities, such as average heating and cooling days, average humidity, whether the county borders the sea coast, etc. The results hardly change when wages are adjusted for these amenities.

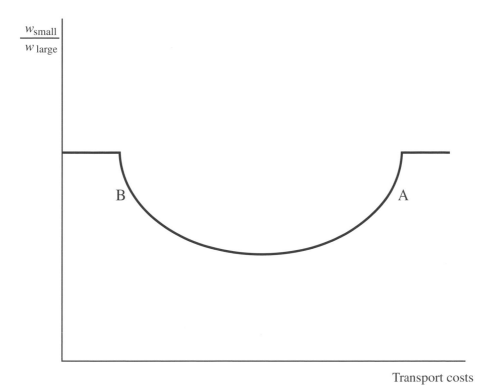

Figure 5.5.   Relative real wage and transport costs.

vantages for firms and workers of the relatively large region. The advantages of market proximity arise from the backward and forward linkages that enable firms in the centers of production to pay relatively higher wages. The disadvantages of agglomeration arise from the higher wage costs for firms and from congestion costs for workers. The latter are incorporated in Thomas (1996), and thus also in Hanson (1998), by a relatively high housing price in the center of production. At a certain point, transport costs get so low that the advantages of market proximity fall short of the disadvantages, and a reloca-tion process starts. This is illustrated in Figure 5.5 (with transport costs rising as one moves from left to right along the horizontal axis).

Why is the theoretical possibility of a non-linear relationship, or U-curve, between transport costs and relative wages important from an empirical point of view? It is because it implies that models of geographical economics can be in accordance with the results found by Hanson (1998), as well as with a tendency toward regional wage equalization, depending on the position of the economy on the U-curve. Without an hypothesis about the initial level of transport costs it is not clear whether increasing regional wage differentials, as in the Hanson study, is evidence in favor of geographical economics or not. Hanson (1998) concludes that the significance of transport costs for regional wages has increased in the period 1970–1990, and that the benefits of spatial agglomeration have also increased over time. This means that either the US economy is on the part of the U-curve where a fall in transport costs stimulates agglomeration and regional wage differentials (point A in Figure 5.5), or the US economy is on the downward-sloping part (point B in Figure 5.5) with *increasing* transport costs.[28]

Hanson (1998) does not deal with the issues raised in Figure 5.5. This may be due to his assumption of real wage equalization across regions, implying that the US economy is always in a long-run equilibrium. This is, however, a very strong assumption. Without knowledge of the initial conditions of the US spatial distribution of economic activity, it is not possible to determine whether or not the observed distribution at any point in time is a long-run equilibrium. If real wage equalization is not imposed, priors for the initial spatial distribution of economic activity, and for the initial values for the three structural parameters in Table 5.2, are called for in order to say what the long-run equilibrium must be. In other words, because geographical economics is characterized by multiple equilibria, it remains difficult to test for the empirical relevance as long as the test does not include a prediction of the equilibrium distribution of economic activity and wages.

We now have come full circle. In section 5.3 it was argued that the bulk of the empirical studies on specialization/concentration/agglomeration are not designed to assess the relevance of a particular theory, and this gave rise to two problems. First, many stylized facts are in accordance not only with geographical economics but also with competing theories. The attempts to test for the home-market effect (section 5.4) and the spatial wage structure (section 5.5) deal with this problem. Second, geographical economics is characterized by multiple equilibria, making it difficult to verify its validity. The second problem remains. The next section tests for a spatial wage structure after the German reunification and here we partly deal with some of these criticisms. We have taken the openness of the German economy into account and have looked at what happens when real wage equalization is not assumed beforehand. Both changes, however, do not affect the results. Also, the case of post-reunification Germany differs from the USA because we know the initial conditions in the case of Germany: when the Berlin Wall fell in 1989 (nearly) all of the profitable manufacturing production was located in the western part of Germany, which in itself gives a reason to expect a spatial wage structure.

5.6   A case study: the spatial wage structure for Germany[29]

5.6.1   *German reunification and geographical economics*

The objective of this case study is to establish whether or not a spatial wage structure exists for Germany. The German case is interesting because of the background of the fall of the Berlin Wall in November 1989, and the formal reunification of West and

---

[28] An increase of transport costs is in line with the results found by Hanson. Thomas (1996), however, concludes that regional wage differentials have narrowed in the USA, which he attributes to the fact that the USA is on the downward sloping part of the U-curve where a fall in transport costs favors the relatively smaller region.

[29] This section is partly based on Brakman, Garretsen, and Schramm (2000) and Brakman, Garretsen, van Marrewijk, and Schramm (2000).

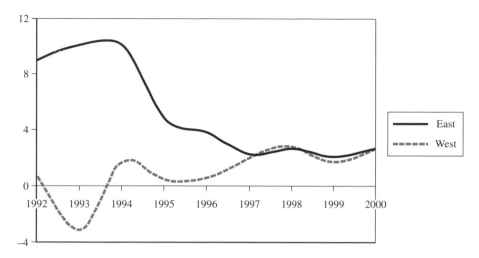

Figure 5.6.   Evolution of growth rates in East and West Germany. *Data source*: See Table
5.3.

East Germany in October 1990. After the initial optimism following the German reunification, it was quickly pointed out that the reasons for this optimism were far from
obvious from the perspective of new trade and new growth theory and geographical
economics. Although some convergence in GDP per capita took place in the period
1991–1995, the clear *lack* of convergence since then indicates that geographical economics, with its emphasis on core–periphery outcomes, might be of some relevance for
post-reunification Germany (see Figure 5.6 and Table 5.3). In fact, the core model of
geographical economics was called upon to show that a so-called Mezzogiorno scenario (with West Germany as the core and East Germany as the periphery) could not
be ruled out for the German case.[30]

Brakman and Garretsen (1993) use the core model of chapters 3 and 4 to investigate
the prospects of East Germany becoming a center of production assuming that initially all manufacturing production is located in West Germany. One of the advantages
of the case of German reunification is that we know the initial conditions; in 1990,
when the formal reunification took place, virtually all (profitable) manufacturing
German production was located in the western part. Given the assumption about the
initial distribution of manufacturing production and the parameter values δ, ε, and T,
the question is whether or not this initial distribution is a stable equilibrium in the long
run; in the terminology of chapter 4, whether or not the core–periphery pattern can be
sustained. To answer this question Brakman and Garretsen (1993) also assume that
labor costs in East Germany are initially higher than in West Germany, which is equivalent to assuming that labor productivity in East Germany is relatively lower.[31] The

---

[30] For a good textbook example of the use of the German reunification to illustrate the potential relevance
of geographical economics, see Krugman and Obstfeld (1994, p. 186).
[31] In the production function $l_i = \alpha + \beta x_i$ it is assumed that marginal labor costs β are higher in East
Germany.

Table 5.3. *GDP per capita, East and West Germany*

a. Convergence

	Real GDP per capita (DM, 1991)		Growth rate (%)		Gap 1 − (1)/(2)
	East (1)	West (2)	East (3)	West (4)	
1991	12,950	41,320	—	—	0.69
1992	14,120	41,520	9.0	0.5	0.66
1993	15,550	40,230	10.1	−3.1	0.61
1994	17,100	40,930	9.9	1.7	0.58
1995	17,900	41,090	4.7	0.4	0.56
1996	18,570	41,320	3.7	0.6	0.55
1997	18,980	42,200	2.2	2.1	0.55
1998	19,470	43,380	2.6	2.8	0.55

b. Forecasts of growth rates of real GDP (%)

	East	West
1999	2.0	1.7
2000	2.6	2.6

Sources: (a) Statistisches Bundesamt; (b) DIW (1999), Wochenbericht, 17.

simulations based on this model lead to the conclusion that it is very difficult for East Germany to become the center of production. Two simulation results tell the story. First, given a moderate value for transport costs T, the initial core–periphery pattern would only fail to be sustained if, and only if, East German labor productivity somehow became *higher* than West German labor productivity. Second, without such a productivity spurt, East Germany could only become a center of production for very high transport costs. In reality, labor productivity in East Germany is not higher, and the fall of the Berlin Wall and subsequent massive investments in infrastructure have lowered transport costs between East and West Germany considerably. Hence, applying the core model to the case of the German reunification yields a rather pessimistic conclusion for the prospects of East Germany in the near future.

The last conclusion is subject to two important caveats. First, the core model is a static model: for a fixed level of overall income it deals with the allocation of economic activity between the two regions. This forecloses the analysis of how economic growth may induce firms to locate and produce in East Germany. As pointed out by Brakman and Garretsen (1993), the introduction of economic growth does not necessarily alter the pessimistic view, since the new growth theory (see section 2.4) also allows for the initial conditions to determine long-run equilibrium in terms of growth of GDP per capita. In fact, some versions of new growth theory are analytically similar to the core model of geographical economics (see, for example, Grossman and Helpman, 1991, ch.

3). We address the topic of geography and growth in chapter 10. The second caveat concerns the empirical relevance of geographical economics for the German case. It is one thing to argue that simulations with the core model show that East Germany may very well remain the periphery. It is something quite different, however, actually to test for the relevance of the main implications of geographical economics for Germany and the convergence prospects. We now turn to the empirical evidence.

5.6.2   *Testing for a spatial wage structure in Germany*

Our empirical analysis is based on the two main specifications used by Hanson (1998, 1999): the market potential equation (equation (5.4)) and the reduced-form wage equation with the three structural parameters (equation (5.4′)). The German case creates several additional challenges. First, unlike the USA, Germany is typically considered to be an open economy, such that one has to take economic activity from abroad into account when testing for a spatial wage structure. Second, the labor market in Germany is considered to be rigid, with sticky wages and centralized wage-setting at the industry level. If one detected a spatial wage structure despite this institutional context, that would constitute a clear case in favor of geographical economics since the bias is against finding such evidence. Third, there are large differences between the West and East German economies. Nominal wages are lower in the east than in the west because of lower labor productivity; see Sinn (2000, p. 19). Moreover, East German firms face severe difficulties entering inter-regional, West German, markets. Despite the relatively high unit labor costs in East Germany, producer prices are estimated to be 20% lower than West German producer prices for equivalent products; see Müller (1999). Market segmentation between East and West Germany is thus something to take into account as well. We will return to the issue of segmentation below when we address the possibility of "mental" distance between East and West Germany (see Figure 5.7 for a map of Germany).

   Before we turn to the estimation results, a few words on the construction of our data-set are in order. Germany is administratively divided into about 440 districts (*Kreise*). Of these a total of 118 districts are so-called city-districts (*kreisfreie Städte*), in which the district corresponds with a city. We use district statistics provided by the regional statistical offices in Germany. The data-set contains local variables, like the value-added of all sectors (GDP), the wage bill, and the number of hours of labor in firms with twenty or more employees in the mining and manufacturing sector. In the empirical analysis we include 114 city-districts in our sample, of which 26 are East German. This group of city-districts represents 47% of total German GDP and about 40% of total German urban population. Since we also want to analyze the hinterland of the cities we included 37 country-districts, formed by aggregation of the 326 administrative country-districts (*Landeskreise*). The total number of districts in our sample is thus 151, namely 114 city districts and 37 country-districts. Transport costs are, of course, a crucial variable. We do not use the geodesic distance between districts, because this measure does not distinguish between primary and secondary roads. Instead, distance is measured by the average travel time by car from A to B. These data are obtained from the *Route*

Figure 5.7.   Germany.

Planner 2000 (Europe, AND Publishers, Rotterdam). For the data on the housing stock, required to estimate equation (5.4), we use the number of rooms in residential dwellings per district. Since we have one observation per district for the average hourly wage and for GDP (1994/5) we have to estimate the wage equations in levels.

5.6.3   *Reduced-form specification*

The reduced form of the (market potential) spatial wage equation to be estimated is:

$$\log(W_j) = \kappa_1 \log\left(\sum_k Y_k e^{-\kappa_2 D_{jk}} \right) + \kappa_3 D_{\text{east}} + \kappa_4 D_{\text{country}} + \text{constant} \qquad (5.5)$$

Table 5.4. *Estimation of the spatial wage structure in Germany*

	Coefficient	Standard error	t-statistic
κ_1	0.167	0.018	8.846
κ_2	0.199	0.045	4.389
κ_3	−0.257	0.045	−5.686
κ_4	−0.500	0.051	−9.992
constant	2.657	0.175	15.173

Note: $R^2 = 0.62$; number of observations $= 151$; estimation method: non-linear least squares.

where W_j is the nominal hourly wage in city-district j, Y_j is the value-added of all sectors in city-district j, and D_{jk} is the distance between city-districts j and k, with distance measured in minutes of travel by car. D_{east} is a dummy variable which takes into account that in East Germany (dummy is 1) wages are relatively low (in 1995 East German wages were about 35% lower than West German wages). $D_{country}$ is a dummy variable which takes into account that country-districts are geographically defined differently from city-districts. The estimation results hardly change when both dummies are excluded.

The main conclusion is that for Germany as a whole (here, 151 districts) we find strong confirmation of the relevance of a spatial wage structure. The coefficients κ_1 and κ_2 are both significantly different from zero. Distance clearly matters and it is noteworthy that the impact of distance seems to be stronger than was found for the USA (see the first part of Table 5.2). Wages in district j depend positively on the economic activity and the resulting demand from other districts (κ_1 is positive), but the impact of this demand on wages in city-district j is localized (κ_2 is positive). In other words, the results confirm the idea that wages will be higher when a district is close to, or part of, an economic center, that is a clustering of districts with relatively high Y. Both dummies are also significant and have the expected sign, indicating that wages are relatively low for East German and/or country-districts.

Another feature worth mentioning is that equation (5.5) assumes that Germany is a closed economy. Germany's main trading partners are the other member-states of the European Union (EU). Adding the market access to these fourteen EU countries has, however, no additional impact whatsoever on wages and the estimation results reported in Table 5.4. The spatial wage structure in Germany does not seem to be affected by economic activity abroad.

To understand the degree to which demand linkages are localized (as measured by the coefficient κ_2), Brakman, Garretsen, and Schramm (2000) conduct an experiment, based on Hanson (1998, 1999), which shows that these linkages are strongly localized for Germany. That is to say, for the wage of district j, only the access to those markets in the near vicinity of this district matters. The following experiment was conducted: the GDP of city-district Essen (see Figure 5.7) was increased by

10%. We then checked what this implied for wages in the various city-districts. The GDP shock leads, not surprisingly, to the largest wage increase occurring in Essen itself (wages in Essen increase by 2.3%). As one moves away from Essen, the magnitude of the wage increase quickly becomes smaller. Travelling more than one hour by car, one arrives at districts where the nominal wages are no longer affected by the GDP shock. This shows that the effect of a local demand shock on wages is geographically limited. Hanson (1999, p. 20), performing a similar experiment for the USA, finds that a local demand shock still has an effect on the nominal wage in a county at a distance of 885 kilometers! Hence, the demand linkages are indeed strongly localized for Germany compared to the USA. The question arises of how to account for the relatively strong impact of distance in Germany. One reason might be the reunification itself; the merger of two very different economies which had been separated for forty-five years may very well imply that there is more to distance and transport costs than is measured by the time to travel between the city-districts (see Box 5.2).

Box 5.2.   Border effects and mental distance: do Ossies and Wessies interact?[32]

Given the potential relevance of border effects for post-reunification Germany in 1995, five years after the reunification, we want to know if distance is less relevant *within* East or West Germany than *between* East and West Germany. In other words, is the former border between West and East Germany still discernible to the extent that it has an impact on the spatial wage structure? To answer this question we changed equation (5.5) as follows:

$$\log(W_j) = \kappa_1 \log\left(\sum_k Y_k e^{(-\kappa_2 - \kappa_3 \varphi_{jk})D_{jk}} \right) + \kappa_4 \text{Dummy}_{\text{east}} + \text{constant} \quad (5.5')$$

where

$\varphi_{jk} = 0$, if j and k are both in West Germany or both in East Germany
$\varphi_{jk} = 1$, otherwise.

Following the studies of Engel and Rogers (1996) or McCallum (1995), we expect that if border effects occur, κ_3 is positive. However, as can be seen from the empirical results in column (1) of Table 5.5, the distance parameter κ_3 is negative. Moreover, the parameters κ_2 and κ_3 cancel out if $\varphi_{jk} = 1$.[33] What do these results with respect to the two distance parameters imply?

First, κ_3 thus has the wrong sign. In this sense, no border effect is observed.

---

[32] This box is based on Brakman, Garretsen, and Schramm (2000), where the sample consists of the 114 city-districts only. Including the country-districts does not change the main results.
[33] The *F*-statistic of the Wald test of the restriction $\kappa_2 + \kappa_3 = 0$ is 1.15. So the sum of the two distance parameters is not statistically significantly different from zero.

Table 5.5. *Estimation results: German district wages and intra-German border*

	East–West Border (1)	North–South Border (2)	North–South Border (only West) (3)
κ_1	1.579	0.174	0.193
	(6.1)	(7.9)	(7.4)
κ_2	0.131	0.170	0.160
	(4.4)	(3.6)	(3.7)
κ_3	−0.131	0.606	0.422
	(−4.4)	(0.0)	(0.0)
κ_4	−3.702	−0.234	—
	(−6.7)	(−4.1)	
Constant	−14.903	2.598	2.417
	(−4.7)	(12.7)	(10.0)
Adjusted R^2	0.472	0.522	0.376
# observations	114	114	88

Note: The t-statistics are in parentheses.

Second, for $\varphi_{jk} = 0$ the distance parameter κ_2 is lower than the estimates shown in Table 5.4 (0.131 compared to 0.199). A reason for the relatively high value for the distance parameter in estimating (5.4) might simply be that we have pooled two groups of city-districts, East and West German districts, whose markets are still segmented five years after the reunification. If this is the case, the pooled estimate for the distance parameter will be biased upwards, as confirmed by the estimation results for $\varphi_{jk} = 0$. Confining our estimations to either West or East German city-districts (with $\varphi_{jk} = 0$), distance clearly still matters but its impact is less for city-district wages. In this respect, demand linkages are geographically stronger within the two parts of Germany than between these parts. As such, our results are consistent with the so-called home-bias effect in trade, indicating that goods markets are far more segmented than is commonly supposed. Our research confirms the theoretical notion of Obstfeld and Rogoff (2000) that transport costs are a possible explanation for this phenomenon.

Our third, and most interesting, result is that κ_2 and κ_3 cancel out when $\varphi_{jk} = 1$. This indicates that the *spatial* distribution of demand in West Germany is not relevant for the spatial wage structure in East Germany and vice versa. The result, therefore, indicates that the East–West German border still matters to the extent that there does not seem to be an effect of the localization of demand for wages across the East–West border.[34] Stated differently, for the level of East German city-district wages only the total West German demand matters, and the geography of this demand is irrelevant, and vice versa. How can this finding be explained? We can only offer some suggestions here. The strong segmentation of East and West German markets could be caused by differences in firm behavior resulting from differences in management style and willingness to adjust to changes in the company environment; see Rothfels and Wölfl (1998, pp. 7–11). The existence of mental borders between the Ossies and Wessies might be relevant. In this case, economic agents impose borders on themselves, for instance because they strongly identify with "their" region and are inclined to stick to this region for their economic transactions. Another possibility, which might be relevant in the initial stage of German reunification, is that agents simply lack knowledge about the other region and are therefore geographically biased when it comes to their economic transactions; see Van Houtum (1998) or Rumley and Minghi (1991). The possible relevance of mental distance (and the norms and values that go along with it) is a reminder of the fact that economic geographers have a point when criticizing the geographical economics approach for paying too little attention to the role of (in)formal institutions in shaping spatial patterns; see Martin (1999). We return to this issue in chapter 11.

To check whether the third result is merely a statistical artifact, columns (2) and (3) of Table 5.5 give the estimation results for different "borders." The first alternative border comes from dividing Germany as a whole into northern and southern parts; see column (2) of Table 5.5. This gives us 26 northern and 88 southern city-districts. The second alternative border comes from splitting West Germany (only) into 15 northern and 73 southern city-districts, see column (3) of Table 5.5. The main point is that for these two additional borders the coefficient κ_3 becomes insignificant, such that the inclusion of those borders is immaterial to the estimation results. The only border that (still) mattered in the mid 1990s was the one between West Germany and East Germany.

5.6.4   Housing specification

In our search for a spatial wage structure in Germany that supports geographical economics we finally turn to an attempt to estimate the structural parameters using equation (5.4′) for Germany. In doing so, we will be able to verify the no-black-hole condition, giving an indication for the convergence prospects in Germany. The data and sample are the same as in subsection 5.6.3. Given that we have already established that the openness of the German economy does not have a bearing on our results, we estimate for the case of a closed economy. Table 5.6 gives the estimation results. We

---

[34] This border effect is quite different from the border effect found by Engel and Rogers (1996) for the USA and Canada, where they find large variations in the movements of prices.

Table 5.6. *Estimating the structural parameters for Germany*

	Coefficient	Standard error	*t*-statistic
δ	1.869	0.887	2.105
ε	3.914	0.618	6.327
$\log(T)$	0.008	0.001	7.257

Note: $R^2 = 0.498$; number of observations $= 151$; estimation method: non-linear least squares; implied values: $\varepsilon/(\varepsilon - 1) = 1.343$, $\rho = 0.745$

also experimented by including a dummy variable for East German districts and a dummy variable for country-districts. As these results proved immaterial for the conclusions with respect to the structural parameters, they are not reported here.

The results are somewhat mixed. The substitution elasticity ε is significant and the coefficient implies a profit margin of 34% (given that $\varepsilon/(\varepsilon - 1)$ is the mark-up) which is fairly reasonable, although higher than found for the USA by Hanson (1998, 1999) (see Table 5.2). The share of income spent on manufactures, δ, is (too) large because it does not differ significantly from 1, which value would mean that Germans do not spend any money on housing, the non-tradable good in the model underlying equation (5.4). Even though Hanson also finds this share to be quite large for the USA (above 0.9 and, in some cases, also not significantly different from 1), this is a somewhat puzzling result. The transport cost parameter has the correct sign and is highly significant. In discussing the Hanson results we criticized his assumption of real wage equalization (imposing a long-run equilibrium). Specifically for the German case this is *a priori* too strong an assumption. We know that real wages in the two parts of Germany were not equal in 1995. So we re estimated equation (5.4) allowing for a real wage differential between (but not within) East and West Germany. The coefficient (not shown here) measuring the real wage differential indeed indicated that real wages are not equal, but (surprisingly) this coefficient did not differ significantly from zero. The results shown in Table 5.6 are therefore a good first approximation for Germany.[35]

To give an idea of the sensitivity of these results and to remedy the somewhat unsatisfactory results for δ, we finally estimated equation (5.4) for a fixed spending share. Instead of estimating δ, we consulted statistical information on German expenditure shares which revealed that the appropriate δ can be chosen either as $(1 - 0.32)$, with 0.32 being the part of income spent on non-tradable services, see Table 5.7a, or as $(1 - 0.17)$, with 0.17 being the part of income spent on non-tradable housing services, (Table 5.7b).[36] We thus re-estimated equation (5.4′), restricting the parameter δ to one of the two values above. The results are reported in Table 5.7.

[35] We also estimated the core model for the case of Germany but the results (not shown here) were clearly inferior compared to the estimation of equation (5.4).
[36] Based on the weights in the German consumer prices index, February 1999, Federal Statistical Office, Germany.

Table 5.7. *Structural parameters for Germany, restricting* δ

a. $\delta = 0.68 = 1 -$ share spent on non-tradable services

	Coefficient	standard error	t-statistic
ε	2.876	0.276	10.409
Log(T)	0.009	0.001	7.278

Note:
Adj. $R^2 = 0.455$; number of observations $= 151$; estimation method non-linear least squares.

b. $\delta = 0.83 = 1 -$ share spent on housing services

	Coefficient	standard error	t-statistic
ε	3.100	0.318	9.734
Log(T)	0.009	0.001	7.568

Note: Adj. $R^2 = 0.465$; number of observations $= 151$; estimation method: non-linear least squares.

As is clear from Table 5.7, restricting the part of income spent on manufactures to 0.68 or 0.83 reduces the estimated elasticity of substitution between manufacturing varieties from almost 4 to roughly 3, and thus increases the estimated mark-up over marginal costs from one-third to a half.[37] The restrictions have virtually no impact on the estimated size and significance of the transport costs T.

We started our discussion about Germany in this section by mentioning the lack of convergence prospects. The estimation results in Table 5.6 as well as in Table 5.7 show that $\rho < \delta$ (with $\varepsilon = 1/(1 - \rho)$). As extensively discussed in section 5.5 this implies in the geographical economics model with a housing sector based on Helpman (1998) that transport costs have an impact on the degree of agglomeration, that is agglomeration is not inevitable if transport costs can be sufficiently reduced. For Germany this seems to indicate that ultimately a lowering of transport costs might lead to more even spreading of economic activity, which is good news for the peripheral districts, the bulk of which are located in East Germany. It also means that the pessimistic view about the German convergence process based on simulations with the core model of geographical economics may be overly so.

5.7   Conclusions

In this chapter we have looked at the empirical relevance of geographical economics. Our analysis gave rise to two main conclusions. First, a large number of empirical

---

[37] A 50%-mark-up may seem rather high. However, Hall (1988) measuring the mark-up in US industry arrives at mark-ups of 120%, 106%, and 210% in the construction, durable goods, and non-durable goods sectors, respectively.

studies and empirical findings are consistent not only with the (core) model of geographical economics, but also with other theories of trade and location. This is not surprising since these studies are mostly not aimed at testing specific theories, such as geographical economics. Second, those studies that try to test directly for the relevance of geographical economics do confirm some of its main predictions, in particular the home-market effect and the existence of a spatial wage structure. Despite this empirical validation, the nature of the geographical economics approach, and specifically the existence of multiple equilibria, make it difficult to test in a conclusive manner for the relevance of this theory.

The analysis in this chapter also raises a number of questions. It remains, for instance, unclear what geographical economics adds empirically to our understanding of the relationships between location and economic activity. Is it that, because of geographical economics, we are now able to discover new facts, or does geographical economics "merely" provide a better theoretical foundation for stylized facts that were established long ago? Another question is whether and how the core model of geographical economics can be extended to deal with a number of issues about the location of economic activity that are not part of the core model that we have used so far in this book. Chapters 6–10 will deal with extensions of the core model. The analysis in these chapters is to a considerable extent aimed at enhancing the relevance of geographical economics.

Exercises

5.1* Take the idea of a spatial wage structure as introduced in this chapter. Do you think it is possible to arrive at such a wage structure using either the neo-classical trade model or the new trade model developed by Krugman and Venables (1990)? (See section 2.3 for a discussion of the latter.)

5.2* On the website for this book you can find the results of the following experiment. Take the estimation results for the wages in German city-districts based on equation (5.5). Now assume that the income in Essen (one of the German city-districts) is increased by 10% and calculate the impact of this income shock for city-district wages. Explain the findings of this experiment in terms of the geographical economics model.

5.3* Suppose we applied the idea of a spatial wage structure on a global level instead of on a country level as in this chapter. Do you think it would be more difficult to find confirmation for a spatial wage structure at this higher level of aggregation? If so, why?

5.4* Take the short-run equilibrium wage equation (5.3). This equation states that low transport costs (low T) are good for regional wages. Why does this equation, however, not tell us what happens with regional wages when transport costs are changed, for instance when T is lowered?

5.5 For Germany we find that the no-black-hole condition holds (see Tables 5.6 and 5.7). Explain, based on the housing model, what this implies for the prospects for convergence between East and West Germany.

5.6 Equation (5.1) is central to the Davis and Weinstein approach to measuring the so-called home-market effect. Discuss how one could amend the measurement of the "neo-classical" variable *END*, referring to labor endowments, in order for it *not* to be subject to the criticism that from a geographical economics perspective the regional allocation of endowments is part of the geographical economics model.

6 Refinements and extensions

6.1 Introduction

Chapter 5 shows that, although difficult, it is possible to test the geographical economics models empirically. At the same time, a number of important phenomena about the location of economic activity are not addressed by the core model of geographical economics. Consequently, the core model has been extended and improved upon in a number of interesting directions since Krugman (1991a). By definition, these extensions focus on aspects that are not part of the core model described in chapter 3. However, a few important building blocks of the core model have hardly been touched (yet), such as firm-specific economies of scale, imperfect competition, pecuniary externalities, and the Dixit–Stiglitz monopolistic competition framework, with its associated love-of-variety effect. Changes in, and extensions of, the core model usually focus on characteristics that can be adapted to better describe stylized facts, or shed new light on familiar problems. Chapters 7 to 11 give detailed examples of such extensions and adaptations, focusing on cities, multinationals, trade, growth, and policy implications, respectively. Instead, this chapter gives a broad overview of three different types of extensions. We label these types I, II, and III extensions, although it is sometimes not crystal clear under which heading a specific geographical economics model should be classified, in particular if there are multiple extensions incorporated in the same model. Table 6.2 at the end of this chapter gives a summary of the types of extension, and an overview of what to expect in the rest of this book.

Type I extensions concern transport costs and the way "space" is handled. It was argued in chapters 3 and 4, that one of the attractive features of the core model of geographical economics is the neutrality of space. Since, by construction, no location is preferred initially over other locations, agglomeration (a center–periphery structure) is not imposed, but follows endogenously from the model. Neutrality of space is, however, not acceptable for applied research, which has to take the actual use of space, and real-world complications, like differences in transport costs for different commodities, hubs, mountain ranges, bridges, etc., into consideration. In other words, some locations are preferred by nature or man-made phenomena over other locations. These locations tend to be natural centers of economic activity. Sometimes, geography is also destiny. Allowing for non-neutral space, the first extension we discuss below, puts, so to speak, more geography in the geographical economics model.

Type II extensions focus on the production side of the core model. Recall that the production structure of the core model is very simple: it uses only labor as a factor of production, and has perfect competition and constant returns to scale in the food sector, and monopolistic competition with increasing returns to scale based on fixed costs in the manufacturing sector. Many extensions analyze a much richer and more detailed production structure, allowing for multiple factors of production, more sophisticated firm behavior, intermediate products, horizontal and vertical integration, etc. These changes enrich, in geographical economics, the forward and backward linkages that are considered to be of primary importance in economic geography and development economics.

Type III extensions stress the role of dynamics and expectations in geographical economics. The dynamics of the core model are rather mechanical. Laborers simply relocate at a certain speed based on differences in real wages, which determines the dynamics of the core model and the final degree of agglomeration. This is not a very sophisticated approach, as it does not allow for the economic agents to form expectations about future developments in the economy, and undertake actions based on these expectations. To the extent that these expectations and actions interfere with the location decision, geography may sometimes not be destiny. We discuss the three types of extensions in turn below: section 6.2 focuses on non-neutral space, section 6.3 focuses on the production structure, and section 6.4 focuses on expectations.

6.2   Type I extensions: non-neutral space and transport costs

6.2.1   Space and history

In his thought-provoking, but not undisputed book *The Wealth and Poverty of Nations* the historian David Landes describes the role of geography in the development of countries. Climate, for instance, can be an enormous advantage or disadvantage in the development of regions. As Landes (1998, p. 17) puts it: "Europe does have winters, cold enough to keep down pathogens and pests . . . Endemic disease is present, but nothing like the disablers and killers found in hot lands." In our terminology, the initial conditions were favorable. Landes stresses the fact that, even though initial conditions were good for Europe, it was not enough (p. 29): "Europe was lucky, but luck was only the beginning." More than a thousand years ago "the probability at that point of European global dominance was somewhat around zero" (p. 44). Internal struggles were the reason for this bleak European future, but this was turned around in the Middle Ages with the beginnings of the modern market economy.

Also, in more recent periods, it has been recognized that geography can be a decisive force in the development process. Gallup, Sachs, and Mellinger (1998), for instance, identify large differences in GDP per capita between rich and poor countries, differences that show little sign of narrowing. They note that in 1820 the average GDP per capita in Western Europe was roughly three times larger than in Africa. In 1992 GDP per capita in Western Europe was more than thirteen times higher. Similar comparisons hold for other parts of the world. The most important conclusions of this study are:

- Tropical and landlocked regions are geographically hindered in development.
- Coastal regions and/or regions linked to the coast by navigable waterways are strongly favored in development. This holds especially if the population density (urbanization) is high. Population density might correspond with positive economies of scale. Recent population growth is a negative factor.

Physical geography, so it seems, is a very important factor in the development process. The main criticism centers on the role of transportation. In a comment on Gallup, Sachs, and Mellinger's paper Henderson (1998) stresses the fact that it is not long-distance shipping cost which determines growth, but insufficient investment in infrastructure to link coastal regions with the (landlocked) hinterland. Navigable waterways, for instance, are often not the result of nature or "geography," but of investment in infrastructure.

Despite the discussions on specific issues, the most striking conclusion of economic geography is verified by Gallup, Sachs, and Mellinger (1998) and Landes (1998), namely the concentration of economic activity in specific locations, most notably cities. Many big cities initially developed by having the advantage of easy access to waterways. Why have cities grown at these places? For geographers this poses no great problem. Ports provide easy access to foreign or overseas markets. One could say that the modeling of port-cities is the geographical counterpart of neo-classical trade theory based on comparative advantage; see, for example, Anas, Arnott, and Small (1998), or Fujita and Mori (1996). Each region has a comparative advantage due to, for example, climatic conditions, natural resources, or production factors confined within the borders. Ports or transport nodes provide some locations with a "comparative advantage" in transportation. The question remains why port-cities continue to be important, despite the fact that the transportation system has changed dramatically; waterways are now less important than they once were. If comparative advantage is the major explanation of the existence of port-cities, one would expect these cities to disappear or become less important. Nothing of the sort has happened; this requires an explanation, possibly provided by geographical economics.

A good illustration is the model developed by Fujita and Mori (1996). The model itself is quite complicated, but can easily be understood by analyzing Figure 6.1 (the example is taken from Fujita and Mori, 1996).

The assumptions are as follows. Space is definitely non-neutral. Space is linear in the sense that in each region activity takes place between the river and the mountain range. Space is one-dimensional – homogeneous – and unbounded; as drawn here there are two regions, one on each side of the river (the regions are the two stretches of land between the river and the mountain range). The quality of the land is the same everywhere and is not mobile. Non-land production factors are freely mobile. Here labor is

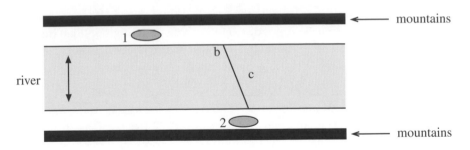

Figure 6.1.   Example of non-neutral space.

the only mobile production factor and each worker is endowed with one unit of labor. A worker can change jobs and location. In principle, regions are identical and the reasons for a cluster of activity to form are the same endogenous forces as described in chapter 3: increasing returns in production, transport costs, market-size effects, and competition effects. Suppose that, because of some initially favorable condition, a cluster of activity has already emerged somewhere, say city 1. This city 1 specializes in manufacturing goods and exports manufactures in exchange for land-intensive imports from both sides of city 1. There are two natural harbors, one at b (with the economic distance from city 1 of b) and one in 2 (this is a potential city in region 2, as will become clear). The economic distance between the two regions is c.

   Now assume that region 1 grows. This will result in a larger city, because agglomeration of manufactured goods production is beneficial; more varieties will be produced without having to import them from elsewhere. This creates a larger market, which stimulates even more agglomeration. As the population grows, more farmland will have to be occupied in order to support the growing city. Eventually, development of farmland in region 2 becomes attractive if the economic distance between region 2 and the city is smaller than the distance from the "marginal" farmland in region 1 to the city; or, where l is the economic distance between the city and the marginal farmland, if $l>b+c$. New farmland in region 2 will be developed on both sides of the port in region 2. Eventually, if the population keeps growing, manufacturing products and farm products will be transported over ever growing distances. At some point new cities will emerge if the (fixed) cost of setting up production is smaller than that of importing manufactured goods.

   The potential locational advantage of ports in this story is obvious (see Box 6.1). What is interesting here is that new cities do not *have* to emerge at ports; self-organizing forces might also stimulate new cities in the same region. It depends on c, the position of b, transport costs in general, and all the other factors that are important in geographical economics. Ports, however, have a natural advantage, because they have an extra *dimension* for trade; they can trade not only on both sides of the port, but also across the river. This is the reason why ports are also known as transport nodes in the geography literature. So, despite the favorable position of ports, non-port cities can still emerge, for example as a result of historical accident. Some examples are identified by Ades and Glaeser (1995), who find evidence that political factors, such as being a capital city which (p. 244) "allows leaders to extract wealth out of the hinterland and distribute it in the capital," are exogenous forces that stimulate city growth. An example of non-neutral space is discussed in chapter 7. Some of its properties are further investigated in chapter 11.

6.2.2 *More on transport costs*

That special features of the landscape can have important effects on the location and emergence of new clusters of economic activity may come as no surprise; special features of the landscape partially translate into specific agglomeration patterns. The intuitive presentation of the model developed by Fujita and Mori (1996) shows that the basic insights of the core model of geographical economics still hold. Some experiments with more complicated transport costs for manufacturing products do not change this conclusion in principle, although the details of the outcome depend, of course, on the precise structure of these transport costs.

Box 6.1. An experiment with non-neutral space: the Stelder approach

Stelder (1998) has implemented the basic model of Krugman (1991a) on non-neutral spaces. Non-neutral space is in his case defined as a grid of *n* locations on a two-dimensional surface. The distance between two locations is calculated as the shortest path, on the assumption that each location on the grid is connected with its direct horizontal and vertical neighbors with distance 1 and with its diagonal neighbors with distance √2 (Figure 6.2).

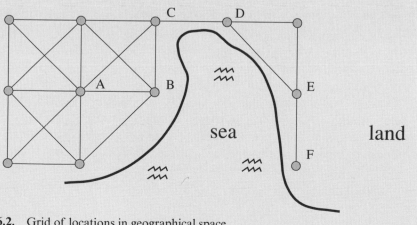

Figure 6.2. Grid of locations in geographical space.

Non-neutral space can now simply be introduced by making "holes" in this grid, for example a sea (Figure 6.2). Assuming no transport across the sea or along the coast, transportation from A to F in the example above would take the route CDE with a total distance of $2 + 2\sqrt{2}$. The model starts with a flat initial distribution in which all locations on the grid are of equal size, an assumption that could be paraphrased as "in the beginning there were only the little villages." The task of the model then is to calculate the optimal distribution of economic activity, given the assumed parameter values for the division of labor between farmers and workers, δ, for the elasticity of substitution, ε, and the distance between grid points. Different parameter configurations result in long-run equilibria with highly asymmetric cities depending on the specific geographical shape of the economy.

The geographical shape of a country is approximated by using a grid resolution as high as possible. Stelder (2000) has built a large geographical grid of Western Europe with over 2,800 locations (see Figure 6.3) in order to find out whether or not the model can simulate the actual city distribution. The enlargements in Figure 6.3 show how sea transport is included by extending the grid with some additional grid-points in the sea. These are part of the network but do not act as potential locations for cities. The model allows for specific costs for transport across land, across sea and in hubs where (un)shipping can take place. In addition, with an extra altitude layer the grid is extended with a third dimension (height). In this way the model can deal with mountains. The shortest distance between grid-points takes these extra transport costs into account when goods have to cross mountains.

Figure 6.4 shows a model run that produces an equilibrium of ninety-four cities with $\delta = 0.5$, $\varepsilon = 5$ and $T = 1.57$.[1] The gray dots are the simulated outcomes and the black dots the ninety-four largest actual cities in 1996. As was to be expected with a flat initial distribution, the model produces an optimal city distribution that is more evenly spread than in reality. Large agglomerations like Paris, London, Madrid, and Rome are not correctly simulated, because population density is for historical reasons higher in the north than in the south. The model predicts too many large cities in Spain and too few cities in the UK, the Netherlands, and Belgium. The results are nevertheless relatively good for Germany. The Ruhrgebiet, Bremen, Berlin, Frankfurt, Stuttgart, and Munich (and also Vienna) are not far from the right place. Some cities in the periphery of various countries also appear in the simulation correctly, like Lille, Rouen, Nantes, Bordeaux, and Nice in France, Lisbon and Porto in Portugal, and Seville and Malaga in Spain.

---

[1] The apparently peculiar choice of T results from a different parameterization used by Stelder, which we have respecified here using our parameterization.

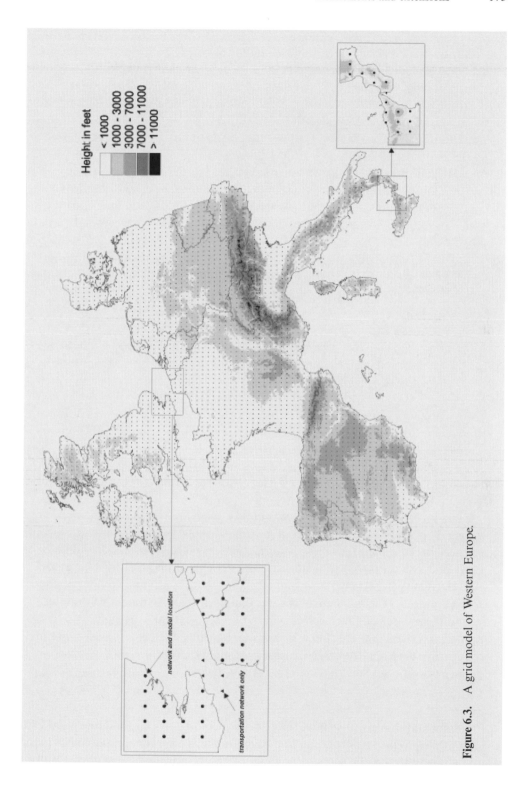

Figure 6.3. A grid model of Western Europe.

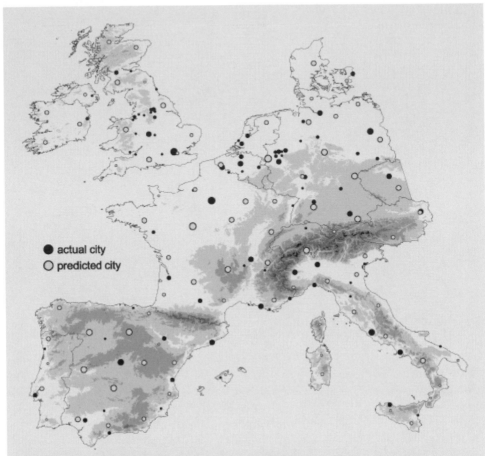

Figure 6.4.   Experimental outcome.

Stelder (2000) points out that these kinds of model results of course *should be* wrong. A good fit would mean "total victory of economics over all other social sciences because then the whole historical process of city formation would be explained with the three parameters δ, ε and T." One of his goals with the model is to clarify to what extent pure economic factors have contributed to the city formation process. The main conclusion is that even the core model can produce very differentiated city hierarchies without any theoretical extensions once it is applied to spaces that are closer to geographic reality. Stelder concludes that in the further development of geographical economics, the "geography" deserves greater priority. See Stelder (2000) for further details.

Fundamental changes arise if we introduce transport costs for food, the good with the immobile production structure. In the core model all the action takes place in the manufacturing sector; the forward linkages of this sector together with the pull or push powers of the labor force determine the strength of agglomerating and spreading forces in the model. Introducing transport costs for food adds an extra spreading force to the model. This may not be immediately obvious, because these transport costs have two effects. First, the region that imports food has a higher wage. This follows from the fact that if both regions produce food, a homogeneous commodity, wages can only differ by the transport cost. In the importing region, say region 1, wages in food will be T times higher than in region 2, where T is the iceberg transport cost for food (see also below). This effect increases the income level in region 1, making it more attractive. Second, the price index also increases, because the cost of living in region 1 increases as a result of the costly import of food. This is an extra spreading force. It turns out that the latter effect dominates the former, because its influence extends to all consumers living in region 1. The main implication of introducing transport costs for food is therefore that, compared to the core model, center–periphery distribution of economic activity is less likely, and spreading is more likely.

More surprising is the consequence of introducing transport costs for food on the so-called home-market effect. Davis (1998) shows that the home-market effect disappears. Recall that the home-market effect arises because the producers of differentiated goods have to choose a location. Locating in the larger market is beneficial because most trade can take place without transport cost. According to the home-market effect, then, the larger region will have a more than proportional share of the differentiated goods, which benefit from economies of scale, and will become an exporter of such goods. The smaller region will be an exporter of food. Davis (1998) shows, by extending the model of Krugman and Venables (1990), that the home-market effect cannot arise in the short-run equilibrium. More specifically, assuming that the larger region exports manufactures and the smaller region exports food, which should be the case if the home-market effect works, leads to a contradiction.

The argumentation is as follows. Since labor is mobile between sectors, wages in the food sector and in the manufacturing sector equalize within a region. Let q^* be the equilibrium amount of a typical manufacturing variety, which as we saw in chapter 3 is calculated as $q^* = \alpha(\varepsilon-1)/\beta$. By choice of units, take $q^*=1$. From the production function it follows that this production level requires $l^* = \alpha + \beta q^* = \alpha + \beta$ labor. Now assume that the larger region sells μ to its own market and delivers $(1-\mu)/T$ to the other region (it ships $(1-\mu)$, and $(1-\mu)/T$ arrives). If this amount is to be produced in the smaller market, total production would have to be equal to $\mu T + (1-\mu)/T = q_s$, say, where the first term reflects the production level needed to ensure that μ units arrive in the larger market. The production level q_s requires $l_s = \alpha + \beta(\mu T + (1-\mu)/T)$ labor. Given equality in the demand structure in both regions, production of manufactured varieties in the larger region can only be viable if the wage bill is lower than in the smaller region. If we let W_l denote the wage in the larger region, and W_s the wage in the smaller region, this is true if $W_l l^* < W_s l_s$, or:

$$W_l(\alpha + \beta) < W_s[\alpha + \beta(\mu T + (1-\mu)/T)] \qquad (6.1)$$

which can be rearranged as

$$\frac{W_l}{W_s} < T\left[\frac{\dfrac{\alpha}{T}+\beta\left(\mu+\dfrac{(1-\mu)}{T^2}\right)}{\alpha+\beta}\right] < T \qquad (*)$$

where the last inequality follows since $T>1$. We can now compare this result with the condition for relative wages if the smaller region exports food. As argued above, the transport costs of food ensure that the importing region has a higher wage rate. Because food is a homogeneous commodity, the price of domestically produced food is the same as the price of imported food in the larger region. The former is equal to the wage rate W_l (perfect competition and constant returns to scale), while the latter is equal to TW_s (also incurring transport costs). Thus, if the smaller region exports food and the larger region also produces food, it follows that $W_l/W_s = T$. This contradicts condition (*) above, so we must conclude that the export of food by the smaller region and the export of manufactures by the larger region are not consistent with each other. The home-market effect does not arise. Allowing for different trade costs for food and manufactures leads to similar conclusions, provided this difference is not too large.

Helpman (1998) develops a variant of this model. Instead of assuming a homogeneous food sector without trade costs, as in chapter 3, or with positive trade costs, as in Davis (1998), he analyzes a non-traded sector, referred to as housing. The advantage of this assumption is that it more closely resembles phenomena studied by regional scientists, who stress the importance of the availability of usable land and of local factors such as climate, good schools, etc. A further advantage is that it deals with the fact that in practice the size of agriculture is simply too small to act as a substantial spreading force. The more important factors are often the non-tradable aspects of a specific region. The consequences for the workings of the model of analyzing a non-tradable housing sector (with mobile workers) rather than a tradable food sector (with immobile workers) are substantial. Suppose that each region has a fixed amount of housing, which is non-tradable. Consumers buy differentiated products and pay for housing. The higher the labor supply in a region, the higher is the number of locally supplied varieties of differentiated products. This raises the living standard of the region. However, in more densely populated regions housing is more expensive, thus lowering the standard of living. These two forces determine the final equilibrium, in which the standard of living is equal for the regions. In general, the housing sector in the Helpman model provides a more powerful spreading force than the food sector in the core model, leading to less agglomeration and to cities of unequal size. Essential in the Helpman model is that, in contrast to the core model, increased demand for non-tradables in the larger region increases its price, and thereby reduces the attractiveness of the region. In the core model, the price of the homogeneous good does not increase in the larger region since food can be traded between regions without costs. As discussed in chapter 5, it is this aspect which ensures that the interpretation of the no-black-hole condition is reversed. The Helpman (1998) extension makes the model more suitable for empirical research than the core model, such that research based on this approach has been extensively discussed in chapter 5.

This section has briefly discussed some aspects of non-neutral space and transport costs. In most cases, the basic insights of the core model still hold, although usually not quite as dramatically. Natural advantages, for example, can give a location a head start in attracting a substantial share of manufacturing production, but the endogenous forces of the core model still play a substantial role. Similarly, the introduction of a non-tradable local sector, such as housing, tends to provide a powerful spreading force, which makes complete agglomeration unlikely. Some of the details of the extensions of the core model require more attention for empirical interpretation. The most vivid example is the correct interpretation of the no-black-hole condition in the core model and in the Helpman model. It is therefore essential in empirical work correctly to apply and interpret different versions of the geographical economics approach. More detailed investigations into the precise roles of hubs, congestion, non-tradables, and differentiated transport costs in geographical economics are clearly necessary.

6.3 Type II extensions: production structure and geography

Type II extensions of the core model of geographical economics focus on the production structure. In the core model this structure is very simple, using only labor as a factor of production, with perfect competition and constant returns to scale in the food sector, and monopolistic competition with increasing returns to scale based on fixed costs in the manufacturing sector. There are essentially three versions of type II extensions. Version 1 modifies the production function in the manufacturing sector itself, allowing for more factors of production or other aspects that may be empirically relevant. This is one of the most fruitful approaches, which we will also use in chapters 7 (cities), 9 (trade), and 10 (growth). A brief example, essentially an introduction to chapter 7, is discussed below. Version 2 of type II extensions introduces interactions in the manufacturing production process. These extensions, also used in chapter 9 (trade), change the way in which factors of production and commodities are combined, and enrich the forward and backward linkages. We will describe an example of a version 2 extension in some detail below. Version 3 allows for more sophisticated firm behavior, with more stages in the decision process, and possibly more strategic considerations. We will encounter an example of this version in chapter 8 (multinationals), when we discuss horizontal and vertical integration.

A simple example of a version 1, type II extension, changing the production function for manufactures, and hence the cost function, is provided by Brakman *et al.* (1996). Arguing that negative feedbacks in the economy, such as the costs of congestion, may be a rationale for the viability of small economic centers, they adapt the production function of manufactures as follows: $l_{ij} = \alpha(N_j) + \beta(N_j)x_i$, where l_{ij} is the amount of labor required in region j to produce x_i units of a variety, and N_j is the number of manufacturing producers located in region j. As in the core model, there are increasing returns to scale at the firm level, resulting from fixed labor costs $\alpha(N_j)$ and marginal labor costs $\beta(N_j)$. This time, however, these costs may vary between regions, in particular according to the number of manufacturing producers N_j located in region j.[2] Note that the production function for manufactures now varies between regions even if there are no technological differences, as long as the number of firms located in the regions is different. In this way, one can deal with special factors determining the cost of production, for example by including positive knowledge spillovers (the cost components α and/or β fall if N_j increases), which introduces an extra agglomerating force into the model. Alternatively, as stressed by Brakman et al. (1996), one can include negative feedbacks (the cost components α and/or β rise if N_j increases) because clustering of economic activity causes congestion, long travel time, high costs of establishment, etc. The congestion case is particularly interesting, as it allows for the economic viability of small centers of activity. This gives rise to the simultaneous existence of regions/cities of different sizes in equilibrium. The latter is a prerequisite for a theoretical model that wants to explain the rank–size distribution of cities as discussed for India in chapter 1. This issue is addressed in Brakman et al. (1999) and in chapter 7, building on Brakman et al. (1996).

We now discuss a version 2 extension in somewhat more detail. A large share of a manufacturing firm's output is not sold as a final good to the consumer, but as an intermediate input to other firms. Indeed, for many firms the greater part of their output, or even all of it, is sold to other firms as an intermediate input. This holds even more strongly for producer services firms, providing a substantial share of total employment in developed economies. In his seminal paper, Ethier (1982) shows that the incorporation of intermediate production in the monopolistic competition framework of Dixit and Stiglitz (1977) is relatively easy. It turns out that this provides a different channel for agglomeration. In principle, the changes to the core model are minimal. Assume that each firm uses an intermediate (composite) good, that itself is an aggregate of all manufactures. Assuming that this aggregate is simply a CES aggregate of all manufacturing firms and is identical to the sub-utility (3.4) in chapter 3, implying that we can use the same price index as defined in (3.6), we only have to change two main equations. First, the unit marginal costs of a firm no longer equals W (omitting indices, because all firms are symmetrical), but $W' = W^{\mu'}I^{1-\mu'}$, where the shares μ' and $(1-\mu')$ indicate the (newly defined) Cobb–Douglas cost shares of labor and manufactures, respectively. Second, demand for manufactures comes not only from labor but also from firms, who use it as an intermediate production factor. This means that the income terms in equation (3.6), δY, change to $E = \delta Y + \mu'Npx$. Spending on manufactures comes from consumers, who as before spend δY on manufactures, and from N firms who spend a fraction μ' of their earnings, px, on manufactures. Now W' replaces W in (3.12) and E replaces all income terms δY. After these changes the analysis proceeds essentially as before.[3]

---

[2] Other specifications, such as fixed or marginal costs in a region depending on the total production level in that region, are of course also possible. This does not alter the analysis in an essential way.

[3] This extension, intermediate inputs, is by now so common in the geographical economics literature that it is looked upon as the second core model; see Neary (2001) and Krugman (2000).

These intermediate production structures are used by Krugman and Venables (1990, 1995), and Venables (1996). One of the advantages of intermediate deliveries is that it can preserve the general structure and characteristics of geographical economics models, and simultaneously allow for labor immobility between countries, a central assumption in international trade theory (see also chapter 9). Firms like to be close to each other not only because of demand linkages through the supply of labor, or pecuniary externalities due to endogenous consumer market sizes, but also because of input-output linkages. This is what Hirschman (1958) meant when he wrote about forward and backward linkages between firms. The central idea is that upstream and downstream firms can benefit from each other. A downstream industry can provide an upstream linkage. If the production of the upstream industry is characterized by increasing returns to scale, an increase in demand for its products induces this firm to produce at a more efficient level of production, which in turn makes the downstream industry more cost-efficient. It is important to note that the agglomeration forces are to some extent different from the core model, where migration of mobile laborers leads to an increase in the number of firms and market size. Here labor is assumed to be immobile between regions, and workers must be pulled away from other sectors of production within a region. This leads to firms each demanding more intermediate products, thus providing a larger market for intermediate goods. The implications of this model are in many respects similar to those of the core model.

The example given by Krugman and Venables (1995) nicely illustrates what happens. This model is closely linked to the core model of chapter 3 by assuming that the upstream and downstream (imperfectly competitive) industries are identical. Furthermore, they assume that the output of this industry is both the final good sold to consumers, as well as an intermediate input to all other firms. Suppose that in a two-country model transport costs decline, starting off from a very high level, and that for some reason the spreading of the manufacturing sector is not symmetric over both countries. As transport costs are lowered the larger market becomes more attractive for the production of intermediate goods. This occurs not only because of the high demand for intermediate products, but also because the production of final goods will become more cost-efficient, which increases the (real) wage of consumers in this region. Below some critical level of transport costs an industrial core and a periphery develop. In the absence of international labor mobility this core–periphery pattern is characterized by a divergence of real wages between the two countries (not within countries, because labor can move between sectors). This difference in labor costs makes the periphery more attractive as transport costs become smaller; being close to the larger market becomes less important when transport costs become relatively small. Thus, the manufacturing sector eventually has an incentive to move out of the economic core and into the periphery. This will set in motion an equalization of real wage rates, suggesting that, in the end, history is not destiny.

Knaap (2000) generalizes the Krugman and Venables (1995) approach by assuming that firms can use various intermediate inputs from various industries in a multi-industry setting, with each industry consisting of many firms. At one extreme, some industries only use labor as an input; at the other, some industries use inputs from all industries (including from itself) as well as labor. All intermediate cases, with industries using inputs from a selection of other industries, can also occur. Knaap shows that in this setting, with all types of industries present, the "history of the world" according to Krugman and Venables becomes less likely. Firms using the outputs of many other industries as inputs tend to be located in the center region, as it avoids the extra costs of transportation and provides a large market at the same time. Firms that do not use any of the outputs of others as inputs have an incentive to locate in the periphery, where labor is cheap because the demand for labor is small. Firms that use only a small part of the output of other industries as an input, have an incentive to locate in the region housing firms producing the necessary inputs for this firm, or on the periphery where labor is cheap, as labor comprises a large part of total costs for these firms. In general the extent of core–periphery patterns is considerably weaker in this setting than in Krugman and Venables (1995).

Box 6.2.   Geographical economics and globalization

As discussed in chapter 2 (see, in particular, Box 2.3), the factor abundance model has been used extensively in recent years to analyze the impact of globalization on labor markets. In particular, the factor abundance model predicts that globalization will hurt the position of low-skilled labor in the OECD countries, to the extent that increased manufacturing imports from non-OECD countries will lead to a decrease in low-skilled wages compared to high-skilled wages in the OECD countries. The empirical evidence indeed shows that manufacturing imports from non-OECD countries has grown relatively fast; see OECD (1997). But empirical evidence also indicates that this trend coincides with very different labor market experiences for the low-skilled workers across the OECD countries. In particular, in countries with a flexible labor market, like the UK and the USA, the relative wages of low-skilled laborers have decreased significantly. But this is not the case in many continental European countries; see the data on the relative income distribution for Germany and the Netherlands in Table 6.1. For this group of countries, characterized by rigid labor markets and sticky wages, the impact of globalization does not show up in relative wage changes, but predominantly in an increase in the relative unemployment of low-skilled laborers (Dewatripont *et al.*, 1999). By comparing the growth rates of the first and the ninth decile (at the bottom and the top of the income distribution, respectively) over a ten-year period, Table 6.1 shows that this income distribution has become more uneven in the USA and in the UK. The opposite is true in Germany, while the income distribution in the Netherlands (already relatively flat) remained more or less the same.

Against this background one should amend the factor abundance model in

Table 6.1. *Growth in real earnings per income decile*

	1st decile		9th decile	
	5 years	10 years	5 years	10 years
USA (1995)	−7.4	−7.2	−2.1	3.1
UK (1996)	4.9	13.8	9.1	24.9
Germany (1994)	30.8	59.6	11.7	21.5
Netherlands (1994)	3.5	8.3	2.7	9.9

Source: OECD, 1997. Changes over 5 and 10 year periods (%); the year in parentheses is the last year of observation; 1st decile: lower end of income distribution; 9th decile: upper end of income distribution.

order to cope with at least three types of economies. This should include a developing economy that has a comparative advantage in low-skilled products, and two types of developed economies, one with a rigid labor market, for example with a fixed minimum wage for low-skilled labor, and one with a flexible labor market; see Krugman (1995c) or Davis (1998). However, the factor abundance model performs poorly "in almost every imaginable way" (Trefler and Zhu, 2000, p. 145). We can conclude that other models might be better suited to analyzing the phenomena surrounding globalization, which to a large extent takes place in an environment in which distance is a dominant factor in determining trade patterns. Almost without exception, the simple gravity model performs better in tests than the factor abundance model. Ideally, a model analyzing globalization should deal with this. Geographical economics constitutes therefore an interesting alternative trade model.

A first attempt to use geographical economics for the analysis of globalization is Krugman and Venables (1995), discussed in this section. They show that the impact of globalization (using a fall in transport costs as a proxy) on relative (real) wages is non-linear; relative real wages in the periphery first fall and then rise again as transport costs decline. This insight is important, because it helps us to understand why OECD countries differ with respect to the impact of globalization. In addition, this model shows that cross-country differences are not necessarily the result of differences in wage flexibility, since wages are flexible throughout the model, but may arise from differences in agglomeration and spreading forces that are central to the geographical economics approach. In the Krugman–Venables model there is, however, only one type of transport costs, only one type of labor, and the labor market always clears. This limits the relevance of the model, if only because the focus is (inevitably) on the relative wage *between* countries and (see above) not on the relative wage *within* countries.

It is possible to extend the Krugman and Venables (1995) analysis in a number of ways. If we stick to a production structure in which intermediate goods are used to produce final manufactures, and we add multiple transport costs, two types of labor (low and high-skilled), and experiment somewhat with the degree of wage flexibility, the following conclusions emerge with respect to the impact of globalization on labor markets.[4] First, the impact of globalization turns out to depend critically not only on the level of transport costs, but also on the type of product for which transport costs are reduced. Similarly, the impact depends on the flexibility of wages and the initial distribution of low-skilled and high-skilled labor. This is in contrast with the factor abundance model, where the only relevant variable is the relative difference in factor endowments between countries. Second, in the geographical economics model globalization is not always bad news for the low-skilled. Specifically, as the globalization process continues (for example, as transport costs continue to fall) the plight of the low-skilled (either in terms of relative wages or unemployment) improves. This suggests that the adverse effect of globalization on low-skilled labor may be temporary; see Wood (1998).

6.4   Type III extensions: the burden of history and the role of expectations

The existence of multiple equilibria is one of the prominent characteristics of the geographical economics approach. The reasons for multiple equilibria are to be found in the non-linear nature of the equilibrium equations, which are based on pecuniary externalities, internal economies of scale, imperfect competition, and love-of-variety. At least to some extent a specific location becomes more attractive if economic activity increases. Sometimes these equilibria are identical from a global welfare point of view; sometimes they are not. Chapter 7 gives many illustrations of the omnipresence of multiple equilibria. The obvious question is, of course, which equilibrium actually gets established. It appears that basically two factors determine the evolution of the economy and the determination of a specific long-run equilibrium; see Krugman (1991c).

First, as discussed in the first part of this chapter, history can be decisive. The term "history" is used here in a very broad sense, and can imply differences in, for example, tastes, technology, or factor endowments. Past circumstances could have a decisive influence on the initial conditions. In his famous, but not undisputed, QWERTY keyboard example, David (1985) argues that relatively small, and at first sight unimportant, factors can mean that certain technologies become "locked in," that is, the initial advantage of a certain technology is almost impossible to overcome by new technolo-

---

[4] For the production structure we refer to De Vaal and Van den Berg (1999) and for the application of this geographical economics model to globalization to Peeters and De Vaal (2000), and Peeters and Garretsen (2000). Final manufactures are produced using two inputs, namely intermediate manufacturing goods and producer services. Both inputs are tradable at input-specific transport costs.

gies (see also Figure 2.5 in chapter 2); in this case, the technology is the QWERTY keyboard layout of typewriters. His example serves to illustrate the importance of historical accident. It is relatively easy to come up with other examples of the same principle, for example the fate of competitive tape recording systems in the early days of video cassette recorders, where the VHS system clearly won, although many experts argued that other systems were technically superior. In a similar fashion, Brakman and Garretsen (1993) discuss the fate of East Germany compared to that of West Germany; here the important role of history (the Berlin Wall) is of course apparent. See also chapter 5.[5]

Second, expectations may be the most important force determining which specific long-run equilibrium gets established. Expectations become particularly important if one takes future earnings into consideration when making decisions. In the examples given above, the initial conditions determine the fate of an equilibrium; new entrants only look at the present situation, and then decide what to do. In expectation-driven equilibria, the importance of future earnings is decisive. This holds, for example, for the role of computer technologies in the so-called new economy discussion, where network externalities are most important. The optimal choice in adopting a new technology depends crucially on what you expect other people will decide to use. The wider a specific technology is adopted, the easier it is to exchange information with other people, and the more attractive this technology becomes. For example, if all other economists use MS Word to write papers, it is easiest for you to do the same, since it makes it simpler for you to exchange information and work together. On the other hand, if all other economists use WordPerfect, it is best for you to also use WordPerfect, and similarly for Scientific Word, etc. The desirability of making a specific choice, therefore, depends on how many others make the same choice and increases with the number of participants. These technology-related network structures result in the possibility of multiple equilibria, in which the outcome is purely a self-fulfilling prophecy; see Krugman (1991c, p. 654).

In the finance literature, it is well known that the models described above can result in (speculative) bubbles or bank runs; see Obstfeld and Rogoff (1996). These models allow for various equilibria, in which not only panics or bank runs but also the absence of such a bank run or panic are possible outcomes. The questions then arise whether a change in expectations can change the equilibrium, and thus cause a panic, and of what determines drastic changes in expectations, and the associated collective behavior of the economic agents. An action of a small investor is often not enough to change the behavior of the "market"; usually nothing happens following the action of an individual small investor, who is unable to change the sentiment in the market. However, an action of a large and influential market-maker, someone like the wealthy speculator (and philanthropist) George Soros, might change the attitude of a large number of investors in a specific market. Actions of such large and influential market-makers

---

[5] For an entertaining collection of examples in which historical accident, initial conditions, and the successive arrival of newcomers in the market determine the final equilibrium, see Schelling (1978).

might determine a specific market outcome or equilibrium, at least if this is considered to be within reasonable bounds by other economic agents in the market. Henderson and Mitra (1996) and Becker and Henderson (2000), for example, also introduce a so-called "large agent," in order to get rid of the indeterminacy of self-organization. These agents are nationally small, but are assumed to control their individual cities. Without such a city developer many equilibria are possible, and in general the outcome will not be efficient. Sometimes, local governments can play this role, if they have the power to determine land use and initiate new projects and thereby balance the interests of various economic agents. To date, very few empirical results exist to help determine whether expectations dominate history or vice versa. Harris and Ioannides (2000) is a first attempt in this direction. History is in principle a strong force but this by no means precludes a strong role for expectations. Harris and Ionannides extend the core model by introducing housing and land explicitly. Furthermore, they assume that labor is forward-looking and workers are able to calculate the present value of wages in a specific city. The migration decisions of workers influence the prices of land and housing, and therefore the expectation of the population in a specific city is reflected in the prices of land and housing and thus influences the calculation of the present values. Conclusions can only be drawn with caution, but, in general, they find for the United States, that "history rules and expectations at best helps history along" (Harris and Ioannides, 2000, p. 11).

The distinction between history and expectations is as such easy to grasp. Difficulties arise, however, if one tries to incorporate these phenomena formally into models with increasing returns and multiple equilibria. This is illustrated by the reaction of Fukao and Benabou (1993) to Krugman (1991c), in which they identify an "error" made by Krugman; they show that rational workers can gain by deviating from the "equilibrium" path identified by Krugman, which is therefore not an equilibrium path. To model the dynamic properties in a geographical economics model is the real challenge, it deals with issues of global stability in non-linear models, which is highly intractable. The models we have discussed in the previous chapters all had in common that the dynamics were *ad hoc*, and not based on forward-looking or rational expectations. Dynamic models such as Krugman (1991c) give up the pecuniary externalities in favor of technological externalities, which are easier to model. But, as we have explained at length, pecuniary externalities are an attractive feature of geographical economics, because they arise endogenously. We would like to incorporate these externalities as well as forward-looking behavior.

This problem is essentially solved by Ottaviano (1999), in a somewhat simpler version of the core model of chapter 3. He shows that lock-in effects can be challenged if the initial advantage of the larger region is not too big, and if trade or migration costs are low enough. The attractive feature of his model is that he motivates the migration decision of workers in the manufacturing sector. Migration is assumed to be costly; the larger the migration flow, the larger the migration costs. One might consider this to be a negative externality on the other migrants. Potential migrants move to another region if the discounted value of the future utility of working in the other

Table 6.2. *Overview of extensions*

Extension	Focuses on	Examples discussed in
Type I	Transport costs and non-neutral space	Chapters 7 and 11
Type II	Production structure	Chapters 7–9
	Version 1 Production function	Chapters 7 and 9
	Version 2 Interactions in production	Chapter 9
	Version 3 Firm behavior	Chapter 8
Type III	Dynamics and expectations	Chapter 10

region minus the costs of migration is larger than the discounted value of the future utility of staying put. If the economies are not too different, the expected path will also be the actual path. In such cases, history is not destiny.

Finally, Baldwin (1999) reaches a similar conclusion, and also shows that the standard (*ad hoc*) migration behavior in geographical economics is consistent with optimal behavior, subject to quadratic migration costs and static expectations. The often-criticized migration equation in the core model is therefore not as primitive as sometimes believed. The relative importance of history versus expectations crucially depends on adjustment costs, and as such might turn out to be mainly an empirical matter. Migration costs in Europe are often thought to be higher than those in the United States, mainly as a result of larger differences in language, historical background, and culture.

6.5 Conclusions

The core model of geographical economics has been extended and improved upon in a number of interesting directions since it was developed by Krugman in 1991. Changes in, and extensions of, the core model usually focus on characteristics that can be adapted to better describe stylized facts, or shed new light on familiar problems. A few important building blocks of the core model have hardly been touched, such as firm-specific economies of scale, imperfect competition, pecuniary externalities, and the Dixit–Stiglitz monopolistic competition framework, with its associated love-of-variety effect. We have given a broad overview of three different types of extensions, briefly discussing some examples of each type along the way. Type I extensions concern transport costs and the modeling of non-neutral space. Type II extensions adapt and enrich the production structure of the model, where we identified three different versions, focusing on the production function, interactions in production, and firm behavior, respectively. Type III extensions analyze the role of dynamics and expectations in geographical economics. We will analyze and discuss examples of each type of extension in more detail in chapters 7–11 below. Table 6.2 gives a summary of the types of extensions, and an overview of what to expect where.

Although the extensions and generalizations of the core model, as discussed above and to be discussed in the chapters to come, add a lot more detail and realism to the core model, which allows us to shed new light on old problems and more easily apply the model to empirical problems and phenomena, it is important to realize that the most important insights of the core model basically hold for all extensions. To mention just a few of these insights: (i) the existence of multiple equilibria, (ii) the role of initial conditions in determining which equilibrium is established in the long run, (iii) the sub-optimality of some long-run equilibria, (iv) the endogenous determination of location decisions based on the interaction of economies of scale, imperfect competition, pecu-niary externalities, monopolistic competition, and love-of-variety, (v) the importance of pecuniary externalities in establishing an equilibrium, and (vi) the possibility, in principle at least (see chapter 11), to influence the future development of the economy as a result of policy actions.

Exercises

6.1 Figure 6.1 suggests that port-cities have a natural advantage over other cities in the sense that they have an extra "dimension" to trade, compared to "landlocked" cities. Can you find evidence that port-cities are indeed on average larger than other types of cities (distinguish between landlocked cities and cities along rivers)?

6.2 In practice almost all commodities are costly to trade. The study by Davis (1998) suggests that in that case the home-market effect probably vanishes. Can you find evidence that this is indeed the case? *Hint*: Are large countries net exporters of commod-ities produced under firm-specific scale economies (use intra-industry trade figures as an indication)?

6.3 The QWERTY story has served as the prime illustratation of the importance of initial conditions in reaching a particular equilibrium. The often implicit assumption is that such an equilibrium is possibly not the most efficient one. Although convincing as a story it is not always the case, even in the QWERTY example. The idea can also be found surrounding information and communication technologies, because these technologies are inherently characterized by increasing returns to scale. Try to find evi-dence that QWERTY might not be that bad, or that "networks" may not always be characterized by increasing returns to scale (just to convince yourself that you have to be careful listening to stories).

6.4 In the USA and the UK the relative wages of low-skilled labor have decreased significantly in the last twenty years or so (see Table 6.1). This has not happened in many continental European countries. Use the discussion in Box 6.2 to explain why this different development might still have occurred even if labor markets in continen-tal Europe had been as flexible as labor markets in the USA and the UK. *Hint*: Use the crucial feature of geographical economics models that the relationship between rela-tive wages and transport costs is non-linear.

7 Cities and congestion: the economics of Zipf's Law

7.1 Introduction

Typically, the long-run equilibrium allocation of footloose economic activity in the core model of geographical economics is characterized either by complete agglomeration or by even spreading. Which equilibrium is established depends critically on the initial distribution of the manufacturing labor force and a few structural parameters, such as the level of transport costs, the elasticity of substitution, and the share of income spent on manufactures. If transport costs, for example, are relatively low, the spreading equilibrium is unstable and agglomeration is the stable long-run equilibrium. Our simulations in chapter 4 with the core model of geographical economics clearly illustrate this; see Figures 4.2 and 4.3. Nevertheless, for many parameter settings the agglomeration forces are stronger than the one spreading force in the core model, the demand for manufactured goods from the immobile labor force (the farm workers). This has been discussed in section 4.10, which generalizes the core model to a racetrack economy, thus allowing for many locations in neutral space. We argued essentially that the forces of agglomeration are so strong in the racetrack economy that economic activity is typically concentrated in one, or only a few, locations. Moreover, if the economy is concentrated in two or three locations, the distribution of economic activity is evenly spread among those locations.

Both facts are hard to reconcile with empirical observations. In reality, we observe at various levels of aggregation multiple centers of economic activity, which differ considerably in size (measured by the share in manufacturing production or the share of the mobile labor force). This is particularly true for the size distributions of cities within a country; see the rank–size distribution for India discussed in chapter 1. The core model of geographical economics has little to say on this, and consequently is ill-suited to deal with a central topic in urban economics: the characteristics of city-size distributions. The balance between the agglomeration and spreading forces in the core model precludes the analysis of an urban system, because it does not allow for an outcome in which large and small centers of economic activity coexist.

This chapter has three objectives. First, it analyzes an extension of the core model of geographical economics, as discussed in chapter 6. In the terminology of chapter 6, the main focus is on a version 1, type II extension (adapting the production structure of the core model by altering the production function for manufactures). At the end of this chapter, however, we also briefly discuss non-neutral space, a type I extension. The second objective of this chapter is to show how the inclusion of an additional spreading force in the core model, namely congestion, changes the nature of the long-run equilibrium allocation of economic activity across space. Following modern urban economics (see section 2.2.1), the introduction of congestion costs or, more generally, of external diseconomies of scale, implies that agglomeration of economic activity is associated with disadvantages to the extent that agglomeration also implies limited local space and resources. The third objective of this chapter is to apply the core model with congestion to the ultimate empirical regularity of city-size distributions, which is thought to hold for many nations, namely Zipf's Law or, in its more general form, the rank–size distribution. We explain the difference between these two terms in section 7.3 below.

This chapter is organized as follows. In section 7.2 we briefly explain how congestion can be introduced in the core model and, subsequently, how the introduction of this additional spreading force alters the workings of the model. Section 7.3 discusses city-size distributions by evaluating attempts to measure Zipf's Law. We also provide our own data analysis on city-size distributions for a large range of countries, providing the requirements that theoretical explanations for Zipf's Law should meet. In section 7.4 we return to the core model with congestion. Most importantly, we use simulations to show how this model can give rise to city-size distributions in accordance with the empirical facts of Zipf's Law. We also compare our explanation with other explanations for Zipf's Law. Section 7.5 concludes. Before we start our inquiry into congestion and city-size distributions, Box 7.1 first gives some background information on the relevance of urbanization and congestion.

Box 7.1.   Urbanization and congestion[1]

According to the World Bank's *World Development Indicators,* 46% of the world's population lived in urban areas in 1998, compared to 40% in 1980. For the middle- and high-income countries these percentages were higher: 65% in 1980 and 77% in 1998. Table 7.1 lists the urban percentage of the population for all countries above 75% in 1998.

Table 7.1 shows that with a few exceptions a level of urbanization of 75% or more is largely confined to the developed countries, Latin America and a number of oil-exporting countries.[2] The outcome should be interpreted with some care because the definitions of urban areas differ across countries; for example, these

---

[1] The data in this box come from the World Bank website at http: //www.worldbank.org
[2] Two city-states, Hong Kong and Singapore, are not included as the urban area coincides with the country.

Table 7.1. *Urban population as a percentage of total population, 1998*

Argentina	89	Germany	87	Russian Federation	77
Australia	85	Israel	91	Saudi Arabia	85
Belgium	97	Japan	79	Spain	77
Brazil	80	South Korea	80	Sweden	83
Canada	77	Kuwait	97	United Arab Emirates	85
Chile	85	Lebanon	89	United Kingdom	89
Cuba	75	Libya	87	United States	77
Czech Republic	75	Netherlands	89	Uruguay	91
Denmark	85	New Zealand	86	Venezuela	86
France	75	Norway	75		
Gabon	79	Oman	81		

Source: World Bank, *World Development Indicators 2000*, Table 3.10.

definitions underestimate the degree of urbanization for China and India. Also, population size alone does not determine the economic relevance of urban agglomeration. Nevertheless, the message from these and similar data is clear and reinforces the conclusion of chapter 1: urbanization is a highly relevant phenomenon that cannot be neglected. It is also clear from the data that within countries the urban population does not live only in a few mega-cities. In the *World Development Report 1999/2000,* the World Bank shows that 63.5% of the world's urban population lived in small and medium-sized cities (population less than 1 million) in 1995, whereas 21.4% lived in large cities (population between 1 and 5 million), and "only" 15.1% lived in mega-cities (population above 5 million). A theory of urban location should therefore also be able to explain the simultaneous existence of cities of varying size. Of course, this is not to say that very large cities are not important (see Box 7.3). In the twentieth century the number of mega-cities increased greatly; in 1900, only London, with a population of 6.5 million, had passed the threshold of 5 million, whereas in 2000 there were sixteen cities with populations exceeding 10 million. Also, the fact that most people around the world live in urban areas helps to explain why in reality the main spreading force in the core model of geographical economics, the demand for manufactures from farm workers in the peripheral regions, is probably not very strong and that in this respect the Helpman (1998) model discussed in chapters 5 and 6 may be preferred.

A major drawback of urban agglomeration is to be found in congestion, which can arise in many different ways, such as limited physical space, limited local resources (such as water for cooling processes), environmental pollution (which may require extra investment), and heavy usage of roads, communication channels, and storage facilities. Congestion and the resulting costs are difficult to

Table 7.2. *Congestion: number of motor vehicles, selected countries*

	Vehicles per 1,000 people		Vehicles per kilometer of road	
	1980	1998	1980	1998
Belgium	349	485	28	33
Finland	288	448	18	30
France	402	530	27	35
Germany	399	522	51	69
Italy	334	591	65	108
Netherlands	343	421	—	57
Poland	86	273	10	28
Spain	239	467	120	54
UK	303	439	50	67

Source: World Bank, *World Development Indicators 2000*, Table 3.12.

measure, but one way to quantify congestion is to look at a specific example for which data are readily available: traffic congestion. Table 7.2 illustrates that the increase in urban agglomeration went along with an increase in the number of motor vehicles (per 1,000 people and per kilometer of road) between 1980 and 1998 for a number of European countries.

Not only has the number of motor vehicles increased, but so has the number of vehicles per kilometer of road, with the exception of Spain. This clearly points to an increase in congestion.[3] By and large a similar picture emerges for other countries (developed and less developed). Reliable estimates of the costs of traffic congestion and other forms of congestion are hard to come by, but it is not doubted that these costs are considerable. Henderson, Shalizi, and Venables (2000) report that world-wide, on average, housing prices are more than 100% higher in an urban agglomeration of 5 million people than in one of 100,000 people.

7.2   Congestion as an additional spreading force[4]

The idea that urban agglomeration, driven by positive external economies, may itself give rise to external diseconomies of scale is, of course, not new. Indeed, in section 2.2 we have already noted that in modern urban economics the main spreading forces are

---

[3] As Spain illustrates, more vehicles need not imply more congestion, in terms of number of vehicles per kilometer of road, if more roads become available at the same time. Conversely, in Poland, after the communist era, road capacity has not kept pace with the strong increase of motor vehicles, leading almost to a tripling of the number of vehicles per kilometer of road.

[4] This section is based on Brakman *et al.* (1996).

precisely external diseconomies of scale, which accompany urban agglomeration. When cities get larger they start to suffer from increasing commuting costs, and higher land or housing rents; see Box 7.1. The costs involved can be quite substantial. For example, according to Arnott and Small (1994), the annual cost of driving delays in the USA alone is about $48 billion or $640 per driver. Similarly, land rents also depend on the relative size of a city. In chapters 5 and 6 we briefly discussed the geographical economics model used by Hanson (1998) and Helpman (1998), where the only spreading force is the increase in regional housing prices as more firms and workers move to a region. External diseconomies of scale also arise from environmental pollution or the drawbacks of crowdedness in general. We will refer to all these diseconomies of scale as examples of congestion, and will not discriminate between the various forms of congestion, because our aim is to analyze the consequences of congestion rather than its origin. The direct consequence of congestion is straightforward since it provides an incentive for firms and mobile workers to relocate from the congested centers to the relatively uncluttered periphery. What is less obvious is how exactly the introduction of congestion affects the equilibrium allocation of firms and workers across space or, in other words, how it affects the balance between agglomeration and spreading forces. To answer this question we must return to the core model of geographical economics.

7.2.1   The modeling of congestion

In the core model, the manufacturing production function is characterized by internal increasing returns to scale. The production structure of the core model can be easily adapted to introduce congestion costs. As briefly discussed in chapter 6, the main idea is that the congestion costs that each firm faces depend on the overall size of the location of production. The size of city r is measured by the total number of manufacturing firms N_r in that city. Congestion costs are thus not industry- or firm-specific, but solely a function of the size of the city as a whole. The specification we use here is somewhat simpler than in Brakman *et al.* (1996):[5]

$$l_{ir} = N_r^{\tau/(1-\tau)}(\alpha + \beta x_i), \qquad -1 < \tau < 1 \tag{7.1}$$

where l_{ir} is the amount of labor required in city r to produce x_i units of a variety, and the parameter τ represents external economies of scale. There are no location-specific external economies of scale if $\tau = 0$. In this case, equation (7.1) reduces to the production function of the core model; see chapter 3. There are positive location-specific external economies if $-1 < \tau < 0$. Such a specification could be used to model, for example, learning-by-doing spillovers. For our present purposes, the case of negative location-specific external economies arising from congestion are relevant, in which case $0 < \tau < 1$. This is illustrated in Figure 7.1.

---

[5] This specification simplifies equations (7.2)–(7.4) considerably. Other specifications, such as dependence of costs on the total production level in a city, are also possible. This does not alter the analysis in any important way. The main advantage of equation (7.1) is that it provides a very general specification for congestion (=negative externalities).

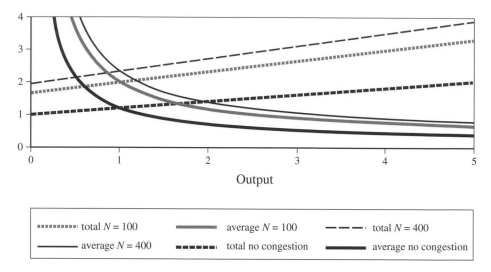

Figure 7.1. Total and average labor costs with congestion (parameter values: $\alpha = 1$; $\beta = 0.2$; $\tau = 0.1$ for $N = 100$ and $N = 400$, $\tau = 0$ for "no congestion").

If the parameter τ lies between 0 and 1 each manufacturing firm i in city r is confronted with a cost increase if other firms also decide to locate in this city. As Figure 7.1 shows, a rise in the number of firms located in city r, raises the fixed and marginal costs of producing in city r, and therefore also the average costs of production. This can be compared in Figure 7.1 to "no congestion," in which case $\tau = 0$ and congestion does not arise. As with any other external effect, we assume that each individual firm does not take into account that its location decision has an impact on the production functions, and thus indirectly on the decision processes, of all the other manufacturing firms.

To keep the analysis tractable, this is the only modification we make in the core model. We must now retrace all the steps taken in chapter 3 when deriving the short-run equilibrium of the core model to see how the introduction of congestion costs affects each step. Details of this process can be found on the website for this book, which also reproduces the normalization analysis of chapter 4 for the core model with congestion. Equations (7.2)–(7.4) give the short-run equilibrium, incorporating the congestion modification of equation (7.1).

$$Y_r = \delta \lambda_r W_r + (1 - \delta)\phi_r \tag{7.2}$$

$$I_r = \left(\sum_{s=1}^{R} \lambda_s^{1-\tau\varepsilon} T_{rs}^{1-\varepsilon} W_s^{1-\varepsilon} \right)^{1/(1-\varepsilon)} \tag{7.3}$$

$$W_s = \lambda_s^{-\tau} \left(\sum_{r=1}^{R} Y_r T_{rs}^{1-\varepsilon} I_r^{\varepsilon-1} \right)^{1/\varepsilon} \tag{7.4}$$

When comparing this short-run equilibrium with the normalized short-run equilibrium of chapter 4 (see equations (4.1′)–(4.3′)), it is immediately obvious that equations

(7.2)–(7.4) reduce to equations (4.1′)–(4.3′) if $\tau=0$. The income equation (7.2) is not affected by the congestion parameter τ.[6] From the wage equation (7.4) it is clear that an increase of congestion in city s, resulting from an increase in the share of manufacturing workers λ_s in that city, tends to reduce the wage rate in city s, and simultaneously tends to reduce the price index in other regions; see equation (7.3). Both forces make other cities more attractive.

Given the distribution of the manufacturing labor force across cities, which determines the number of varieties produced and hence the number of manufacturing firms in each city, equations (7.2)–(7.4) determine the short-run equilibrium. We will not use the short-run equilibrium for the congestion model except in Box 7.2 where the welfare implications of congestion will be discussed. To assess the relevance of congestion for the long-run equilibrium allocation of economic activity, when the distribution of the mobile labor force is not fixed, we rely on simulations and proceed in two steps. In the first step, we illustrate the relevance of congestion in the two-city model. This allows us to make comparisons with the simulations of chapter 4. Since it is one of the objectives of this chapter to apply the core model with congestion to the empirical phenomenon of city-size distributions, a two-city model will not do. In the second step, we therefore introduce many cities and congestion in the racetrack economy of the core model. Remember that in the racetrack economy space is neutral, that is to say by construction no location is preferred over any other location. Any results derived in such a setting can be attributed to the workings of the model, rather than the geometric construction of space. The racetrack economy with congestion will therefore be used in our attempt to give a theoretical basis for Zipf's Law in section 7.4.

Box 7.2.   Congestion, love of variety, and welfare

In chapter 4 (in particular, sections 4.8 and 4.9), it was concluded that it is often not possible to analyze the welfare implications of the core model of geographical economics. This is also the case for the congestion model, but there we can arrive at an interesting conclusion with respect to welfare by making use of the love-of-variety effect. In the core model of chapters 3 and 4, once we know the distribution of the labor force between the two regions, we also know the equilibrium number of varieties N of the manufactured good. Equation (3.15) makes this clear for region r: $N_r = \gamma L \lambda_r / \alpha \varepsilon$. Any change in λ_r leads to an equiproportional change in N_r. In our congestion model this is no longer the case. Equation (7.1) shows that the fixed costs α are now a function of the number of varieties, and with $0 < \tau < 1$ this means, for instance, that an increase in λ_r now leads to a less than proportional increase in the equilibrium number of varieties N_r. Instead of equation (3.15) we now have $N_r = (\lambda L l_r / \alpha \varepsilon)^{1-\tau}$. What does this imply for welfare? Here we need to rely on the love-of-variety effect as it has been described

---

[6] This clearly also holds for the real wage equation, not shown here.

in chapter 3. The love-of-variety effect states that, other things being equal, an increase in the number of varieties increases each consumer's welfare level. Now suppose that $\lambda_1 > \lambda_2$ and that the two regions are equal in all other respects. Then a movement of some manufacturing workers from region 1 to region 2 (while still keeping $\lambda_1 > \lambda_2$) will increase welfare because the migration of labor to the less densely populated region implies that the total number of varieties produced ($N_1 + N_2$) will increase. An increase in the number of varieties means, through the love-of-variety effect, that each consumer's welfare is enhanced.

7.2.2   Two locations and congestion

In the simulations of the core model with congestion, where food production is again evenly divided over the two cities, we focus on the real wage of city 1 relative to that of city 2 to determine the direction of change of the distribution of the manufacturing labor force, and thus the stability of long-run equilibria. This is identical to the approach in chapter 4 (see, for example, Figure 4.1), although this time we simultane-ously plot the total welfare achieved in the two cities together for each distribution of the manufacturing labor force. That is, for each value of λ_1, the share of the manufac-turing labor force in city 1, we first determine the short-run equilibrium by solving equations (7.2)–(7.4). Second, we calculate the relative real wage of city 1 and total welfare. Third, we plot the latter two variables as a function of the share of the manu-facturing labor force in city 1; see Figure 7.2.

A long-run equilibrium is reached either when the real wages in the two cities are equal, that is when the relative real wage in Figure 7.2 is equal to 1, or when the entire manufacturing labor force is agglomerated in one city. The long-run equilibrium is stable if, going from left to right, the relative real wage cuts the "$w_1/w_2 = 1$ line" from above (the latter is not drawn to avoid cluttering). To illustrate how the introduction of congestion alters the long-run equilibrium and its stability, we vary the transport costs T in Figure 7.2; Panels a–i are in *decreasing* order of transport costs. Recall that we concluded in chapter 4 that, if there are no congestion costs, the spreading equilibrium is stable for high transport costs, whereas full agglomeration in either city is stable for low transport costs; see Figure 4.2. As explained at the end of chapter 4 and in the introduction of this chapter, this "bang-bang" tendency of the stable long-run equilib-rium without congestion (it is either a spreading equilibrium or complete agglomera-tion) is not a very satisfactory outcome from an empirical point of view. As demonstrated in Figure 7.2, even if we add only a small amount of congestion ($\tau = 0.01$) the possibilities for long-run equilibria change drastically.

Considering the panels of Figure 7.2 sequentially, that is for steadily decreasing transport costs, five different stages can be identified.

(1) For very high transport costs, spreading is the only stable (and welfare-maximizing) equilibrium; see panels a and b.

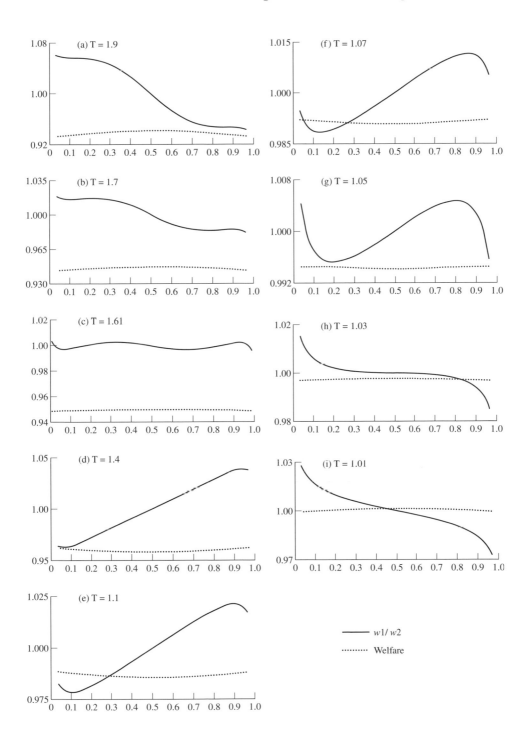

Figure 7.2. The two-region core model with congestion ($\varepsilon = 5$; $\delta = 0.4$; $\tau = 0.01$).

(2)   As transport costs decrease, spreading is still a stable (and welfare-maximizing) equilibrium, but there are now also two other stable equilibria with *partial* agglomeration; see panel *c*. Apparently, the introduction of congestion costs enriches the possible long-run equilibrium outcomes considerably, in particular by allowing partial rather than complete agglomeration as a stable equilibrium. Also note that there are seven long-run equilibria in panel *c* (including complete agglomeration); going from left to right these are alternately unstable and stable.

(3)   Complete agglomeration in either city is a stable (and welfare-maximizing) equilibrium as transport costs continue to fall; see panels *d–f*. The range of transport costs for which this holds is fairly large.

(4)   As transport costs become very small, their impact relative to congestion costs is limited. Initially this implies that *partial* agglomeration in either city is a stable (and welfare-maximizing) equilibrium; see panel *g*.

(5)   For very low transport costs, spreading is again the only stable (and welfare-maximizing) equilibrium; see panels *h* and *i*.

Three conclusions emerge from this analysis. First, the range of possible long-run equilibrium outcomes with congestion is considerably wider than without congestion. Second, the phenomenon of partial agglomeration establishes the possibility of the simultaneous existence of small and large centers of economic activity as a stable long-run equilibrium outcome in a model with neutral space. Third, keeping the qualifications of chapter 4 in mind, the welfare implications of the geographical economics model have a tendency, by and large, to coincide with stable long-run equilibria. We get back to this observation in chapter 11.

7.2.3   *Many locations and congestion*

After analyzing the two-city version of the core model with congestion, it is time to extend the analysis to the neutral-space racetrack economy with congestion. As already mentioned in chapter 4 and in the introduction to this chapter, without congestion the racetrack economy usually ends up with only one city having manufacturing production, or at best with two cities of equal size, in the long-run equilibrium. Now that we have seen in the previous subsection that the two-city model with congestion allows for the viability of small economic centers of manufacturing production, we extend this analysis to a structure with many cities.

   Figure 7.3 shows the results of two simulations of a twenty-four-city racetrack economy with congestion, one with $T=1.2$, the other with $T=1.3$. The initial distribution of the manufacturing labor force was chosen randomly, but was the same in the two simulations. Panels *a* and *b* of Figure 7.3 show both the initial and the final (long-run equilibrium) distribution of the manufacturing labor force. The greater the distance from the center of the circle, the larger is the manufacturing labor force in that city. So, for example, cities 1 and 21 are initially very small, while cities 20 and 23 are initially very large. Panels *c* and *d* of Figure 7.3 show column charts of just the final distributions of the manufacturing labor force.

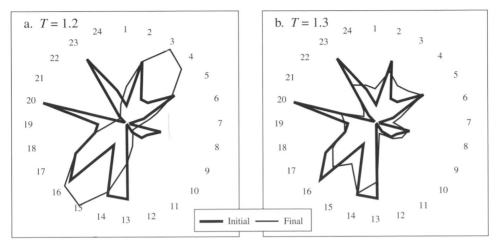

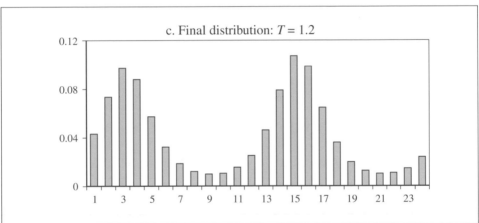

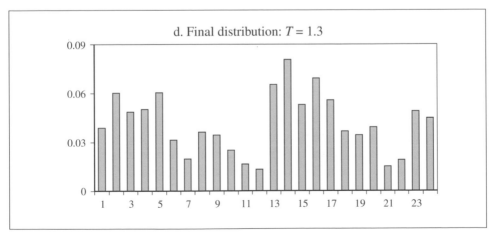

Figure 7.3.   The racetrack economy with congestion ($\varepsilon = 5$; $\delta = 0.7$; $\tau = 0.1$).

Panels *a* and *c*, depicting the simulation results for transport costs $T=1.2$, lead to the following observations. First, with congestion, many cities, not just one or two, still have manufacturing production in the long-run equilibrium. Second, these cities vary considerably in economic size, which is promising from an empirical point of view. Third, the final distribution of manufacturing production is well-structured around two centers of economic activity in cities 3 and 15; see, in particular, panel *c*. Fourth, whether an individual city increases or decreases in economic size during the adjustment process toward the long-run equilibrium largely depends on its relative place in the initial distribution of city sizes, that is on the size of cities in its neighborhood. Cities 20 and 23, for example, are initially very large, but isolated. Consequently, they both shrink considerably during the adjustment process. City 15, on the other hand, is initially quite small, but surrounded on both sides by large cities, namely cities 13, 14, 16, and 17. This allows city 15 to eventually become the largest city of all, even larger than cities 20 and 23 were initially. The cluster of cities 2, 3, and 4 thrives in particular because they are exactly opposite the "agglomeration shadow" imposed by the cluster surrounding city 15.

Relative to the above discussion, panels *b* and *d*, for $T=1.3$, show two additional results, namely that, depending on the parameter values, the final distribution may be much more determined by the initial distribution (see panel *b*) and thus be less structured (see panel *d*). In this sense the importance of the initial conditions, or in other words "history," may vary.

Before we turn to the empirical evidence for Zipf's Law, it must be emphasized that we certainly do not want to pretend to offer a fully fledged analysis of the economics of congestion. However, the core model with congestion does illustrate that the inclusion of an additional spreading force may give rise to many centers of economic activity which vary considerably in size, even in a setting of neutral space. This is a necessary condition for applying such a model to explain urban systems and city-size distributions. This is addressed in section 7.4, but first we have a closer empirical look at city-size distributions.

7.3　Zipf's Law: definition, data, and estimation results

7.3.1　Urban systems and Zipf's Law

In chapter 2 it became clear that any convincing story about the existence and growth of cities is ultimately based on the existence of increasing returns to scale. The exact nature of the increasing returns need not concern us here but both so-called *localization* and *urbanization* externalities (see, in particular, section 2.2.1 of chapter 2) were thought to be important in explaining the existence and growth of cities.[7] In chapter

---

[7] For a quick and useful introduction to the main concepts involved in the analysis of the existence and growth of cities, such as localization and urbanization economies of scale, see World Bank (2000, pp. 125–138). For a useful survey of the main concepts involved in urban economics see Fujita and Thisse (1996) or the extended version, Fujita and Thisse (2000).

5 we briefly discussed empirical evidence with respect to the determinants of the agglomeration or specialization of cities. There it was also concluded that increasing returns are relevant. In addition to increasing returns, endowments and political factors are also thought to be important in determining the formation and growth of cities.

Externalities and cities

A number of additional observations about externalities and cities are in order before we actually turn to city-size distributions and Zipf's Law. First, the distinction between localization and urbanization externalities is also important from a theoretical point of view. In the core model of geographical economics, firms group together in a city because local demand is high and demand is high because firms have decided to produce in that city. What matters is that the positive externality is associated with the number of firms (and their workers) in the city and its surrounding cities and not with whether or not firms specialize in the production of the same type of goods. The core model is therefore a model in which, if anything, urbanization and not localization externalities are present. There is no advantage for cities in being specialized. In many theoretical models in urban economics, however, the positive externality is assumed to come from specialization. Hence, in these models localization externalities are the driving force behind city formation and growth. The model developed by Black and Henderson (1999b) is a good example of this approach. In reality (see Glaeser et al., 1992, pp. 1148–1149), cities are both specialized and diversified: a typical city is at the same time characterized by firms producing the same kind of goods, but also by the production of many very different (and unrelated) goods. This means that both localization and urbanization externalities are relevant. To a large extent both types of externalities drive urban agglomeration, but at a different level of aggregation: "even if local diversification is important, we still expect specialization in broader classes of traded goods across cities. Even with enormous diversification, New York's industrial composition with a relative focus on finance, publishing and fashion looks very different from that of Gary, Indiana" (Black and Henderson, 1999b, p. 256). Having said this, it is good to keep in mind that urbanization externalities, which are thus present in the core model of geographical economics, are found to be relevant. Glaeser et al. (1992, p. 1150), for instance, find for a sample of US cities, that within a city the smaller industries display employment growth when the four largest city industries increase their employment. The smaller industries, which are not related to the four largest ones, show an employment increase of 0.5% when the four largest industries in a city increase their employment by 1%.

In a dynamic or growth context, the distinction between urbanization and localization externalities is, following Glaeser et al. (1992), nowadays referred to in the literature as a distinction between, respectively, so-called Jacobs externalities and Marshall–Arrow–Romer (MAR) externalities. These two dynamic externalities were briefly mentioned in chapter 2 and both externalities refer to knowledge spillovers between firms. With MAR externalities, which are at home in modern growth theory (see chapter 10), knowledge spillovers occur between firms that belong to the same industry. In this case, city growth is fostered by specialization. With Jacobs externalities, based on the work of Jane Jacobs (1969), knowledge spillovers are not industry-specific but take place among firms of different industries. Here city growth is stimulated by diversity. Glaeser *et al.* (1992) conclude that Jacobs externalities are the most important externalities for employment growth in US cities. There is, however, also evidence in favor of MAR externalities. Black and Henderson (1999a) and also Beardsell and Henderson (1999), for instance, find that MAR externalities are to be found in the high-tech industries. To measure static as well as dynamic industry-specific externalities or, in other words, to measure localization and MAR externalities, Black and Henderson (1999a, pp. 325–326) proceed as follows. They analyze whether for a high-tech industry located in area Z its output at time t is positively affected by a current or a past increase in either the number of own-industry plants in Z or by the number of new own-industry plants in area Z. A positive output effect of a current increase in these two determinants is taken as evidence in favor of localization externalities, whereas a similar lagged output response is evidence of MAR externalities. It turns out that both externalities matter in the high-tech industry and that MAR externalities matter in particular for non-affiliate (single-plant) high-tech firms. That is, the output of such a firm at a particular location depends positively on the number of other high-tech firms at the same location.

It is beyond the scope of this chapter to deal extensively with the research on the empirical relevance of within-city industry concentration or industry diversity for city formation and growth. It suffices to note that the various positive externalities mentioned above all seem to matter. Or, in the words of Glaeser (2000, p. 92), "for the moment, the role of concentration and diversity does not seem to have been resolved by the literature."[8] Our brief discussion also makes clear that the empirical research is about agglomeration forces. The spreading forces are not part of the analysis. Differences between cities are therefore attributed to differences in the way the *positive* externalities influence cities. Negative externalities, arising from for instance congestion, are neglected. Other potential spreading forces like the need for city firms to serve non-city markets at positive transport cost are also not part of this kind of empirical investigation. This is unfortunate because we want to stress spreading rather than agglomeration in this chapter. In our view, the main reason for this neglect is that the empirical research on the various positive externalities driving urban agglomeration focuses upon the determinants of the size and growth of *individual* cities, and far less upon the ways in which these cities and their hinterlands, the rural areas, work together. The nationwide space, which includes both cities and rural areas, is simply not a prime object of research in urban economics. In geographical economics it is precisely the

---

[8] Given our discussion in chapter 5 this should not come as much of a surprise because there it was concluded that the empirical evidence on spatial (here, urban) agglomeration is typically consistent with a variety of theories. Following Hanson (2000) the main problem is that we cannot identify the precise nature of the externalities underlying urban agglomeration.

interaction between the centers with their production (cities) and the rest of the economy that matters.

Until quite recently, it proved to be difficult to come up with a sound micro-economic foundation for systems in the nationwide space and the "old" central place theory has long remained the work-horse in discussing why a system of cities exists and how it hangs together. In chapter 2 we have already dealt with the drawbacks of central place theory. Eaton and Lipsey (1982) were among the first to develop a model in which a micro-economic foundation could be given for a central place outcome. But their model only verifies that such an outcome could be an equilibrium. When it comes to deriving central place theory from the underlying behavior, Fujita, Krugman, and Venables (1999, ch. 11) are among the first to show that this can be done in a model of geographical economics. But their approach, as we shall see in the next subsection, suffers from the serious drawback that it is at odds with the observed regularities in actual city-size distributions.

Black and Henderson (1999b) and also Eaton and Eckstein (1997) follow a different route when it comes to city-size distributions since they take these observed regularities as their starting point and then attempt to find a theoretical model that can deal with these facts. The facts we refer to concern the relative similarity both across countries and across time of city-size distributions.[9] The model developed by Black and Henderson (1999b, p. 259) uses the trade-off, well known in urban economics, that firms in each city face between localized economies of scale and congestion costs. But now they use this basic idea to show that the growth of cities (driven by this trade-off) can result in a stable city-size distribution. Eaton and Eckstein (1997) develop a similar, somewhat simpler model of city growth and explicitly use their model to address the central (and hotly debated) stylized fact about city-size distributions: Zipf's Law or the rank–size rule. In the remainder of this chapter we will use Zipf's Law as an empirical yardstick for the analysis of various theories (including our own congestion version of the core model) of city-size distributions. Before doing so, we will define Zipf's Law and provide relevant data on this "law."

What is Zipf's Law?

Zipf's Law is a special case of the rank–size distribution. How can this distribution be measured? First, as we did for India in chapter 1, collect data on the size of all cities in a particular region of the world, say defined by the number of inhabitants in a city. Second, order these observations in decreasing size; this defines their rank. Now take the natural logarithms of the rank and the size. According to the rank–size distribution, this relationship should be approximately linear. In a formula:

$$\log(M_j) = \log(c) - q\log(R_j) \tag{7.5}$$

where c is a constant, M_j is the size of city j (measured by its population), and R_j is the rank of city j (rank 1 for the largest city, rank 2 for the second largest city, etc.). In

---

[9] Of course, there are other well-established patterns with respect to urbanization as well, such as the observed growth in the number and size of cities over time (Black and Henderson, 1999b, p. 254).

empirical research q is the estimated coefficient, giving the slope of the supposedly log-linear relationship between city size and city rank. It is said that *Zipf's Law holds if, and only if, $q = 1$.* If Zipf's Law holds, that is if $q = 1$, the largest city is precisely k times as large as the kth largest city.[10] If q is smaller than 1, a more even distribution of city sizes results than predicted by Zipf's Law (if $q = 0$, all cities are of the same size). If q is larger than 1, the large cities are larger than Zipf's Law predicts, implying more urban agglomeration, i.e. the largest city is more than k times as large as the kth largest city. Empirically, we have to establish if the rank–size distribution holds. If it does, the question arises of whether Zipf's Law holds, that is whether $q = 1$ or not.[11]

Using mostly US data, a number of authors have recently stressed that (i) Zipf's Law holds (that is $q = 1$), and (ii) the estimated coefficient q hardly changes over time; see Krugman (1996a, 1996b), Gabaix (1999a, 1999b), and Fujita, Krugman, and Venables (1999, ch. 12). Indeed, when equation (7.5) is estimated, q is usually close to 1 when US data are used. Carroll (1982), however, surveys the empirical evidence on the rank–size distribution and finds that Zipf's Law does not always hold for the United States. In an influential paper on Zipf's Law, or the Pareto distribution as they call it, Rosen and Resnick (1980, p. 167) find that $q = 0.84$ for the USA, which would imply a much more even city-size distribution than if Zipf's Law holds. Similarly, Black and Henderson (1998, pp. 11–12) find not only that the slope coefficient in equation (7.5) slowly increased over the course of the twentieth century for the USA, but also that this coefficient clearly is not equal to 1. In fact, they find that for the USA q is greater than 1 (around 1.17), which would imply that the US urban system is more concentrated than Zipf's Law predicts.[12] For other countries a mixed picture also emerges. Eaton and Eckstein (1997) find for Japan and France that Zipf's Law nearly holds, and also that q has hardly changed over time. Rosen and Resnick (1980, p. 167), however, show that for both countries q is smaller than 1 (France: 0.75; Japan: 0.78). If one wants to give a theoretical explanation for (deviations from) Zipf's Law it obviously matters a great deal whether one concludes from the available empirical evidence that $q = 1$ and/or q is stable over time.

---

[10] Equation (7.5) is the log-linear specification of the rank–size distribution as used in empirical tests. Carroll (1982) shows that the rank–size distribution had been discussed prior to Zipf (1949), notably by Auerbach and Lotka. Equation (7.5) is also referred to as the Pareto distribution with q as the Pareto parameter; see Rosen and Resnick (1980). Our specification follows Zipf, but many empirical studies prefer to use $\log(R_j) = \log(c) - q' \log(M_j)$. To avoid confusion all estimates for q mentioned in the text are based on equation (7.5).

[11] Zipf (1949) attempts to capture a broad range of observed social and spatial regularities by means of simple equations. His book is part of a larger tradition, sometimes referred to as the literature on gravity models, which, inspired by Newtonian physics, typically stipulates that economic or social interaction between the objects of interest is a function of the mass (economic size) of these objects weighted by their distance. These equations are not meant to explain the social or spatial phenomenon at hand. Their objective is simply, analogously to the physical sciences, to describe the phenomenon. This "un-deductive" approach, called *social physics* by Krugman (1995a), led not only to Zipf's Law, but also to the gravity model and the market potential function. George Zipf, a lecturer in linguistics at Harvard, argues that the rank–size distribution holds for many phenomena. A well-known example is in the use of language, where the expressions that are most frequently used are also the least complex. Zipf had a reputation for being eccentric. The story goes that he applauded the *Anschluss* of Austria to Nazi Germany in 1938 because the resulting city-size distribution was more in line with the rank–size rule!

[12] This is also concluded by Dobkins and Ioannides (2000).

Fortunately, the evidence on Zipf's Law is somewhat less muddled than the previous paragraph suggests because the differences are to a considerable extent due to differences in city definitions and sample sizes. To start with the latter, it turns out that if the size of cities drops below a certain threshold level (which is neither constant through time nor the same for every country), there is hardly any negative correlation between size and rank left for the group of very small cities. Inclusion of very small cities makes it therefore more likely that one finds that $q < 1$. So an important issue in comparing studies on Zipf's Law is the choice of the sample size. Two strategies are followed: (i) use a fixed number of cities (say, the largest fifty); or (ii) define a threshold level below which cities will not be included in the sample. In accounting for the different conclusions with respect to the size of the q coefficient the definition of a city is also a very relevant factor. There are two main options for the empirical studies on city-size distributions when it comes to the definition of a city. The first one is to confine the city to its legal boundaries, the so-called *city proper*. Hence the size of New York is measured by the population of the legal entity "New York City." The second option is to define the city as the agglomeration that is thought to constitute an economic unit and to disregard official city definitions. According to this definition, the city of New York is the urban agglomeration, and includes parts of New Jersey and Connecticut. As our own estimates of equation (7.5) show (see below), estimations based on the city proper usually result in a more evenly spread distribution of city sizes (a lower value for q) compared to urban agglomeration. This is to be expected, because the inclusion of suburbs favors the already relatively large cities. Rosen and Resnick (1980) use the city proper definition. Based on a sample of forty-four countries their mean value for q is equal to 0.88, which indeed implies a relatively even city-size distribution. Studies that find confirmation for Zipf's Law are mostly based on the urban agglomeration definition of cities.

Two additional problems that beset the estimation of equation (7.5) are the special role of the largest city, the so-called *primate city*, and the possibility of a non-linear relationship between the rank of cities and their size. The role of the primate city is discussed in Box 7.3. Rosen and Resnick (1980, pp. 174–175) and Black and Henderson (1998) conclude that a quadratic specification provides a somewhat better fit.[13] Since we want to compare our findings with the the literature on Zipf's Law that uses equation (7.5) we retain the linear specification.

Box 7.3.   Primate cities

One reason why actual rank–size distributions need not to be in accordance with Zipf's Law is that the largest city, with rank 1, is much larger for many countries than predicted by Zipf's Law. This holds for certain developed countries, like

---

[13] Black and Henderson (1998), Dobkins and Ioannides (1999), and Ioannides and Overman (2000) use a non-parametric approach for the USA.

Table 7.3. *Primacy ratio, selected countries*

France (1982)	0.529
Austria (1991)	0.687
Mexico (1990)	0.509
Peru (1991)	0.753
Indonesia (1995)	0.523
Czech Republic (1994)	0.550
Romania (1994)	0.605
Iran (1994)	0.556
UK (1994)	0.703
Egypt (1992)	0.499
Chile (1995)	0.769
South Korea (1990)	0.532
Vietnam (1989)	0.570
Hungary (1994)	0.726
Russian Federation (1994)	0.504
Iraq (1987)	0.643
Sample mean	0.500

Note: Year of observation in parentheses.
Source: Own calculations based on UN data that can be found at http://www.un.org/Depts/unsd/demog/index.html

Japan (Tokyo), France (Paris), or the UK (London), but it holds especially for many developing countries, where we can think of mega-cities like São Paulo, Shanghai, Mexico City, Seoul, Lagos, or Cairo. To measure the relative size of the largest, or primate, city, urban as well as development economists use primacy ratios, which give an indication of the dominance of the primate city in the urban system of a country. Following Rosen and Resnick (1980), we calculated the primacy ratio for fifty-six countries; see Table 7.3 for a selection of countries with a primacy ratio equal to or above the sample mean of 0.5. The primacy ratio calculates the ratio of the size of the largest city to the sum of the sizes of the five largest cities.[14] For reasons of data availability we used city proper, rather than urban agglomeration, which underestimates the importance of the largest city.

As the results show, the primacy ratio is greater than 50% for quite a few countries. Analytically, the question is how the existence of the large primate city, particularly of mega-cities in developing countries, can be explained. Krugman and

[14] Other indicators of primacy are possible. The World Bank, for instance, gives the population in the largest city as a percentage of *urban* population. For the group of low-income countries this percentage is 27, compared to 15 for the EMU countries, and 8 for the USA.

Livas Elizondo (1996) offer an interesting theoretical explanation from a geographical economics perspective. Their model loosely builds on the case of Mexico. As we noted in chapter 5 when discussing Hanson's (1997) work, wages in Mexico City are relatively high compared to those in other Mexican regions. Why do firms want to locate in Mexico City despite the relatively high wages? According to the core model of geographical economics, it is because of the high demand for their products. In extensions, it is also because their main suppliers are located there. Similarly, the workers, and hence the demand, are located in Mexico City because the suppliers (the firms) are there. By now, all of this will sound familiar. Krugman and Livas Elizondo (1996) argue that this line of reasoning depends on the assumption that Mexico is a *closed* economy. Suppose, however, that Mexican firms produce largely for the world market and buy their inputs on these markets, and that Mexican demand for goods is also directed at the world market. Suppose also that agglomeration is accompanied by high land rents in the center, which then act as a spreading force. In that case, it no longer makes sense for Mexico City to be the center of production or, in other words, for Mexico to have a disproportionally large primate city. One would expect a more even distribution of economic activity, with agglomeration in regions with good access to foreign markets (near the Mexican–US border or near ports). Krugman and Livas Elizondo show that as the economy in their model moves from a closed to an open economy, the initial stable equilibrium of full agglomeration at one location is replaced by spreading as the only stable equilibrium.

This suggests that increased openness of the economy goes along with a relatively smaller size of primate city. For Mexico this seems to be the case, since the change from a trade policy of import substitution toward one of trade liberalization has resulted in a decline in the relative importance of Mexico City. For a sample of eighty-five countries, Ades and Glaeser (1995) indeed find that higher levels of international trade usually imply a smaller size for the primate city. There are two caveats. First, the direction of causality remains unclear. The causality could also run from size to trade: "concentration of population in a single city might give local firms a transport cost advantage over foreign suppliers and thus lower the amount of foreign trade" (Ades and Glaeser, 1995, p. 213). Second, the empirical results point to the relevance of political (non-economic) factors in explaining the existence of large primate cities. In particular, countries with a totalitarian regime have large primate cities. Under such a regime, and assuming that the primate city is also the political center of the country, firms and workers outside the primate city are at a disadvantage in the situation where the political regime has considerable control over the operation of the economy, and does not respect the economic or political rights of peripheral regions. It may then be cost-effective for workers and firms to ensure that they are located in the political center, that is in the primate city. These political costs give a stimulus to the size of the primate city in addition to the economic agglomeration forces. The relatively high primacy ratio of countries like Iraq or Iran, or of the former communist countries in eastern Europe, are consistent with this line of reasoning. Given these kinds of consideration, is there is an "optimal" degree of primacy, in the sense that it maximizes economic growth? Henderson, Shalizi, and Venables (2000, p. 22) argue that this is the case. According to them, for low-income countries ($1,100 per capita), middle-income countries ($4,900) and high-income countries ($13,400), the optimal degree of urban primacy (percentage of population in the largest city) is respectively 15%, 25%, and 23%.

Finally, Diego Puga (1998) develops a geographical economics model that can account for the relatively large size of primate cities in many developing countries. His model is similar to the core model of chapters 3 and 4 but there are also some notable differences, like the fact that labor can move between the manufacturing and agricultural sectors; the degree to which inter-sector labor migration occurs depends crucially on the elasticity of labor supply. Puga shows that when transport costs are becoming very low and increasing returns to scale are relatively strong, an urban system with a large primate city develops. With relatively high transport costs and weaker economies of scale a more balanced urban system takes shape. According to Puga the latter applies to nineteenth-century European urbanization whereas the former applies to late-twentieth-century urbanization in developing countries.

7.3.2   Estimating Zipf's Law

We now turn to our own estimation results using equation (7.5). All data were collected from the United Nations website at http: //www.un.org/Depts/unsd/demog/index.html. This website lists city sizes (measured by number of inhabitants) for many countries around the world. When available, both "city proper" and "urban agglomeration" data are given for all cities with at least 100,000 inhabitants. The rank–size distribution was estimated for all countries with at least ten cities above this cut-off value. Depending on data availability, we estimated equation (7.5) for city proper and urban agglomeration. Only forty-eight countries appear in at least one of these data categories: forty-two countries appear in the city proper list, twenty-two countries in the urban agglomeration list, while only sixteen countries are in both lists. Table 7.4 gives the summary statistics for the q coefficient that result after estimating equation (7.5) for forty-two countries (city proper data) and twenty-two countries (urban agglomeration data), respectively.

Table 7.4 shows that for the city proper definition the mean value for q is clearly below 1. In fact, at 0.88 our mean value for cities proper is exactly the same as the one found by Rosen and Resnick (1980). As was to be expected, the mean q value for the urban

Table 7.4. *Summary statistics for q*

	City proper	Urban agglomeration
Mean	0.88	1.05
Standard error	0.030	0.046
Minimum	0.49	0.69
Maximum	1.47	1.54
Average R^2	0.94	0.95
# observations	42	22

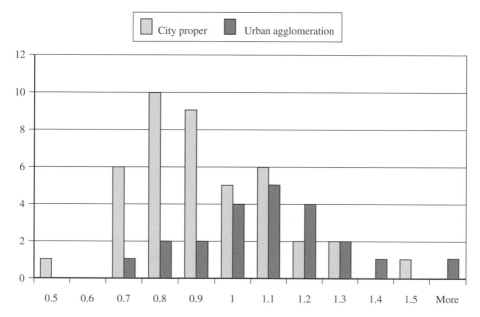

Figure 7.4. Frequency distribution of estimated coefficients.

agglomeration definition is larger than for the city proper one, namely 1.05 compared to 0.88. For urban agglomerations we therefore find a value close to 1, that is, close to Zipf's Law. However, as indicated by the standard errors, there is considerable variation in the estimated coefficients. For city proper the estimated coefficients range from 0.49 to 1.47; for urban agglomeration, the range is from 0.69 to 1.54. Figure 7.4, giving the frequency distribution of the estimated coefficients, clearly illustrates that Zipf's Law does not hold for many countries, irrespective of the city definition used, that is q is often found to differ from 1. Most importantly, however, the average goodness of fit of the rank–size distribution, as measured by the average R^2, is impressive: 94% for cities proper, and 95% for urban agglomerations (Table 7.4). In general, therefore the rank–size distribution provides a good characterization of city-size distributions.

To summarize: more often than not the estimated coefficient q is found to be different from one. Too much attention to the value of $q = 1$ (and hence to Zipf's Law) is therefore unwarranted. This does not imply that we do not find confirmation for the rank–size distribution. On the contrary, for almost every country the fit of the estimated equation is very good. The idea of a stable city-size distribution across countries is certainly confirmed by our estimations. This is illustrated in Table 7.A1 in the appendix to this chapter, which gives the q coefficients, the number of observations and the R^2 for every country in our data-set, both for cities proper and for urban agglomerations. For the USA (on which most of the empirical research has been focused), our results are in line with Rosen and Resnick (1980) for cities proper and with Black and Henderson (1998) for urban agglomerations. In both cases Zipf's Law is not confirmed. For readers interested in the individual country data, as well as full estimation results and graphical analysis for each country, the website for this book should be consulted.

Our country estimates for q point to two requirements that a theoretical explanation of the rank–size distribution must meet. First, that the relationship between rank and size should be able to account for deviations from Zipf's Law. This is in marked contrast with Gabaix (1999a, 1999b), Krugman (1996a, 1996b) and Fujita, Krugman, and Venables (1999, pp. 216–217), who take as their starting point $q = 1$, and try to come up with a theoretical explanation of that "fact." The second, and related, requirement refers to the stability of the q coefficient over time. Our estimations, as reported in Table 7.A1, have nothing to say on this issue, because we estimated q for a single year. We can at most discuss cross-sectional stability. Some authors put great emphasis on the fact that q hardly changes over time. Krugman (1996a, pp. 40–41) for example concludes that "the rank–size rule seems to have applied to US cities at least since 1890!" Similar observations are made by Eaton and Eckstein (1997) and Gabaix (1999a, 1999b). The idea of a constant value of q over time does, of course, have different implications for a theoretical explanation from the notion, to which we adhere, that q often changes over time, as a result of structural changes in the economy. Black and Henderson (1998, pp. 11–12) present evidence for the USA that q has increased over time. In Box 7.4 we show that for the Netherlands, one of the earliest intensively urbanized countries in Europe, the city-size distribution has also changed over time.[15] The non-constancy of q over time implies that urban growth is not proportional; see also Parr (1985).

7.4   Explanations for Zipf's Law: the congestion model and other approaches[16]

One of the objectives of this chapter is to see whether the geographical economics approach can be used as a foundation for actual regularities in city-size distributions; see section 7.1. To focus our discussion we have picked one such regularity: the rank–size distribution, or Zipf's Law if $q = 1$. Since the tension between agglomerating

---

[15] A third stylized fact that a theoretical explanation for the rank–size distribution should address is that the ranking of *individual* cities is not constant over time.
[16] This section is based on Brakman *et al.* (1999).

and spreading forces is crucial in determining the spatial allocation of economic activity in geographical economics, it is clear that an attempt to explain Zipf's Law based on these models must focus on this tension. In urban economics, the analytical foundation for cities and city systems is also based on the balance between agglomerating forces (economies of scale, such as localization economies) and spreading forces (diseconomies of scale, such as congestion costs). In both geographical economics and urban economics, the size of cities matters, and differences in city sizes must be the result of the fact that the balance between agglomerating and spreading forces differs between individual cities. In this section, we use the core model of geographical economics with congestion, as discussed in section 7.2, to explain Zipf's Law. So it is clear from the beginning that we think that the tension between agglomerating and spreading forces facing each city is a useful way of thinking about city-size distributions. There is, however, another route that can be taken to explain Zipf's Law. This alternative route takes as its starting point the assertion that the relative size of cities does *not* matter. Two main examples are the application of Simon (1955) to Zipf's Law and the use of Gibrat's Law by Gabaix (1999a, 1999b) to explain Zipf's Law. Before we return to the congestion model of section 7.2, we briefly discuss these two examples, mainly to bring out the differences from our explanation.[17]

7.4.1   Other approaches

Although the basic idea of Simon (1955) is simple, the mathematics underlying the model is not.[18] Imagine a population characterized by random growth. The "newly born," who for some unexplained reason arrive in cohorts, and not one by one, may begin a new city (with probability π), or they may cling to an existing city (with probability $1 - \pi$). If they cling to an existing city, the probability that they choose any particular city is proportional to the size of the population of that city. It can then be shown (provided the cohorts of newly born are neither too large nor too small) that the random growth of the population will eventually result in Zipf's Law ($q = 1$). The point to emphasize is the lack of economic content in this explanation for Zipf's Law, which contrasts sharply with the geographical economics approach. The size of the city, and hence the aforementioned tension between agglomerating and spreading forces, is not an issue. This also implies that changes in the rank–size distribution are thought to be random. There are other difficulties; see Fujita, Krugman, and Venables (1999, pp. 222–223), or Gabaix (1999a, p. 129) who points out that "the ratio of the growth rate of the number of cities to the growth rate of the population of existing cities . . . is in reality significantly less than 1." (This ratio is assumed to be 1 by Simon.)

   Gabaix (1999a, 1999b) provides a different explanation for Zipf's Law, where the relative size of cities does not matter and where the economics of city formation are not part of the explanation. He calls upon Gibrat's Law which, when applied to cities, states that the growth process of a city is independent of its size. He proves that if every

---

[17] Another example is Krugman (1996a).   [18] Our discussion of Simon (1955) is based on Krugman (1996a).

city, large or small, shares the same common mean growth rate, and if the variance of this growth rate is also the same for every city, then Zipf's Law follows. Again, the point to notice is that this explanation is not based on an economic model. Nonetheless, it is an interesting question as to which type of city-growth model gives rise to a steady-state growth rate leading to Gibrat's Law. Gabaix shows that Gibrat's Law (and hence Zipf's Law) results if cities are characterized either by constant returns to scale, or by external economies of scale with positive and negative externalities canceling out. The latter would mean that a geographical economics model can give rise to Zipf's Law only if for each city the agglomeration forces are exactly equal to the spreading forces.[19]

There are two main problems with these explanations. First, they are not founded on a coherent framework of economic principles. Second, they do not meet the requirements for an explanation of the empirical city-size distribution as formulated at the end of section 7.3, namely that the explanation must take account of the fact that q often deviates from one, and that q can change over time. Both Simon's model and the approach of Gabaix using Gibrat's Law predict that $q = 1$. The explanation we want to offer instead is based on the congestion model of section 7.2. In a nutshell, this explanation combines the geographical economics approach with modern urban economics, where the spreading force arises from the congestion costs associated with urban agglomeration. This additional spreading force is important to ensuring that the geographical economics approach can reasonably explain city-size distributions. Fujita, Krugman, and Venables (1999, ch. 11), for example, develop an intricate urban hierarchy model, in fact a central place model. Simulations with this model, however, give rise to city-size distributions that clearly do not match the empirical facts discussed in the previous section.[20] As we shall show, this is no longer true when the balance between agglomeration and spreading forces is altered by the introduction of conges-

---

[19] The idea of using Gibrat's Law to explain the rank–size distribution may be new to economists, but it is not to geographers. See, for instance, an early edition of the well-known introductory textbook on economic geography by Dicken and Lloyd (1990), or the survey paper by Carroll (1982, sect. 2). The assumption that the variance of the growth rate is the same for every city has been criticized by Fujita, Krugman, and Venables (1999, p. 224), who argue that this variance must be larger for smaller, less-diversified cities. Gabaix (1999b) agrees with this point, but says that this is precisely why the rank–size distribution does not hold in the lower tail of the city-size distribution. Dobkins and Ioannides (1999) do not find empirical support for the "uniform variance" assumption.

[20] This is also acknowledged by Fujita, Krugman, and Venables (1999, p. 217); see, in particular, their Figure 12.2. The central place model in Fujita, Krugman, and Venables (1999) is based on Fujita, Krugman, and Mori (1999). The basic idea can be understood as follows. Suppose we add to our core model of chapters 3 and 4 that instead of one manufacturing good (which is produced in many varieties, one variety per firm) we now have two of these manufacturing goods. Suppose also that the first manufacturing good consists of many highly differentiated varieties with a low elasticity of substitution and the second good consists of varieties that are close substitutes, i.e. have a high substitution elasticity. It can be shown that *ceteris paribus* the first good will be produced at a single location (the largest or central city) whereas the second good will be produced at both locations. Extending this idea to a large number of locations and a large number of manufactured goods (with a different substitution elasticity) leads to a hierarchy of locations as in Christaller's central place theory in which the largest or central location produces all manufacturing goods and the locations lower in the hierarchy only produce the good with highest substitution elasticity. The fact that a high (low), substitution elasticity may induce spreading (agglomeration) has already been discussed in chapter 4; see, in particular, Figure 4.3a.

tion. To illustrate the merits of the model for a discussion on city-size distributions, we use the actual history of Dutch urbanization as our benchmark. Box 7.4 briefly discusses the main features of the urbanization process in the Netherlands.

Box 7.4.   Zipf's Law and economic changes in the Netherlands

The Netherlands were one of the earliest intensively urbanized countries in Europe. Kooij (1988) distinguishes three periods of urbanization that will be used below in the simulations of the rank–size distributions. These periods are thought to be characteristic not only for the Netherlands, but also for other countries in continental Europe.

(1) *Pre-industrialization: approximately 1600–1850*. Characterized by high transport costs and production being dominated by immobile farmers.
(2) *Industrialization: approximately 1850–1900*. Characterized by declining transport costs and the increasing importance of "footloose" industrial production with increasing returns to scale.
(3) *Post-industrialization: approximately 1900–present*. Characterized by the declining importance of industrial production, and the increasing importance of negative externalities, like congestion.

With regard to the first of these periods, it may be noted that as early as 1600 the Netherlands contained twenty cities with more than 10,000 inhabitants. The size distribution of these cities was relatively even. Until halfway through the nineteenth century, which marks the start of the era of industrialization in the Netherlands, there was no integrated urban system at the national level. Apart from the fact that the industrialization process had, by and large, yet to begin, the relatively high transport costs between cities are thought to have provided an important additional economic reason for this lack of a truly national urban system.

Considering the second period, the estimation of equation (7.5) for the Netherlands reveals that q increased from 0.55 in 1600 to 1.03 in 1900 (own calculations; see Figure 7.5). In the second half of the nineteenth century an integrated urban system was formed. Two interdependent economic changes were mainly responsible for this formation. First, the development of canals, a railroad network, and, to a lesser extent, roads significantly lowered transport costs between cities and this enhanced trade between cities. Second, because of lower transport costs, the industrialization process accelerated and cities often became more specialized. This stimulated trade between cities. Even though the industrialization process did not lead to significant changes in the overall rank–size distribution, it can nevertheless be concluded that as time went by the initially large cities gained a larger share of the urban population.

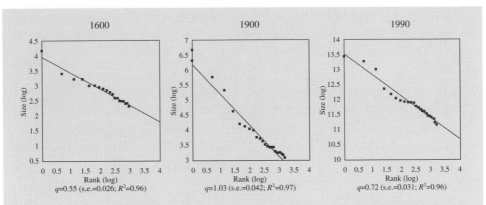

Figure 7.5. Rank–size distribution in the Netherlands. *Source*: Own calculations. Data are from Kooij, 1988, and CBS, 1995. The sample consisted of nineteen cities for 1600 and twenty-three cities for 1900.

With regard to the final period, structural changes in the rank–size distribution take decades to materialize, so it was only well into the twentieth century that the industrialized countries, including the Netherlands, gradually entered the post-industrialization era. The share of the services sector in total employment became ever more important, at the expense of the footloose industrial sector. Comparing the Dutch rank–size distributions for 1900 and 1990 it is evident that the size distribution of cities has become more even. In 1900 q was 1.03 compared to 0.72 in 1990. The declining importance of industry (and hence of production characterized by increasing returns to scale) may be one factor contributing to this change in the size distribution. Increased congestion, especially in the large cities such as Amsterdam, Rotterdam, and The Hague, is thought to have stimulated the (relative and absolute) decline of these cities.

We conclude this brief discussion by noting that the second period, the industrialization period, was special in its power of agglomeration, as also noted by Kooij (1988, p. 363): "this was the era of the large cities." For all three periods, however, the rank–size distribution holds. This is illustrated in Figure 7.5 which shows the results of estimating equation (7.5) for our sample of Dutch cities in 1600, 1900, and 1990: at least 96% of the variance in city size is explained by the rank–size distribution. Industrialization apparently led to an increase of q and it is during this period (around 1900) that the Dutch rank–size distribution mimics Zipf's Law ($q = 1$). Finally, these three periods in which changes in economic variables have a demonstrable impact on the rank–size distribution enable us to simulate the impact of these changes with the core model of geographical economics with congestion; see section 7.2.

7.4.2   Simulating Zipf: the core model with congestion

To mimic the rank–size distribution using the core model with congestion, we start with twenty-four cities located on the racetrack economy. Initially, each city receives a random share of the manufacturing labor force. Furthermore, in the subsequent analysis we only include cities with a long-run manufacturing sector; pure agricultural areas are not included as they do not represent a city. In this respect, the number of cities is endogenous (but at most twenty-four). The rest of the model used to simulate the rank–size distribution is exactly the same as the model discussed in section 7.2.[21] On the basis of the three stylized periods of urbanization for the Netherlands, as discussed in Box 7.4, we now change the economic parameters in our model between these three periods, with the aim of explaining changes in the rank–size distribution over time.

The first period is *pre-industrialization*. The small manufacturing sector in this period produces close substitutes and production is dominated by immobile farmers. We simulate the small manufacturing sector by choosing a relatively high value for the share of agricultural workers in the total labor force $(1 - \delta = 0.5)$. The manufacturing sector is modeled as homogeneous (i.e. it does not yet produce many varieties) by choosing a relatively high value for the elasticity of substitution between varieties $(\varepsilon = 6)$. This simultaneously implies that increasing returns to scale are relatively unimportant; see chapter 3. The low level of regional integration (high transport costs) is described by choosing $T = 2$. Negative economies of scale are not very important in this period, although not absent (think of the disease-ridden large cities in the Middle Ages). This is simulated by choosing a moderate value (0.2) for τ.

The second period is referred to as *industrialization*. The basic characteristic in this period is the spectacular decrease in transport costs and the increasing importance of "footloose" manufacturing production with increasing returns to scale. At the same time negative externalities are not absent, but also not very important, in the sense that they do not prevent large cities from becoming even larger. In the model we simulate these factors by lowering transport costs to $T = 1.25$, and increasing the share of the manufacturing labor force in total employment to $\delta = 0.6$. The increased importance of economies of scale and differentiated manufactured products are represented by choosing $\varepsilon = 4$. In this period the strong industrialization leads to the disappearance of relatively small cities. This corresponds with the idea that agglomerating forces dominate during the era of big-city growth.

The last period is called *post-industrialization*. In this period, transport costs remain low and, as before, the manufacturing sector is characterized by differentiated products and increasing returns to scale. The notable difference from earlier periods is congestion, reflected in growing traffic jams, increased air pollution, rising land rents in larger cities, etc. Smaller cities are less troubled by such effects and therefore have a tendency to grow faster. In the model we simulate this by increasing the congestion parameter τ to 0.33.

---

[21] The specification for the production function in the simulations is $l_{ir} = \alpha N_r^{\tau(1-\tau)} + \beta x_i$.

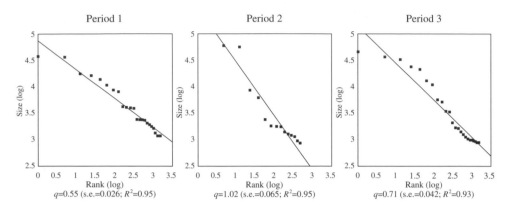

Figure 7.6.   Simulating Zipf.

Figure 7.6 presents the simulation results for the above three periods. At least 93% of the variance in city size is explained by the rank–size distribution. More importantly, these simulations suggest that the *n*-shaped pattern of *q* over time, identified by Parr (1985), depends on the economic parameter changes. According to this pattern, economic development starts off with *q* well below one. As economic development gathers pace, *q* increases. When the economy matures, *q* starts to decrease. With the congestion version of the core geographical economics model, actual rank–size distributions can be reproduced by varying those model parameters that have been identified in the literature as relevant to understanding the changes in the size distribution of cities.

7.4.3 Structural analysis

An objection that can be raised against the simulations in the previous subsection is that it is possible that by sheer coincidence our congestion model can mimic actual (changes in) city distributions. One would like to know whether or not the rank–size distributions are a structural outcome of the model. Fortunately, as shown by Brakman *et al.* (1999), this is the case. To prove their case they analyze the outcome of many simulations, but these are beyond the scope of this book. Instead, it is more illuminating to focus on the adjustment process of a particular simulation.

Analyzing more closely the adjustment over time of a typical simulation example is the best way to get an intuitive feel for the adjustment process. Figure 7.7a depicts a random initial distribution of city size over the twenty-four cities of the racetrack economy.[22] Given this initial distribution we solve for the short-run equilibrium. Since

---

[22] The uniform random distribution is used to determine the industrial labor force for the twenty-four cities. Note, however, that Figure 7.7 depicts total city size, that is the sum of industrial and agricultural workers.

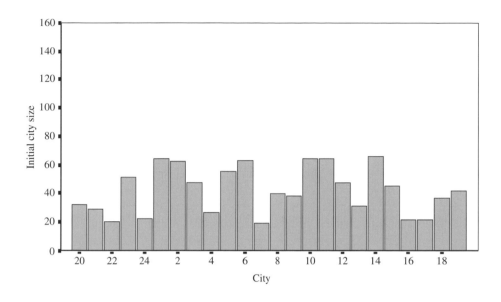

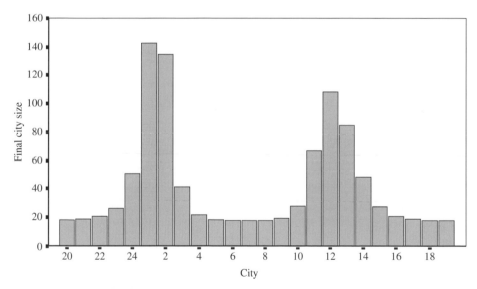

Figure 7.7.   Change in city sizes.

the real wages for manufacturing workers differ among the twenty-four cities, this starts a migration process of workers from cities with low real wages to cities with high real wages. The redistribution of workers determines a new short-run equilibrium, which starts a second migration process, because the real wages are still not equal for all cities. This process continues, for this simulation example, until the long-run equilibrium is reached after sixteen migration processes. Figure 7.7b depicts the final distribution of city size over the twenty-four cities at the long-run equilibrium. There are ultimately two agglomerations of economic activity, one around city 1 and one around city 12.

Inspecting both panels of Figure 7.7 shows that the two final centers of economic agglomeration are close to the initial centers of high economic activity. At the same time, the two final centers are rather evenly spread over the racetrack economy, that is they are not too close to each other. This is also clear from Figure 7.8a, showing the evolution of size over time as a result of the migration processes for cities 1, 2, 11, and 12 (ultimately ranked as numbers 1–3 and 5 in size). After two migration processes, cities 2 and 11 are the two largest cities. However, as agglomeration centers these two cities are too close to each other; therefore city 2 ultimately becomes smaller than city 1, and city 12 becomes substantially larger than city 11. As demonstrated by city 11 the adjustment process is not monotonic over time.[23] The prosperity of individual cities does not depend only on their own size, but also on that of their neighbors. City 14, for example, is initially the largest city. Since it is surrounded by smaller cities it ultimately drops in the rankings to number 7. Nonetheless, initial size matters: eight of the ten ultimately largest cities were also in the initial top ten list.

Figure 7.8b, finally, suggests that the model increases the predictive power of the rank–size distribution: as the city-size distribution is adjusting to the long-run equilibrium the share of the variance explained by the rank–size distribution is increasing (up to $R^2 = 0.95$). Simultaneously, the level of agglomeration, as measured by the q-value, is increasing over time after a small initial drop.

Non-neutral space

Another objection to the analysis in the previous subsection might be that the modeling of space by means of the racetrack economy is rather special. With the racetrack economy each city enters symmetrically and there is no structural bias toward either agglomeration or spreading for any particular city. Although this has the advantage that any results are derived from the economic workings of the model rather than the pre-imposed geometric structure, we would also like to deal with some real-world phenomena arising from non-neutral space; see chapter 6. Nature often provides specific locations favoring agglomeration, such as valleys or natural harbors. We complete this chapter by giving an example indicating how non-neutral space in the core model with congestion may affect agglomeration. This thus means that we give an example of a type I extension here (see Table 6.2).

The so-called *Manhattan circles*, introduced to spatial economics by Kuiper *et al.* (1990), are a simple way of analyzing non-neutral space. Figure 7.9 depicts a

---

[23] The size of cities 1, 12, 13, and 24 is monotonically increasing; of cities 5, 6, 8, 14, 15, 18, 19, 20, 21, and 23 is monotonically decreasing; and of the remaining ten cities is first increasing and then decreasing.

a. Adjustment of some cities over time

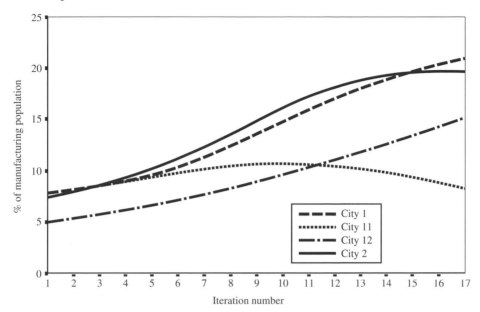

b. Adjustment of q-value and R^2 over time

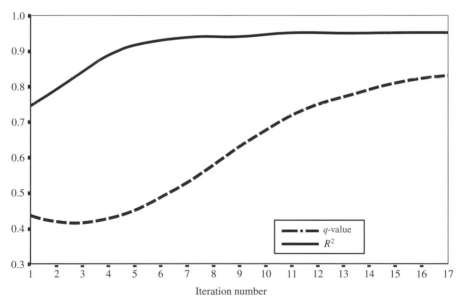

Figure 7.8.   Stepwise evolution.

		6		
	13	2	7	
12	5	1	3	8
	11	4	9	
		10		

Figure 7.9.   Manhattan circle with radius 2.

a. Center location is largest

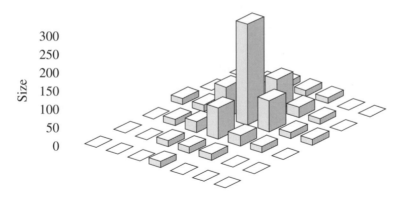

b. Center location is not largest

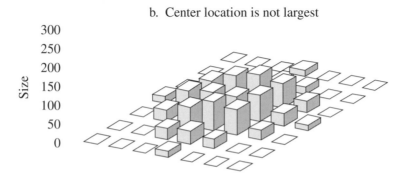

Figure 7.10.   Simulations with Manhattan circles.

Manhattan circle with radius 2. The distance between two locations is measured step-wise; thus the distance between locations 1 and 6 equals 2, and the distance between locations 13 and 4 equals 3. By construction location 1 is the most favorable location for agglomeration as the average distance to the other locations is minimal. One would expect that simulations of the core model with congestion using Manhattan circles instead of the racetrack economy lead to complete agglomeration of manufacturing production and mobile workers at location 1, which is by construction the most advantageous location.

For our present purposes, the main point that we want to bring across is that, despite its structural advantage in the center of the Manhattan circle, location 1 is not always the largest location in the long-run equilibrium. This is illustrated in Figure 7.10 where panel *a* depicts a typical outcome in which location 1 is the largest and panel *b* depicts an equilibrium outcome in which an off-center location is the largest. It is a reminder of the fact that in the model with congestion the structural advantage of location 1 need not be decisive in making this location the largest location. See Brakman *et al.* (1999) for further details.

7.5 Conclusions

In this chapter we have added an additional spreading force, congestion, to the core model of geographical economics. This extension came about by changing the production structure of the core model. It is therefore a type II extension (Table 6.2). The introduction of congestion as an additional spreading force served two main aims. The first was to make clear that this introduction has an impact on the nature of the long-run equilibria. With congestion, the model typically results in a more even equilibrium allocation of the manufacturing labor force. Complete agglomeration is now the exception and not, as in the core model, the rule. The second aim of this chapter was to apply the congestion version of the geographical economics model to an important topic in urban economics, the stability of city-size distributions. With respect to what is probably the best example of this stability, the version of the rank–size distribution known as Zipf's Law, we showed that the congestion model can replicate (changes in) actual rank–size distributions. This serves as an example that geographical economics is useful for the study of urban economics, but we want to stress that the model discussed in this chapter is certainly not meant as a fully fledged model of urban economics. In fact, the usefulness of (adaptations to) the core model of geographical economics for urban economics is thought by some to be limited (see Henderson, 2000). We will return to this topic in chapter 11. The analysis in this chapter is also certainly not the last word on Zipf's Law, if only because our model, like all other economic explanations, merely simulates the rank–size distribution. One obvious shortcoming of the model, when applied to urban economics, is its static nature, like all geographical economic models discussed so far. The question of how geographical economics can be used to analyze (urban) growth will be dealt with in chapter 10.

Appendix

Table 7.A1. *Country overview of rank–size distributions*

Country	City proper			Urban agglomeration		
	q	R^2	# obs.	q	R^2	# obs
Argentina	0.90	0.96	32	1.39	0.95	15
Australia	1.47	0.93	14	1.54	0.90	12
Bangladesh	—	—		1.17	0.95	18
Belarus	1.00	0.96	13	—	—	
Belgium	0.78	0.97	10	1.04	0.96	11
Brazil	0.81	0.99	193	—	—	
Bulgaria	1.01	0.97	10	0.95	0.95	10
Canada	0.75	0.93	36	1.15	0.98	30
Chile	0.88	0.81	20	—	—	
China	0.83	0.89	371	—	—	
Colombia	—	—		1.03	0.97	28
Congo	1.09	0.95	12	—	—	
Ecuador	1.18	0.86	10	—	—	
Egypt	1.22	0.96	23	—	—	
Ethiopia	1.07	0.71	10	—	—	
France	0.70	0.94	35	0.97	0.96	38
Germany	0.77	0.99	84	—	—	
India	0.89	0.99	300	1.05	0.99	175
Indonesia	1.10	0.98	50	—	—	
Iran	0.97	0.99	46	—	—	
Iraq	0.82	0.88	18	—	—	
Israel	0.62	0.94	12	—	—	
Italy	—	—		0.87	0.99	52
Japan	0.75	0.99	217	—	—	
Kazakhstan	0.70	0.95	21	0.69	0.96	20
Korea	1.24	0.99	39	—	—	
Malaysia	0.80	0.84	13	0.72	0.96	11
Mexico	0.89	0.97	72	—	—	
Morocco	—	—		1.07	0.98	16
Netherlands	0.67	0.94	21	0.77	0.96	21
Nigeria	0.63	0.95	27	—	—	
Pakistan	—	—		1.30	0.98	23
Peru	1.16	0.90	17	—	—	
Philippines	0.71	0.97	62	—	—	
Poland	0.76	0.99	42	—	—	
Romania	0.70	0.87	25	—	—	
Russia	0.82	0.96	168	0.86	0.96	104
South Africa	0.70	0.96	32	—	—	
Spain	0.74	0.98	55	—	—	
Sweden	0.86	0.93	11	0.90	0.93	11
Thailand	—	—		1.29	0.76	11
Turkey	1.03	0.99	47	0.90	0.98	38
Ukraine	0.87	0.97	50	—	—	

Table 7.A1. (*cont.*)

Country	City proper			Urban agglomeration		
	q	R^2	# obs.	q	R^2	# obs
United Kingdom	0.49	0.94	234	—	—	
United States	0.75	0.99	209	1.10	0.95	115
Uzbekistan	0.90	0.90	15	—	—	
Venezuela	0.94	0.98	28	1.20	0.97	16
Vietnam	1.03	0.96	23	1.15	0.91	23

Notes: q = estimated coefficient; # obs. = number of available observations.

Exercises

7.1* Explain why equation (7.1), with τ not equal to 0, displays *external* economies of scale. Also explain why, irrespective of the value of τ, equation (7.1) is characterized by internal economies of scale as well.

7.2 One possible criticism of the application of our multiple region model with congestion costs to urban systems is that it cannot deal with the evolution of these systems in *frontier states* like the USA. Another possible criticism is that the model of chapter 7 cannot deal with urban growth. Address both criticisms.

7.3 Have a look at Table 7.A1. Compare the rank–size distributions (using data for cities proper) for developing countries with those for the developed countries and give possible explanations for the relative difference in the importance of primate cities in these countries.

7.4* What would happen in terms of core–periphery equilibria if in equation (7.1) we choose $-1 < \tau < 0$?

7.5* Compared to the core model of chapters 3 and 4, the two-region model with congestion costs favors spreading instead of complete agglomeration. The main reason why this is the case is very similar to the housing model of geographical economics due to Helpman (1998) and discussed in chapters 5 and 6. In Box 7.1 some information on the variation of housing prices across city sizes was given. Explain the corresponding differences in nominal as well as real wages across these cities.

8 Agglomeration and international business

8.1 Introduction

Globalization has many faces. The most characteristic aspect of globalization is that it appears that the world becomes smaller; transport costs are reduced, trade barriers disappear, and information becomes less expensive and becomes itself an internationally traded product. Although spreading of economic activity is certainly possible, the lessons of the geographical economics approach might increase fears of an ever-growing gap between nations, in which, because of decreases in trade costs, center–periphery structures become the rule instead of the exception. One of the major actors in this process of globalization is the multinational firm, or multinational for short. This is probably the most mobile among all firms, with sufficient "international" knowledge to seize a profitable opportunity when it presents itself. Without specific cultural ties to individual nations, it can rapidly move in and out of countries, acting only on economic incentives. Given the recent growth in foreign direct investment (FDI), which at the moment is growing faster than international trade, one might expect multinational firms to be decisive in at least some of the agglomeration and spreading trends going on today. It will turn out that the geographical economics approach is an excellent and promising methodology to look at multinationals. Together with the general equilibrium models developed in the 1980s by Helpman and Krugman (1985), they provide an improvement to the useful taxonomic OLI framework of Dunning (1977, 1981); see section 8.3.

In chapter 6 we explained how the introduction of intermediate goods can change the mechanisms leading to spreading or agglomeration. Firms, rather than labor, were assumed to be mobile. Agglomeration can come about if workers move to other sectors; in other words, workers are immobile between regions or countries, but mobile within those regions and countries. That model did not incorporate the decisions of firms to set up (part of) production in a foreign market. This is what we will do in this chapter. In section 8.2 we present some stylized facts about multinational production. Section 8.3 discusses modern developments in explaining multinational production. Section 8.4 studies a more formal modeling approach, using the framework of geographical economics. Section 8.5 presents some (indirect) evidence on the relevance of multinationals. Section 8.6 presents our conclusions.

8.2 Multinational production: stylized facts

Geography has traditionally been a very important factor in describing and explaining the behavior of multinationals, and for describing the flows of FDI. Obviously, the choice of locations for headquarters and production facilities is critical in describing multinational production. Firms seem to be able to change location very often and have to decide where to locate a particular part of the firm. Data on multinationals are notoriously difficult to obtain, not only because of data availability, but also because of conceptual difficulties. A multinational is a firm that controls, by means of ownership, productive assets in more than one country. But ownership and control may vary between 0% and 100%. It is therefore a matter of definition when one speaks of multinationals; see Markusen (1995).[1] Data on FDI are systematically collected by UNCTAD and the World Bank, thus providing the best sources for data on FDI. They show that since the 1980s FDI has grown astonishingly fast, even faster than international trade. This is illustrated in Figure 8.1.

On average, world-wide nominal GDP has grown by more than 7% per year between 1970 and 1997. During this period, international trade, measured by world-wide nominal imports, grew by more than 12%, whereas nominal FDI grew by almost 31%. Not only has the level of FDI increased, but it has also changed from investments in manufacturing to investment in services. Furthermore, investments increasingly take place in the form of mergers.

Not all types of firms seem to become multinational. We can distinguish four characteristics: multinationals (i) appear to be concentrated in industries characterized by a high ratio of R&D to sales, (ii) tend to have high values of intangible assets, (iii) are often associated with new or technologically advanced and differentiated products, and (iv) are often relatively old, large and more established firms within their sector; see Markusen (1995).

As illustrated in Figure 8.2, the predominant sources of FDI are the high-income developed countries. In the period 1987–1992, the developed countries accounted for more than 90% of outflowing FDI, and for more than 85% in the period 1993–1998. The main destinations of FDI are also the advanced countries. In the period 1988–1998 they received more than 70% of the inflowing FDI. As such, these data reflect what also holds for inter- and intra-industry trade, namely that most economic interaction takes place between the developed countries; see chapter 9. Most of these observations can be explained, of course, by the difference in the economic sizes of developed and developing countries. As Figure 8.2c clearly shows, in recent years Western Europe has been the main net source of FDI flows.

Table 8.1 gives the Foreign Direct Investment position of the USA, Japan, and the EU–15 countries, which are the major investors. From the table it is again obvious that the advanced countries are the main destinations for FDI. Although developing countries are relatively unimportant for FDI, it is interesting to note that just ten developing

---

[1] The US Bureau of Economic Analysis distinguishes majority-owned foreign subsidiaries of US parents from affiliates, where the latter have at least 10% non-US ownership. The criteria are of course subject to discussion.

a. World FDI, GDP, and trade (1970 = 100)

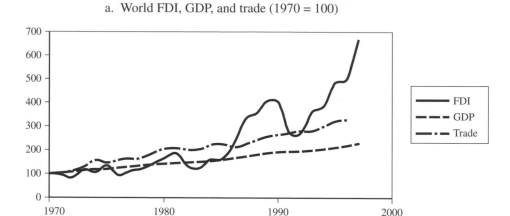

b. FDI (% of GDP)   c. Trade (% of GDP)

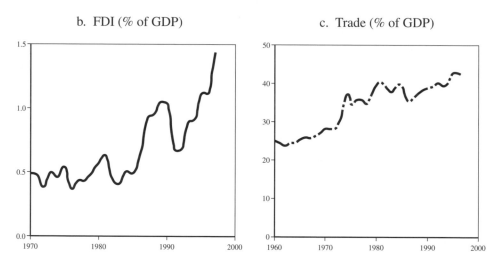

Figure 8.1. Development of world GDP, FDI, and trade. *Source*: World Bank, *World Bank Development Indicators*, CD-ROM, 1999.

countries accounted for two-thirds of inward FDI to all developing countries; see Shatz and Venables (2000).[2] China received 30.6% of this. Recently China has witnessed a fourfold increase of FDI in relative terms: in the period 1988–1992 it received 2.9% of total world FDI, compared to more than 12% in the period 1993–1997.

8.3   Explaining multinational production

The field of international economics mostly studies trade in goods, although it has focused somewhat more on services recently. Indeed, the central lesson of the

[2] Argentina, Brazil, Chile, China, Hungary, Indonesia, Malaysia, Mexico, Poland, Singapore.

a. FDI inflows (billion $)

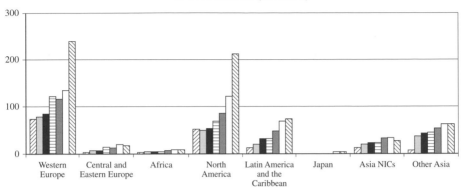

b. FDI outflows (billion $)

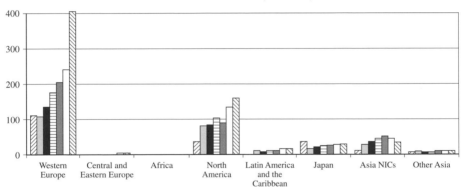

c. Net FDI flows (billion $)

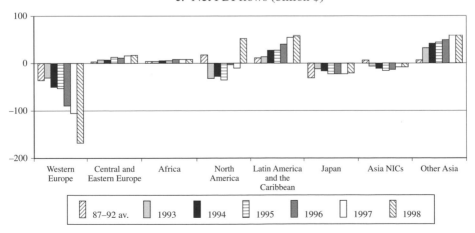

Figure 8.2. Foreign direct investment (FDI) flows. (*Data source*: UNCTAD, 1999.)

Table 8.1. *Outward foreign direct investment, billion US $ (%)*

	All countries	Advanced countries	Developing countries
USA	777.2 (100%)	536.3 (69%)	240.9 (31%)
Japan	463.6 (100%)	317.0 (68%)	146.6 (32%)
EU–15	76.0 (100%)	61.4 (87%)	14.6 (13%)

Source: Shatz and Venables (2000); USA stock, 1996; Japan stock, 1994; EU–15 flows, 1994.

neo-classical workhorse of international trade theory, the factor abundance model, suggests that trade in goods and trade in production factors are substitutes; see chapter 2. In general, however, this is only true for the simple two country, two factors of production, and two goods model without transport costs and not too different factor endowments. In most other cases, trade in goods and trade in production factors might be complements; see, for example, Wong (1986). The implication is that, even in the neo-classical factor abundance context, it is worthwhile to look at the effects of trade in production factors, of which FDI represents a special case.

The existence of multinationals influences the behavior of variables like the volume of trade and the share of intra-industry trade. However, it was not trade theory which first tried to explain the existence of multinationals, but the descriptive industrial organization literature. The best example is the OLI approach of Dunning (1977, 1981a, 1981b). According to Dunning (1977), three conditions need to be satisfied in order for a firm to become a multinational. These three conditions are known as OLI: Ownership advantage, Location advantage, and Internalization advantage. Ownership advantage means that a firm has a product which enjoys some market power in foreign markets; location advantage implies that foreign production is more profitable than exports; internalization advantage makes it more profitable for a firm to exploit the product itself than to license it to a foreign firm.

The OLI methodology has been extended in various directions, mostly concentrating on better data and more advanced tests; for a survey, see Bowen, Hollander, and Viaene (1998). In this type of literature, variables describing existing multinationals are correlated with variables which represent the O, the L, or the I (in one way or another) of the OLI model. This method provides a useful categorization scheme of variables and gives clues as to what set of variables best characterize multinationals.[3] It is at best a partial equilibrium approach, which focuses on characteristics of individual firms or even plants, but does not explain why or how multinationals come about, or answer the question of what triggers multinational behavior in the first place. In contrast, this is central in the modern theories of multinationals.[4]

---

[3] Among the frequently mentioned variables are knowledge capital, which can easily be transported or transferred, large trade barriers of one kind or another, and less expensive inputs in other countries.

[4] A somewhat separate strand of literature stresses strategic oligopolistic interaction between firms. In such models one can show, for example, that because of strategic interaction between firms, foreign production is the preferred option even when cost considerations might suggest exporting.

Box 8.1. Michael Porter

The OLI literature has provided useful insights on the factors that determine the decision to become a multinational firm. In the management literature one can also find elements describing essential characteristics of multinationals. The management literature, however, seems to develop more or less separately from the economics literature. The most famous example of this phenomenon is Michael Porter, the management superstar and writer of the bestseller *Competitive Advantage: Creating and Sustaining Superior Performance* (1985). He produces impressive lists of characteristics of firms and regions, and suggests how they influence each other. The term "competitiveness" is central in his analysis. According to Porter, competitiveness is the ability to innovate and to improve processes and products. Local competition is important, and even necessary, for international success. Case study analyses are used to prove his point.

Multinationals can compete only when they have a strong position in their home market. Sales are most easy to multinationalize according to Porter. R&D, on the other hand, is much harder to multinationalize. He notes that businesses are becoming more global, which introduces greater competition in each country. From his research, Porter concludes that the conditions at a company's home base are crucial for its competitiveness abroad. In particular, innovative vitality appears to be established at home. Moreover, geographical clusters of activity seem to be very important. Basically his list comprises the forward and backward linkages already described by Marshall and the classical geographers and discussed in chapter 2. He does not analyze why these clusters establish themselves or how they evolve from the characteristics he identifies. His analysis gives *ex post* rationalizations of clusters. Once a cluster is successful, firms can try to establish themselves as multinationals.

Why is it that some countries are wealthier than other countries, and that some industries are more successful than others? According to Porter, location also matters. Not because of "location" advantages, as in the OLI literature, but because rivalry stimulates "innovation," and most competition occurs among competitors who are geographically concentrated. These clusters of excellence could be defined as a city, a region, or a continent, but nations are the most important level of aggregation. On this level, demand conditions are affected by macro-economic policy; the dynamism of competition by national antitrust and trade policy; the level and type of skills by the national education system; and the attitudes of managers, workers, and customers by a national culture. A global strategy merely supplements the competitive advantage created in the home base. National success creates the opportunity to cross borders. It is crucial that companies cling on to those virtues when they expand abroad. Going global comes from "home."

Although the elements Porter puts forward are familiar, and his analysis points relevant factors, he does not give causal relationships between all his characteristics, or explain in what sense they influence each other, nor does he discuss the choice between exporting or going multinational, or how the difference between horizontal and vertically differentiated multinationals is established. In a sense, Porter returns to the state of affairs of the 1950s when Myrdal was discussing issues like cumulative causation, but was unable, at that time, to formalize his ideas into a consistent model. The lists that Porter produces are good starting points for further analysis to understand which factors determine the "competitiveness" of firms and which factors are most relevant. Nevertheless, it turns out that the work by Porter has been an inspiration for Paul Krugman; see Box 11.2.

8.3.1   *Multinationals in trade theory*

The modern theories alluded to above try to model the behavior of firms, and identify under what circumstances they become multinational. There are two main reasons for a firm to go multinational. One is to serve a foreign market more profitably at the foreign location, and the other is that the foreign market provides lower-cost inputs. The first reason to become multinational is associated with so-called horizontal multinationals. They simply duplicate their business in a foreign country, because local provision of goods is more profitable. It usually substitutes for exports from the home country. So-called vertical multinationals, on the other hand, are in the business of "slicing up the value chain" to use a phrase from Paul Krugman. The idea is that certain stages of the production process can be made more cost-efficient by relocating them to low-cost locations. This type of multinational behavior is complementary to trade and usually trade-creating, because the (intermediate) products from different countries have to be shipped to other countries in order to be assembled. A brief case study was given in chapter 1, when discussing the hard disk drive industry. The distinction is not always very clear, as vertically differentiated firms might also sell to foreign markets.

The now classic theory of vertically differentiated multinationals has been developed primarily by Helpman (1984a), and Helpman and Krugman (1985). At its most basic level, it is a general equilibrium model in which large differences in factor endowments between countries are crucial for the decision to become multinational or not. The existence of multinationals thus becomes endogenous in this model, which is basically an extended version of the factor abundance model. In Helpman and Krugman (1985) there are two sectors, food and manufactures. Food is produced using only capital and labor, which have to come from the same location, and is produced according to a standard linear cost function. The production of differentiated manufactures requires capital and labor, but also so-called headquarters services. These (differentiated) services can be used in plants at different locations, but once specific headquarters services are adopted they become a firm-specific asset and tied to the entrepreneurial unit or plant that uses them. Headquarters services are produced using capital and labor. The production of manufactures is characterized by increasing returns to scale. It therefore pays to concentrate the production in a single plant. As usual, all varieties have the same cost structure. The central idea is that different stages in the production process have different (production) factor intensities. For example, headquarters services are the most capital-intensive, and the production of food is the least capital-intensive. The production of manufactures, therefore, has intermediate capital intensity.

It is now easy to understand how multinationals might develop in the Helpman and Krugman model. Free trade in goods can bring about factor price equalization if factor endowments in the two countries are not too different. If this is the case, there is no incentive to form a multinational. Now suppose that factor endowments differ between the two countries in such a way that factor prices are not equalized. Then firms have an incentive to become multinational, because factor price differentials offer an opportunity to look for cost efficiency. Not surprisingly, headquarters services are located in the capital-rich country. This country therefore becomes a net exporter of headquarters (capital-intensive) services to its production location in the labor-rich country, and a net importer of labor-intensive products. Clearly the presence of multinationals influences the structure of intra-industry trade if the products of multinationals are traded, although the precise link between trade and the existence of multinationals can be quite complicated; see Helpman and Krugman (1985, ch. 12). This specialization increases relative demand for labor in the labor-rich country and for capital in the capital-rich country, thus increasing the probability of factor price equalization.

The Helpman and Krugman model provides a step forward compared to the more descriptive OLI models, but seems at odds with the stylized facts of multinational production. First, the model assumes that international trade of goods and trade in headquarters services are both without costs. In this model, multinationals arise in the absence of transport cost or other trade barriers, the driving force being the uneven distribution of production factors over countries. More specifically, the model assumes that splitting the production of headquarters services and the production of the final (or intermediate) good can be done at no additional cost. Most importantly, however, the model implies that no (FDI) investment takes place between similar countries (meaning similar factor endowments and thus factor price equalization). As we have seen, most foreign direct investment in fact takes place between similar countries. So, the model might provide a well-designed way to incorporate multinationals endogenously in a general equilibrium model, but leaves a large part of these investments to be explained.[5]

Introducing trade barriers to the model is illuminating. From standard trade theory, we know that trade barriers diminish the chances of factor price equalization, and as

---

[5] Venables (1999) has extended this strand of literature, stressing fragmentation and its effect on international trade more than agglomeration or spreading (in fact, his model assumes constant returns to scale and perfect competition).

such stimulate splitting up production and vertical multinationals. This tendency toward splitting up production is, however, counterbalanced by more costly trade due to the barriers themselves; location of production sites in various countries increases trade, and thus increases total trade costs. The further one locates from the center, the higher trade costs are. Whether or not to locate in a remote location depends on the balance between these two factors: low factor prices stimulate investment of those activities which use these factors intensively; high trade costs discourage these investments. This reasoning suggests that similar countries and high trade costs stimulate horizontal multinationals, the more so if these distant markets are large. The elements mentioned here must sound familiar from our earlier discussions of the geographical economics literature in chapters 3 to 7.

8.4 Multinationals in geographical economics

Various models have been developed incorporating the notion of multinationals in the core model of geographical economics, allowing for the endogenous formation of vertically and horizontally differentiated multinationals; see, for example, Ekholm and Forslid (1997), or Markusen and Venables (1998). These studies have in common that a less simplistic notion of the firm is adopted compared to that in the core model. In the terminology of chapter 6, they thus provide a type II, version 3 extension of the core model, by adapting the production structure of that model, more specifically in terms of firm behavior. In the core model, the firm is essentially identical to the plant and no decisions have to be taken on the organization of the firm. A less restrictive view on the firm is the distinguishing feature of the modern literature on multinationals. How do the results of such a model compare to those of the core model with respect to agglomeration and spreading forces?

We take Ekholm and Forslid (1997) as an example in our discussion, because they closely follow the core model, and at the same time illustrate how the existence of multinationals, both horizontally integrated and vertically integrated, changes the tendencies for agglomeration and spreading. We concentrate on two countries only. The basic structure is straightforward. In chapter 3 the cost function for a firm producing x_{ir} units of variety i in country r was represented as: $W_r l_{ir} = \alpha W_r + \beta W_r x_{ir}$, that is both fixed labor costs α and variable labor costs β are incurred in the same location. From the discussion above, we know that horizontally integrated multinationals arise if factor prices differ between locations. Since the only production factor in this framework is labor, we only have to analyze the impact of firm's decisions on wage differentials between locations, provided the firms are able to split up the production process. Now suppose that headquarters services are produced only in one country, whereas actual production can take place either in the other country (vertical integration), or in both countries (horizontal integration). Typically, headquarters services are associated with R&D, financial services and other specialized services, such as marketing, accounting, etc., produced and organized at a firm's headquarters. If we assume that these headquarters services are available, without any extra cost, in the production sites, they can be seen as goods traded at no cost. Because of the fixed-cost nature of these services it pays to choose a single location for the headquarters of the firm. In general, the cost function for firm i with its headquarters in country r is:

$$W_r l_{ir} + W_k l_{ik} = \alpha W_r + \beta(W_r x_{ir} + W_k x_{ik}) \qquad r = 1,2\,; k = 1,2 \qquad (8.1)$$

where

$\quad l_{ir}$ = labor used by firm i in location r
$\quad l_{ik}$ = labor used by firm i in location k
$\quad x_{ir}$ = production level of firm i in location r
$\quad x_{ik}$ = production level of firm i in location k

We can distinguish three separate logical possibilities. The latter two are discussed in more detail below. To be concrete, this is illustrated in Figure 8.3 for the firm producing variety 5, assuming that its headquarters are in country 1.

Figure 8.3a. It is not possible to separate the production of headquarters services from the manufacture of goods in the production site, that is both have to be produced simultaneously in the same country. This has been analyzed in the core model of chapters 3 and 4.

Figure 8.3b. It is possible to separate the production of headquarters services from the manufacture of goods at the production site. Moreover, it is possible to supervise several production locations simultaneously. The firm can thus set up production plants in both countries simultaneously, and it must choose where to set up its headquarters. This is the case of *horizontal integration*.

Figure 8.3c. It is possible to separate the production of headquarters services from the manufacture of goods at the production site. However, the manufacture of goods must take place at one location, perhaps because the headquarters can supervise only one production plant at a time. The firm must now choose where to set up its production plant as well as its headquarters. This is the case of *vertical integration*.

Horizontally integrated multinationals

We first have a look at horizontal multinationals in this model. With positive trade costs and no extra costs of setting up an extra plant in the other country, the symmetric division of production over the two countries is stable, because transport costs can be avoided by starting production in the second country. The complete agglomeration situation, where the whole firm is located in either country 1 or country 2, can never be a stable equilibrium because a firm starting production in the periphery can capture the whole "foreign" market, as no transport costs have to be charged. Furthermore, if all firms produce symmetrically in both regions, the price indices in both countries are identical. The location of the firm's headquarters is now straightforward: headquarters services are produced in the country with the lowest wage. In this case its location

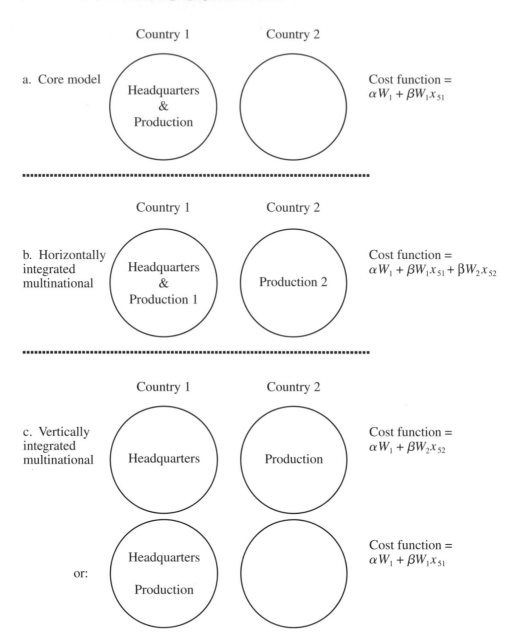

Figure 8.3.   Production structure for variety 5 if headquarters are in country 1.

is undetermined.[6] Note that this result is in contrast to the core model. For positive trade costs, spreading of manufacturing is the only stable equilibrium; agglomeration is no longer possible. Introducing extra costs into the model, such as extra costs to open a second production plant, reduces the extreme nature of this conclusion. In general, however, agglomeration in the presence of horizontal multinationals becomes less likely. It is interesting to note that this conclusion corresponds to the work of Markusen (1995), where multinationals arise when countries are similar with respect to their respective factor endowments. In the geographical economics approach, however, countries become more similar because multinational production arises.

Vertically integrated multinationals

If we turn to vertically integrated multinationals, the firm has to choose where to locate the headquarters and where to locate the production plant of the firm. As with horizontal multinationals, the symmetric division of firms over both regions is a possible equilibrium. This time, however, it is possibly an unstable equilibrium. In fact, the spreading equilibrium is stable for exactly the same parameter values as in the core model analyzed in chapters 3 and 4; in effect the two models are identical in this respect.

For parameter values for which the symmetric spreading equilibrium becomes unstable, what happens depends on how fast headquarters can relocate relative to production. If the symmetric equilibrium becomes unstable and headquarters are slow to move, first production will move to the larger region, and then headquarters will follow, because, in contrast to the case described above, one can by assumption not avoid transport costs by locating part of the production unit in the other country. Here the larger market has a cost advantage, because in the (relative) absence of transport costs, wages will be lower in the larger region. Headquarters and production will therefore eventually locate in the larger country or region, and this will eventually lead to complete agglomeration.

The analysis is more interesting, and intuitively more plausible, if headquarters are either fast movers, or cannot move at all once they are established. For ease of exposition, we assume throughout the remainder of this chapter that all headquarters are located in country 1. In this case, stable equilibria between symmetric spreading and agglomeration are possible with vertical multinationals. Note, first of all, that headquarters services have to be paid for from operating profits, that is firms charge a higher price than marginal costs (the mark-up) to recover the outlay for fixed costs. The basic decision problem facing a firm with headquarters in country 1 is illustrated in Figure 8.4. If the firm decides to produce in country 1 its marginal production costs are βW_1, which determine the price the firm charges, the production level at which the firm recuperates its operating profits, and the number of laborers required for this production level. Similarly, if the firm decides to produce in country 2 its marginal production

---

[6] Once a firm chooses a site for its headquarters, the local demand for labor increases (in order to produce headquarters services) and drives up wages. Because the location of the headquarters is indeterminate and there are many firms making this decision at the same time, headquarters will be symmetrically distributed.

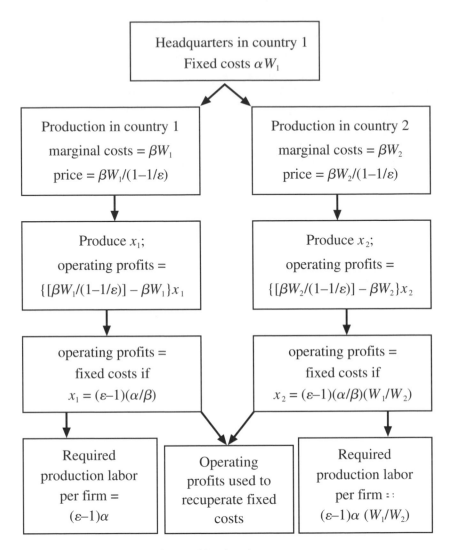

Figure 8.4. Decision problem for vertical multinationals.

costs are βW_2, which has different repercussions for the price the firm charges, the production level at which it recuperates fixed costs, and the number of laborers required for this production level. Note in particular that if the firm decides to set up a production facility in country 2, it will repatriate the operating profits ("transferring" these to country 1) to recuperate the fixed costs of production. Multinationals are often criticized for this type of practice, which in this setting is entirely unwarranted.

In the short-run equilibrium the equations in Figure 8.4 must hold exactly because an individual firm should, in its production, be indifferent between country 1 and country 2, and there is entry and exit of firms producing in either country until profits are zero. The most important thing to note is that the production level for firms producing in country 2 depends on the wage level in country 2 relative to the wage level in country 1. This obviously arises from the fact that the fixed costs arising from head-quarters services are paid at the wage rate, W_1, in country 1, while the marginal costs from the production plant are paid the wage rate W_2. To be more precise, a firm producing in country 2 has an equilibrium production level equal to W_1/W_2 times that of a firm producing in country 1. Thus, if the wage rate is *higher* in country 2 than in country 1, a firm with a production plant in country 2 will produce *less* output in equilibrium. This implies, other things being equal, that a given number of manufacturing laborers in country 2 will produce a higher number of varieties locally, giving rise to a positive welfare effect through love of variety. Other things are, moreover, not equal, but reinforce this effect. Remember that the production of headquarters services all takes place in country 1, such that all manufacturing workers in country 2 are available for production activities to reinforce the above effect of a larger locally produced number of varieties in country 2. In essence, this gives two spreading effects, which may result in partial, rather than complete, agglomeration.

Following a similar procedure to that in chapters 3 and 4 we can derive the short-run equilibrium for the model with vertical multinationals, that is the equilibrium that arises given the distribution of the manufacturing workforce. This is given in equations (8.2)–(8.5) below, with the impostion of the normalization of chapter 4 so that these equations can be compared to equations (4.1′)–(4.3′).

$$\lambda_1 = N_1 + (1/\varepsilon)N_2 \tag{8.2}$$

$$\lambda_2 = (1-1/\varepsilon)(W_1/W_2)N_2 \tag{8.2'}$$

$$Y_r = \delta\lambda_r W_r + (1-\delta)\phi_r \qquad r = 1, 2 \tag{8.3}$$

$$I_r = \left(\sum_{s=1}^{2} N_s T_{rs}^{1-\varepsilon} W_s^{1-\varepsilon} \right)^{1/(1-\varepsilon)} \qquad r = 1, 2 \tag{8.4}$$

$$W_1 = \left(\sum_{r=1}^{2} Y_r T_{r1}^{1-\varepsilon} I_r^{\varepsilon-1} \right)^{1/\varepsilon} \tag{8.5}$$

$$W_2 = (W_2/W_1)^{1/\varepsilon}\left(\sum_{r=1}^{2} Y_r T_{r2}^{1-\varepsilon} I_r^{\varepsilon-1} \right)^{1/\varepsilon} \tag{8.5'}$$

Equations (8.2) and (8.2′) are the full-employment equations for manufacturing labor in the two countries, which determine the number of varieties produced in country 1 and in country 2. In the core model of chapters 3 and 4 these two equations simplify to $\lambda_r = N_r$ for $r = 1, 2$. Since in the model with vertical multinationals all fixed labor is located in country 1 and, as discussed above, all manufacturing labor in country 2 is thus available for production activities, other things being equal country 2 will produce more, and country 1 will produce fewer varieties than in the core model. Equation (8.3), giving the income level in both countries, is identical to equation (4.1′). Equation (8.4), giving the price index in both countries, is almost identical to equation (4.2′). The only difference is that N_r replaces λ_r because equations (8.2) and (8.2′) indicate that these two variables are not (through a normalization) identical in the framework with vertical multinationals. Finally, the wage equation (8.5) is identical to (4.3′) for country 1, since the equilibrium conditions for a firm producing in country 1 have not changed, as summarized in Figure 8.4. However, equation (8.5′) is not identical to (4.3′) for country 2 because the fixed costs occur in country 1, and not in country 2. Only if the wage rate in the two countries is the same is this equation identical, as is obvious from its formulation.

As argued above, we can analyze in this context two situations, namely where headquarters cannot move (but manufacturing labor can), and where headquarters can be relocated quickly (as well as manufacturing labor). Both situations are illustrated simultaneously in the simulations of Figure 8.5, which solve equations (8.2)–(8.5) for different distributions of the manufacturing labor force. If headquarters cannot relocate, both the solid and the dashed lines of the short-run equilibrium hold. As always, manufacturing labor will relocate if the real wage is higher in one country than in the other. Figure 8.5 shows that for relatively low transport costs ($T = 1.1$) the partial agglomeration equilibrium is unstable. For somewhat higher transport costs ($T = 1.19$ and $T = 1.64$) partial agglomeration is a stable equilibrium. If headquarters can relocate quickly, only the solid lines in Figure 8.5 represent a short-run equilibrium. This holds because the firms will only locate the headquarters in country 1 if the wage rate is lower in country 1 than in country 2. Otherwise, they will quickly relocate the headquarters to the other country. We therefore have to verify whether or not $W_1 < W_2$ in the short-run equilibrium. In Figure 8.5 this holds only for the solid lines, and not for the dashed lines. In any case, the results indicate again that a stable equilibrium with partial agglomeration is possible.

In a similar model Markusen and Venables (1998, p. 201) find that "multinationals tend to be found in equilibrium when firm-level scale economies and tariff/transport costs are large relative to plant-level scale economies." Among the extensions they consider are two production factors, instead of one, which facilitates the analysis of country differences. Furthermore, they distinguish plant from firm economies of scale, implying that each good is produced by only one firm, but can be produced at different plants at different locations, because of the existence of transport costs. In general, they find that multinational production becomes more important as countries become similar in size. The analysis also implies that further (trade) liberalization shifts multinational production to the smaller and less developed countries. Gao (1999) reaches similar conclusions in an encompassing model which allows for more elaborate demand and cost linkages between firms. Baldwin and Ottaviano (2000), show that this approach can easily be extended to create a link between trade and FDI; FDI might replace trade, but if varieties are sold to third markets, it also implies trade creation instead of trade diversion.

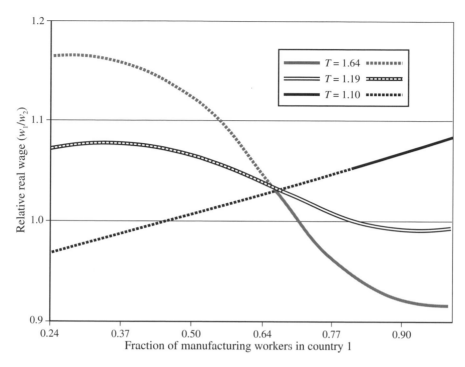

Figure 8.5.　Agglomeration with vertically integrated multinationals (parameters $\delta = 0.4$ and $\varepsilon = 5$).

8.5　Empirical evidence

The literature providing empirical evidence of the determinants of multinational production is quite large; see Markusen (1995) for a survey. Much attention has been devoted to finding specific variables in the OLI approach. Although useful, these studies do not answer the questions on the relevance of different economic models. We do not survey this literature, but select and discuss only those studies which can shed some light on the relevance of geographical economics. This will illustrate the significance of agglomeration or spreading with respect to FDI.

As is the case with empirical results on geographical economics in general, empirical evidence on the agglomeration or spreading effects of investment decisions by multinational firms is in short supply. Not only do different models predict different outcomes, but the various equilibria in a geographical economics model also depend on specific values of the relevant parameters. Both agglomeration and spreading can result from the same geographical economics model, according to the values of those parameters. This becomes especially awkward if parameter values change over time, or differ across space. At present, evidence is indirect and one must hope that all this evidence assembled together will give a broader understanding.

First of all, one can look at the location behavior of firms with the characteristics of

Table 8.2. *Top twenty transnational corporations, ranked by foreign assets, 1997*

Corporation	Country	Industry	Assets		Sales		Employment		TNC index
			Foreign	Total	Foreign	Total	Foreign	Total	
1 General El.	USA	Electronics	97	304	25	91	111	276	33
2 Ford Motor	USA	Automotive	73	275	48	154	174	364	35
3 Shell Group	NL/UK	Petroleum	70	115	69	128	65	105	59
4 Gen. Motors	USA	Automotive	–	229	51	178	–	608	29
5 Exxon	USA	Petroleum	55	96	105	120	–	80	66
6 Toyota	Japan	Automotive	42	105	50	89	–	159	40
7 IBM	USA	Computers	40	82	49	79	135	269	54
8 Volkswagen	Germ.	Automotive	–	57	43	65	134	280	57
9 Nestlé	Switz.	Food	32	38	48	48	220	226	93
10 Daimler	Germ.	Automotive	31	76	46	69	75	300	44
11 Mobil	USA	Petroleum	30	44	37	64	22	43	60
12 FIAT	Italy	Automotive	30	69	20	51	95	242	41
13 Hoechst	Germ.	Chemicals	29	34	24	30	–	137	77
14 Asea BB	Switz.	El. equip.	–	30	30	31	201	213	96
15 Bayer	Germ.	Chemicals	–	30	–	32	–	145	83
16 Elf	France	Petroleum	27	42	26	42	41	84	58
17 Nissan	Japan	Automotive	27	58	28	50	–	137	51
18 Unilever	NL/UK	Food	26	31	45	46	263	269	92
19 Siemens	Germ.	Electronics	26	67	40	61	201	386	52
20 Roche	Switz.	Pharmac.	–	38	13	13	42	52	82

Source: UNCTAD (1999). Sales and assets in billion $, employment in thousands, TNC index = Transnationality Index (%); average of the foreign shares of assets, sales, and employment ($\times 100$).

multinationals. As mentioned earlier in this chapter, multinationals are characterized by (i) a high ratio of R&D, (ii) the employment of relatively skilled labor, (iii) being associated with new or complex products, and (iv) having a minimum threshold of production size (above this threshold, firm size is less important); see Markusen (1995). If firms with these characteristics cluster together, this suggests that it also holds for multinationals.

Looking at the top twenty multinationals and the sectors in which these firms operate, as listed in Table 8.2, suggests that multinationals are indeed active in sectors in which R&D and new and complex products are very important. The study by Midelfart-Knarvik *et al.* (2000), is particularly illuminating in this respect. Using different measures of specialization for at least thirteen EU countries and at least thirty-six industries for the period 1970 to 1997, they find evidence of increased specialization during the years 1994 to 1997, which might indicate that relatively few industries become dominant in a few locations. Further regional disaggregation shows that increased specialization is found in either relatively poor regions or relatively rich regions which have undergone a major structural change, that is become more services-oriented than manufactures-oriented; see Hallet (2000). This evidence might reflect trade liberalization within the EU, which allows more industry-level specialization, especially affecting intra-industry trade. But, in which industries are countries specializing? Midelfart-Knarvik *et al.* (2000) also answer this question. Identifying industries by key characteristics, like economies of scale, R&D intensity, skill intensity, inter-industry linkages, and technology level, they find a clear distinction between "North" and "South" Europe. Industrial structures of France, Germany, and the United Kingdom are best described by high returns to scale, high technology, and a relatively highly educated workforce. These countries are the home of industries like motor vehicles, motorcycles, aircraft, chemicals, electrical apparatus, and the petro-chemical industry; these are industries in which multinationals are active. The industrial structure of Spain, Portugal, and Greece is characterized by low returns to scale, low technology, and less skilled labor. They are relatively unable to attract the industries with the characteristics of the North.

Hallet (2000) also finds that the most spatially concentrated industries are to be found within manufacturing (which is more concentrated than GDP). Products which are not characterized by knowledge content and related factors are found all over Europe. One could call these "day-to-day products," which due to lack of economies of scale do not benefit from clustering in specific regions or countries. These findings corroborate the fact that the EU is a popular host for FDI. This holds especially for the northern part of the EU. Also the increased specialization patterns in the EU are consistent with the predictions of the geographical economics models which include multinationals; if multinationals are present, core–periphery patterns, or clustering of all activity, is less likely. All countries have become more specialized (although increased specialization does not imply agglomeration). The broad picture within the EU is consistent with what we expect to find on the basis of the theoretical models, but these findings only indirectly confirm the relevance of the geographical economics approach in the presence of multinationals.

Table 8.3. *Geographical distribution of the activities of US foreign affiliates (%)*

| Country | Gross product | | | | Employment |
	1977	1982	1989	1995	1995
Europe	*56.5*	*54.9*	*57.8*	*60.0*	*45.1*
UK	14.9	17.3	15.9	12.2	11.6
Germany	16.8	15.3	15.0	17.2	10.8
France	8.7	7.4	6.9	8.2	6.0
Italy	3.8	3.9	4.5	4.1	3.6
Netherlands	3.1	2.6	4.5	3.7	1.8
Belgium	3.6	2.4	2.9	3.3	1.7
Ireland	0.7	1.3	2.0	3.2	1.4
Spain	2.1	1.9	3.3	2.9	2.5
Total world production	$71.6 bn	$99.8 bn	$172.0 bn	$232.8 bn	3.66 m
Share in EU	44.4	44.6	53.8	50.2	61.3

Data source: Barrell and Pain (1999); US majority-owned manufacturing foreign affiliates.

More direct evidence is also available. As noted by Barrell and Pain (1999), obvious examples of multinationals can easily be found, such as the concentration of financial services in the City of London. Non-UK banks can better serve Europe from within, which provides an example of horizontal multinationals. Specialized branches of EU banks also like to have a subsidiary in London to benefit from spillovers in the City. Table 8.3 presents gross product (a value-added measure) and employment of majority-owned US foreign affiliates. As the USA is the world's largest foreign direct investor, this provides a good example.

Barrell and Pain (1999) note that Table 8.3 provides some evidence of agglomeration, because the largest four economies in Europe are also the largest destinations of US FDI. Furthermore, the table illustrates that Europe has become more important as a destination for US FDI since 1982. A closer look at more disaggregated data reveals that the EU is becoming more attractive to foreign investors as a result of the ongoing process of EU integration and the associated diminishing of trade costs.[7] Differences in national labor costs are important in determining the location of these investments since nations with relatively low labor costs are preferred. Most importantly, Barrell and Pain (1999) also find evidence of the relevance of agglomeration economies, measured by the scale of production (national to EU production) and the size of the research base (national to EU stock of R&D). The agglomeration variables contribute significantly to the explanation of FDI. Also some indication of cumulative causation is found: a 1% increase in the output share raises FDI by 1.7%, and a 1% increase in the relative share of R&D raises inward

---

[7] For the period 1978–1994 panel data for six countries and five sectors are used. The countries considered are France, Germany, Italy, the Netherlands, Spain, and the UK. The sectors are food and drink, metals and metal products, mechanical and electrical engineering, chemicals, and other manufacturing.

investment by 1.5%. These results are rather characteristic for this type of research. Markusen and Maskus (1999) and the literature they cite (especially Brainard, 1997) find that local sales of multinationals depend strongly on the market size of the host country and trade costs. But the results also depend on the motive of the investments. If investments are made to serve the local markets, they find a positive relationship of the ratio of export to local sales with the skilled-labor abundance of the parent, and a negative relationship with market size in the host country, and with investment costs or trade costs. If firms invest in host countries to serve third markets, high trade and investment costs stimulate firms to invest elsewhere. The bottom line of all this work is again that tendencies for agglomeration, if they arise, are generally smaller in the presence of multinational investment than if multinationals are absent.

Head, Ries, and Swenson (1995) provide direct evidence by looking at Japanese investments in the United States. They try to determine whether or not variables which are important in the geographical economics approach determine Japanese greenfield investments (new manufacturing plants) in the USA. The geographical pattern of 751 investments in 225 different four-digit manufacturing industries, is established (using investment data since 1980). The central idea is that trade theory indicates that firms in the same industry tend to cluster together in regions with adequate factor endowments, but that these location advantages (low factor prices), are enhanced through the presence of agglomeration externalities which add to the attractiveness of the location. Head, Ries, and Swenson (1995) analyze the difference in the geographical distribution of Japanese investments from that of US establishments. They hypothesize that two major explanations can be responsible for a distinctive Japanese investment pattern. Japanese firms choose a location for specific geographical reasons (near a harbor, for instance). Or they cluster in different regions from their US counterparts because of specific externalities only important for Japanese firms. Using proxies for agglomeration externalities, such as the number of US firms in the same four-digit group, the number of Japanese plants operating in the same four-digit group, the number of Japanese establishments in the same *keiretsu*, and a variable measuring linkages with nearby states, it turns out that Japanese investments in the US are significantly influenced by the previous location decisions of other Japanese firms in the same industry or *keiretsu*. These results do not indicate that specific location factors are *un*important in determining new Japanese investments, in particular since these factors might have been important in attracting the initial investments. Proximity to Japanese suppliers of intermediate products seems important. Furthermore, the existence of technological externalities specific to Japanese firms might be important. Most of the Japanese investments in the United States are carried out by multinationals. Again, the evidence is consistent with the modern theory of multinational investments, although no clear distinction was made between horizontal and vertical investments.

A descriptive analysis of the Dutch Ministry of Economic Affairs (1998) into the determinants of new Japanese and US investments in northwest Europe also reveals

Table 8.4. *New US and Japanese investments in northwest Europe, 1981–1995*

Host country	European headquarters		Distribution centers		Greenfield investments		Total	
	Number	%	Number	%	Number	%	Number	%
Belgium	199	25	26	15	53	11	278	19
Germany	132	16	32	18	108	22	272	18
France	108	13	20	11	192	38	320	22
Luxembourg	4	0	2	1	18	4	24	2
Netherlands	283	35	94	54	110	22	487	33
Austria	6	1	0	0	17	3	23	2
Switzerland	69	9	0	0	3	1	72	5
Total	801	100	174	100	501	100	1476	100

Source: Dutch Ministry of Economic Affairs (1998).

the importance of these kinds of externalities. Table 8.4 shows the distribution of new investments of Japanese and US firms in northwest Europe. The most important hosts, in this sample, are Germany and France, which is not surprising given what we already know from Tables 8.1 and 8.2. Belgium and the Netherlands, however, are also large hosts, which may be more surprising.

A closer look at these data reveals that most of the European headquarters are located in large city agglomerations like Paris, Brussels, Berlin, Vienna, or Amsterdam. Proximity to airports, local networks or a prestigious location is very important for the decision on the location of European headquarters. In the terminology of the core model: externalities are decisive in this decision. For distribution centers and greenfield investments, location in so-called corridors between the large cities is preferred. Easy access to the large cities and low investment costs seem to be the most important factors. The location decisions are also influenced by easy access to large markets, forward and backward linkages, and the proximity of other companies in the same industry. This could explain why the Netherlands and Belgium are among the most popular hosts. For greenfield investments, proximity to large cities is less important than for other types of investment. The price of production factors and low investment costs, combined with low transport costs, are more important for this type of investment. This descriptive analysis, performed for policy reasons, again indicates that elements familiar to geographical economics are important in explaining multinational investments.

8.6 Conclusions

The study of multinational firms has long been a descriptive, rather than an analytical field of economics. The focus has been on taxonomy and classification, and on empirical studies producing a large number of interesting stylized facts on multinationals, multinational behavior, and the characteristics of the source and destination countries of FDI. These facts were subsequently used to select the most relevant theoretical models. In the last two decades, theoretical models on multinationals have been developed. These explain in a consistent framework why multinationals exist. At first, in the 1980s, this was done using extended versions of neo-classical trade theory. These models are elegant, but largely at odds with the stylized facts on multinationals identified before. The fact that these models can only explain the existence of multinationals if relative factor endowments between countries are very different presents a problem, since FDI mostly takes place between similar countries. Moreover, a substantial proportion of multinationals are horizontally integrated, while the extended trade models mostly emphasize the vertical nature of multinationals.

The geographical economics approach has only recently started to analyze multinational behavior. The results so far seem promising. Not only can the models incorporate stylized facts of multinational behavior, but they also predict how multinational behavior affects clustering or spreading. In general, agglomeration of economic activity becomes less likely if multinationals exist, that is multinationals tend to make countries more similar. The framework discussed in section 8.4 can explain both horizontal and vertical multinationals, and is consistent with the fact that most FDI takes place between similar countries. Given the recent nature of these developments, empirical evidence is scarce. In general, elements that play a role in the geographical economics approach to explaining multinational firms seem to drive FDI and the location choices of multinationals.

Exercises

8.1 Find more empirical evidence on the relevance of the separate factors in the OLI approach with respect to the explanations of multinationals. Which factors are most important, those that stress the O, the L, or the I in this approach?

8.2 The neo-classical trade theory provides an explanation for the existence of (vertical) multinationals. Can you find evidence for the combination of (i) the absence of international factor price equalization, and (ii) the presence of multinationals?

8.3 Apply the same procedure as in chapters 3 and 4 to derive the equations that describe the short-run equilibrium of (8.2)–(8.5′).

8.4* Figure 8.5 suggests that if transport costs become arbitrarily large ($T \rightarrow \infty$), the fraction of manufacturing workers in country 1 can be determined precisely; this fraction appears to be in the neighborhood of 2/3. Can you derive this fraction analytically (or approximately) and can you explain it in economic terms? *Hint*: Use the fact that in the long-run equilibrium real wages are equal and then calculate λ.

8.5 The geographical economics approach stresses the importance of transport costs. Can you find evidence that multinationals that produce commodities subject to high transport costs are of the horizontal type?

9 The structure of international trade

9.1 Introduction

Untill recently, the modern literature on geography and trade paid relatively little attention to the relationship between agglomerating and spreading forces on the one hand and the structure and volume of (international) trade on the other. International trade flows are undoubtedly largely determined by the spatial distribution of economic activity. Taking the core (symmetric) two-country model of chapters 3 and 4 as a point of departure, the predictions on the structure and size of trade flows are simple. If economic activity is evenly spread, food is not traded internationally, so there is only intra-industry trade of manufactures between the two countries. If there is complete agglomeration of manufacturing activity, the only other possible long-run outcome, there is exclusively inter-industry trade (food for manufactures) between the two countries. Although these basic predictions are in line with empirical observations, that is trade is large between similar countries and dominated by intra-industry trade (see Box 9.1), the basic structure is too extreme in its predictions and too rigid in structure to allow for different types of international trade flow. The objective of this chapter is to demonstrate how international trade models may be combined with the geographical economics structure to allow for a diversified and rich explanation of international interactions. In doing so it partially fills the gap in the literature observed by Bertil Ohlin in 1933, namely the need to develop a theory of location which may serve as a background for a theory of international trade; see chapter 1.

The core model of chapters 3 and 4 analyzes the forces of economic agglomeration and spreading by allowing mobile laborers to migrate between regions. This assumption is in stark contrast to the standard procedure in international economics, one of the building blocks of the geographical economics literature, which assumes labor to be immobile between countries. The words "region" and "country" were used synonymously earlier in this book, but this may not be quite appropriate when referring to labor mobility. In general, labor is allowed to migrate more easily between different regions in one country than between countries. Naturally, there are exceptions to this rule. In China and the Soviet Union, for example, there were severe restrictions on labor migration between regions. On the other hand, inhabitants of the European Union are allowed to migrate to any other nation of the EU.

To discuss the structure and size of international trade in a geographical economics setting as clearly as possible, we first assume that labor is immobile between nations. In addition, as in the core model of chapters 3 and 4, we assume that there are two countries which are symmetric in all aspects, except one. To enrich the range of possibilities we will investigate two manufacturing sectors, *A* and *B*, as explained in the next section. As long as labor is not mobile between locations we will assume mobility between the two sectors. We analyze this model allowing for comparative advantage, resulting from either Ricardian-style technological differences or Heckscher–Ohlin-style factor abundance. Next, we briefly discuss the extent of international labor migration. We conclude by discussing the gravity equation in geographical economics models when allowing for labor migration, using the congestion model of chapter 7.

Box 9.1.   International trade flows

There are three world-wide centers of economic agglomeration, formed by, as the reader will have guessed, the United States of America (USA), the countries of the European Union (EU), and Japan. These centers dominate world trade flows in goods and services. This is illustrated in Figure 9.1, where the EU is treated as one country (thus excluding intra-EU trade flows). As panel *a* shows, the USA is the world's largest importer (21%), followed by the EU (18%) and China (8%, including Hong Kong). Panel *b* shows that the EU is the world's largest exporter (19%), followed by the USA (16%), Japan (9%), and China (also 9%).

As we have seen before, for example for German exports in chapter 1, there is a strong local orientation of international trade flows. Another example is given in Figure 9.2. The European Union currently consists of fifteen member-states,[1] and is contemplating an enlargement toward Central and Eastern Europe. Figure 9.2 shows that the trade flows of the prospective EU member-countries are already heavily oriented toward the EU. For example, 63% of Hungarian imports come from the EU, while 71% of Hungarian exports go to the EU. Previous experience with other countries joining the EU indicates that the EU trade flows will increase substantially, thus lifting the already high EU orientation, once the Central and Eastern European countries join the EU.

Table 9.1 summarizes data for selected countries on the extent of intra-industry trade, that is trade between nations of similar types of goods (for example, the export of cars in exchange for the import of cars), in contrast to inter-industry trade, that is trade between different types of goods (for example, the export of cars in exchange for the import of oil); details are explained in section 9.3. Take the USA as an example. Averaged over all countries no less than 60.7% of US trade can be categorized as intra-industry trade. This is, however,

---

[1] Finland, Sweden, Denmark, Ireland, the United Kingdom, the Netherlands, Belgium, Luxembourg, Germany, France, Austria, Portugal, Spain, Italy, and Greece.

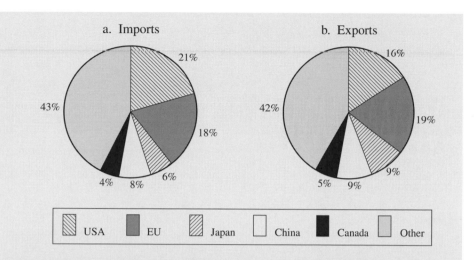

Figure 9.1. Shares of world trade flows. *Source*: Eurostat, 1998. EU is exclusive of intra-EU trade; China includes Hong Kong.

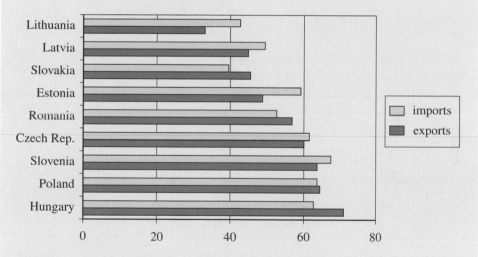

Figure 9.2. EU trade orientation of prospective EU member-countries. *Source*: Eurostat, 1997. Percentage share of European Union in trade flows.

very unevenly divided over its trading partners. Trade with the Asian newly industrialized countries (26.5% intra-industry trade), the less developed countries (35.0% intra-industry trade), and the centrally planned economies (37.9% intra-industry trade) have a relatively low intra-industry trade component, that is this trade is largely of the inter-industry type (trading different types of goods).

Table 9.1. *Intra-industry trade*

| Country | All countries | Trade with | | | |
		Asian NICs	Less developed	Developed	Centrally planned
Australia	35.8	26.9	29.2	22.7	5.5
Belgium	79.9	29.8	40.1	77.6	29.0
Canada	58.5	15.7	33.0	56.7	18.1
France	80.4	29.7	44.2	79.2	40.0
Germany	65.4	24.4	34.6	74.1	31.6
Italy	65.4	36.0	44.3	59.8	40.2
Japan	28.8	27.2	17.6	33.6	11.8
Sweden	66.5	15.1	17.4	72.5	30.7
UK	79.1	27.4	44.2	77.5	30.9
USA	60.7	26.5	35.0	66.7	37.9

Source: Culem and Lundberg (1986), data for 1980. Value of the Grubel–Lloyd index (see section 9.3), averaged (unweighted) across goods at the four-digit level of the ISIC, for: all countries, Asian newly industrialized countries, less developed countries, developed countries, and centrally planned economies.

US trade with other developed countries, on the other hand, is largely categorized as intra-industry trade (66.7%), that is trade of similar types of goods. Apparently, similar developed nations are largely engaged in trading similar types of goods among themselves.

9.2   Two manufacturing sectors

Integrating location theory with international trade theory, which focuses on comparative advantage as a reason for two nations to trade, requires the introduction of two sectors which may benefit from differences in comparative advantage between the two nations. For sections 9.2–9.4 the demand structure and notation, as well as some of its consequences, is therefore explained below, and summarized in Figure 9.3. There are two manufacturing sectors, A and B, and two countries, 1 and 2. For simplicity the food sector is dropped from the analysis. The countries are identical in all aspects, except one. This ensures that the resulting equilibrium always has a mirror-image structure, which considerably simplifies the exposition. The aspect in which the countries differ depends on the problem investigated. In section 9.3 they have different technologies, while in section 9.4 they have different endowments.

The demand side of the economy has the familiar nested Cobb–Douglas, constant elasticity of substitution structure, ensuring that there is no consumption bias:

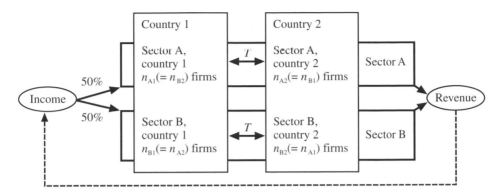

Figure 9.3. Demand and symmetry structure.

$$U = M_A^{1/2} M_B^{1/2} \tag{9.1}$$

$$M_A = \left(\sum_{i=1}^{n_A} c_{ai}^\rho \right)^{1/\rho}; \quad M_B = \left(\sum_{i=1}^{n_B} c_{bi}^\rho \right)^{1/\rho} \tag{9.2}$$

where M_A is the composite index for sector A manufactures, and similarly for sector B and M_B. Equation (9.1) indicates that 50% of a consumer's income is spent on sector A manufactures, and thus also 50% on sector B manufactures. Equation (9.2) indicates that manufacturing sector A consists of n_A different varieties. The elasticity of substitution between those varieties, important in determining the mark-up of price over marginal cost, is equal to $\varepsilon = 1/(1-\rho) > 1$. Similarly for sector B. The two sectors have the same elasticity of demand, and thus will follow the same pricing rule; see section 3.5. The imposed symmetry, described below, ensures that whatever holds for sector A in country 1 also holds for sector B in country 2 and vice versa.

Let A_2^1 be the demand facing a country 2, sector A producer in country 1, and similarly for A_1^1, B_1^2, etc. Moreover, let n_{A1} be the number of sector A firms in country 1, and similarly for n_{B2}, etc. By symmetry $A_1^1 = B_2^2$, $A_2^1 = B_1^2$, $n_{A1} = n_{B2}$, $n_{A2} = n_{B1}$, etc. This implies that if we let s denote the share of sector A firms residing in country 1, that is $s = n_{A1}/n_A$, then s is also equal to the share of firms in country 1 producing in sector A since $s = n_{A1}/(n_{A1} + n_{A2}) = n_{A1}/(n_{A1} + n_{B1})$. As the country 1–sector A versus country 2–sector B symmetry holds throughout sections 9.2–9.4, we will henceforth focus on country 1.

9.3   Comparative advantage: Ricardo

This section is based on the work of Luca Ricci (1997, 1999), integrating Ricardian-style comparative advantage and the geographical economics approach. The production function uses labor as the only input and is characterized by increasing returns to scale, ensuring that each variety is supplied by only one producer. There is, however, a technological difference between the two countries:

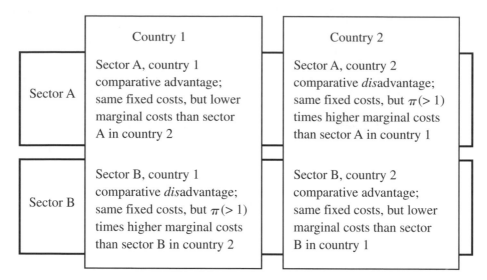

Figure 9.4.　Comparative advantage structure: Ricardian model.

$$l_{A1i} = \alpha + \beta x_{A1i}; \qquad l_{B1i} = \alpha + \bar{\beta} x_{B1i}$$

$$l_{A2i} = \alpha + \bar{\beta} x_{A2i}; \qquad l_{B2i} = \alpha + \beta x_{B2i}; \qquad \pi \equiv \bar{\beta}/\beta > 1 \tag{9.3}$$

where l_{A1i} represents the amount of labor a sector A producer, i, in country 1 must use to produce x_{A1i} units of output, etc. Note that the marginal labor requirement is lower in country 1 for sector A, such that country 1 has a comparative (and absolute) advantage in sector A manufactures (and country 2 in sector B). The ratio of the marginal labor requirements, the variable π, measures *the extent of comparative advantage*; the larger π, the larger the technological differences between the two countries. This is summarized in Figure 9.4. Transport costs between the two countries are of the iceberg type, equal to T, and are the same for sectors A and B.

As usual, the firms in the manufacturing sector behave according to monopolistic competition. They thus charge a constant mark-up over marginal cost, which is the same for the two sectors since the price elasticities of demand are identical. Sector B firms in country 1 are confronted with higher marginal costs and thus charge a higher price than sector A firms in country 1, that is $p_{B1}/p_{A1} = \pi$. Obviously, the price charged abroad is T times higher than the price charged at home for all firms to cover the transport costs. There is entry and exit of firms in each sector and country until profits are zero. This implies, as the reader may wish to verify, that a sector B producer in country 1 sells a lower quantity of goods than a sector A producer in country 1, but that the firms use the same amount of labor to produce these quantities. The number of firms active in each sector is therefore directly proportional to the number of laborers working in that sector. Moreover, the total sales revenue is the same for firms in the two sectors (although the distribution of foreign to domestic sales may differ; see below).

The higher productivity for sector A in country 1 than in country 2 gives firms an incentive to locate sector A production in country 1. In a standard Ricardian framework, specialization will be complete. Will the same occur in this Ricardian–geographical economics framework, or will some firms locate production in the less advantageous country? If so, why? The answer, as discussed below, is that both situations may occur. There may be *incomplete specialization*, in which case both countries produce goods in sectors A and B, although production of the sector with a comparative advantage will be larger than production of the sector with comparative disadvantage. The reasons are straightforward. Increasing returns to scale ensure that production is located in only one country. On the one hand, agglomeration of sector A in country 1 is promoted by the productivity advantage. On the other, spreading of sector A production to country 2 is promoted by competition for segmented markets as transport costs create a price wedge which results, through the substitution effect (see below), in higher demand for domestic goods. If there is a balance between these two forces, specialization will be incomplete. However, there may be *complete specialization* if the productivity advantage dominates the spreading advantages, that is if transport costs are low and substitution of one variety for another is easy relative to the productivity difference.

It can be shown (Ricci, 1997, p. 55) that the share of sector A firms residing in country 1, which is equal to the share of firms in country 1 active in sector A (see section 9.2), if there is incomplete specialization, is given by:

$$s = \frac{n_{A1}}{n} = \frac{1}{2} + \frac{T^{\varepsilon-1}(\pi^{2(\varepsilon-1)}-1)}{2[\pi^{\varepsilon-1}(1 + T^{2(\varepsilon-1)}) - T^{\varepsilon-1}(1 + \pi^{2(\varepsilon-1)})]} \equiv f(T,\varepsilon,\pi) \qquad (9.4)$$

Thus, as intuitively explained above and illustrated in Figure 9.5, the extent of specialization increases if the extent of comparative advantage increases, the transport costs decrease, or the elasticity of substitution decreases. Figure 9.5 measures the extent of specialization by the share of sector A firms in country 1 (= the share of sector B firms in country 2). The most important effect of combining the Ricardian approach with the geographical economics approach is the mitigation of the extent of specialization within countries, that is, for a range of parameter values, countries will only partially, and not completely, specialize in the production of the good for which they have a comparative advantage. Note, finally, that one of the strong points of the Ricci (1997, 1999) Ricardian–geographical economics approach is that it leads to a *closed form* solution for the share of firms in the sector with comparative advantage, that is we can explicitly derive a function for this share, as given in equation (9.4).

Now that we have seen the impact of comparative advantage on the distribution of manufacturing activity we look more closely at the volume and structure of international trade. The ratio of sales for a good produced domestically to those of an imported good depends on the price ratio and the demand elasticity. Since the wages at home and abroad are the same, as is the mark-up, the price ratio depends on the

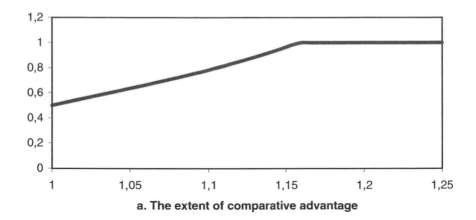

a. The extent of comparative advantage

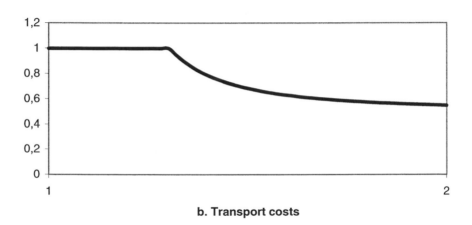

b. Transport costs

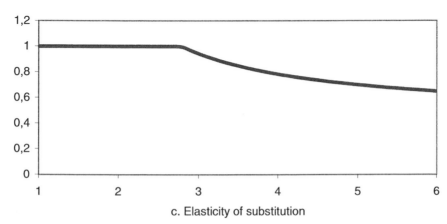

c. Elasticity of substitution

Figure 9.5.   The share of sector A firms in country 1 (default parameters: $T=1.4$, $\varepsilon=4$, and $\pi=1.1$).

transport costs T and the extent of comparative advantage π only. The ratio of domestic to foreign demand for a good with domestic comparative advantage, that is sector A in country 1 and sector B in country 2, and the revenue ratio are given by (see also sections 3.4 and 3.5):

$$\text{demand} = A_1^1/A_2^1 = (\pi T)^\varepsilon; \quad \text{revenue} = (\pi T)^{\varepsilon - 1} \tag{9.5}$$

Note that both aspects, transport costs and comparative advantage, increase the demand of domestic firms relative to foreign firms, as both result in a lower price for domestically produced goods. The lower foreign sales are only partially compensated for by a higher price, so the domestic to foreign revenue ratio equals $(\pi T)^{\varepsilon - 1}$. Similarly, the ratio of domestic to foreign demand for a good with a domestic comparative disadvantage, that is good B in country 1 and good A in country 2, and the revenue ratio are given by:

$$\text{demand} = B_1^1/B_2^1 = (T/\pi)^\varepsilon; \quad \text{revenue} = (T/\pi)^{\varepsilon - 1} \tag{9.6}$$

Note that this time transport costs increase, and comparative disadvantage decreases, the demand of domestic firms relative to foreign firms. Using equation (9.5) and the definition of s above, it follows that of the income spent on the good with a domestic comparative advantage, the share spent on domestically produced goods, dom_{A1}, is

$$dom_{A1} = \frac{n_{A1}p_{A1}A_1^1}{n_{A1}p_{A1}A_1^1 + n_{A2}p_{A2}TA_2^1} = \frac{s(\pi T)^{\varepsilon - 1}}{s(\pi T)^{\varepsilon - 1} + (1 - s)} \tag{9.7}$$

Similarly, of the good with a domestic comparative disadvantage, the share spent on domestically produced goods, dom_{B1}, equals

$$dom_{B1} = \frac{n_{B1}p_{B1}B_1^1}{n_{B1}p_{B1}B_1^1 + n_{B2}p_{B2}TB_2^1} = \frac{(1 - s)(T/\pi)^{\varepsilon - 1}}{(1 - s)(T/\pi)^{\varepsilon - 1} + s} \tag{9.8}$$

Knowing the distribution of domestic to foreign spending for the two sectors as given in equations (9.7) and (9.8), and keeping in mind that half of a country's income is spent on each sector, makes it easy to calculate the share of income spent on imports (namely $[(1 - dom_{A1}) + (1 - dom_{B1})]/2$) and the extent of intra-industry trade as measured by the Grubel–Lloyd index (defined by $1 - |export - import|/(export + import)$, which gives $2(1 - dom_{A1})/[(1 - dom_{A1}) + (1 - dom_{B1})])$. The various shares are illustrated in Figure 9.6. Panel a shows both the increasing share of firms in the sector with comparative advantage and the preference for spending on domestic goods as the extent of comparative advantage increases. Panel b shows the declining share of firms in the sector with comparative disadvantage and the associated declining preference for spending on domestic goods as the extent of comparative advantage increases. Finally, panel c shows that the proportion of intra-industry trade falls from 1 to 0, and thus the proportion of inter-industry trade rises, while the share of income spent on imports rises to 50% as the extent of comparative advantage rises. Again, we see a mitigation of the strong "bang-bang" results found in the standard Ricardian model. More

a. Industry with comparative advantage: domestic shares

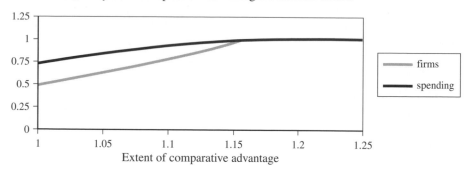

b. Industry with comparative disadvantage: domestic shares

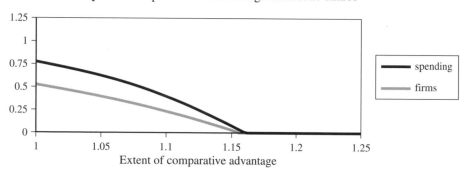

c. Intra-industry trade and share spent on imports

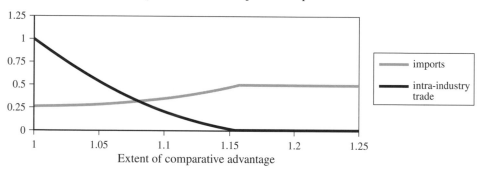

Figure 9.6.   Ricardo and geographical economics ($T=1.4$, $\varepsilon=4$).

importantly, as countries are becoming more similar, that is as the extent of comparative advantage decreases, they are increasingly engaged in intra-industry trade, as supported by empirical evidence (see Box 9.1).

9.4   Comparative advantage: factor abundance

As demonstrated in the previous section, the general implications of the Ricardian
framework, focusing on technological differences between countries, can be integrated
in the geographical economics approach, focusing on imperfect competition, increasing returns to scale, and forward and backward linkages, to create an intricate picture
of the various forces underlying international trade flows, sometimes reinforcing one
another, sometimes working in opposite directions. This section completes the mar-
riage of neo-classical theory to geographical economics by integrating the factor abundance international trade theory into the geographical economics approach. To ease
the exposition as much as possible we will use an almost identical structure to that in
section 9.3, again imposing super-symmetry, and point out similarities and differences
whenever appropriate.

The demand structure is explained in section 9.2. There are two countries, 1 and 2,
and two sectors, A and B, each producing a variety of manufactures which are imperfect substitutes for one another. Naturally, to investigate a setting where relative factor
abundance plays a role requires the use of at least two factors of production, instead
of the single factor, labor, used thus far. An elegant way to do this was developed by
Kenen (1965) and later applied by Ethier and Horn (1984) to analyze customs unions,
Brakman and Van Marrewijk (1995a, 1998) to analyze international transfers, and
Fujita, Krugman, and Venables (1999) in a geographical economics setting. The production process takes place in two stages (Figure 9.7). In the first stage, primary inputs,
labelled capital, K, and labor, L, are used to produce two sector-specific intermediate
goods, D_A and D_B. In the second stage, these intermediate goods are used as inputs in
the production process for varieties, as usual under internal increasing returns to scale.

Since the second-stage production process, essentially representing the geographical
economics part of the model, is more familiar we start by briefly describing this second
stage. Since we have already analyzed technological differences in section 9.3, we
assume that the production function for varieties is the same for both sectors and both
countries. If D_{A1i} is the amount of intermediate good D_A used by sector A producer i
in country 1, the resulting output x_{A1i} is given by

$$D_{A1i} = \alpha + \beta x_{A1i} \tag{9.9}$$

Similarly for D_{B2i} with respect to x_{B2i}, etc. The fixed costs α and the marginal costs β
are therefore the same for both sectors in both countries when measured in terms of
the intermediate goods. The rest of the second-stage structure is the same as in section
9.3. So each manufacturing firm charges a constant mark-up over marginal cost
($\rho p_{A1} = \beta p_{DA1}$, analogously for other indices), while entry and exit of manufacturing
firms in each sector and country ensure that all varieties are produced in the same

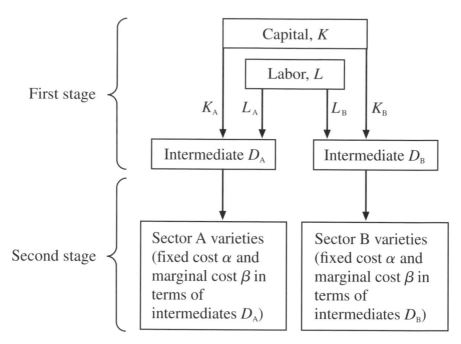

Figure 9.7. Production stages of the factor abundance model.

quantity, using the same amount of intermediate goods ($x = (\varepsilon-1)\alpha/\beta$ and $D = \varepsilon\alpha$, respectively). Transport costs for varieties are of the iceberg type, equal to T, and the same in the two sectors.

Now we move to describing the first stage of the production process, essentially representing the factor abundance part of the model, where the intermediate goods D_A and D_B are produced using primary inputs, capital and labor, under perfect competition with a standard, constant-returns-to-scale, neo-classical Cobb–Douglas production function, which is identical in the two countries.

$$D_A = [\mu^{-\mu}(1-\mu)^{-(1-\mu)}]K_A^\mu L_A^{1-\mu}; \qquad D_B = [\mu^{-\mu}(1-\mu)^{-(1-\mu)}]K_B^{1-\mu}L_B^\mu \quad (9.10)$$

Note that we imposed symmetry in the production functions, that is the capital intensity of sector A is the labor intensity of sector B and vice versa. Without loss of generality we will assume $\mu > 1/2$, that is sector A is relatively capital-intensive. To complete the symmetry, we assume that the total amount of capital available is equal to the total amount of labor available.

The first-stage production process for intermediate goods gives rise to a standard concave transformation curve, substituting one type of intermediate good for another. We start by analyzing a situation in which countries 1 and 2 have the same amount of labor and capital, such that they are symmetric in all respects.[2] The transformation curve is illustrated in Figure 9.8. The curvature is rather pronounced since we chose a

---

[2] Fujita, Krugman, and Venables (1999) analyze stability for this setting.

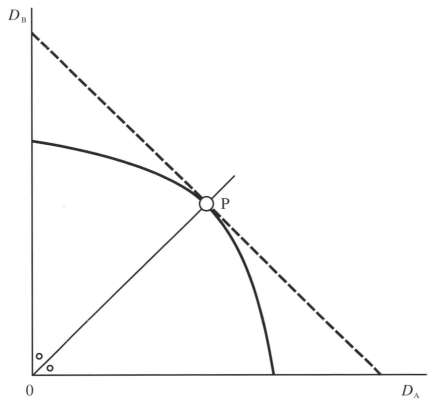

Figure 9.8.   Intermediate goods transformation curve ($\mu = 0.9$).

high value of μ, sector A's capital share, for illustrative purposes. The large difference in capital intensity for the production of the two intermediates ensures that they are relatively difficult to substitute one for another, which results in the high curvature. In the symmetric equilibrium the wage rate is equal to the rental rate, say equal to 1. Total income in each country is then equal to the sum of the available capital stock and labor stock. The cost-minimizing capital–labor intensity of production is equal to $k_A = K_A/L_A = \mu/(1 - \mu)$ for intermediate good A and $k_B = K_B/L_B = (1 - \mu)/\mu$ for intermediate good B. From the identity $k_A(L_A/L) + k_B(L_B/L) = K/L = 1$ it follows that $L_A/L = 1 - \mu$, that is the share $1 - \mu$ of labor is employed in sector A. From the normalization of the wage rate and rental rate it follows that the price of the intermediate goods in both sectors in both countries is equal to 1, if a suitable choice is made of the constant in the production functions for intermediate goods; see (9.10).

The equilibrium production point for the intermediate goods sectors, with an equal distribution of capital and labor, is given by point P in Figure 9.8. Both countries have the same distribution of capital and labor over the two sectors and produce the same number of varieties in each sector. International trade between the two countries is purely intra-industry trade. We are, however, interested in the impact of different factor endowments on the structures and size of the international trade flows. At the same time we want to preserve the mirror-image structure of the model. Thus, we shift capital from country 2 to country 1 in return for an equal amount of labor from country 1 to country 2. Any adjustments in the production structure of country 1 will be mirror-mimicked in country 2. Since country 1 becomes relatively well endowed with capital, we expect country 1 to specialize (partially) in the production of the capital-intensive sector A manufactures.

There are two ways to continue, namely (i) the easy way and (ii) the interesting way, and these will be discussed in turn.

The easy way to continue is to assume that the sector-specific intermediate goods can be costlessly transported from one country to another and that the share of total capital available in country 1 does not exceed μ, the share of capital employed in sector A in the symmetric equilibrium. Under those circumstances the original symmetric equilibrium can be replicated. This is illustrated in Figure 9.10 by the production points Pr_{10} for country 1 and Pr_{20} for country 2. The shift of capital from country 2 to country 1 in return for labor from country 1 to country 2 affects the transformation curves of the two countries. Country 1's transformation curve is biased toward the production of sector A intermediate goods, which are capital-intensive, because country 1 is relatively well endowed with capital. Similarly, country 2's transformation curve is biased toward the production of sector B intermediate goods, which are labor-intensive, because country 2 is relatively well endowed with labor. In fact, it is a well-known result from neo-classical international trade theory, partially discussed in chapter 2, that a country which increases the endowment of a factor of production, say capital, will increase the production of the capital-intensive good and reduce production of the labor-intensive good, at given prices for these goods. These changes are proportional to the size of the change in the endowment, that is we can trace out a straight line for these changes, the so-called Rybczynski line (see Box 9.2), in goods space (in this case the space for intermediate goods D_A and D_B). Similar lines hold for equiproportional simultaneous changes in both endowments.

Box 9.2.   Factor endowments and the Rybczynski line

One of the classic results of neo-classical trade theory is the Rybczynski theorem. If there are two final goods, say X and Y, and two factors of production, say capital K and labor L, the theorem states that, for *given* prices of the final goods X and Y, an increase in one of the factors of production, say K, leads to an increase in output of the final good using this production factor relatively intensively, and a decrease in output of the other final good. Moreover, these changes are equiproportional.

This is illustrated in Figure 9.9, where Tr_0 is the initial transformation curve, A is the initial production point, and we assume that good X uses capital K relatively

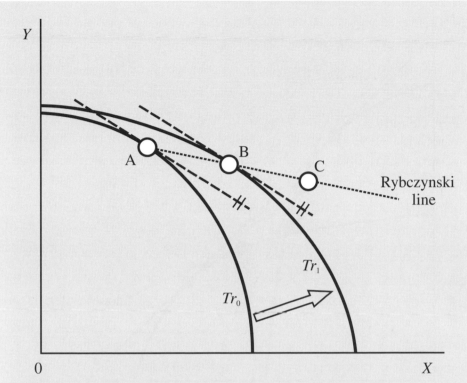

Figure 9.9.   The Rybczynski line.

intensively. If the available capital stock increases by ΔK the transformation curve will shift out to Tr_1, relatively more in the direction of good X, the capital-intensive good, than in the direction of good Y, as indicated by the arrow in Figure 9.9. At the same final goods prices (indicated by the parallel dashed price lines) the economy will now produce at point B, increasing production of good X, the capital-intensive good, and reducing production of good Y, the labor-intensive good.

Moreover, as mentioned above, the changes are equiproportional. A second increase in capital of equal size, ΔK, will lead to an identical change in final goods production, from point B to point C. The line connecting all such production points is called the capital Rybczynski line. A similar line can be derived for changes in labor.

Given the prices for intermediate goods in the symmetric equilibrium the original world production level for intermediate goods can be replicated, in essence by both countries adjusting their production of intermediate goods along the Rybczynski lines. Does this mean that the original symmetric equilibrium can be replicated? Yes, but only

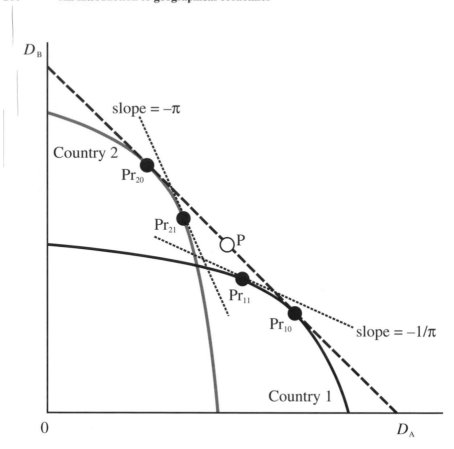

Figure 9.10. Transformation curves ($K_1/K=L_2/L=2/3$; $\mu=0.9$).

if the intermediate goods are costlessly tradable. In that case, country 1 would produce intermediate goods at point Pr_{10} and export intermediate good D_A in return for inter-mediate good D_B to reach point P. The same number of varieties as before would be produced in both countries, such that at the manufacturing level there would again be only intra-industry trade. This is complemented by pure inter-industry trade at the intermediate goods level to compensate for the differences in factor endowments.

The main disadvantage of the easy way to continue just described is the assumption that intermediate goods can be traded costlessly, while final goods produced from these intermediate goods are costly to trade. Although it makes the analysis simple, this assumption, which essentially makes primary inputs costlessly tradable, is not very appealing. The remainder of this section will therefore analyze the interesting way to continue, by making the opposite assumption: sector-specific intermediate goods cannot be traded internationally.[3]

---

[3] The arguments below are similar if intermediate goods are tradeable at high costs. See also De Vaal and Van den Berg (1999).

What will the production structure look like if sector-specific intermediate goods cannot be traded? We expect capital-rich country 1 to specialize in the production of capital-intensive sector A intermediate goods, but to what extent? A first guess might be up to production point Pr_{10}, which would enable the world as a whole to produce the same number of varieties for both types of manufactures. In that case, country 1 would make a larger share of sector A manufactures, and country 2, of sector B manufactures. There would be more intensive trade relations, both intra-industry and inter-industry. However, since trade of manufactures is costly the production points Pr_{10} and Pr_{20} cannot be an equilibrium. Indeed, the Ricci equation (9.4) in section 9.3 determining the share of sector A firms in country 1 in a Ricardian setting gives us an indication that a higher share of sector A firms in country 1 requires a higher price of sector B manufactures relative to sector A manufactures in country 1. There must thus be a price wedge $p_{B1}/p_{A1} \equiv \pi > 1$ for final goods, which translates directly into an equal price wedge π for intermediate goods. Since at points Pr_{10} and Pr_{20} the price ratio of intermediate goods, which is equal to minus the slope of a line tangent to the transformation curve, is 1, it cannot be an equilibrium point.

Now that we have established the need for a price wedge π for intermediate goods it is immediately clear from Figure 9.10 that the equilibrium production points must be something like points Pr_{11} and Pr_{21}. Obviously, the higher price for sector B intermediate goods in country 1 at point Pr_{11} implies a substitution away from the production of sector A intermediates relative to point Pr_{10}, thus reducing the size of sector A and the need for costly transportation of manufactures. The same holds for sector B in country 2. In other words, the comparative advantage of capital-rich country 1 in the production of capital-intensive sector A intermediate goods translates into a lower price for sector A intermediate goods relative to country 2.

The analogy with the Ricardian technology-driven comparative advantage is almost complete if we take the price wedge π as a measure of comparative advantage. Almost, but not quite. Remember that all firms in all sectors use the same amount of intermediate goods in equilibrium. Since the price of sector B intermediate goods in country 1 is higher than the price of sector A intermediate goods this implies that the revenue from sales for a sector B firm in country 1 must be higher than the revenue of sales from a sector A firm in country 1. One firm in sector B in country 1 therefore has a higher impact on this country's income than one firm in sector A.[4] It can be shown (Van Marrewijk, 2000) that as a result of this higher impact on a country's income, the share of sector A firms residing in country 1, which is equal to the share of firms in country 1 active in sector A (see section 9.2), if there is incomplete specialization is given by

$$\frac{n_{A1}}{n} = \frac{\pi g(T,\varepsilon,\pi)}{1 + (\pi-1)g(T,\varepsilon,\pi)} \tag{9.11}$$

where

---

[4] To be precise: income $= (n_{A1}P_{DA1} + n_{B1}P_{DB1})\alpha\varepsilon = (n_{A1} + \pi n_{B1})P_{DA1}\alpha\varepsilon$.

$$g(T,\varepsilon,\pi) = \frac{1}{2} + \frac{T^{\varepsilon-1}(\pi^{2\varepsilon}-1)}{2[\pi^{\varepsilon}(1 + T^{2(\varepsilon-1)}) - T^{\varepsilon-1}(1 + \pi^{2\varepsilon})]}$$

As in the Ricardian–geographical economics framework we can thus derive a *closed form* solution for the share of firms in the sector with comparative advantage.

As illustrated in Figure 9.11 the larger impact of sector *B* firms for the income level in country 1 affects the extent of specialization. Panel *a* shows that the same level of specialization translates into a lower price wedge, or alternatively that the same level of comparative advantage as measured by the price wedge translates into a higher degree of specialization for the factor abundance model than for the Ricardian model. Panels *b–e* compare the resulting differences in impact for the Ricardian and factor abundance models for domestic spending in the sector with comparative advantage and disadvantage, for the share of income spent on imports, and for the extent of intra-industry trade, respectively. As with the Ricardian model, comparative advantage based on factor abundance integrated in the geographical economics model results in higher levels of intra-industry trade between similar countries and, *ceteris paribus*, larger trade flows between dissimilar countries.

9.5   Migration

According to Krugman and Venables (1995), a crucial difference between international economics and regional economics concerns the mobility of labor across space. In international economics it is often assumed that labor is not mobile between countries, whereas in regional economics, the contrary assumption is made. We have maintained this distinction so far in this chapter since in our analysis of international trade with the geographical economics model, labor remained immobile. In the core model of geographical economics, however, labor is mobile between locations in the long run. In fact, in chapters 2–4 we emphasized that labor mobility is a defining characteristic of the geographical economics approach. A natural question to ask is therefore whether and how a geographical economics model *with* labor mobility can be used for the analysis of international trade. This question will be addressed in the next section. In this section we briefly present and discuss some data to show that the international migration of labor matters. The process of globalization can be defined as the increasing cross-country economic interdependencies through increased trade and increased factor mobility; see IMF (1997). Compared to international trade flows and capital mobility, the international mobility of labor is (still) less relevant in this process, but it is nevertheless increasingly becoming a factor to take into consideration.

In a recent study for the International Labour Organization (ILO), Stalker (2000) argues that for many countries migration, though still relatively small as a percentage of a country's total population, has been on the rise in the post-World War II period and is expected to increase further in the near future. To illustrate the phenomenon at hand, Table 9.2 gives the *stock* of migrants for the world as a whole for various regions. The data illustrate that as a percentage of the respective populations, the developed

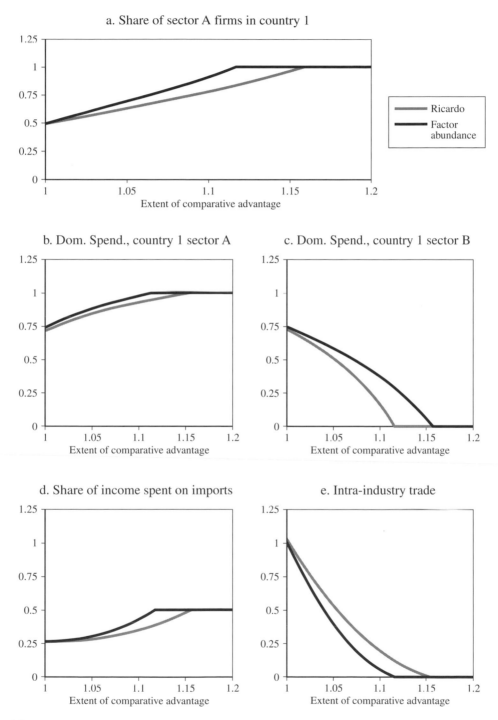

Figure 9.11.   Ricardo and factor abundance ($T=1.4$, $\varepsilon=4$).

Table 9.2. *World migrant stock by region, 1965–1990*

| | % of total population | | | |
	1965	1975	1985	1990
Industrial countries	3.1	3.5	4.1	4.5
Developing countries	1.9	1.6	1.6	1.6
Africa	2.5	2.7	2.3	2.5
Asia	1.7	1.3	1.4	1.4
Latin America and Caribbean	2.4	1.8	1.6	1.7
North America	6.0	6.3	7.8	8.6
Europe/former USSR	2.2	2.7	3.0	3.2
Oceania	14.4	15.6	16.9	17.8

Source: Stalker (2000).

countries have witnessed an increase in their stock of migrants. "Migrants" in this table refers to either foreign-born population or non-citizens, and the term also includes refugees. For the world as a whole, the total migrant stock increased between 1965 and 1990 from 75 million to 120 million people (Stalker, 2000, p. 6).

People migrate for various reasons, and to some extent migration is not driven by economic factors but, for instance, by political motives and the desire to be reunited with family members who live abroad. Having said this, a large part of migration is economically determined. The (ever-increasing) income difference per capita between rich and poor countries (see chapter 1) is the main force behind economic migration. This helps to explain why we observe that the flow of international migration is predominantly from countries with a relatively low GDP per capita to countries with a higher GDP per capita. This is not only important for the migration between the regions mentioned in Table 9.2 but also for the migration within these regions. Within the EU, stimulated by the gradual abolition of legal restrictions on intra-EU labor mobility, the migration flow is from the southern periphery to the northern core of the EU. In a similar vein, within Asia migration is from the poorer countries to countries like South Korea or Singapore, where wages are considerably higher. To illustrate the importance of these intra-regional migration flows: in 1995, almost 90% of migrants to Germany, which had by far the largest annual inflow of all EU countries, came from other European countries.

The fact that migration flows are from low-wage countries to high-wage countries is important from the perspective of geographical economics because in the core model (see section 3.9 and chapter 4) the decision of labor to move between locations is entirely driven by (real) wage differences between locations. Also relevant from a geographical economics perspective, and in line with the idea of a spatial wage structure (see chapter 5), is that migration from "poor" to "rich" countries reinforces agglomeration patterns. In the next section we present evidence that a spatial wage structure can indeed also be observed at the global level.

Many observers expect that economic migration will become more important in the near future. The main reason for this expectation is that increasing wage differentials between countries will increase the expected net return of migration for many people. Migration obviously also involves costs and it can be looked upon as a risky investment. The costs of migration are often substantial and they include not only the actual cost of moving but also the (immaterial) cost of leaving friends and family behind and the costs of finding a job in your new country. The migration decision is also a risky one because of the uncertainty surrounding the job and earning prospects in the new country; see Stalker (2000, p. 24).[5] *Given* these costs and risks the ever-increasing wage differentials alone will induce more migration. But it is not unlikely that the costs and risks of migration will decrease in the future, thereby providing a further incentive for migration. Improvements in transport and communications technology may decrease the actual costs of moving, and may also make it easier for future migrants to be informed about the prospects of migrating.

Finally, the experience with migration in what is sometimes called the first era of globalization (late nineteenth and early twentieth centuries) shows that migration flows can increase dramatically in a relatively short span of time (see below). For migration to matter from an economic point of view it is not absolutely necessary that migration flows increase further nor that the stock of migrants, as a percentage of total population, must become larger than the stocks reported in Table 9.2. Even the present migration flows can exert an influence on (marginal) wages in the rich countries, especially for lower-skilled labor. The idea that the mobility of labor (similarly to the trade of goods) may exert an influence on wages is, of course, at home in old and new trade theories alike, and there is evidence that migration can be important for relative wages within or between countries. O'Rourke and Williamson (1999), for instance, show that in the second part of the nineteenth century and the early part of the twentieth century not only did the migration from European countries to the USA increase strongly, but also this movement of labor exerted a significant influence on factor prices in Europe and the USA.[6] Table 9.3, based on O'Rourke and Williamson (1999, p. 122), illustrates for a number of European countries and two labor-receiving countries, the USA and Canada, the emigration and immigration rates for the three decades between 1880 and 1910. This era remains even until today, especially for (now) developed countries, the heyday of international labor mobility. To put this era of transatlantic migration into perspective: in 1901–1910 foreign-born citizens in the USA formed 14.2% of the total US population. This is a considerably larger share than the 8.6% for North America in 1990 shown in Table 9.2.

9.6 Gravity

One of the topics briefly discussed in chapter 1 is the empirical success of the "gravity equation" to describe international trade flows between nations; see section 1.4 on

---

[5] A very simple equation that has performed well from an empirical point of view is the so-called Harris–Todaro equation which states that migration from "poor" country i to "rich" country j will occur until $W_j(1 - U_j) = W_i(1 - U_i)$, where W is the wage and U is the unemployment rate. The Harris–Todaro equation was originally devised to explain migration from rural to urban areas within developing countries.

[6] In line with the factor abundance theory this migration flow led to a rise in wage–rental ratios in Europe and a fall in wage–rental ratios in the USA (in the USA the in-migration of people made labor relatively less scarce).

Table 9.3. *Migration rates per decade (per 1,000 mean population)*

	1881–1890	1891–1900	1901–1910
European emigration rates			
British Isles	70.2	43.8	65.3
Germany	28.7	10.1	4.5
Ireland	141.7	88.5	69.8
Italy	33.6	50.2	107.7
Norway	95.2	44.9	83.3
Portugal	38.0	50.8	56.9
Spain	36.2	43.8	56.6
Sweden	70.1	41.2	42.0
"New World" immigration rates			
Canada	78.4	48.8	167.6
USA	85.8	53.0	102.0

Source: O'Rourke and Williamson (1999).

German export flows. A "demographic gravitation" model of interactions between two locations was first developed by the Princeton astronomer James Q. Stewart (1947, 1948). In analogy to the Newtonian gravity model, he found strong correlations for traffic, migration, and communication between two places, based on the product of their population size and inversely related to their distance squared. A similar procedure was first applied to international trade between nations by Jan Tinbergen (1962). This became known as "the gravity model" in international economics; see also Pöyhönen (1963) and Linneman (1966). There have been many attempts, increasingly successful and increasingly complicated, to provide a solid theoretical basis for the gravity equation based on imperfect competition and trade costs, for example Anderson (1979), Bergstrand (1985, 1989, 1990), Harrigan (1994, 1995), and Box 2.5. ˙˙here was a strong need for this theoretical basis in view of the empirical success of the gravity equation and in view of its popularity in tackling difficult policy-related questions; see, for example, Tinbergen (1962), Pollins (1989), and Van Bergeijk and Oldersma (1990).

We believe that the geographical economics approach can provide a simpler theoretical basis for the gravity equation. We could proceed in various ways, for example by identifying several regions within a country for a number of countries and assuming labor migration between different regions of one country and not between countries. As before, however, we want to keep the analysis as simple as possible. Now that we have briefly discussed the sizeable migration flows between countries in section 9.5 we will assume that manufacturing labor is mobile between locations. Naturally, a discussion of the gravity equation requires the analysis of many, not just two, locations. Moreover, the empirical observations in chapter 1 indicate that there must be considerable variation in the size and intensity of economic activity at these locations. Finally, we would like the gravity equation to be endogenously generated by the model, not preimposed by its geographic structure or some parameters which differ between loca-

Table 9.4. *Estimates for the basic gravity equation*

Income origin ($\theta1$)	0.69
	(85.24)
Income destination ($\theta2$)	0.87
	(99.11)
Distance ($\theta3$)	−1.01
	(−43.38)
$\bar{R}^2$	0.58

Note: t-values in parentheses.
Source: Brakman and Van Marrewijk (1995b).

tions. A suitable geographical economics model that fits all these requirements is the neutral-space, many-location model with negative feedbacks (congestion), developed and discussed in chapter 7. We proceed by briefly discussing some simulations with this model in relation to the gravity equation. Recall that the model has an immobile food sector and a single mobile manufacturing sector, that δ is the share of income spent on manufactures, ε is the elasticity of substitution between different varieties of manufactures, and τ measures the extent of congestion costs.

The basic version of the gravity equation, which we have already discussed in chapters 1 and 2, relates the size of the international trade flows to the economic size of the two countries and their distance as follows:

$$Tr_{ij} = CY_i^{\theta1} Y_j^{\theta2} D_{ij}^{\theta3} e_{ij} \tag{9.12}$$

Where Tr_{ij} is the international trade flow from country i to country j, C is a constant, Y_i is the income level of the origin country, Y_j is the income level of the destination country, D_{ij} is the distance between the two countries, e_{ij} is an error term, and the parameters $\theta1$, $\theta2$, and $\theta3$ have to be estimated. Brakman and Van Marrewijk (1995b) estimate *inter alia* the most basic version of the gravity equation using 1992 trade data for 199 countries (Table 9.4). The gravity equation is thus a (successful) attempt to show that location matters in international trade. In chapter 5 of this book we used the idea of a spatial wage structure to illustrate that location matters on a regional level. In Box 9.3 we argue that such a wage structure can also be observed on a global level.

Table 9.4 shows clearly that the main parameters of the basic gravity equation are significant, and that even this simple version explains almost 60% of the variation in international trade flows.

Box 9.3.   Wages around the world

The estimation results for the gravity equation (9.12) show that distance matters for international trade. In previous chapters (see especially sections 5.5 and 5.6), we have emphasized that distance is also important for the determination of regional wages. The basic idea of a spatial wage structure is that wages fall the further one moves away from economic centers. On a regional or national level, evidence can be found for a spatial wage structure; see the discussions in chapter 5 of the work of Hanson (1997, 1998) for Mexico and the USA, and our estimations for Germany. It turns out that there is also evidence for a spatial wage structure on a global level. To illustrate this, the following simple wage equation, essentially the same as equation (5.2), has been estimated:

$$\ln(W_{it}/W_{ct}) = \kappa_0 + \kappa_1 \ln(t_{ic}) + err_{it}$$

where:

W_{it} = manufacturing wage in country i in year t;
W_{ct} = manufacturing wage in center c in year t;
t_{ic} = geodesic distance between country i and center c;
err_{it} = error term.

This relative wage equation has been estimated for sixty-eight countries (those countries for which the World Bank has data on manufacturing labor costs) for the years 1982 and 1994 under the assumption of three centers of agglomeration: the USA, Germany, and Japan. For each country the nearest of these three centers was taken to represent c in the regression. So for Spain, for example, only the distance to Germany (and hence German wages as W_{ct}) matters, whereas for Korea and Brazil the relevant centers are respectively Japan and the USA. The estimation results in Table 9.5 suggest that a spatial wage structure also makes sense on a global level.

Comparing the distance coefficients for 1982 and 1994, it is interesting to note that distance apparently has become more important, and not less important. Given that manufacturing wages are largely determined by *national* variables, like the system of wage bargaining or the minimum wage, it is far from obvious that a supranational spatial wage structure exists. Similarly, given the often erratic behavior of exchange rates, the conversion of wages expressed in national currencies into US dollars also makes it less likely that, compared to the national level, a spatial wage structure will be found for the world as a whole.[7] In order to examine the link between spatial wages and the gravity equation more closely, a wage equation was also estimated in which a country's manufacturing wage was specified as a function of the GDP of all other countries corrected for distance. Or, in other words, a market potential function as given by equation (5.3) was also subject to estimation. Here the evidence is somewhat less conclusive,

---

[7] The estimation results are based on current exchange rates; the use of purchasing power parity (PPP) exchange rates (not shown here) did not change the main result.

Table 9.5. *A spatial wage structure*

	1982	1994
κ_0	−0.994 (−5.170)	−1.242 (−5.004)
κ_1	−0.098 (−2.324)	−0.140 (−2.577)

Notes: # observations = 68; *t*-values in parentheses.
Source: Peeters (2001).

probably because, given the labor productivity differences between countries, the inclusion of GDP (though correct from the point of view of the core model) is a rather imperfect proxy for the market potential when one compares countries. Countries like China or India have a relatively large GDP but are located in an area with relatively low manufacturing wages. The opposite holds for small European countries like the Netherlands or Belgium. The use of GDP per capita is one way to correct for this problem.

Using the congestion model of chapter 7 in a setting with twenty-four locations we report four simulations, in which we change the size of the transport costs T, but not the initial distribution of the mobile labor force (λ initial). Naturally, the size of the transport costs has an impact on the long-run equilibrium distribution of the mobile labor force (λ final). This is illustrated in the series of panels in Figure 9.12. Clearly, higher transport costs imply a more uneven long-run distribution of the mobile labor force, and hence of economic activity; moving from panel *a* to panel *d* the final distribution moves from almost circular to spiked.

Can the agglomerating forces at work in the congestion model shed some light on the underpinning of the gravity equation? To answer this question we calculated the distribution of international trade flows for the final equilibrium. This poses, of course, no problem for the manufacturing sector. However, since there are no trade costs involved in the food sector these flows could in principle be from any exporting location to any importing location. To determine the food flows we therefore imposed the simple rule that each food-exporting location exports food to all food-importing locations in proportion to that location's relative demand for food imports. More details are given in the appendix to this chapter.

It is important to note that the calculation of the simulated trade flows between different locations involves detailed knowledge not only of the income levels of the locations and their geographic distance, but also of wages, prices, and price indices for all locations, as well as parameters pertaining to the elasticity of substitution

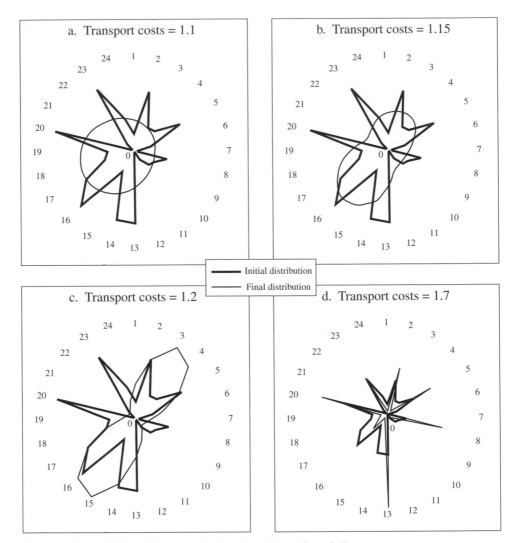

Figure 9.12. Initial and final distribution ($\delta = 0.7$; $\varepsilon = 5$; $\tau = 0.1$).

between different varieties, the impact of congestion, etc. This is much more detailed information than will generally be available in any data-base. The basic gravity equation reported above, on the other hand, uses only income levels for the various locations, as well as their geographic distance. We should be surprised, therefore, if the gravity equation is able to explain a fair share of the variation in the trade flows between locations. In this respect the performance of the congestion model is impressive: at least 67% of the variation of the trade flows is explained by the basic gravity equation. The estimates for the distance parameter θ_3 and the income level of the destination θ_2 are also reassuring: both are highly significant and of the correct sign. The parameter estimates for the income level of the origin are more

Table 9.6. *Overview of the basic gravity equation in simulations*

	$T=1.1$	$T=1.15$	$T=1.2$	$T=1.7$
Income origin ($\theta1$)	−0.866	0.840	0.698	−0.827
	(−6.94)	(7.26)	(6.35)	(−2.67)
Income destination ($\theta2$)	2.633	0.810	1.232	6.615
	(21.11)	(7.00)	(11.19)	(21.33)
Distance ($\theta3$)	−1.027	−2.286	−2.881	−7.459
	(−24.81)	(−55.34)	(−39.23)	(−27.14)
$\bar{R}^2$	0.670	0.851	0.755	0.686

Note: t-values in parentheses.

problematic, as they have the "wrong" sign twice, both for high and low transport costs.

9.6   Conclusions

This chapter has partially fulfilled Bertil Ohlin's objective of analyzing international trade flows against the background of a theory of location. For the latter we use the core model of geographical economics, which itself is largely based on the new trade theory. We combine this with two traditional approaches in trade theory: Ricardian comparative advantage, based on differences in technology; and factor abundance theory. In both cases we derive an intricate picture of the forces underlying international trade flows, enabling us to explain both intra- and inter-industry trade flows, as well as the locational aspects of firm decisions. The geographical impact shows up in both cases through a mitigation of the effects of comparative advantage, that is, other things equal, an increase in trade costs reduces the extent of industrial specialization within countries. This is intuitively plausible as firms are relatively sheltered from the forces of international competition as transport costs increase, such that they benefit more strongly from the home-market effect. We conclude the chapter by briefly discussing the gravity equation of international trade, and showing that the geographical economics model can explain this empirically observed phenomenon using the many-location version with congestion discussed in chapter 7.

Appendix

Using the notation of chapter 7 and the normalization we give the international trade flows for the congestion model of chapter 7. Food import in location r is simply the difference between demand for food $(1 - \delta) Y_r$ and local production $\phi_r(1 - \gamma)L$:

$$\text{food import} = (1 - \delta) Y_r - \phi_r(1 - \gamma)L \tag{9.A1}$$

The distribution of food exports over the locations is as described in the main text. Demand for a product in location r from location s equals $\delta Y_r W_s^{-\varepsilon} T_{rs}^{-\varepsilon} I_r^{\varepsilon-1}$. Recall that T_{rs} units have to be shipped from s to r and that location s has N_s firms to see that total export of manufactures from location s to location r is given by:

manufacturing exports from s to $r = \delta Y_r p_s^{-\varepsilon} T_{rs}^{1-\varepsilon} I_r^{\varepsilon-1} N_s = \delta Y_r W_s^{-\varepsilon} T_{rs}^{1-\varepsilon} I_r^{\varepsilon-1} \lambda_s^{1-\tau-\tau\varepsilon}$

$$(9.A2)$$

Exercises

9.1 According to the cost functions given by equation (9.3), country 1 (country 2) has a comparative and absolute advantage in sector A (sector B) manufactures. Modify equation (9.3) such that country 1 has an absolute advantage in the production of both sector A and B manufactures, but still only a comparative advantage in the production of sector A manufactures. *Hint*: Introduce four types of βs in equation (9.3).

9.2 On the website for this book you can find a small user-friendly "Ricardo" simulation for the model described in section 9.3. Download the simulation and start it up. Now vary the elasticity of substitution from 2; 3; 4; ...; to 10 by changing the numbers in red. Describe and explain what happens, as the elasticity of substitution varies, to:

(i)   the domestic share of the industry with comparative advantage;
(ii) the domestic share of the industry with comparative disadvantage;
(iii) intra-industry trade and the share of GNP imported.

9.3 On the website for this book you can find a small user-friendly "Ricardo" simulation for the model described in section 9.3. Download the simulation and start it up. Now vary the transport costs from 1.1; 1.2; 1.3; ...; to 2 by changing the numbers in red. Describe and explain what happens, as the transport costs vary, to:

(i)   the domestic share of the industry with comparative advantage;
(ii) the domestic share of the industry with comparative disadvantage;
(iii) intra-industry trade and the share of GNP imported.

9.4 In the core model of geographical economics there is international labor mobility. In the factor abundance model discussed in this chapter there is no labor mobility between countries. Explain why the introduction of labor mobility is at odds with the analysis underlying the factor abundance model. *Hint*: Remember that labor is the endowment.

9.5 On the website for this book you can find a small user-friendly "factor abundance" simulation, comparing the models described in sections 9.3 and 9.4. Download the simulation and start it up. Now vary the elasticity of substitution from 2; 3; 4; ...; to 10 by changing the numbers in red. Compare, describe, and explain what happens, as the elasticity of substitution varies, to:

(i)   the share of sector A firms in country 1;
(ii) domestic spending on sector A in country 1;
(iii) the share of sector B firms in country 1;
(iv) domestic spending on sector B in country 1;
(v)   the share of income spent on imports;
(vi) intra-industry trade.

9.6 On the website for this book you can find a small user-friendly "factor abundance" simulation, comparing the models described in sections 9.3 and 9.4. Download the simulation and start it up. Now vary the transport costs from 1.1; 1.2; 1.3; ...; to 2 by changing the numbers in red. Compare, describe, and explain what happens, as the transport costs vary, to:

(i)   the share of sector A firms in country 1;
(ii) domestic spending on sector A in country 1;
(iii) the share of sector B firms in country 1;
(iv) domestic spending on sector B in country 1;
(v)   the share of income spent on imports;
(vi) intra-industry trade.

9.7* According to Alan Deardorff (1998), the gravity equation (9.12) can also be founded on neo-classical trade theory (see section 2.2 for the neo-classical trade theory). Try to think of a neo-classical trade story that could result in a gravity equation and the kind of empirical results shown in Table 9.4.

9.8* In the core model of geographical economics (see equation (3.25)) manufacturing workers migrate if there are real wage differentials between regions. The speed at which they react to inter-regional real wage differences is given by the parameter η. A low (high) value for this parameter implies a weak (strong) reaction by manufacturing workers to real wage differences. Given the information in section 9.5 why do you think that η is low for most countries? How could the reluctance of people to migrate, even if real wage differences are significant, be modeled?

10 Dynamics and economic growth

10.1 Introduction

So far we have not paid much attention in this book to the intermediate dynamics underlying the geographical economics models. Instead, we have usually focused attention on the relationship between a long-run equilibrium outcome and the structural parameters, given an initial geographical distribution of labour and production. For that reason we argued in chapter 2 that the novelty of geographical economics relative to new trade theory is to be found in the endogenous determination of market size, fostered by the migration of mobile workers towards regions with higher real wages. The dynamics underlying the adjustment path, that is how we evolve over time (see our remark below on "time") from an initial distribution to a final distribution, and the intricacies of economic growth and development have been virtually absent in the analysis so far. This chapter partially fills this void. In doing so we will distinguish among three types of dynamics, increasing in complexity and in importance:

(i)   adjustment dynamics
(ii) simulation dynamics
(iii) economic growth.

Adjustment dynamics
This type of dynamics analyzes the adjustment path over time, from an initial distribution of manufacturing production across regions to a final long-run equilibrium, by showing the sequence of short-run equilibria leading to the long-run equilibrium. The driving force behind this adjustment process in the core model of geographical economics is therefore the migration decision of individuals who move towards regions with higher real wages, arising from the tensions between the home-market effect and the price index effect in this sequence of short-run equilibria. Adjustment dynamics are discussed in section 10.2. The reader should realize that the time dimension in that section (and in section 10.5) is "simulation time," where ten simulation reallocations might represent a time frame of six months, or three weeks, or some other "real" time frame.

274

Simulation dynamics

At various places in this book we give interpretations of the geographical models of the "suppose" type, such as "suppose the economy is initially in a long-run spreading equilibrium and transport costs T gradually decrease over time." The story then continues to discuss what may happen in the model to the distribution of manufacturing activity as transport costs fall. In essence, we then invoke an exogenous fall in a structural parameter to discuss how the model may be useful in explaining the evolution of some phenomenon over time. So far we have done this almost always without explicitly performing and showing such simulations (chapter 7 provided some exceptions). We label this type of reasoning "simulation dynamics" and discuss it in sections 10.4 and 10.5.

Economic growth

The most important, but also the most complex, type of dynamics is the investigation and modeling of "real" economic growth. In terms of the geographical economics models this implies not only modeling the forces giving rise to agglomeration or spreading of economic activity, as we have done so far, but also modeling traditional and novel forces explaining the increase in economic prosperity over time. This increase may result from rising production levels or the invention and availability of new goods and services, requiring for example investment in capital goods or research and development. To model economic growth properly therefore requires the analysis of the investment decisions of economic agents, which in turn implies the modeling of intertemporal optimization. This is a complicated technical issue, certainly in a model with multiple long-run equilibria. However, important breakthroughs on this issue have been made recently by Richard Baldwin and Rikard Forslid. An in-depth analysis of these issues is beyond the scope of this book, but the most important modeling details and results are discussed in section 10.6.

Section 10.3 provides some stylized facts of economic growth, as a prelude to the discussion on simulation dynamics and economic growth in sections 10.4–10.6. Section 10.7 concludes. We start, however, with a discussion of the adjustment path from an initial distribution towards a long-run equilibrium.

10.2 Adjustment dynamics

Throughout this book we have focused attention almost exclusively on the long-run equilibria of the various geographical economics models we have presented and investigated. It is time to pay more attention to the adjustment paths used to get from an initial distribution of the manufacturing labor force to a final distribution as represented by a long-run equilibrium. To focus the analysis in this section, we analyze adjustment paths using the two-region base scenario of the core model, also used in chapter 4, in which the elasticity of substitution $\varepsilon = 5$, the share of income spent on manufactures $\delta = 0.4$, and the transport costs $T = 1.7$. As a reminder, the short-run equilibrium real wage of region 1 relative to region 2 for all distributions of the manufacturing workforce is reproduced here as Figure 10.1a (see also Figure 4.1). In the interior, a long-run equilibrium is reached if the relative real wage is 1. As the reader may recall, this setting gave rise to five possible long-run equilibria: three stable equilibria (spreading [point C], agglomeration in region 2 [point A], or agglomeration in region 1 [point E]) and two unstable equilibria (in this particular case where the share of the manufacturing workforce in region 1 is roughly 16% [point B] or 84% [point D]).

The rest of this section addresses two main issues. First, in subsection 10.2.1 we briefly describe the "regular" adjustment of the economy over time. The term "regular" conveys the idea that this type of adjustment occurs most frequently in the simulations of the various geographical economics models. Second, in subsection 10.2.2 we draw attention to some "special" cases that may arise in an adjustment process. As suggested, these special cases will rarely occur, but the reader should be conscious of the fact that they may arise when performing simulation exercises.

10.2.1   Regular adjustment

Before we can analyze the adjustment path of the economy over time, we must choose an initial distribution. This choice is largely arbitrary, as long as it is not a long-run equilibrium. Here, we choose an initial distribution in the "basin of attraction" of the spreading equilibrium, with 30% of the manufacturing workforce in region 1, as illustrated by the square in Figure 10.1a. The reader may recall the adjustment equation of the manufacturing workforce, based on migration decisions, invoked in chapter 3 (see equation (3.25), in which laborers move gradually to the region with the highest real wage:

$$\frac{d\lambda_1}{\lambda_1} = \eta(w_1 - \overline{w}), \qquad \text{where } \overline{w} = \lambda_1 w_1 + \lambda_2 w_2 \tag{10.1}$$

In this differential specification, starting from an initial distribution with 30% of the manufacturing workforce in region 1, manufacturing workers would gradually migrate from region 2 to region 1, as indicated by the arrow in Figure 10.1a, until the stable long-run spreading equilibrium is reached in which 50% of the manufacturing workforce is located in region 1. The swiftness of this migration process depends on the speed-of-adjustment parameter η (equation (10.1)), which is the focus of analysis in this section. It is important to realize, however, that in the simulations of the geographical economics models, differential equation (10.1) is approximated by equation (10.2), where a subscript t denotes the number of the reallocation:

$$\begin{bmatrix} \lambda_{1,t+1} \\ \lambda_{2,t+1} \end{bmatrix} = \begin{bmatrix} \lambda_{1,t} \\ \lambda_{2,t} \end{bmatrix} + \eta \begin{bmatrix} (w_{1,t} - \overline{w}_t)\lambda_{1,t} \\ (w_{2,t} - \overline{w}_t)\lambda_{2,t} \end{bmatrix} \tag{10.2}$$

For most simulations reported in this book, we chose a relatively low speed-of-adjustment parameter, namely $\eta = 2$. For this setting, Figure 10.1b depicts the adjustment of the economy over time, where time is measured in terms of the number of reallocations, that is the number of times λ is adjusted, before a long-run equilibrium is reached. The broken horizontal lines in Figure 10.1b, and in similar figures to follow, depict the interior long-run equilibria of the economy, in accordance with points B, C,

a. Two-region base scenario

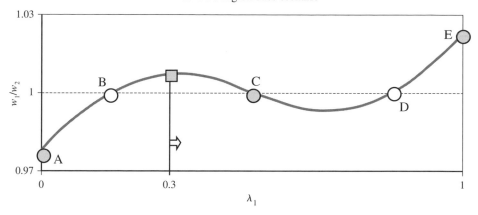

b. Share of manufacturing workers in 1, $\eta = 2$

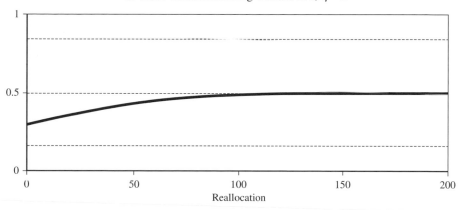

c. Number of reallocations toward spreading

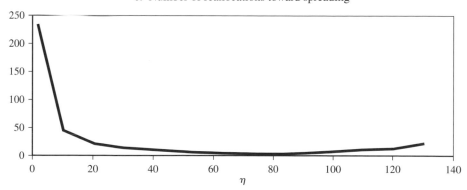

Figure 10.1.   Regular adjustment dynamics.

and D in Figure 10.1a. As illustrated, the share of manufacturing workers in region 1 rises slowly (from 30% to 50%) until the long-run spreading equilibrium is reached. If the speed-of-adjustment parameter $\eta=2$, this occurs after 233 reallocations.[1]

Increasing the speed-of-adjustment parameter η, first to 10 and then by increments of 10, shows that the adjustment process illustrated in Figure 10.1b holds for a large range of adjustment speeds.[2] The most important difference is, as would seem obvious, that the long-run spreading equilibrium is reached using fewer reallocations if the speed of adjustment increases. As illustrated in Figure 10.1c, this reasoning only holds up to a certain point, in this case until the speed-of-adjustment parameter $\eta=80$ (with only three reallocations). For even higher speeds of adjustment, there is some "over-shooting" of the long-run spreading equilibrium, that is at some point a reallocation increases the manufacturing workforce in region 1 above 50%, necessitating a reduc-tion to reach the long-run spreading equilibrium. This overshooting then leads to a gradual rise in the number of reallocations, as illustrated in Figure 10.1c.

Figure 10.1c shows clearly why it is tempting for researchers to increase the speed of adjustment η when performing simulations of geographical economics models: the end result is the same (the economy converges towards the long-run spreading equilib-rium), while the number of reallocations (and thus the computing time involved) reduces drastically. The next subsection will illustrate, however, that there are also serious, and perhaps unexpected, costs associated with increasing the speed of adjust-ment (although we must admit that some of the issues and problems explained in the next subsection can in principle also arise if a low speed of adjustment is chosen, although usually in a less extreme form, as illustrated by the discussion of the "pancake" economy in chapter 11).

10.2.2   Special adjustment

When performing computer simulations one should be aware in general of some special cases that may arise while the economy is adjusting over time from one short-run equilibrium to another on its path towards a long-run equilibrium. We will focus attention on three issues, all of which can be clearly illustrated and understood using the two-region core model example, namely:

(i)   the dynamic path of the economy may converge to "cycles";
(ii)   the dynamic path of the economy may lead to an unstable equilibrium;
(iii) the dynamic path of the economy may not lead to the "nearest" stable equilibrium.

First, the dynamic path of the economy may converge to "cycles." Figure 10.2a shows the adjustment of the economy over time for the first 1,000 reallocations if the speed-of-adjustment parameter $\eta=200$. The figure appears not to be very clear, or at least

[1] The number of reallocations is actually the number reported minus 1 and depends not only on the speed-of-adjustment parameter η, but also on the tightness of the stopping criterion as measured by the param-eter σ and discussed in section 4.2: $\left| \dfrac{W_{r,iteration} - W_{r,iteration-1}}{W_{r,iteration-1}} \right| < \sigma$. In this case, $\sigma=0.00001$.

[2] Details of these simulations are available on the website for this book.

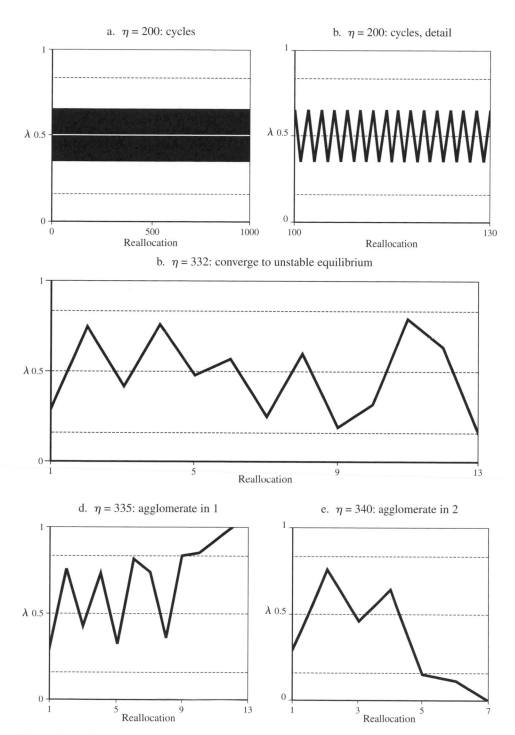

Figure 10.2.   Special adjustment dynamics.

does not give a clear picture of the adjustment process, since there is one thick line centered around 0.5. Figure 10.2b, therefore, enlarges a small part of Figure 10.2a. As is evident from this enlargement, showing reallocations 100–130, the dynamic path of the economy is zigzagging around the stable spreading equilibrium (in this case for a manufacturing workforce in region 1 of roughly 36% and 64%). The specified dynamics imply that the economy will continue to do so forever. This process is called a two-period "cycle." By implication, the computer program will never stop, unless you unplug the power supply or, as is customary, have a built in safety device. Our built in safety device makes the computer program stop if a long-run equilibrium is reached or if a maximum number of reallocations is exceeded. The maximum number of reallocations we used was 1,000. On the website for this book we have labeled the adjustment process "infinity" for the two-region program if this number was exceeded. Cyclical behavior, in general, characterizes the dynamics of the economy if η is in between 140 and 331.[3]

Case (ii) occurs when the dynamic path of the economy leads to an unstable equilibrium. At first sight, an adjustment path leading to an unstable equilibrium seems like a contradiction. In principle it should be, but Figure 10.2c gives an example where this happens nonetheless. As is clear from the figure, at this high speed of adjustment the economy appears to be moving around randomly within the boundaries of the unstable long-run equilibria (the dashed lines). Then, "by accident" the economy hits the unstable long-run equilibrium with roughly 16% of the manufacturing workforce in region 1 on the thirteenth reallocation. Thus, as specified, a long-run equilibrium is reached and the dynamic adjustment process stops.[4] One should therefore be aware that if the dynamic adjustment path converges to a long-run equilibrium, this does not necessarily imply that it is a stable equilibrium, although it usually does.

Finally, case (iii) is where the dynamic path of the economy may not lead to the "nearest" stable equilibrium. The term "nearest" in the sentence above should be interpreted as follows: if the initial equilibrium is within the "basin of attraction" of a certain long-run equilibrium, this does not necessarily imply that the adjustment process leads the economy toward this long-run equilibrium. Instead, depending on the speed-of-adjustment parameter η, the economy may converge to a different stable long-run equilibrium. Figures 10.2d and 10.2e show two examples of this phenomenon, one in which manufacturing production agglomerates in region 1 (if $\eta = 335$) and one in which manufacturing production agglomerates in region 2 (if $\eta = 340$).

We want to make two general remarks. First, the special adjustment cases illustrated above may be relatively clear to understand and easy to avoid in the two-region example, but are less easy to understand and less easy to avoid in a more general setting, with many locations, complicated transport structures, congestion costs, and distinctions among different industrial sectors with intermediate deliveries; in particular, it is then very hard to identify the stable long-run equilibria. Second, it is clear from the dis-

---

[3] We say "in general" because there are cases in which the long-run spreading equilibrium is reached "by accident", for example if $\eta = 280$ or $\eta = 300$. This phenomenon is similar to case (ii) described in this subsection.
[4] Because of the stopping criterion discussed in section 4.2 the adjustment process stops whenever the allocation is within a small range around the unstable long-run equilibrium.

cussions and examples above that the "special" adjustment phenomena arise more easily if the speed of adjustment is high. We can be confident that in general it is less likely for such special cases to occur if the speed of adjustment is not so high. This seems to be more in line with the gradual processes empirically observed for migration decisions, which are not taken lightly. It is nonetheless important to be aware of the possibilities which may arise, as these may also occur for moderate speeds of adjustment. An example of this is given in the pancake model of chapter 11. Moreover, high speeds of adjustment may be relevant in a different economic setting, for example when examining adjustment processes in financial markets.

Now that we have seen in more detail the adjustment processes that may arise while the economy is moving from an initial distribution to a long-run distribution of manufacturing activity, it is almost time to take the next step and analyze simulation dynamics. The aim of simulation dynamics is to show the most important model implications of parameter changes. That is, it tries to understand a model by telling a story. Before you can do this, however, you must know which story to tell. The next section therefore briefly discusses some important characteristics in this respect.

10.3 Some stylized facts of economic growth

The field of economic growth basically deals with two questions: "why do countries grow over time?" and "why do some countries grow faster than others?" These questions are interesting because, as briefly discussed in chapter 2 within a neo-classical framework, diminishing returns to capital ensure that "poor" countries grow faster than "rich" countries. In the extreme case, similar countries will have the same income per capita in the long run. In the absence of technological growth, income per capita will eventually not grow at all. Neither is the case in practice.

Table 10.1 presents economic growth and income per capita data for a selection of currently developed countries over an extended time period (1890–1990), as pioneered by Angus Maddison. The table shows twenty-year intervals of income per capita (in 1985 US dollars) and the growth rates over each twenty-year period. The evolution of income per capita as given in Table 10.1 is illustrated in Figure 10.3 for a selection of four countries, Australia, USA, France, and Japan. Figure 10.3 uses a logarithmic scale, on which a straight line depicts a constant growth rate, and the steepness of this line the extent of economic growth. Income per capita in the United States, for instance, has grown in a fairly stable manner from more than $3,000 to more than $18,000. In contrast, economic growth in Japan has been less stable, with an enormous increase in the period 1950–1980.

Several important facts given in Table 10.1 and illustrated in Figure 10.3 are worth noting. First, there is no sign that economic growth rates are falling as time passes by. Second, there are large swings in economic prosperity. In particular, there are long periods with stagnant or declining incomes per capita, followed by (rapidly) rising income levels; see for example Australia and Japan in Figure 10.3. In this sense, the experience of the USA is the exception, not the rule. Third, and related to the second observation, the relative income per capita position may change for long periods of

Table 10.1. *Economic growth and income per capita, selected developed countries*

| | USA | | UK | | Germany (West) | | Japan | | Netherla |
Year	Growth	Income	Growth	Income	Growth	Income	Growth	Income	Growth	I
1890	1.6	3,101	1.1	3,383	1.4	1,624	—	842	—	
1910	1.9	4,538	0.7	3,891	1.6	2,256	1.2	1,084	—	
1930	1.1	5,642	0.5	4,287	0.9	2,714	1.8	1,539	2.0	
1950	2.1	8,605	1.4	5,651	1.3	3,542	0.2	1,620	0.3	
1970	1.9	12,815	2.3	8,994	4.8	9,257	8.1	8,168	3.4	
1990	1.7	18,258	2.1	13,589	2.2	14,288	3.4	16,144	1.7	1

Note: The observations are per capita averages over the twenty-year periods preceding the indicated year, 1985 US dollars.
Source: Maddison (1992).

Table 10.2. *Economic growth and income per capita, selected developing countries*

| | China | | India | | Indonesia | | Philippines | | Brazil | |
Year	Growth	Income	Growth	Income	Growth	Income	Growth	Income	Growth	Income
1900	—	401	—	378	—	499	—	718	—	436
1913	0.3	415	0.4	399	0.5	529	2.4	985	1.4	521
1950	−0.6	338	−0.3	359	−0.2	484	−0.2	898	1.9	1,073
1973	3.6	774	1.6	513	2.1	786	1.9	1,400	3.7	2,504
1987	5.8	1,748	1.8	662	3.0	1,200	0.6	1,519	2.2	3,417

Note: The observations are per capita averages over the twenty-year periods preceding the indicated year, 1985 US dollars.
Source: Maddison (1992).

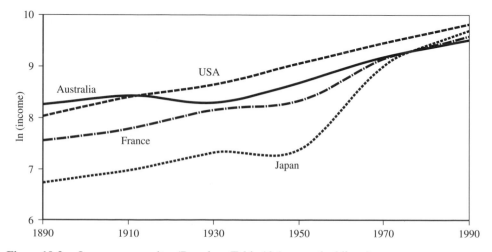

Figure 10.3.   Income per capita. (Based on Table 10.1; smoothed lines.)

…stralia		France		Italy		Canada		Switzerland	
ª Income	Growth	Income	Growth	Income	Growth	Income	Growth	Income
3,949	1.1	1,955	0.5	1,352	1.6	1,846	—	—
4,615	1.0	2,406	1.7	1,891	2.7	3,179	—	2,979
3,963	2.0	3,591	1.1	2,366	1.1	3,955	2.1	4,511
5,970	0.7	4,176	0.9	2,840	2.2	6,112	1.9	6,546
9,747	3.9	9,245	5.1	7,884	2.6	10,200	3.1	12,208
13,514	2.2	14,245	2.6	13,215	2.6	17,070	1.2	15,650

time. In Table 10.1, Australia dropped from first place in 1890 to eighth in 1990. The USA moved from third place in 1890 to first in 1930, and stayed there. Japan moved from last place in 1890 to third in 1990, etc. This phenomenon is known as "leap-frogging." These observations are at odds with the simplest neo-classical growth models. Since technological knowledge is a non-rival and non-excludable good,[5] at least in the long run, it is difficult to convince oneself that over a period of more than a hundred years, differences in the growth of technological knowledge can explain the differences in growth rates and per capita income.

Is there, at least, conditional convergence of income per capita, as argued by the neo-classical growth model and maybe suggested by Figure 10.3? No, there is not (see also the discussion in chapter 5). Note that Table 10.1 presents data for currently developed countries, and not randomly chosen countries. If we had selected countries of approximately equal income per capita in 1890, we would of course have observed diverging income levels. Table 10.2 presents data for a selection of currently developing countries in a slightly different time frame. Note in particular, when comparing the entries in Tables 10.1 and 10.2, that the growth rates in less-developed countries are by no means higher than those in the developed world. There seems to be no long-term trend for less-developed countries to grow faster than more-developed countries. Again, for each country there are large swings in economic prosperity, indicative of some localized influences as dramatically illustrated by the initially weak, but eventually strong, performance of China.

Now that we have seen the large swings in economic prosperity at the national level we briefly return to the global regions identified by the World Bank, as discussed in chapter 1. Recall that the World Bank divides the world into seven global regions: (East) Europe and Central Asia (ECA), East Asia and Pacific (EAP), Latin America and Caribbean

---

[5] A good is non-rival if two people can use it at the same time. This applies, for example, for ideas which can be used simultaneously (such as the concept of adding numbers). A good is non-excludable if I cannot prevent you from using it, such as breathing air.

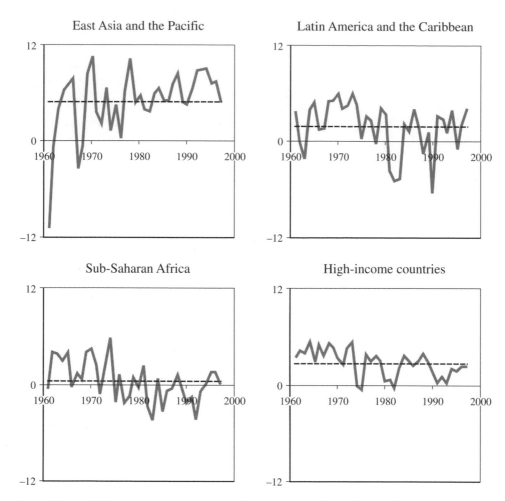

Figure 10.4. GNP per capita growth rates. *Source*: The World Bank, *World Development Indicators*, CD-ROM, 1999. The broken horizontal lines indicate the average growth rate; see Table 10.3.

(LAC), Middle East and North Africa (MNA), South Asia (SAS), Sub-Saharan Africa (SSA), and the high-income countries (High). Figure 10.4 shows the evolution of GNP per capita for those four global regions (EAP, LAC, SSA, and High) for which data are available on the World Bank's *World Development Indicators* CD-ROM (1999) for the entire period of observation (1960–1997). Table 10.3 provides summary statistics for those regions. What is striking is that the core–periphery discussion seems to repeat itself, but now in terms of growth rates. Going back forty years we can clearly distinguish two growth cores (EAP and High) and two growth peripheries (LAC and SSA).

As is clear from Figure 10.4 and Table 10.3, annual economic growth in the past four decades has on average been highest in East Asia and the Pacific (4.9%), followed by the high-income countries (2.7%), Latin America and the Caribbean (1.7%), and

Table 10.3. *Summary statistics of GNP growth per capita (average annual growth, 1960–1997)*

	EAP	LAC	SSA	High
Mean	4.90	1.76	0.45	2.71
Standard deviation	4.04	3.06	2.46	1.65
Minimum	−10.7	−6.3	−4.3	−0.6
Maximum	10.5	5.8	5.6	5.4

Note: EAP = East Asia and Pacific; LAC = Latin America and Caribbean; SSA = Sub-Saharan Africa; High = high-income countries.

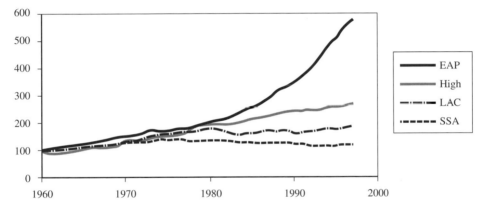

Figure 10.5. GNP per capita (index) *Source*: World Bank, *World Development Indicators*, CD-ROM, 1999. The index in 1997 for EAP = 570, for LAC = 188, for SSA = 117, and for High = 267.

Sub-Saharan Africa (0.5%). It is also evident that economic growth is more stable in the high-income countries, that is the ups and downs in economic growth are more pronounced in poor regions, particularly for East Asia and the Pacific (see the standard deviation in Table 10.3, and note that the scale is the same for all regions in Figure 10.4).

The difference in average annual economic growth between, for example, East Asia and the Pacific and the high-income countries, that is 4.9% compared to 2.7%, may not seem impressive at first sight. Note, however, that this difference in economic growth continues year after year, which even over a relatively short period of thirty-seven years leads to remarkable differences in economic development and well-being. This is dramatically illustrated in Figure 10.5, where GNP per capita in each region is indexed at 100 in 1960. Economic well-being for the average person in East Asia and the Pacific, which, as the reader may recall, includes China and contains about 1.8 billion people, has increased almost sixfold in those thirty-seven years. This is roughly twice as much as the increase in well-being for the average person in the high-income countries. The average person in Sub-Saharan Africa saw virtually no increase in economic well-being in the same period. Apparently, there are local influences on economic growth not only at the national level but also at the level of global regions. The appendix to this chapter illustrates this for a much longer period (1820–1992), using a somewhat different regional division of the world.

We can summarize the most important facts on economic growth as follows.

(i)　For almost all countries, there is an ever-increasing level of income per capita.
(ii)　Differences in economic growth rates between countries may persist for a long time.
(iii)　There may be long periods of stagnation, followed by periods of rapid economic growth.
(iv)　There are frequent changes in economic ranking, known as leap-frogging.

All four observations occur both at the national level and the global regional level. It is time to see how some of these observations can be explained.

10.4　Explaining the facts: endogenous growth and simulation dynamics I

Two different fields of economics can play a role in understanding the empirical observations summarized at the end of section 10.3, namely endogenous growth theory and geographical economics. We will argue below that the former is useful for understanding facts (i) and (ii), while the latter is useful for understanding facts (iii) and (iv).

10.4.1　Endogenous growth

Our discussion on the usefulness of endogenous growth for explaining facts (i) and (ii) will be brief. Some more details are given in chapter 2, and a good survey is given in Barro and Sala-i-Martin (1995). The essence of this literature is quite simple. The aim is to construct models capable of explaining facts (i) and (ii), that is persistent increases in income per capita and persistent differences in economic growth rates. Essentially, this is done as follows. Take the standard neo-classical production function $Y = Af(K,L)$, in which production (income) Y rises if the variable A rises, or if the available inputs, capital K or labor L, rise. In the endogenous growth models the variable A is some function of other economic factors, for example capital K with technological spillovers, or research and development expenditures, or some kind of Schumpeterian innovation process. Consequently, instead of decreasing returns to capital, the model now has constant or increasing returns, which enables the economy to grow forever. This explains fact (i): ever-increasing per capita income levels.

Most endogenous growth models analyze a closed economy. If the structural influence on the variable A is then different in one country from another country this can vacuously explain fact (ii): long-lasting differences in economic growth rates. The analysis is more interesting, and more challenging, in an open economy setting, as pioneered by Grossman and Helpman (1991).[6] Their aim is to analyze along which channels international trade affects long-run innovation and growth. This depends fundamentally on what is assumed with respect to knowledge spillovers and the extent to which countries differ in factor endowments. The opening of trade might stimulate growth or diminish it. If knowledge spillovers are geographically localized in specific countries, the smaller country might find that fierce competition from abroad can reduce the returns on investment in knowledge, which in turn might reduce the growth rate. Alternatively, if a country is relatively well endowed with unskilled labor, it might specialize in traditional sectors rather than the R&D sector, which also reduces the growth rate. To the extent than the structural influences on the variable A are localized in an international setting fact (ii) may still hold, that is there may be long-lasting differences in economic growth. Facts (iii) (periods of stagnation and rapid growth) and (iv) (leap-frogging) cannot be explained in endogenous growth models, which focus strongly on, and are constructed to lead to, balanced-growth equilibria.

10.4.2 Geographical economics (simulation dynamics)

The geographical economics approach cannot contribute in explaining facts (i) (persistent rising income levels) and (ii) (persistent growth differences), simply because there is no mechanism in the models discussed so far through which there is an increase in production levels or investment in R&D leading to the invention and development of new manufacturing varieties. Fortunately, however, facts (iii) and (iv) naturally arise within the geographical economics framework, as indicated below.

Krugman and Venables (1995) analyze a two-country model in which there is no labor mobility between countries, but there is an intermediate input (see also chapter 6). Labor combined with intermediate inputs produces the final product, which can be used for consumption and the intermediate product. The central questions in this particular structure are: what determines the allocation of manufacturing industry over the two countries and what determines the allocation of the labor force over potential activities? If for some reason one country has a larger market for intermediate products this will be an attractive place for other firms because all varieties are available without transport cost, which also lowers the cost of producing a final product.

Starting from an initially very high level of transport costs, Krugman and Venables discuss at length what happens in this model if transport costs start to fall, taking this description as representative of actual developments in the world economy. Essentially, therefore, they give an interpretation of the workings of the model by investigating what happens if an exogenous parameter falls over time. We have termed this practice "simulation dynamics" in section 10.1. In any case, the sequence of events is roughly as follows. Initially, manufacturing production is evenly spread over the two countries.

---

[6] They also cite related work by Rivera-Batiz and Romer (1991).

As transport costs start to fall, the world spontaneously divides itself into a core–periphery pattern. If the manufacturing sector is large enough this will also result in different real wages between the two countries (different income per capita levels). Eventually, as transport costs continue to fall, the core–periphery pattern disappears again. Both the appearance and the disappearance of the core–periphery pattern is in accordance with fact (iii) (periods of stagnation and rapid economic growth).

Puga and Venables (1996) extend the Krugman and Venables (1995) model, not only by assuming three instead of two countries, but also by analyzing how industrialization spreads from country to country. They assume that some exogenous force increases the size of the industrial sector in one of the countries relative to agriculture (which makes their analysis "simulation dynamics" in our terminology). Since it is assumed that the income elasticity of consumer demand for manufactures is larger than 1, this increases demand for manufactures relative to agriculture, which leads to wage increases. Starting with the situation in which industry is agglomerated in country 1, this implies that wages become higher but it is still profitable for firms to agglomerate because they benefit from inter-firm relationships. As wages increase further, at some point it becomes beneficial to relocate to a low-wage country. The process then repeats itself and might finally result in waves of industrialization.[7] This phenomenon of a sequence of industrialization and the descriptions given in Puga and Venables (1996) are in accordance with fact (iv) (leap-frogging).

Redding and Venables (2000) give some evidence as to the relevance of the approach. The empirical implications are that the distance of countries to the markets in which they sell and the distance to countries which supply intermediates are crucial determinants for explaining cross-country wage differentials. The further away are the final markets and suppliers of the intermediate products, the lower the wages firms in these countries can pay. Redding and Venables give a simple example to illustrate the potential impact of transport costs in such a model. If the prices of all goods are set on the world market and transport costs are borne by the producing country, and if intermediates account for 50% of the total value, the effects of small changes in transport costs can be quite large. Transport costs of 10% on both final products and intermediate products reduce the value-added by 30%. Transport costs of 20% reduce value-added by 60%. This example makes intuitively clear why Redding and Venables are able to explain more than 70% of cross-country variation in income per capita and 50% of the variation in manufacturing wages.

---

[7] The resemblance to Murphy, Shleifer, and Vishny (1989) is not coincidental. In this model too, firms are characterized by increasing returns to scale and, furthermore, pecuniary externalities are important. The central question here is: if a country finds itself in an "underdevelopment trap" or has become a periphery can it do something to industrialize itself? The answer basically is yes; coordinated investments and adopting the increasing-returns technologies simultaneously might tilt the balance, because each firm creates income and a market for all other firms. Without such coordinated action the investments might very well turn out to be unprofitable, and the country may forever stay in an underdevelopment trap. However, the analysis does not deal with the question of how the core–periphery pattern itself came into existence; it is a closed-economy exercise and therefore only provides a start on the questions we are dealing with in this chapter. Furthermore, the model does not provide a description of the stylized facts of growth; the underdevelopment trap does not necessarily come before the development path.

This section has briefly described how the endogenous growth literature is useful for understanding empirical facts (i) and (ii) identified in section 10.3, while the geographical economics literature is useful for understanding facts (iii) and (iv) (by using simulation dynamics). It would be desirable to have the best of both worlds by merging the endogenous growth approach and the geographical economics approach. We return to this issue in section 10.6 below. First, however, we must point out that the discussion above used insights for the geographical economics approach based on simulation dynamics. Before we continue the analysis of economic growth in section 10.6, we must, therefore, explain in somewhat more detail what simulation dynamics entails.

10.5 Simulation dynamics II: an experiment

As explained in the introduction, and discussed in detail in section 10.4, many insightful interpretations of the geographical economics models are of the "suppose" type, where the reader is "talked through" what might happen over time if some important parameter in the model is changing. Fujita, Krugman, and Venables (1999) refer to such thought experiments as a "history of the world"; see also Neary (2001). We prefer to call these experiments "simulation dynamics." A fall over time of the transport cost parameter T has been particularly popular in such thought experiments, as in Krugman and Venables (1995), but the same principle of course also applies for changes in other parameters, such as the share of income spent on manufactures or the degree of congestion, or a simultaneous change in more than one parameter; see, for example, chapter 7.

10.5.1 Structure of the simulation dynamics experiment

Two general observations on simulation dynamics can be made. First, they are almost always literally thought experiments, that is the model simulations underlying the discussions in the text are not actually performed.[8] In some cases this is understandable, for example if the author wants to emphasize the arbitrariness of a certain outcome in a situation with multiple long-run equilibria. Second, the large majority of discussions on simulation dynamics restrict attention to a two-region or two-country setting. In contrast, this section will perform and report a series of simulation dynamics in a multi-region setting.

For the remainder of this section we use the twelve-region (neutral-space) racetrack economy model. To allow for the simultaneous existence of economic centers of different size and avoid "bang-bang"[9] (corner) solutions, we use the model with congestion costs discussed in chapter 7. This model has an additional advantage, because it does not require small perturbations of manufacturing activity around a long-run

---

[8] If simulations were undertaken, they are not reported.
[9] See Van Marrewijk and Verbeek (1993).

equilibrium to set the dynamic process in motion. Thus, once we have chosen an initial distribution of manufacturing activity over the twelve regions, the entire simulation dynamics experiment is determined, as explained below.

In the discussion we focus attention on the impact of a gradual, but stepwise, fall in transport costs T. The other parameters of the model will remain fixed. We have used empirically reasonable estimates. More specifically, the elasticity of substitution $\varepsilon = 5$, the share of income spent on manufactures $\delta = 0.6$, the speed-of-adjustment parameter η, discussed in section 10.2, equals 2, and congestion costs are modest at $\tau = 0.05$. The experiment runs as follows.

(i)   We set the transport costs at a very high level, namely $T = 3$.
(ii) We randomly select an initial distribution of manufacturing production across the twelve regions.
(iii) Since the initial distribution is not a long-run equilibrium, manufacturing workers migrate to regions with higher real wages until a long-run equilibrium is reached (as discussed in section 10.2). It can take many reallocations.
(iv) Given the long-run equilibrium established in step (iii), we now give a shock to the system by lowering the transport costs from $T = 3$ to $T = 2.9$.
(v)   The distribution of manufacturing activity over the twelve regions, which was a long-run equilibrium in step (iii), will, in general, no longer be an equilibrium after the change in transport costs in step (iv). This sets in motion further labor migration to regions with higher real wages until a new long-run equilibrium is reached for the new level of transport costs (similar to step (iv)).
(vi) We continue to shock the system along the lines of steps (iv) and (v) by gradually, but in a shockwise manner, lowering transport cost to $T = 2.8$, $T = 2.7$, etc.

10.5.2   Measuring agglomeration: the Herfindahl index

The fact that we analyze a twelve-region setting has the advantage that it allows for a much richer structure and more surprising economic interactions than the usual two-region setting. The disadvantage is, however, that it is more difficult to succinctly present and interpret the results of the simulations. The phenomenon we have been interested in throughout this book is the degree of agglomeration of economic activity. Part of the discussion that follows will therefore concentrate on this. To do so we will report a widely used empirical measure of industry concentration, the Herfindahl index, that is also used for policy purposes; see, for example, Martin (1994).

The Herfindahl index (Herfindahl, 1950), is simply defined as the sum of the squared shares of manufacturing in each region (or of a firm in industry output). Thus, for example, if there are three regions and all manufacturing is located in one region, the Herfindahl index is $1^2 + 0^2 + 0^2 = 1$. If manufacturing activity is equally divided over two of the three regions the Herfindahl index is $0.5^2 + 0.5^2 + 0^2 = 0.5$. If the manufacturing activity is equally divided over all three regions the Herfindahl index is: $0.33^2 + 0.33^2 + 0.33^2 = 0.33$, etc. In general, therefore, the Herfindahl index is lower if

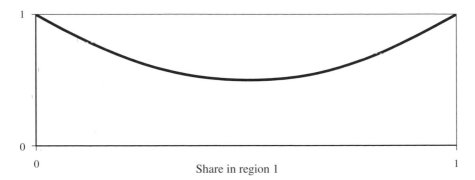

Figure 10.6.   Distribution of manufacturing between two regions and the Herfindahl index.

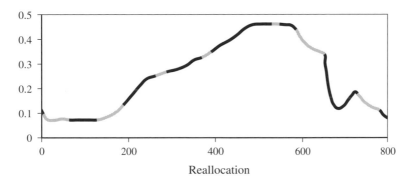

Figure 10.7.   Evolution of agglomeration measured by the Herfindahl index.

manufacturing activity is more equally spread over the regions, and higher if economic activity is more agglomerated. It can therefore be used as a measure of agglomeration. The index is illustrated for all possible divisions of manufacturing activity in a two-region setting in Figure 10.6. Some of the shortcomings of the Herfindahl index as a measure of agglomeration are illustrated in subsection 10.5.3.

10.5.3   Discussion of the results of the experiment

During the simulation experiment explained in subsection 10.5.1, manufacturing activity is reallocated over the twelve regions 800 times. This subsection will briefly describe the most interesting and remarkable aspects of the simulation dynamics; more complete details can be found on the website for this book. Figure 10.7 gives an overview of the evolution of the extent of agglomeration, as measured by the Herfindahl index, during the reallocation process as the transport costs fall. Each time the line in Figure 10.7 changes tone there has been an exogenous fall in transport costs (the length of each segment indicates the number of reallocations). There does not appear to be much change in economic structure in the initial phase of the experiment, approximately as

Table 10.4. *Overview of reallocations and the Herfindahl index*

T	# reallocations	Herfindahl index
3.0	4	0.091
2.9	18	0.074
2.8	7	0.074
2.7	16	0.075
2.6	1	0.075
2.5	2	0.076
2.4	1	0.076
2.3	0	0.076
2.2	3	0.075
2.1	74	0.074
2.0	58	0.130
1.9	77	0.252
1.8	23	0.266
1.7	80	0.323
1.6	22	0.342
1.5	144	0.460
1.4	14	0.462
1.3	36	0.448
1.2	70	0.342
1.1	75	0.188
1.05	58	0.109
1.01	16	0.080
Sum	800	

far as reallocation number 130. Further reductions in transport costs then start to set in motion a long process of increasing agglomeration of economic activity, reaching a peak of about 0.46 approximately between reallocations 480 and 580. As transport costs continue to fall the agglomeration of economic activity starts to decrease again. There seems to be a slight revival during the transition process, approximately between reallocations 650 and 730, which will be discussed below. Eventually, as transport costs continue to fall (in the end, $T = 1.01$) manufacturing activity is about equally spread over the twelve regions.

Table 10.4 gives an overview of the number of reallocation steps after each exogenous reduction in transport costs, as well as of the Herfindahl index once the long-run equilibrium is reached. Thus, for example, if $T = 3$ there are four reallocations from the random initial distribution until the long-run equilibrium is reached (where the Herfindahl index $= 0.091$). If T then falls to 2.9, eighteen reallocations are required to reach a new long-run equilibrium (where the Herfindahl index $= 0.074$), etc.

In the initial phase, when transport costs are very high and manufacturing activity is relatively evenly spread, reductions in transport costs have very limited effects (roughly the range from $T = 3.0$ to $T = 2.2$). This is illustrated by the very small number of reallocations after a fall in transport costs needed to reach a new long run equilibrium (sometimes only one, two, or three reallocations; in one case, no reallocation is required). In this phase the Herfindahl index is about 0.075. Note that this is *lower* than what the index would be if manufacturing activity were perfectly evenly spread over the twelve regions (in which case the index would be 0.083), an indication that the Herfindahl index is not a perfect measure of agglomeration.[10]

The first long adjustment process occurs when transport costs fall from 2.2 to 2.1 and seventy-four reallocations are needed. This reallocation process has, however, virtually no impact on the Herfindahl index (which falls from 0.075 to 0.074). As shown in Figure 10.8a the stability of the Herfindahl index is deceptive, because in the course of this long reallocation process the distribution of manufacturing activity becomes "spiked," after being almost equally distributed. The spikiness continues for a long time as transport costs continue to fall, becoming even more pronounced along the way; see Figures 10.8b–e. If $T = 2$ we have five spikes (at locations 1, 3, 6, 8, and 11); if $T = 1.9$ we have four spikes (the spike at 1 disappears); if $T = 1.7$ we have three spikes (the spike at 8 disappears); and if $T = 1.5$ we have two spikes (the spike at 3 disappears). The adjustment processes in this phase are usually quite long. It transport costs fall from 1.6 to 1.5, for example, the number of spikes reduces from three to two, which requires 144 reallocations of manufacturing activity. As transport costs become quite small, at $T = 1.1$, the spikes disappear and a lopsided distribution emerges in which region 9 (half-way between the previously largest manufacturing centers 6 and 11) attracts most manufacturing activity (Figure 10.8f). Finally, the lopsidedness disappears as well if transport costs become very small, to yield an almost even distribution of manufacturing activity (not illustrated).

The evolution of manufacturing activity during the simulation is shown in Figure 10.9 for a selection of regions (3, 6, and 9). Again, as in Figure 10.7, a change in the tone of a line in Figure 10.9 indicates an exogenous change in the transport costs, which sets in motion a new adjustment process to reach a new long-run equilibrium. Figure 10.9 dramatically illustrates the leap-frogging phenomenon. We now look at the dynamics of these regions in somewhat more detail.

(i)   There is an initial phase, in which all regions are roughly equal in size.
(ii) The process of agglomeration starts. Region 6 rapidly attracts a lot of manufacturing activity, while region 3 increases in size more slowly. In contrast, manufacturing activity in region 9 disappears quite quickly.
(iii) There is an intermediate phase in which the size of region 6 falls and region 3 takes over as the largest region.
(iv) The further reduction in transport costs causes a long gradual decline of manufacturing activity in region 3, and a simultaneous long-lasting rise of production in region 6, which for some time attracts almost half of all manufacturing activity.

---

[10] Any one-dimensional measure of agglomeration has its disadvantages.

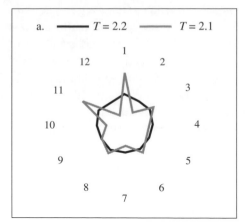

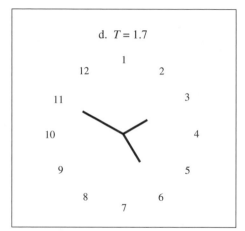
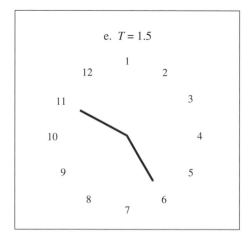
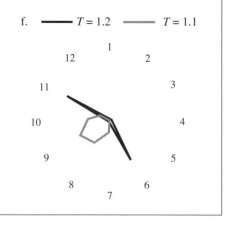

Figure 10.8.   Several phases of the reallocation process.

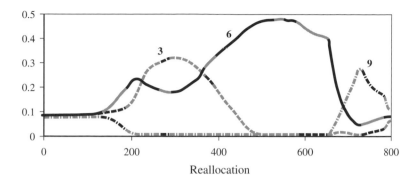

Figure 10.9. Evolution of share of manufacturing in regions 3, 6, and 9.

(v) When transport costs become very low, economic production in region 6 falls dramatically in a short period of time. Simultaneously, production in region 9 increases rapidly to a peak of almost 30% of total production. This is remarkable in view of the fact that production in region 9 virtually disappeared when the process of agglomeration started.

(vi) Eventually, manufacturing production in all three regions is approximately of the same size, as transport costs are virtually absent.

We have discussed the general practice in what we have dubbed simulation dynamics in section 10.4. In this section we have actually performed and discussed in detail a particular simulation dynamics experiment, namely modeling a gradual but shockwise reduction in transport costs in the twelve-region racetrack economy with congestion. The experiment substantiated and enriched the practice of simulation dynamics; see the discussion of the Krugman and Venables (1995) paper in section 10.4. We indeed saw that as transport costs were falling from an initially high level, the distribution of manufacturing activity was agglomerating in ever fewer and larger manufacturing centers. Only as transport costs became very small, did the degree of agglomeration decrease and manufacturing production become more evenly distributed. In addition, we have seen many examples of the leap-frogging phenomenon. During the course of the experiment, the economic size of regions changed drastically, and sometimes rapidly, with different regions being the largest manufacturing center at different phases; see Figure 10.8. This important empirical aspect of economic growth, as discussed in section 10.3, cannot be explained using either neo-classical or endogenous growth theories, but is more readily understood in a geographical economics framework. However, the simulation dynamics discussed in this section do not allow for an increase in the number of varieties produced, or for an increase in output per capita (as explained by endogenous growth theories), which is another important empirical fact discussed in section 10.3. It is therefore time to see if we can integrate the two approaches.

10.6   Economic growth

The first steps in developing a truly dynamic geographical economics model were taken by Martin and Ottaviano (1999, see also the literature cited there) and Baldwin, Martin, and Ottaviano (1998).[11] This literature combines the insights of the endogenous growth literature and the Krugman (1980) and Krugman and Venables (1995) first-generation geography models; all elements of the core model are present, except for labor mobility between countries. If knowledge spillovers are localized, agglomeration of firms can stimulate growth in the core region. The process of cumulative causation is enhanced in a growth model. Global knowledge spillovers do not influence regional growth rates, because everyone can benefit from the same knowledge. Interestingly, Baldwin, Martin, and Ottaviano (1998) show that an adapted version of this model can explain four well-known stages in economic development following the Industrial Revolution: (i) industrialization of the core, (ii) the subsequent growth take-off, (iii) the global income divergence, and (iv) the rapid trade expansion.

Baldwin and Forslid (2000b) provide the first endogenous economic growth version of the core model of geographical economics, that is including labor mobility between regions. It combines the structure of the core model with a dynamic framework of inter-temporal optimization to explain increases in output per capita. The Baldwin–Forslid model thus gives an explanation of the interaction among economic integration, for example through a fall in transport costs, the location of manufacturing activity, and economic growth. The model incorporates the fact that economic growth affects location and location affects economic growth. More precisely, the technical externalities or knowledge spillovers that are the driving force behind endogenous growth theories are related to the distribution of manufacturing activity across space. The empirical study of Eaton and Kortum (1996), for example, shows that knowledge creation at a distance gives rise to lower knowledge spillovers than locally produced knowledge; see also Coe and Helpman (1995) and Coe, Helpman, and Hoffmaister (1997). It is important to realize that trade in goods and services is only one aspect of international beneficial exchange. Trade in ideas is equally, if not more, important. Sharing knowledge internationally, about businesses, cultures, technology, etc., through personal and business travel, cross-border mergers and acquisitions, and the like, has reduced the localization of commercially relevant knowledge, such as product and process innovation. Many governments stimulate knowledge flows to peripheral regions, setting up universities or high-technology industrial parks. These changes, in turn, have an impact on the interaction between economic growth and localization, as we shall see below. This section first presents the basic structure of the Baldwin–Forslid model, and then discusses its main findings.

---

[11]   Another forerunner is Englman and Walz (1995), based on Grossman and Helpman (1991).

10.6.1 Structure of the Baldwin–Forslid model

The basic structure of the Baldwin–Forslid model is identical to the two-region core model of chapters 3 and 4. There is an even distribution of immobile food production in two regions, on which a share $1 - \delta$ of income is spent, as well as production of many different varieties of manufactures, with an elasticity of substitution ε. Manufacturing production may relocate if workers decide to move to a region with a higher real wage. To allow for economic growth in the model we must explicitly model the time structure, and explain the driving force behind economic growth. To start with the latter, producing a manufacturing variety requires a one-time fixed cost of one unit of capital K, as well as the traditional variable costs in terms of labor; see Van Marrewijk, Stibora, and Viaene (1994) for an identical structure. Capital K can be viewed as human capital, knowledge capital, or physical capital (see Van Marrewijk, 1999 for a discussion), but within this framework it is probably best seen as new knowledge embedded in a manufacturing facility that is immobile across regions. The cost function is therefore given by $R + W\beta x_i$, where R is the rental rate of capital, W is the wage rate, β is the unit labor requirement, and x_i is the output of variety i.

Box 10.1.   Discounting the future

Consumers care not only about current consumption levels, but also about future levels. This is important in determining their savings decisions, that is the supply of funds which can be used by firms to finance their investment decisions. To reflect the preference for current consumption by consumers, and take uncertainty about future developments into account, economic growth models assume that consumers discount future consumption using the discount rate θ (>0). Consumption t periods from now is then "discounted" by the factor $[1/(1 + \theta)]^t$.

Suppose we take into consideration only three periods, rather than the infinite number of periods in equation (10.2), in which contemporaneous utility derived from consumption is 10 in each period. Total utility derived from this consumption pattern if the discount rate $\theta = 0.1$ is then:

$$\left(\frac{1}{1.1}\right)^0 10 + \left(\frac{1}{1.1}\right)^1 10 + \left(\frac{1}{1.1}\right)^2 10 = 10 + 9.09 + 8.26 = 27.35$$

The weight given today to the utility derived from consumption two periods from today is therefore only 8.26, rather than 10. This effect is stronger if the discount rate rises. For example, if $\theta = 0.2$:

$$\left(\frac{1}{1.2}\right)^0 10 + \left(\frac{1}{1.2}\right)^1 10 + \left(\frac{1}{1.2}\right)^2 10 = 10 + 8.33 + 6.94 = 25.27$$

which shows that consumption two periods from now is given a weight of only 6.94, rather than 10. These examples show that savings today, which are equivalent to foregone consumption today, require a higher return to make up for this foregone consumption in the future if the discount rate is high.

The capital needed for the production of manufactures must in turn be manufactured in the investment good (or innovation) sector, which produces under perfect competition using only labor as an input. One unit of capital is made using α_I units of labor. Individual firms in the investment goods sector view α_I as a parameter. However, the investment goods sector benefits from technological externalities (knowledge spillovers): as output rises, the unit labor requirement for the investment goods sector falls; see Lucas (1988), Romer (1990), or Grossman and Helpman (1991). This fall in the unit labor requirement is necessary within the model for long-run economic growth to occur; without it, output per capita would ultimately reach an upper limit. As suggested by the empirical work of Eaton and Kortum (1996), the distribution of manufacturing activity will affect the degree of knowledge spillovers. In particular, firms will benefit more from locally accumulated knowledge than from knowledge accumulated in the other region. The production function is

$$Q_K = \frac{L_I}{\alpha_I}; \qquad \alpha_I = \frac{1}{K_{-1} + \kappa K^*_{-1}}; \qquad 0 \le \kappa \le 1 \qquad (10.3)$$

Where Q_K is the flow of new capital, L_I is employment in the investment sector, K is the stock of knowledge, κ is a parameter, an asterisk denotes the other region, and the subscript -1 indicates a one-period lag. Note that this specification implies knowledge spillovers with a one-period lag, leading to a gradual fall in the unit labor requirement α_I. The term κ measures the degree of knowledge spillovers, that is the extent to which knowledge accumulated in the other region contributes to this region's stock of knowledge. If $\kappa = 0$ knowledge is only locally generated; any knowledge generated in the other region does not contribute at all to this region's stock of knowledge. Similarly, if $\kappa = 1$ knowledge is a global phenomenon; any knowledge generated in the other region leads to an identical increase in this region's stock of knowledge. Baldwin and Forslid assume, for analytic convenience, that capital depreciates in one period.

Analyzing economic growth also requires inter-temporal preferences. Consumers care not only about current consumption levels of food and manufactures, but also about future consumption levels. To reflect their preference for current consumption and their uncertainty about future developments, consumers discount future consumption using the discount rate $\theta\,(>0)$ (see Box 10.1). Preferences U are given by

$$U = \sum_{t=0}^{\infty} \left(\frac{1}{1+\theta} \right)^t [\ln(F_t^{1-\delta} M_t^{\delta})]; \qquad M_t = \left(\sum_{i=1}^{N_t} c_{it}^{\rho} \right)^{1/\rho} \qquad (10.4)$$

where the subscript t is a time index and all other variables are as defined in chapter 3. The specification of utility derived from contemporaneous consumption is therefore identical to that in chapter 3. This is crucial for the demand functions, implying that the price elasticity of demand for a variety of manufactures is again $\varepsilon \equiv 1/(1-\rho) > 1$. Consequently, the producer of a particular manufacturing variety applies the same optimal pricing rule as in the core model.

Labor migration between the two regions arises from differences in real wages. To allow for forward-looking behavior in this economic growth model, rather than the static expectations of the core model, the wage pressure is related to the log of the difference between the present values of the real wages in regions 1 and 2. Manufacturing workers therefore take (expected) future developments in the real wages into account in the migration decision; see also chapter 6.

10.6.2 Discussion of the main results

A complete analysis and derivation of the main results of the Baldwin–Forslid model described in the previous subsection is beyond the scope of this book as it requires knowledge of inter-temporal optimization techniques. Fortunately, the three main conclusions of their approach, discussed below, can be readily understood without going into the technical details.

First conclusion

Baldwin and Forslid show that there are only three possible stable long-run equilibria in which the distribution of the manufacturing workforce remains stable over time: (i) complete agglomeration in region 1, (ii) complete agglomeration in region 2, or (iii) even spreading of manufacturing activity across the two regions.[12] These three long-run equilibria are identical to those of the core model. The main difference is, of course, that in this economic growth version of the model, firms indefinitely keep investing in knowledge and inventing new varieties of manufactures. The ceaseless increase in the number of varieties raises contemporaneous utility without bound through the love-of-variety effect.

Second conclusion

Baldwin and Forslid analyze the stability properties of the steady-state equilibria. To illustrate the stability properties of the model in a compact space, as is convention, they define the "free-ness of trade" parameter $T^{1-\varepsilon}$. Note that this parameter varies from 0 to 1. It depends both on the transport costs T and the elasticity of substitution ε, as

---

[12] There may be other interior long-run equilibria, but they are always unstable.

illustrated in Figure 10.10. As transport costs increase for a given value of ε, the free-ness of trade parameter falls from 1 to 0. The parameter also falls if the elasticity of substitution ε increases.

The stability properties of the steady-state equilibria crucially hinge upon the size of two parameters: the free-ness of trade parameter as defined above, and the degree-of-knowledge-spillover parameter κ as used in equation (10.3). Both parameters may vary from 0 to 1, so we can summarize the stability properties in a compact space as given in Figure 10.11. The plane in Figure 10.11 is subdivided into three different areas: (i) an area in which spreading is a stable equilibrium and agglomeration is not, (ii) an area in which agglomeration is a stable equilibrium and spreading is not, and (iii) an area in which both agglomeration and spreading are stable equilibria. If we fix the degree of knowledge spillovers, for example by analyzing the horizontal solid line in Figure 10.11, we see a perfect correspondence between the stability properties of the Baldwin–Forslid model and the core model. As transport costs fall over time (following the arrows on the horizontal line), initially spreading is the only stable equilibrium, then agglomeration and spreading are both stable equilibria, and finally only agglomeration is a stable equilibrium. It is most reassuring that the simple dynamics of the core model can be reproduced in this more sophisticated dynamic framework.

In addition, Figure 10.11 shows that Baldwin and Forslid have enriched our insights into the dynamic interaction between location and economic growth by incorporating the degree of inter-location knowledge spillovers. The European Union, for example, is much more closely integrated economically now than it was forty years ago. This arises not only from a reduction in trade costs as measured by the transport costs parameter T, but also from improved information transmission across borders. Think of increased traveling possibilities, watching foreign television channels, increased foreign direct investment, improved communication possibilities, the rise in intra-European mergers and acquisitions, and the funds spent on fostering intra-European knowledge exchanges. Arguably, then, the degree of knowledge spillovers between locations, κ, has also increased across time. Rather than the horizontal movement over time illustrated by the solid line in Figure 10.11, which brings us quite rapidly into the area where only agglomeration is a stable equilibrium, we have been witnessing a simultaneous rise in knowledge spillovers and a reduction in transport costs, that is a movement as illustrated by the broken curve in Figure 10.11. Evidently, this keeps the economy much longer in the area where both agglomeration and spreading of manufacturing activity are stable equilibria, implying that it is less likely that economic integration leads to complete agglomeration. This may be one of the reasons why we did not find much evidence in chapter 5 of increasing agglomeration within the European Union.

Third conclusion
In the welfare analysis of the core model of geographical economics (chapter 4), we concluded that agglomeration of manufacturing activity benefits the manufacturing workers and the farmers in the region in which agglomeration occurs as a result of the local provision of all manufacturing varieties (so that transport costs are avoided). On the other

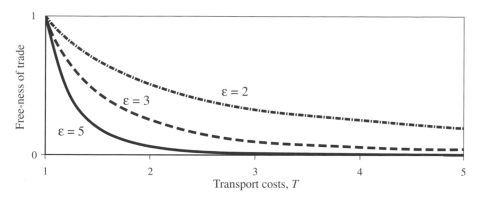

Figure 10.10. Free-ness of trade index.

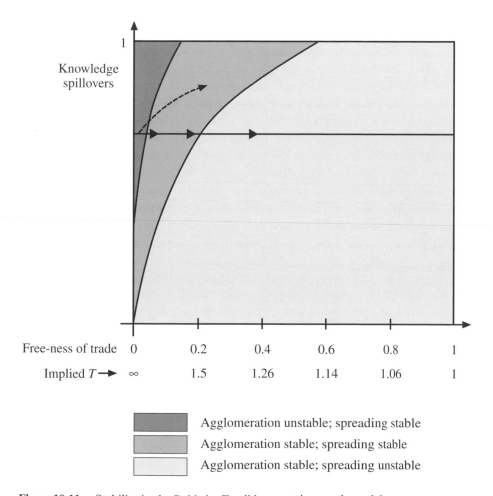

Figure 10.11. Stability in the Baldwin–Forslid economic growth model.

hand, farmers in the periphery are hurt, because they have to import all manufacturing varieties from the other region and incur high transport costs; see also chapter 11. The net effect on welfare for the economy as a whole depends on the specific parameter values, as explained and illustrated in chapter 4. Baldwin and Forslid point to a mitigating effect in their economic growth model for the farmers in the periphery when economic agglomeration occurs, namely the dynamic gains from agglomeration. As explained in the previous subsection, economic growth arises from knowledge spillovers which reduce the unit input requirement for the investment sector. However, knowledge created in the other region only partially contributes to the local stock of knowledge, as measured by the parameter κ. Agglomeration of manufacturing activity in only one region implies that all knowledge is locally generated, which therefore increases the growth rate of the economy. Farmers in the periphery therefore face a static welfare loss (they have to import all varieties of manufactures) and a dynamic welfare gain (the number of varieties increases faster if manufacturing activity agglomerates; this benefits them as consumers through the love-of-variety effect). Baldwin and Forslid also show (for some parameter values) that the dynamic welfare gain mitigates, but does not reverse, the static welfare loss.[13] Again, it is reassuring to see that the conclusions derived in the core model are reproduced in the dynamic Baldwin–Forslid model.

So, can extensions of the Baldwin–Forslid model explain the four empirical facts (rising income levels, lasting differences in growth rates, periods of stagnation followed by rapid growth, and leap-frogging) mentioned at the end of section 10.3? Perhaps, but it is too early to tell. The model will have to be extended to a setting with many regions, incorporating a mechanism, such as congestion costs, to allow for the simultaneous existence of large and small regions. Analyzing such a model will be technically daunting. However, by combining endogenous growth with simulation dynamics from geographical economics it incorporates in principle all elements necessary for understanding the four empirical facts.

10.7   Conclusions

We have identified three types of dynamics: adjustment dynamics, simulation dynamics, and economic growth. Adjustment dynamics analyze the reallocation processes within a geographical economics model that brings us from an initial distribution to a long-run equilibrium. This process is usually quite smooth, but the reader should be aware of some special cases that may arise during the adjustment process, in particular for high speeds of adjustment (cycles, movement to a non-stable equilibrium, and movement away from the nearest stable equilibrium).

Simulation dynamics involve discussion and interpretation of a model based on a series of exogenous changes in some parameter. Before you can perform this type of story-telling, you have to know which story to tell. We therefore had a brief look at some stylized facts of economic growth and development, and focused attention on four facts: (i) rising income levels, (ii) lasting differences in growth rates, (iii) periods of

---

[13] In the area where the dynamic gain is larger than the welfare loss the spreading equilibrium is unstable.

stagnation followed by rapid growth, and (iv) leap-frogging. We argued that the endogenous growth literature can help us understand the first two facts, while geographical economics can help us understand the last two, in particular by using simulation dynamics. We discussed this claim at length in an experiment based on a twelve-region version of the racetrack economy with congestion.

The most complex type of dynamics is the analysis of economic growth. This requires the modeling of forces explaining the increase in economic prosperity over time, forces which result from rising production levels, or the invention and availability of new goods and services based on investment in capital goods or research and development. This can only be satisfactorily modeled in a framework of inter-temporal optimization, which makes the technical analysis more complex, certainly in a model with multiple long-run equilibria. We briefly discussed the Baldwin–Forslid model, a merger of the core model of geographical economics with an endogenous growth model. Fortunately, and most reassuringly, the main conclusions derived in this framework are consistent with our findings in the core model of chapters 3 and 4, in particular with respect to the stability and welfare analysis. It justifies the shortcuts we have been taking in other chapters of this book. The Baldwin–Forslid model also gives us some new insights, for example on the importance of inter-location knowledge spillovers, and on the distinction between static and dynamic welfare effects.

Appendix

Section 10.3 illustrates long-lasting growth differences in the period 1890–1990 for selected developing and developed countries (Tables 10.1 and 10.2). Similarly, it gives an overview of such differences for the aggregate global regions identified by the World Bank, although for a shorter period (1960–1997); see Table 10.3 and Figure 10.4. Thanks to the pioneering work of Angus Maddison, we can also show the long-lasting differences in income growth per capita for aggregate global regions for a longer time period (1820–1992), albeit for a different division of the world into global regions (Table 10.A1).

Table 10.A1. *Growth in GDP per capita (annual average compound percentage rate)*

	1820–1870	1870–1913	1913–1950	1950–1973	1973–1992	1820–1992
Western Europe	1.0	1.3	0.9	3.9	1.8	1.5
Western offshoots	1.4	1.8	1.6	2.4	1.4	1.7
Southern Europe	0.6	1.1	0.4	4.9	1.7	1.4
Eastern Europe	0.7	1.0	1.2	3.5	−1.1	1.1
Latin America	0.2	1.5	1.5	2.5	0.5	1.1
Asia[a]	0.1	0.6	0.1	3.8	3.2	1.0
Africa	0.1	0.4	1.0	2.0	−0.1	0.6
World	0.6	1.3	0.9	2.9	1.2	1.2

Note: [a] Includes Oceania.
Source: Maddison (1995).

Exercises

10.1 Economists often use the idea of instantaneous price adjustment, meaning that after a shock has occurred prices adjust so fast that everybody and everything in the economy remains in equilibrium. In the model of geographical economics this is, however, not the case for labor (see equations (10.1) and (10.2)). Discuss why a very swift reallocation of labor across regions may not necessarily be a good thing. Also (*) what is the (implicit) assumption in the models of geographical economics in this book about the adjustment behavior of manufacturing firms?

10.2 In chapter 5 (section 5.2.2) it was argued that in terms of GDP per capita, convergence has taken place in the post-war period in the countries of the European Union, e.g. Portugal has caught up with Germany. Use the endogenous growth theory to explain this.

10.3 At the end of section 10.3 four "stylized facts" about economic growth were formulated. Discuss how these four facts can in principle be explained by the Baldwin–Forslid model of economic growth and location.

10.4 World-wide there has been a clear reduction in transport costs associated with international trade in the last decades (think of the GATT/WTO-inspired reduction in tariffs, the decrease in the costs of communication, etc.). Despite this reduction, there has not been a clear convergence in GDP per capita at the global level. Use Figure 10.11 and equation (10.3) to explain why this might be the case.

10.5 Section 10.4 deals with so-called simulation dynamics. Suppose globalization (defined as ever-decreasing transport costs) ultimately results in a truly global economy. What would this mean for the degree of economic agglomeration? *Hint*: Use Figure 10.7.

10.6 Figure 10.3 shows some examples of "leap-frogging" (USA over Australia around 1900; Japan over France around 1975). How can this phenomenon be explained in a geographical economics model? *Hint*: Look at Figure 10.9.

11 The policy implications and value-added of geographical economics

11.1 Introduction

The core model of geographical economics was introduced and explained in chapters 3 and 4 of this book. In our analysis of various extensions and applications in chapters 5–10 we investigated relatively small modifications of the core model, usually only affecting the cost function, and thus the production structure, of the core model. This was done on purpose. Not only for didactic reasons (each time returning to the familiar territory of the core model), but also to demonstrate that (seemingly) small changes in the core model can drastically increase its applicability and have interesting and sometimes far-reaching consequences. In our discussions of these adaptations of the core model two important questions have, however, been unduly neglected. First, what are the policy implications (if any) that arise from the core model and its extensions? Or, more generally, can geographical economics be used for policy analysis? Second, now that we have come to the end of our inquiry into geographical economics, what are the strong and weak points of this approach? In other words, how should geographical economics be assessed? The closing chapter of this book therefore deals with the *policy implications* and with the *value-added* of geographical economics. The latter is, inevitably, a subjective undertaking, but it gives us the opportunity to express our own views on the advantages and disadvantages of geographical economics.

This chapter is organized as follows. In the next section, we will conduct a simple policy experiment by doing simulations with the congestion model of chapter 7 in a world of non-neutral space. Section 11.3 discusses the policy relevance of geographical economics. We will conclude that at present this relevance is limited, but that models of geographical economics can be of use to policy-makers in a qualitative sense. Section 11.4 reviews the criticisms that have been raised against geographical economics and subsequently tries to answer the critics. In doing so, we conclude the section with an assessment of geographical economics. Finally, section 11.5 addresses the future of the subject, and provides some educated guesses as to what this future might look like.

11.2   Building a bridge: a simple policy experiment in non-neutral space

We adapt the racetrack economy that was introduced in chapter 4 to demonstrate the effects of a simple policy-inspired and highly stylized experiment. The model to be used in this section is the core model with congestion as it has been discussed at length in chapter 7. The example that will be the topic of this section not only serves to illustrate some of the policy implications, but also provides an example of non-neutral space and hence of a type I extension of the core model (see Table 6.2). In addition, Appendix 1 to this chapter gives the reader a final opportunity to study some of the basics of the core model with congestion. This appendix can be looked upon as a final exercise.

11.2.1   The pancake economy

Suppose that we take the circle of the racetrack economy as introduced in section 4.10, say with twelve cities, and flatten this circle to the "pancake" shape illustrated in Figure 11.1a.[1] Assume, moreover, that the manufacturing workforce and the farm workers are uniformly distributed over the twelve cities, each city thus hosting and producing one-twelfth of the economy total. As we know from chapters 3 and 4 such a symmetric structure implies that this initial distribution represents a long-run equilibrium, which Fujita, Krugman, and Venables (1999) call the "flat-earth" equilibrium. We will analyze the consequences of disturbing this long-run flat-earth equilibrium as a result of an active policy intervention involving two of the twelve cities. Throughout the following we will refer to it as an infrastructure project, namely building a bridge (but it could have been a road or a tunnel), which directly connects the two cities and thus reduces the distance between them. The policy project can, however, also be interpreted as a reduction in distance between the two cities as a result of closer cooperation, say resulting from economic integration or monetary unification. Building a bridge between two cities in the pancake economy implies that space can no longer be considered to be neutral, as in the racetrack economy of chapter 4.

We analyze three possible infrastructure projects, namely

- building a bridge between cities 2 and 12 (Figure 11.1b),
- building a bridge between cities 3 and 11 (Figure 11.1c), and
- building a bridge between cities 4 and 10 (Figure 11.1d).

In all cases, it is assumed that the link between the two cities reduces the distance between those two cities to 1 unit. In principle, there could be five "vertical" bridges (in addition to the three mentioned above, one could also envisage a bridge between cities 6 and 8 [but this would be analytically equivalent to a bridge between cities 2 and 12] or between cities 5 and 9 [analytically equivalent to a bridge between cities 3 and 11]).

The cities not directly linked by the vertical bridge may or may not benefit from the bridge in terms of reducing the distance to other cities. In particular, cities 1 and 7 never

[1] Some people might argue that it now looks more like a racetrack than it did before.

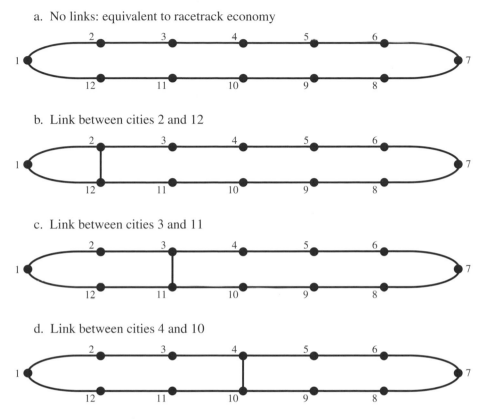

a. No links: equivalent to racetrack economy

b. Link between cities 2 and 12

c. Link between cities 3 and 11

d. Link between cities 4 and 10

Figure 11.1.   The pancake economy.

benefit in this sense from any of the possible bridges. The other cities do benefit, either directly or indirectly. For example, the bridge between cities 3 and 11 (Figure 11.1c) not only reduces the distance between those two cities (which falls from 4 to 1), but also reduces the distances between cities 3 and 11 and some other cities, as well as reducing the distances between some of the other cities. An example of the former is the distance between cities 3 and 10 (which falls from 5 to 2), and an example of the latter is the distance between cities 4 and 12 (which falls from 4 to 3). Table 11.1 gives an overview of the impact, in terms of the average distance to other cities (including the city itself), for all cities when there are no bridges, and when there are the three different bridges mentioned above. In this structure it suffices to analyze only these six cities.[2] As is intuitively expected, the bridge between cities 4 and 10 leads to a larger reduction in average distance than the bridges between cities 3 and 11, or cities 2 and 12. Similarly, the greatest reduction in average distance arises, of course, for the linked cities themselves. Tables 11.A1–11.A4 in Appendix 2 to this chapter give more detailed information.

---

[2] By construction, the impact on average distance for cities 2 and 12, 3 and 11, 4 and 10, 5 and 9, and 6 and 8 are identical, while there is no impact for cities 1 and 7. It therefore suffices to list just the first six cities.

Table 11.1. *Average distances in the pancake economy*

City	No links	Link 2–12	Link 3–11	Link 4–10
1	3	3.00	3.00	3.00
2	3	2.58	2.67	2.75
3	3	2.67	2.08	2.33
4	3	2.75	2.33	1.92
5	3	2.83	2.58	2.33
6	3	2.92	2.83	2.75
Average	3	2.79	2.58	2.51

11.2.2 Bridges and manufacturing distribution

To analyze the general impact of the infrastructure projects on the distribution of man-ufacturing activity, we calculate the long-run equilibrium for each of the three bridges, starting from a uniform initial distribution. For our base scenario we chose the follow-ing parameter values: the share of income spent on manufacturing δ is equal to 0.6, the elasticity of substitution ε is 5, the transport costs parameter T is 1.2, and the conges-tion parameter τ is equal to 0.1. It is important to note that in the absence of a bridge the flat-earth equilibrium is a stable equilibrium for the base scenario parameter setting. We have thus essentially specified initial conditions with a bias *against* eco-nomic agglomeration.[3] Nonetheless, as is clear from Table 11.2 and is illustrated in Figure 11.2 (with the share of manufacturing activity, λ_i, on the vertical axis), building bridges in the pancake economy has a large impact on the distribution of manufactur-ing production, and leads to considerable agglomeration of economic activity (see especially the bold entries in Table 11.2).

The reduction of transport costs that results from the building of a bridge benefits the cities that undertake such a project by enabling them to attract a large share of man-ufacturing production. The rationale behind this phenomenon is straightforward. If manufacturing activity is evenly distributed, the workers in the two cities at each end of the bridge have the highest real wage as they have to pay the lowest transport costs. This attracts other manufacturing workers into the linked cities, which on the one hand rein-forces the process, but on the other leads to more congestion and makes demand in the more remote markets more attractive. These forces are balanced in the long-run equi-librium. In general, the impact of building the bridge, an obvious example of non-neutral space, is remarkably high. Even the link "on the edge" between cities 2 and 12 leads to a doubling of manufacturing activity in cities 2 and 12. In Appendix 1 to this chapter we analyze the impact of parameter changes on the equilibrium distribution of economic activity for the case of building a bridge between cities 4 and 10. We urge the reader to have a look at this appendix, if only to test the understanding of the geograph-

---

[3] In fact, we have done this rather strongly. Even the simulations with an initial distribution far away from the uniform distribution lead to the flat-earth equilibrium in the absence of links.

Table 11.2. *Distribution of manufacturing workers (%)*[a]

city	Link 2–12	Link 3–11	Link 4–10
1	8.2	4.1	2.7
2	**16.4**	7.0	3.8
3	10.3	**20.7**	8.5
4	7.1	9.8	**22.8**
5	5.4	5.3	8.5
6	4.6	3.5	3.8
7	4.3	3.0	2.7

Note:
[a] The impact on cities 8, 9, 10, 11, and 12 is identical to the impact on cities 6, 5, 4, 3, and 2, respectively.

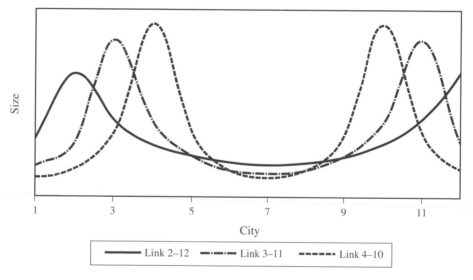

Figure 11.2. Impact of building a bridge on spatial distribution: base scenario, pancake economy.

ical economics approach developed during the study of this book. For the most important parameter, transport costs T, Box 11.1 at the end of this section gives a brief discussion.

11.2.3 Welfare implications

To complete our bridge experiment, we now come to the reasons for building a bridge and consider the welfare implications. After all, such an endeavor is costly, so the authorities must have a good reason to start and complete such a project. Although one can think of various reasons for building a bridge, we will concentrate in this sub-

Table 11.3. *Overview of welfare effects at long-run equilibrium (%)*

	Link 2–12	Link 3–11	Link 4–10
Average change in real income	0.9	1.9	2.2
Average change in real farm income	−0.3	0.2	0.2
Average change in real manufacturing income	1.6	2.8	3.5

section on its welfare implications, where a city's welfare is given by its real income and total welfare is the summation of real income over twelve cities.

The basic effect of building a bridge is, of course, to reduce the distance between cities, either directly or indirectly, as shown in subsection 11.2.1. Here we are more interested in its long-run welfare implications, that is to say in the welfare implications *once we allow manufacturing workers to migrate* in reaction to the building of the bridge. As is clear from the above description and the uneven distribution of the reduction in average distance over the cities, inhabitants in different cities enjoy different welfare effects from the completion of the bridge. Initially, the inhabitants of the linked cities enjoy the largest welfare gain. This sets in motion a process of migration which, as we have seen in the previous subsections, leads to substantial economic agglomeration in the linked cities. Thus this second effect, the migration process, also influences the distribution of welfare gains. In general, the cities that grow in size enjoy a positive welfare effect in the second stage as they can purchase a larger number of manufacturing varieties locally. As we shall see below, the second effect can dominate the first effect.

There are essentially thirteen different economic agents in the long-run equilibrium, namely the farm workers in the twelve cities and the manufacturing workers. Since the manufacturing workers will migrate to other cities until their real wage is equalized, the long-run welfare impact of building a bridge is the same for all manufacturing workers. Table 11.3 summarizes the average long-run welfare effects of building a bridge – for the economy as a whole, for the average farm worker, and for a manufacturing worker. For the economy as a whole the effect is always positive, although the economy will obviously benefit more from a centrally located bridge, linking cities 4 and 10, than from a more peripherally located bridge, linking cities 2 and 12. This reasoning holds more strongly for the manufacturing workers, that is they benefit more than the economy on average, and the size of their welfare increase is greater the more centrally the bridge is located.

The welfare picture is not so positive for the average farm worker. In particular, if the bridge is peripherally placed, linking cities 2 and 12, the average farm worker suffers a reduction in real income of 0.3% as a large share of manufacturing activity is moved to peripherally placed cities, requiring the average farm worker to pay large transport costs. Even if the bridge is more centrally placed, linking cities 3 and 11, or cities 4 and 10, the average farm worker experiences only a small gain (0.2%) in real income. Calculation of averages can be deceptive, however, which is clearly the case here.

As is illustrated in Figure 11.3, the information in Table 11.3 on the welfare of the average farm worker is a poor indicator of what happens to any particular farm worker.

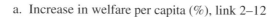

a. Increase in welfare per capita (%), link 2–12

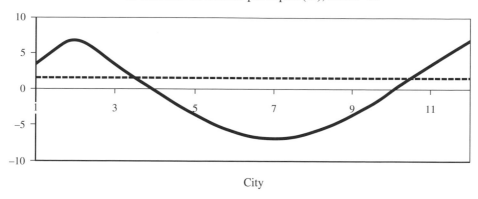

City

b. Increase in welfare per capita (%), link 3–11

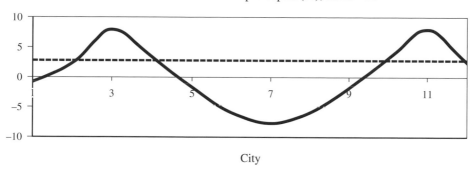

City

c. Increase in welfare per capita (%), link 4–10

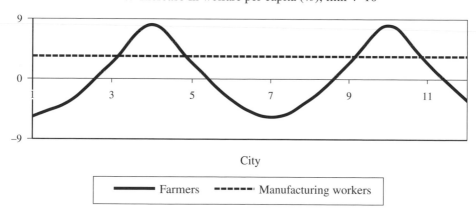

City

—— Farmers ------- Manufacturing workers

Figure 11.3. Real income and welfare changes

The welfare increase for the farm workers in the linked cities is always positive, and much larger than the average increase for the manufacturing workers (up to an 8.1% improvement for the farm workers in cities 4 and 10 when there is a bridge between these cities). In contrast, the welfare impact for the farm workers in the cities far away from the linked cities is always negative, and substantially so (as low as −6.9% for the farm workers in city 7 if there is a bridge between cities 2 and 12).

What are the lessons of this policy and simulation example? First, it shows that policy experiments, however simple, can be performed with straightforward applications of the core model; second, that even a simple policy experiment with a simple model can have quite complex implications.

Box 11.1.   Changing transport costs with a bridge between cities 4 and 10

We have, of course, already become used to the fact that the impact of transport costs on the resulting long-run equilibrium is non-monotonic. This holds in particular if we allow for negative feedbacks such as congestion; see, for example, Figure 7.2. A similar observation holds in this case, where we analyze the impact of building a bridge between cities 4 and 10 in our pancake economy, as illustrated in Figure 11.4 for cities 1–4.

Let's first look at the two extreme cases, that is (i) very large, and (ii) very small transport costs. If the transport costs become very large (in Figure 11.4 this is the case if T is close to 2), the impact of building a bridge is minimal. City 4 becomes somewhat larger, but the possibilities for welfare improvement are limited because of the high transport costs, that is each city is almost autarkic. As a result, the linked cities are only able to attract some extra manufacturing production. Again, if transport costs become very small, that is to say T is very close to 1, the impact of building a bridge is also minimal. In the absence of any transport costs, that is if $T = 1$, there is no impact of building a bridge because trade of manufactures is costless. This reasoning extends to a situation of small transport costs, that is it holds in the neighborhood of $T = 1$. As illustrated in Figure 11.4, however, this neighborhood is very small. Even for very modest transport costs, say $T = 1.05$, the impact of building a bridge is already substantial. In this sense the neighborhood of small transport costs appears to be smaller than the neighborhood of large transport costs.

For intermediate values of transport costs, the impact of building a bridge is substantial There are two local maxima, namely for low intermediate values (around $T = 1.35$) and for high intermediate values (around $T = 1.8$). The impact is largest for low intermediate values. More specifically, cities 4 and 10 combined will attract more than 50% of total manufacturing activity if transport costs are between $T = 1.25$ and $T = 1.45$. The peak for high intermediate transport costs is much smaller (cities 4 and 10 combined attract almost 28% of total manufactur-

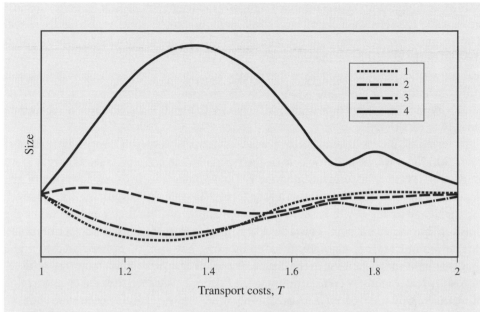

Figure 11.4.   Impact of transport costs: bridge between 4 and 10

ing activity). The contrast between the two peaks is fascinating. For high intermediate transport costs (around $T = 1.8$), when trade is difficult, cities 4 and 10
grow only at the expense of their immediate neighbors (cities 3, 5, 9, and 11).
There is virtually no impact on the cities that are further away (cities 1, 2, 6, 7, 8,
and 12) which, as a result of high transport costs, mostly trade amongst themselves. In contrast, for low intermediate transport costs, say in the range $T = 1.1$
to $T = 1.5$, when trade of manufacturing goods is much easier, cities 4 and 10
grow mostly at the expense of the cities that are far away (cities 1, 2, 6, 7, 8, and
12). In this case, the opportunities for trade are easier, which allows the manufacturing producers in the central cities 4 and 10 to serve the remote markets in the
cities further away.

11.3   Policy relevance of geographical economics

At various instances throughout this book it has been suggested that geographical economics can be applied to real-world issues relevant for policy-makers. To give just a few
examples: in chapter 5 we used an extension of the core model to analyze the wage
structure in post-reunification Germany; in chapter 6 we discussed how geographical
economics might be useful for analyzing the impact of globalization; and in the preceding section we discussed a simple policy experiment, namely the building of a bridge
in our pancake economy.

In general, geographical economics is mostly mentioned in economic policy discussions when the consequences of large-scale economic integration are being discussed. The prime example here is the debate about the Economic and Monetary Union (EMU) in the countries of the European Union (EU). Right from the start, geographical economics has been used heavily in these discussions.[4] The main question was, and still is, whether and how the ongoing process of economic integration, as well as the establishment of a monetary union, will change the spatial distribution of economic activity across the EU.

In terms of the models of geographical economics, what will happen if transport costs fall? Who will benefit, the core or the periphery? In chapter 5 (see Figure 5.3) we showed that economic integration in the EU has coincided with some lowering of the degree of agglomeration at the country level. "Peripheral" countries, like Ireland, Portugal, and Spain, saw their share in overall manufacturing activity increase while the opposite happened in "core" countries like France and the UK. With respect to monetary union in Europe, geographical economics has, however, often been used to argue that we might see an *increase* in the degree of agglomeration of manufacturing production and greater industry concentration in the future. This is then thought to undermine monetary union itself because it could imply more country-specific economic shocks.[5] Suppose all manufacturing activity ends up in the core countries, Germany, France, and the UK, and also that the car industry ends up in Germany and the fashion industry in France. The EMU could then be vulnerable to shocks to industry production that would hit the core but not the periphery (in which there is only agricultural/services production). Within the core, economic developments might also diverge if, for instance, the car industry is booming while the fashion industry is in recession.

This kind of use of geographical economics for policy issues like the EMU is, however, indirect to the extent that the policy issue itself (EMU), the policy-makers (European Central Bank) or the policy instruments (e.g. interest rates, money supply) are *not* analyzed within the context of a geographical economics model. At the moment there is simply no widely accepted geographical economics model of the EMU. Geographical economics is only used as background material in the policy discussions (Neary, 2001). In general, policy-makers are absent in geographical economics models. In addition, even if policy-makers and policy instruments were included, there would be a need to address the policy implications of one of the defining characteristics of geographical economics, the existence of multiple equilibria. This would need to be addressed if one really wanted to apply geographical economics to policy issues. We will briefly deal with both topics in the remainder of this section.

---

[4] In a way, the idea that the analysis of core–periphery patterns is important for economic integration in the EU even predates the geographical economics approach because Krugman and Venables (1990), a crucial forerunner of the approach, was explicitly aimed at analyzing the core–periphery implications of EU integration. Also Paul Krugman's (1991b) *Geography and Trade* even then mentions the potential relevance of geographical economics for the analysis of the feasibility of monetary union.

[5] Good examples of this use of geographical economics in the EMU discussions are Krugman (1993e) and, from the side of geography, Martin (2001).

Recently, a number of papers have explicitly introduced policy into geographical economics. A good example is Baldwin and Krugman (2000); see also Ludema and Wooton (1998). Baldwin and Krugman set out to analyze whether economic integration requires a harmonization of tax rates. In the context of economic integration in the EU this is a highly debated topic because of the well-known idea of a "race to the bottom," the idea that economic integration forces countries to have a uniform tax rate at the lowest conceivable level. A country which has a tax rate that is higher than this common rate would not be able to hold on to its mobile factors of production. In particular, the core countries of the EU, with a higher than average tax rate, fear that they would need to lower their tax rates (and their spending levels) to the levels of the peripheral countries.

Baldwin and Krugman (2000) show that in a world where agglomeration implies positive external economies of scale, the "race to the bottom" need not result. For our present purposes it is especially interesting that a policy instrument (a tax rate) and the policy-maker's objective function are part of the model. The geographical economics model they use is a two-region (North and South) model with two factors of production, labour L and human capital K. It resembles the Baldwin–Forslid growth model discussed in section 10.6. Both factors of production are necessary to produce a variety of the manufactured good X, which requires one unit of K and a_x units of labor per unit produced, where a_x is the input–output coefficient. The cost function for a manufacturing firm i is then $R + Wa_x x_i$, where R is the wage rate for human capital and W is the wage for labor. Apart from this production structure, the model is essentially the same as the core model, although with one further exception: labor is assumed to be immobile between countries, only capital can move between North and South. Capital moves to the region with the highest *after-tax* real wage.

Let s_k be the share of capital in the North. Given the structure of the model, the resulting equilibria are well known and not surprising against the background of the core model; they are (i) $s_k = 1$, (ii) $s_k = 0$, or (iii) spreading. Depending on the level of iceberg transportation costs for manufactures X (a proxy for the degree of economic integration), these equilibria are either stable or unstable. Assume now that the level of trade costs is relatively low, to the extent that $s_k = 1$ is a stable long-run equilibrium, and assume also that the economy finds itself in this equilibrium, with all human capital and all manufacturing production in the North. We know from chapter 4 that in this case real wages for the mobile factor of production, here human capital, will be higher in the North (compare with Figure 4.1). This creates what Baldwin and Krugman call an *agglomeration rent* for human capital. It is immediately clear that capital will not move from North to South as long as this agglomeration rent is positive. Hence, if North taxes human capital it has to make sure that the tax rate is set at such a level that capital does not migrate. If this condition is fulfilled, the equilibrium tax rate in the North can be higher than the tax rate in the South. There is thus no need of tax harmonization. In this case, the South need not bother to try to attract capital and its tax rate will depend only on "domestic" considerations. Crucial for the "no tax harmonization" result is that capital is fully agglomerated in the North and that the level of economic integration (that is the level of transport costs) is such that agglomeration is a stable equilibrium.

The Baldwin and Krugman (2000) analysis demonstrates how geographical economics can be used in a *direct manner* (because the policy question is explicitly modeled) to address a specific policy issue. It is also relevant to showing how in the models of geographical economics the presence of agglomeration may lead to different policy conclusions than those reached in the tax competition literature, where perfect competition is the norm. There is, however, also a problem with the use of such a model for policy applications, related to the welfare implications of agglomeration. In the core model of chapters 3 and 4, as well as in the Baldwin and Krugman model, the mobile factors of production are always better off with full agglomeration because this maximizes their real income. Given the relatively strong bias in the bulk of geographical economics models toward agglomeration, this has a very strong policy implication which "tempts" regional policy-makers to try to make sure that the mobile workers agglomerate in their region. This is precisely what drives the behavior of the policy-maker in the North in the Baldwin and Krugman model. Apart from the fact that agglomeration has potentially many drawbacks (such as congestion costs), too strong a reliance on agglomeration also tends to neglect the effect on total welfare (North and South combined), and thereby neglects the predicament of the immobile workers, which might be considerable, as we saw in the example of section 11.2 (Figure 11.3).

Finally, as pointed out by Neary (2001), the tendency to view agglomeration as the "best" equilibrium seems to have clear policy implications in models characterized by multiple equilibria, such as the models of geographical economics. The presence of multiple equilibria suggests that policy-makers, when faced with an equilibrium which they do not like, can try to pick a "better" equilibrium. This supposes that equilibria can indeed be ranked from a welfare perspective and that policy-makers know how to get the economy from one equilibrium to another. These are no small requirements, to say the least. The experience with actual industrial and trade policies, for instance, shows that governments are more then willing to (mis)use models with multiple equilibria to rationalize their interventionist policies. As Neary (2001, p. 27) puts it:

> it is tempting to suggest a role for government in "picking equilibria". This in turn may encourage a new sub-field of "strategic location policy", which . . . has produced much interesting theory but no simple robust rules to guide policy making. All these are temptations to be resisted, since they take too literally the neat structure of the [geographical economics] model, and ignore the econometric difficulties in estimating the non-linear, non-monotonic relation it predicts.[6]

In the previous section we analyzed a policy experiment in non-neutral space, the building of a bridge in the pancake economy. In this sense we have given in to the temptation mentioned by Neary because the bridge example shows in a very simple and general manner how the introduction of non-neutral space, which may come about

---

[6] This is probably the reason why Fujita, Krugman, and Venables (1999, p. 349) are reluctant to discuss policy implications.

through policy intervention, affects the equilibrium outcome and welfare. Given the above verdict on the usefulness of geographical economics for policy analysis, two important questions now arise with respect to our own simulation experiment.

First, does this kind of simulation experiment have any relevance for "real-world" policy issues? When it comes to policy applications, simulations with such a highly stylized model are only of limited relevance. There is clearly not enough flesh on the bone of the core model to tackle the costs and benefits of a particular plan to build a bridge. Clearly, when deciding on the costs and benefits of a specific issue, one first has to construct a model taking the most important aspects of this issue into consideration, possibly using elements from geographical economics models. In a qualitative sense, we do think that simulation examples, such as that of building bridges in the pancake economy, are useful thought-experiments for policy-makers. It forces them to think in general equilibrium terms about policy proposals and their geographical implications. A major lesson for policy-makers is that the core and the periphery are mutually dependent and cannot be dealt with separately, as is often done.

Suppose, for example, that the European Commission has a large sum of money at its disposal with which it could finance either a bridge between Denmark and Sweden (e.g. the new bridge across the Sont) or a "bridge" between France and the UK (e.g. the Channel Tunnel between Calais and Folkestone). In a multi-country, instead of a multi-city, setting, our pancake economy can be thought of as representing the European Union lying on its back, with Norway as country 1 and Spain as country 7 (recall Figure 11.1 for the depiction of the pancake economy). A bridge across the Sont could then be thought of as a bridge between countries 2 and 12 and the Channel Tunnel as linking countries 4 and 10. Our simulations show that the European Commission, in deciding which of the two projects it wants to carry out, must take into account not only the net benefits of the "bridge" for the two countries directly linked but also the benefits for the other EU countries. This would mean that, other things being equal, the financing of the Channel Tunnel would be a better idea than the bridge across the Sont connecting Denmark and Sweden.

The second, more general, question is whether the current state of affairs in geographical economics permits any substantial policy analysis at all. Is it possible to go beyond the simple simulations discussed above? In this section we saw that there are early attempts to incorporate policy instruments into the geographical economics model. This is no doubt an improvement upon the exogenous role of policy in our bridge example, but it remains to be seen whether models like that of Baldwin and Krugman (2000) can be applied to policy issues. This brings us to the important issue of an overall assessment of geographical economics: when all is said and done what is the value-added of geographical economics? It is to this topic that we now turn.

11.4   An assessment of geographical economics

After the discussion of the core model of geographical economics and its extensions in the previous chapters, and following the analysis of some policy implications in the first part of this chapter, it is time to take stock. We are now in a position to evaluate the contribution of geographical economics to our understanding of the location of economic activity. We will start with some of the main criticisms and then comment on these criticisms. In doing so, we will clarify our own position. In chapter 2, the role of geography in various theories that predate but nevertheless foreshadow geographical economics has been extensively discussed. It is precisely from these fields that some objections to the geographical economics approach have been raised. To a large extent, these criticisms reduce to the observation that geographical economics is either not new, not about geography, or deemed not to be relevant for practical purposes. In some cases all three charges are raised against geographical economics. As was stated on various occasions throughout this book, geographical economics can be looked upon as an attempt to answer Bertil Ohlin's call for a unification of international economics and regional economics (Ohlin, 1933). It is clear that Paul Krugman, the founding father of geographical economics, sees it this way (Krugman, 1995a, 1999). He has, however, an international economics background, while most doubts about the usefulness of geographical economics have been raised from the various branches of regional economics. We therefore present the critical reflections on geographical economics of leading scholars within regional economics in the next two subsections, followed by an assessment from a leading scholar in international economics.

11.4.1 *Comments from economic geography*

In chapter 2 (section 2.2) we dealt with the role of geography in urban and regional economics. The latter includes economic geography, whose scholars have been particularly critical of the main features of geographical economics. Ron Martin (1999) is a prime example. He argues that geographical economics must first and foremost be seen as a belated attempt to cast the old insights of Christaller and Lösch into a neo-classical framework, that is a framework in which the decisions of profit-maximizing firms and utility-maximizing consumers are explicitly modeled. Martin (1999) has two main (related) objections to geographical economics; see also Martin and Sunley (1996) or Clark (1998).[7] First, economic geography has moved on since the days of Christaller and Lösch, mainly because of the limitations associated with the work of these and other "old" economic geographers. It is beyond our scope in this book to discuss modern economic geography, but the main criticism of the early work, that it was ultimately more an exercise in geometry (see Figure 2.3 on the central place system) and contained too little real-world economic geography, was addressed in much of the later work in economic geography. Second, the neo-classical framework, and the deductive theorizing upon which it is based, are ill suited, according to Martin, to deal with the analysis of economic geography. This neo-classical framework is thought not

---

[7] See also various contributions by economic geographers to the *Oxford Handbook of Economic Geography* (Clark, Feldman, and Gertler, 2000). The contributions by geographers like Scott and Peck in this book are very critical of geographical economics. Scott (p. 23) even suggests not referring to geography at all and referring instead to the approach of our book as the *new regional science*.

to be able to deal with the role of institutions, uncertainty, and the resulting non-optimizing behavior of agents, all of which are decisive for the location of economic activity in the real world. To put it more bluntly, the complaint is that the new economic geography is neither new (but merely a restatement of outdated earlier insights of economic geographers) nor is it economic geography (since there is no place for real-world geography).

Given this position it is hardly a surprise that most economic geographers think that geographical economics cannot and should not be applied to policy issues because spatial policy-making is far too complicated for the models of geographical economics. Here, economic geographers point not only to the limitations of the neo-classical framework, but also to the alleged oversimplification in geographical economics by, for instance, not discriminating between various levels of spatial aggregation. Indeed, in the previous chapters the location r interchangeably represented a city, a region, or a country.

11.4.2   Comments from regional and urban economics

As became clear in chapter 2, there is also a substantial group of researchers within regional economics who, at least since Walter Isard (1956, 1960), have continued to build on the work of Christaller, Lösch and, from a growth perspective, Perroux, by formalizing and extending the initial insights on the location of economic activity. This sub-field, regional science, makes heavy use of the neo-classical framework that the economic geographers reject. Compared to economic geography, regional science has therefore much more in common with geographical economics. Notwithstanding the similarities in the toolkits, regional scientists are rather critical of the contents of geographical economics. For example, in his review of Fujita, Krugman, and Venables (1999), Peter Nijkamp (2000), a leading regional scientist, issues five complaints. In his view, geographical economics, and the aforementioned book in particular:

(i)   neglect the work done by forerunners;
(ii)   have too narrow a view of geography through reliance on iceberg transport costs, neglecting psychological transport costs, or mental distance;
(iii) pay no attention to spatial competition among firms, since there is no well-developed theory of the firm within geographical economics;
(iv)   pay scant attention to the role of institutions; and
(v)   rely too much on numerical simulations, resulting in a lack of quantitative and empirical research.

Whether these criticisms are valid in our view will be addressed below, but it is already noteworthy that the first, second, and fourth issues are also mentioned by economic geographers. In a similar vein, urban economists who have criticized geographical economics also point to the lack of empirical support, the overly simple depiction of (urban) geography, and too strong a reliance on simulations. In his criticism of the core model of geographical economics, Vernon Henderson (2000) concludes that for these reasons the core model is not suited for urban economics.

11.4.3   Comments from international economics

How about the position of international economics, the other half involved in the merger of regional and international economics proposed by Ohlin (1933)? One of the main themes in chapter 2 was that the core model of geographical economics is to a large part an extension of the new trade model developed by Krugman (1979, 1980). Trade economists have also made this point. In their prominent advanced textbook on trade theory, Bhagwati, Panagariya, and Srinivasan (1998, pp. 187–192) discuss both the Krugman 1980 and the Krugman 1991 models in their section on economic geography. They show that both models belong to the same line of research. In his excellent review of Fujita, Krugman, and Venables (1999), Peter Neary (2001) also leaves no doubt that geographical economics is firmly based in (new) trade theory. In Neary's view, "in stressing the relevance to regional issues of models derived from trade theory, Krugman has not so much created a new sub-field as extended the applicability of an old one" (Neary, 2001, p. 28; see also Box 11.2). In addition to questioning the antecedents of geographical economics, Neary criticizes the contents of geographical economics. Given that in his view geographical economics is rather close to existing and well-established trade theories, his overall judgment is far more positive then the comments mentioned above by economic geographers and regional and urban economists. Neary nonetheless points out the following weak spots:

(i)   a lack of analysis of individual firms; there is no strategic interaction between firms;
(ii)   the depiction of geography is too simple; here the use of iceberg transport costs is criticized, as well as the depiction of space as being (mostly) one-dimensional;
(iii) the reliance on specific functional forms and numerical simulations; the effect is that welfare and policy analyses are nearly absent;
(iv)   a lack of strong empirical evidence (until recently) to back up the theoretical work.

It is clear that the points raised by Neary have a lot in common with the comments made by regional and urban economists. Are the critical remarks therefore valid?

Box 11.2.   The $100 bill on the sidewalk between 1980 and 1991

In chapter 2 we came to the conclusion that the core model of geographical economics in Krugman (1991) is essentially the same as the new trade model of Krugman (1980), except for one crucial difference: factor mobility. In the core model, the mobility of manufacturing workers implies that each region's market size, as well as the regional distribution of manufacturing firms and labor, is no longer given. This has been emphasized before. On the continuity of the Krugman 1980 and Krugman 1991 approach it is illuminating to quote Krugman himself at some length (1999, p. 6):

[The observation] that something special happens when factor mobility interacts with increasing returns . . . is . . . obvious in retrospect; but it certainly took me a while to see it. Why exactly I spent a decade between showing how the interaction of transport costs and increasing returns at the level of the plant could lead to the "home market effect" (Krugman, 1980) and realizing that the techniques developed there led naturally to simple models of regional divergence (Krugman, 1991) remains a mystery to me. The only good news was that nobody else picked up that $100 bill lying on the sidewalk in the interim.

In addition, when asked by us, Paul Krugman wrote the following about the origins of the core geographical economics model:

Michael Porter had given me a manuscript copy of his book on *Competitive Advantage of Nations*, probably late 1989. I was much taken by the stuff on clusters, and started trying to make a model – I was on a lecture tour, I recall, and worked on it evenings. I started out with complicated models with intermediate goods and all that, but after a few days I realized that these weren't necessary ingredients, that my home market stuff basically provided the necessary. I got stumped for a while by the analytics, and tried numerical examples on a spreadsheet to figure them out. It all came together in a hotel in Honolulu . . .

11.4.4   An evaluation

So, are the critical remarks on geographical economics reported in the preceding sub-sections valid? Our answer is threefold: (i) yes, (ii) no longer so, and (iii) no.

The "yes" answer

It is true that the state of the art in geographical economics analysis implies that most models are short on analytical solutions, which hampers the welfare and policy analyses. This does not mean that there no analytical solutions; see, for instance, chapter 9. It is, of course, true that numerical solutions are part and parcel of the geographical economics approach. The observation that the core model of geographical economics, like new trade theory, relies heavily on specific functional forms and specific assumptions, such as Dixit–Stiglitz monopolistic competition and iceberg transport costs, is no doubt also valid. Similarly, a racetrack (or pancake) depiction of space is indeed very simple and difficult to accept for anyone who believes Copernicus was right and the believers in the "flat earth" were wrong.[8] As for the handling of geography, the idea that it only matters because a proportion of manufactured goods melts away during transport from one location to another is surely too stringent; not only can the transport sector itself have an influence on spatial developments, because in reality this

---

[8] An important advantage of the neutral-space racetrack economy, mentioned previously, is that the agglomeration outcome cannot be the result of a pre-imposed geographic structure.

sector is not a neutral bystander (imperfect competition in the transport industry), but also geography has, to an extent, a sociological and psychological component (see section 1.1). This last remark also refers to the criticisms about the neo-classical model of individual behavior underlying geographical economics and its neglect of institutions that are needed to understand how the coordination of economic activity across space comes about. Finally, it cannot be denied that geographical economics at times leads to theoretical and empirical conclusions that appear not to be new. The analysis of core–periphery patterns and the testing of market potential functions or gravity equations can, for instance, be traced back to the 1950s.

The "no longer so" answer

These and related critical remarks are well taken but they clearly paint too dark a picture of geographical economics for two reasons. First, and this is our "no longer so" part of the answer, geographical economics has moved on since the development of the core model by Krugman (1991). Chapters 5–10 of this book give many examples of extensions of the core model of chapters 3 and 4. Second, and more importantly, the assessment of geographical economics depends very much on what the aim of geographical economics is considered to be, and also what the proper framework is thought to be for the analysis of the location of economic activity. On that point we will answer below with a loud and clear "no" on the validity of the critique.

Most scholars criticizing the geographical economics approach cannot resist the temptation to use the core model of geographical economics as a scapegoat. The comments made above by economic geographers (Ron Martin), regional scientists (Peter Nijkamp) and urban economists (Vernon Henderson) focus attention too strongly on the shortcomings of the core model. Recent developments in geographical economics have dealt effectively with a number of criticisms. We give some examples here that have not already been mentioned in the previous chapters. Baldwin *et al.* (2000), for instance, derive important analytical results for the core model, in particular with respect to the stability of equilibria. There is also progress on the policy and empirical front. The model of Baldwin and Krugman (2000), discussed in section 11.2, is just one recent example of incorporating policy into geographical economics models. On the empirical side, papers by, for instance, Redding and Venables (2000) and Harris and Ioannides (2000) try to test for specific versions of the geographical economics model. There are also attempts to move away from the notion of iceberg transport costs, and to focus instead on the costs of (intra-firm) communication; see Gersbach and Schmutzler (2000). In the previous chapters, we ourselves have given simple examples to show that welfare and policy analyses are feasible even if one sticks rather closely to the core model. The introduction of (housing) services (chapter 5), intermediate goods and non-neutral space (chapter 6), congestion (chapter 7), fragmentation of production (chapter 8), other determinants of trade (chapter 9), and the possibility of more complex dynamics and economic growth (chapter 10) address some of the other criticisms.

The "no" answer

We come now to the third part of our answer about the validity of the criticisms, where we arrive at the two most important contributions of geographical economics. As has already been argued in chapter 2, the real novelty of geographical economics is to be found not so much in its research topic, but instead in the way it tackles the relationships between economics and geography. True in spirit to Ohlin (1933), geographical economics succeeds in lowering the fences between International and Regional Economics. By using highly stylized models, which no doubt neglect a lot of specifics about urban/regional/international phenomena, geographical economics is able to show that the same mechanisms are at work at different levels of spatial aggregation. The idea that at least to some extent the same underlying economic forces are relevant for explaining the spatial organization of cities, the interaction between regions within a nation, as well as the uneven distribution of GDP across countries is very important. In order to lay the foundations for a unified approach, there is a price to be paid in terms of a neglect of institutional and geographical details, as the aforementioned criticisms make clear. But this is a price well worth paying initially, certainly in view of our optimism that a number of these voids will be filled as geographical economics keeps developing in the future.

The second major contribution of geographical economics is that the clustering of economic activity, which can be observed at various levels of aggregation, is not taken for granted. By this we mean that, in contrast to the existing fields (international and regional economics), geographical economics does *not* assume beforehand what has to be explained. It is crucial that geographical economics is above all an attempt to bridge the gap between economics and geography from the perspective of mainstream economic theory. The clustering of economic activity is inextricably linked with the existence of increasing returns to scale. Geographical economics shows how in such a world the decisions of individual economic agents may give rise to clustering or agglomeration. By explicitly modeling the choices of firms, consumers, and workers in a general equilibrium framework, within a market structure of imperfect competition, geographical economics is the *only* field of economics which provides a micro-economic foundation in a consistent general equilibrium framework for the spatial distribution of economic activity. Of course, the importance one attaches to such a foundation depends crucially on the question of whether one thinks the deductive reasoning central in neo-classical or mainstream economics provides a good place to start the inquiry into the relationships between economics and geography.[9] We think it is. Not only because a well-developed alternative is simply lacking, but also because the meta-approach of geographical economics towards the *why*, *who* and *where* of the location of economic activity offers additional insights compared to approaches that focus only on cities, regions, trade, or growth.

To sum up, despite some well-argued criticisms, the value-added of geographical economics for both international and regional economics, and their integration, is

[9] Again, this attempt to lower the fence between international and regional economics is why we prefer the phrase "geographical economics" instead of "new economic geography."

clearly positive. This is not only because it gives a sound theoretical foundation for a fruitful combination of these two fields of economics, which enriches international as well as regional economics, but also because in doing so it clearly points out the similarities in these approaches and the common economic forces underlying various empirical phenomena at different levels of aggregation. A final question to address in this book is where does geographical economics go from here?

11.5   Geographical economics in 2020

It is, of course, very difficult (if not simply impossible in the absence of 20–20 vision) to predict what geographical economics will look like, say twenty years from now. At the end of our book, we can only offer some tentative suggestions about the direction of future research as our "predictions."

Given that the core model of geographical economics is in many ways too simple, one feasible line of future research is to combine the basic elements and insights of the core model with well-established causes and determinants of trade and location from international and regional economics. With respect to trade theory, one can think of models in which, alongside the interaction between factor mobility, increasing returns and transport costs that are central to geographical economics, there is also a role for more "classical" determinants of trade, like relative factor endowments or productivity. We have already discussed some simple examples of this possibility in chapter 9. It also seems reasonable to expect that the main elements of geographical economics will merge with existing models of endogenous growth, simply because there is a clear kinship between geographical economics and models of international economic growth as summarized, for instance, in Grossman and Helpman (1991). Such a development would allow a larger role for geography in economic growth theory, while at the same time (see chapter 10) it would provide an opportunity to go beyond the simple simulation dynamics that characterize the bulk of geographical economics at present.

Similarly, we think that despite the criticisms raised in regional economics against geographical economics, there will be more interaction between these two fields in the near future. There is a mutual interest in taking better notice of each other's work and in trying to incorporate elements of geographical economics into separate sub-fields, and vice versa. Geographical economics has at present not much to say on the role of institutions in the determination of location decisions, but we think that this will also change in view of the empirical work within geographical economics itself. Take, for instance, the empirical research on a spatial wage structure in Germany in chapter 5. It was found that border effects between eastern and western Germany are still relevant. If one tries to come up with an explanation, it is hard to neglect the role of formal (market segmentation) or informal (Ossies and Wessies do not interact) institutions. There are also signs that part of modern economic geography is taking geographical economics more seriously, to a large extent out of dissatisfaction with the descriptive modes of analysis currently dominant in economic geography.

The launching of a major new periodical in 2001, the *Journal of Economic Geography*, with an editorial board firmly rooted in economic geography, urban economics, *and* geographical economics, is an encouraging sign of more cooperation, or at least of more conversation. In urban economics it seems more than likely that basic elements of geographical economics, notably the (Dixit Stiglitz) model of imperfect competition and the inclusion of trade costs between cities, will be integrated with existing systems-of-cities models (Henderson, 2000). Given the similarities in the analytical toolkits of urban economics and geographical economics we predict that the difference between these two fields will become fuzzy. This will probably also occur because for various applications geographical economics needs a richer menu of agglomerating and spreading forces, such that variables like congestion/commuting costs or land, which have long been emphasized by urban economists, could receive more attention (see also Fujita, Krugman, and Venables, 1999, p. 346). In addition, the theory of the firm is rather ill developed in geographical economics (Neary, 2001). When it comes to urban systems and the establishment of new cities, modern urban economics, with its emphasis on the land development market, can be crucially important in our view.

All of the above examples have in common that they point to future research in geographical economics along the lines of "general to specific" – from the highly abstract and simple core model of chapters 3 and 4 to models which are more or less geared to a specific research question. Such a trend would not be surprising, because that is what happens when a research field matures. So here is another prediction: in geographical economics, researchers will increasingly tailor the model to the locational issue at hand, and adapt their set of agglomerating and spreading forces accordingly. Now that the basics of geographical economics are well known, one can also expect more empirical research.[10] In this respect there is a similarity with the new growth theory, where, after the theoretical developments in the second half of the 1980s, the emphasis in the following years was on empirical research. More empirical research will probably also mean that greater attention will be given to policy issues in the years to come.

Finally, is it to be expected that geographical economics will become established as a field on its own? This is an open question. If, as we believe, the integration with other fields within international and regional economics is on the research agenda it might very well be that the label geographical economics (or new economic geography) will become less fashionable than it is now. This does not really matter. What matters is the content of geographical economics. In this respect we are optimistic about its contribution in the long run. Geographical economics will have a lasting impact on trade and growth theory, translated into more attention for geography in these theories. Similarly, insights from geographical economics will also become part of the core literature for the various branches of regional economics. In this respect, Ohlin can be satisfied: geographical economics is the most fruitful and promising attempt thus far to bring international economics and regional economics together.

---

[10] For the core model of geographical economics this feeling of "completion" is also due to the fact that its basic structure and the nature of the resulting equilibria can be understood via analytical as well as numerical solutions; see in particular Baldwin *et al.* (2000, ch. 1).

Appendix 1   Effects of parameter changes with a bridge between cities 4 and 10

In this appendix we illustrate the impact of changes of important model parameters on the ability of linked cities to attract more manufacturing activity. For ease of exposition we concentrate on building a bridge between cities 4 and 10. We investigate, in turn, the impact of changes in the share of income spent on manufactures δ, the elasticity-of-substitution parameter ρ, the congestion cost parameter τ, and the speed-of-adjustment parameter η. The first three parameters, together with the transport cost parameter that was discussed in Box 11.1, determine the long-run equilibrium and these parameters cannot be "eliminated" by normalization. The last parameter, η, determines the responsiveness of manufacturing workers to real-wage differences between cities.

Before proceeding to the answers below to see what happens when the parameters are changed, the reader might first want to come up with an answer herself, because the previous discussions about the impact of parameter changes in chapters 4–10 and also, of course, Box 11.1 on the impact of changing T, provide important information as to what to expect when δ, ρ, τ, or η is changed.

Share of income spent on manufactures, δ

An increase in δ implies that the mobile economic activity becomes more important and the immobile one becomes less so. We therefore expect that an increase in δ will make building a bridge more attractive by allowing a larger agglomeration of economic activity in the linked cities. This is indeed what happens, as illustrated in Figure 11.A1a, where we note that the size of city 4 increases as δ becomes larger.

Elasticity-of-substitution parameter, ρ

An increase in ρ implies that it becomes easier for the consumer to substitute between different varieties of manufactures. This essentially reduces the impact of transport costs on welfare (real wages), so that we expect an increase in ρ to reduce the impact of building a bridge. This is confirmed in Figure 11.A1b, where the size of city 4 falls as ρ becomes larger, that is as it becomes easier to substitute between different varieties.

Congestion cost parameter, τ

An increase in τ implies that economic agglomeration of manufacturing activity becomes less attractive, as it leads to high congestion costs. The attractiveness of building a bridge therefore diminishes as congestion costs increase, by reducing the extent of economic agglomeration. This is illustrated in Figure 11.A1c, where the size of city 4 falls as τ becomes larger.

Speed-of-adjustment parameter, η

As has already been discussed in chapter 10, depending on the speed of adjustment of manufacturing labor, that is the speed of migration flows, the economy may end up in different (stable) long-run equilibria. In chapter 10 this was shown for very high speeds of adjustment, but here we illustrate it for two relatively low speeds of adjustment

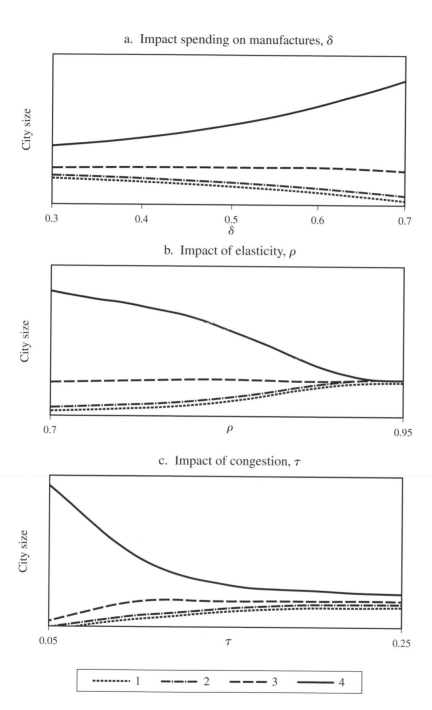

Figure 11.A1. Impact of some parameters: bridge between 4 and 10.

a. Impact of adjustment speed, η

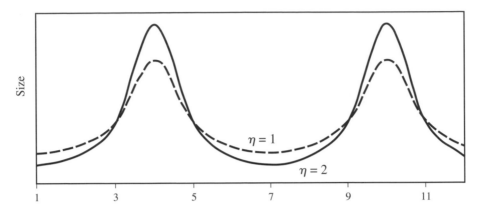

b. Adjustment speed and long-run equilibrium

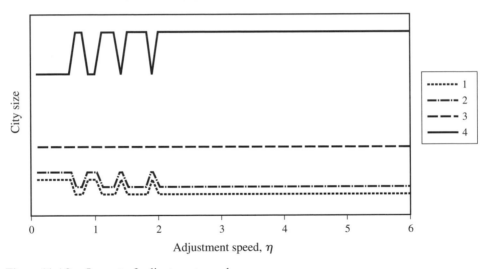

Figure 11.A2.   Impact of adjustment speed.

($\eta = 1$ and $\eta = 2$); see Figure 11.A2a. Apparently, cities 4 and 10 are able to attract more manufacturing activity in the base scenario ($\eta = 2$) than when $\eta = 1$. Figure 11.A2b shows the long-run equilibrium to which the economy converges for a large range of adjustment speeds (η ranges from 0.1 to 6 in steps of 0.1). It shows clearly that the economy converges to one of only two possible long-run equilibria, namely the two equilibria illustrated in Figure 11.A2a.[11] For all adjustment speeds above 2 the economy converges to the equilibrium illustrated in the base scenario of Figure 11.2. For all adjustment speeds below 0.6 the economy converges to the other long-run equilibrium, with somewhat less economic agglomeration, as illustrated in Figure 11.A2a.

---

[11] This does not imply that these are the *only* two long-run equilibria.

In the range between 0.6 and 2 the long-run equilibrium to which the economy converges is very sensitive with respect to the speed of adjustment η, as illustrated by the comb-like section in Figure 11.A2b.

Appendix 2

Table 11.A1. *Distances: pancake economy, no link*

	1	2	3	4	5	6	7	8	9	10	11	12
1	0	1	2	3	4	5	6	5	4	3	2	1
2	1	0	1	2	3	4	5	6	5	4	3	2
3	2	1	0	1	2	3	4	5	6	5	4	3
4	3	2	1	0	1	2	3	4	5	6	5	4
5	4	3	2	1	0	1	2	3	4	5	6	5
6	5	4	3	2	1	0	1	2	3	4	5	6
7	6	5	4	3	2	1	0	1	2	3	4	5
8	5	6	5	4	3	2	1	0	1	2	3	4
9	4	5	6	5	4	3	2	1	0	1	2	3
10	3	4	5	6	5	4	3	2	1	0	1	2
11	2	3	4	5	6	5	4	3	2	1	0	1
12	1	2	3	4	5	6	5	4	3	2	1	0

Table 11.A2. *Distances: pancake economy, link between 2 and 12*

	1	2	3	4	5	6	7	8	9	10	11	12
1	0	1	2	3	4	5	6	5	4	3	2	1
2	1	0	1	2	3	4	5	5	4	3	2	1
3	2	1	0	1	2	3	4	5	5	4	3	2
4	3	2	1	0	1	2	3	4	5	5	4	3
5	4	3	2	1	0	1	2	3	4	5	5	4
6	5	4	3	2	1	0	1	2	3	4	5	5
7	6	5	4	3	2	1	0	1	2	3	4	5
8	5	5	5	4	3	2	1	0	1	2	3	4
9	4	4	5	5	4	3	2	1	0	1	2	3
10	3	3	4	5	5	4	3	2	1	0	1	2
11	2	2	3	4	5	5	4	3	2	1	0	1
12	1	1	2	3	4	5	5	4	3	2	1	0

Note: Shaded cells indicate where distance deviates from that in the racetrack economy.

Table 11.A3. *Distances: pancake economy, link between 3 and 11*

	1	2	3	4	5	6	7	8	9	10	11	12
1	0	1	2	3	4	5	6	5	4	3	2	1
2	1	0	1	2	3	4	5	5	4	3	2	2
3	2	1	0	1	2	3	4	4	3	2	1	2
4	3	2	1	0	1	2	3	4	4	3	2	3
5	4	3	2	1	0	1	2	3	4	4	3	4
6	5	4	3	2	1	0	1	2	3	4	4	5
7	6	5	4	3	2	1	0	1	2	3	4	5
8	5	5	4	4	3	2	1	0	1	2	3	4
9	4	4	3	4	4	3	2	1	0	1	2	3
10	3	3	2	3	4	4	3	2	1	0	1	2
11	2	2	1	2	3	4	4	3	2	1	0	1
12	1	2	2	3	4	5	5	4	3	2	1	0

Note: Shaded cells indicate where distance deviates from that in the in racetrack economy.

Table 11.A4. *Distances: pancake economy, link between 4 and 10*

	1	2	3	4	5	6	7	8	9	10	11	12
1	0	1	2	3	4	5	6	5	4	3	2	1
2	1	0	1	2	3	4	5	5	4	3	3	2
3	2	1	0	1	2	3	4	4	3	2	3	3
4	3	2	1	0	1	2	3	3	2	1	2	3
5	4	3	2	1	0	1	2	3	3	2	3	4
6	5	4	3	2	1	0	1	2	3	3	4	5
7	6	5	4	3	2	1	0	1	2	3	4	5
8	5	5	4	3	3	2	1	0	1	2	3	4
9	4	4	3	2	3	3	2	1	0	1	2	3
10	3	3	2	1	2	3	3	2	1	0	1	2
11	2	3	3	2	3	4	4	3	2	1	0	1
12	1	2	3	3	4	5	5	4	3	2	1	0

Note: Shaded cells indicate where distance deviates from that in the racetrack economy.

References

Abdel-Rahman, H.M. (1994), Economies of scope in intermediate goods and a system of cities, *Regional Science and Urban Economics*, 24, 497–524.

Abdel-Rahman, H.M. and M. Fujita (1993), Specialization and diversification in a system of cities, *Journal of Urban Economics*, 33, 189–222.

Ades, A. and E. Glaeser (1995), Trade and circuses: explaining urban giants, *Quarterly Journal of Economics*, 110, 195–228.

Agenor, P.R. and P.J. Montiel (1996), *Development Macroeconomics*, Princeton University Press.

Allen, P.M. and M. Sanglier (1979), A dynamic model of growth in a central place system, *Geographical Analysis*, 11, 256–272.

Alonso, W. (1964), *Location and Land Use*, Harvard University Press, Cambridge, Mass.

Amiti, M. (1998), New trade theories and industrial location in the EU: a survey of the evidence, *Oxford Review of Economic Policy*, 14, 45–53.

(1999), Specialization patterns in Europe, *Weltwirtschaftliches Archiv*, 135, 573–593.

Anas, A., R. Arnott, and K.A. Small (1998), Urban spatial structure, *Journal of Economic Literature*, 36, 1426–1464.

Anderson, J.E. (1979), A theoretical foundation for the gravity equation, *American Economic Review*, 69, 106–116.

Arnott, R. and K. Small (1994), The economics of traffic congestion, *American Scientist*, 82, 446–455.

Bairoch, P. (1988), *Cities and Economic Development: From the Dawn of History to the Present*, reprint, trans. Christopher Braider, University of Chicago Press.

Balassa, B. (1961), *The Theory of Economic Integration*, Allen and Unwin, New York.

Baldwin, R.E. (1999), The core–periphery model with forward looking expectations, NBER Working Paper, no. 6921, Cambridge, Mass.

Baldwin, R.E. and R. Forslid (2000a), Trade liberalisation and endogenous growth: a q-theory approach, *Journal of International Economics*, 50, 497–517.

(2000b), The core–periphery model and endogenous growth: stabilizing and destabilizing integration, *Economica*, 67, 307–324.

Baldwin, R.E., R. Forslid, P. Martin, G. Ottaviano, and F. Robert-Nicoud (2000), The core–periphery model: key features and effects, draft chapter 1 of manuscript *Public Policies and Economic Geography*.

Baldwin, R.E. and P. Krugman (2000), Agglomeration, integration and tax harmonization, CEPR Discussion Paper, no. 2630, London.

Baldwin, R.E, P. Martin, and G.I.P. Ottaviano (1998), Global income divergence, trade and industrialization: the geography growth take-offs, NBER Working Paper, no. 6458, Cambridge, Mass.

Baldwin, R.E. and G.I.P. Ottaviano (2000), Multiproduct multinationals and reciprocal FDI dumping, mimeo., Graduate Institute of International Studies, Geneva.

Barrell, R. and N. Pain (1999), Domestic institutions, agglomeration and foreign direct investment in Europe, *European Economic Review*, 43, 925–934.

Barro, R. and X. Sala-i-Martin (1995), *Economic Growth*, McGraw-Hill, New York.

Batty, M. and P. Longley (1994), *Fractal Cities*, Academic Press, London.

Beardsell, M. and V. Henderson (1999), Spatial evolution of the computer industry in the USA, *European Economic Review*, 43, 431–457.

Becker, R., and V. Henderson (2000), Intra-industry specialization and urban development, in J.-M. Huriot and J.-F. Thisse (eds.), *The Economics of Cities: Theoretical Perspectives*, Cambridge University Press, 138–166.

Begg, D.K.H. (1982), *The Rational Expectations Revolution in Macroeconomics: Theories and Evidence*, Philip Allen, Oxford.

Berg, M. van den, and J.-E. Sturm (1997), The empirical evidence of the location factors modelled by Krugman, SOM Research Report, no. 97C01, University of Groningen.

Bergeijk, P.A.G. van, and H. Oldersma (1990), Détente, market-oriented reform and German unification: potential consequences for the world trade system, *Kyklos*, 43, 599–609.

Bergstrand, J.H. (1985), The gravity equation in international trade: some microeconomic foundations and empirical evidence, *Review of Economics and Statistics*, 67, 474–481.

(1989), The generalized gravity equation, monopolistic competition, and factor-proportions theory in international trade, *Review of Economics and Statistics*, 71, 143–153.

(1990), The Heckscher–Ohlin–Samuelson model, the Linder hypothesis, and the determinants of bilateral intra-industry trade, *Economic Journal*, 100, 1216–1229.

Berry, B.J.L., E.C. Conkling, and D.M. Ray (1993), *The Global Economy; Resource Use, Location Choice, and International Trade*, Prentice Hall, London.

Bhagwati, J.N., A. Panagariya, and T.N. Srinivasan (1998), *Lectures on International Trade*, 2nd edn., MIT Press, Cambridge, Mass.

Black, D. and V. Henderson (1998), Urban Evolution in the USA, Working Paper, no. 98–21, Brown University.

(1999a), Spatial evolution of population and industry in the United States, *American Economic Review*, Papers and Proceedings, 89, 321–327.

(1999b), A theory of urban growth, *Journal of Political Economy*, 107, 252–284.

Blaug, M. (1984), *Economic Theory in Retrospect*, Cambridge University Press.

Bowen, H.P., A. Hollander, and J.-M. Viaene (1998), *Applied International Trade Analysis*, Macmillan, London.

Brainard, S.L. (1997), An empirical assessment of the proximity–concentration trade-off between multinational sales and trade, *American Economic Review*, 87, 520–544.

Brakman, S. and H. Garretsen (1993), The relevance of initial conditions for the German unification, *Kyklos*, 46, 163–181.

Brakman, S., H. Garretsen, R. Gigengack, C. van Marrewijk, and R. Wagenvoort (1996), Negative feedbacks in the economy and industrial location, *Journal of Regional Science*, 36, 631–652.

Brakman, S., H. Garretsen, and C. van Marrewijk (1998), De moderne lokatie-handelstheorie: ongelijkheid als evenwichtsuitkomst, *Economisch en Sociaal Tijdschrift*, 52, 479–509.

Brakman, S., H. Garretsen, C. van Marrewijk, and M. van den Berg (1999), The return of Zipf; towards a further understanding of the rank–size curve, *Journal of Regional Science*, 39, 183–215.

Brakman, S., H. Garretsen, C. van Marrewijk, and M. Schramm (2000), Empirical research in geographical economics, paper presented at the conference *The Monopolistic Competition Revolution after Twenty-Five Years*, University of Groningen, October 30–31.

Brakman, S., H. Garretsen, and M. Schramm (2000), The empirical relevance of the new economic geography: testing for a spatial wage structure in Germany, CESifo Working Paper, no. 395, Munich.

Brakman, S. and C. van Marrewijk (1995a), Transfers, returns to scale, tied aid and monopolistic competition, *Journal of Development Economics*, 47, 333–354.

(1995b), Megalopolis op Mezzogiorno: locatie en handel in de wereld economie (Megacity or Mezzogiorno: location and trade in the world economy), mimeo, University of Groningen and Erasmus University, Rotterdam.

(1996), Trade policy under imperfect competition: the economics of Russian Roulette, *De Economist*, 144, 223–258.

(1998), *The Economics of International Transfers*, Cambridge University Press.

Brezis, E.S., P.R. Krugman, and D. Tsiddon (1993), Leapfrogging in international competition: a theory of cycles in national technological leadership, *American Economic Review*, 83, 1211–1219.

Broecker, J. (1989), How to eliminate certain defects of the potential formula, *Environment and Planning A*, 21, 817–830.

Brülhart, M. (1998a), Economic geography, industry, location and trade: the evidence, *World Economy*, 21, 775–801.

(1998b), Trading places: industrial specialisation in the European Union, *Journal of Common Market Studies*, 36, 319–345.

Brülhart, M. and J. Torstensson (1996), Regional integration, scale economics and industry location in the European Union, CEPR Discussion Paper, no. 1435, London.

Brülhart, M. and F. Trionfetti (1999), Home-biased demand and international specialisation: a test of trade theories, mimeo., Centre for Economic Performance, London School of Economics.

Bura, S., F. Guérin-Pace, H. Mathian, D. Pumian, and L. Sanders (1996), Multiagent systems and the dynamics of a settlement system, *Geographical Analysis*, 28, 161–178.

Carroll, G. (1982), National city-size distributions: what do we know after 67 years of research?, *Progress in Human Geography*, 6, 1–43.

CBS (1995), *Stand van de Bevolking*, The Hague.

Cheshire, P. and C. Carbonaro (1995), Convergence-divergence in Regional Growth rates: an empty black box?, in H. Armstrong and R. Vickerman (eds.), *Convergence and Divergence among European Regions*, Pion, London, 89–111.

Christaller, W. (1933), *Central Places in Southern Germany*, trans. Fischer, Prentice Hall, London.

Clark, G.L. (1998), Stylized facts and close dialogue: methodology in economic geography, *Annals of the Association of American Geographers*, 88, 73–87.

Clark, G.L., M.P. Feldman, and M.S. Gertler, eds. (2000), *The Oxford Handbook of Economic Geography*, Oxford University Press.

Coe, D.T. and E. Helpman (1995), International R&D spillovers, *European Economic Review*, 39, 859–887.

Coe, D.T., E. Helpman, and A.W. Hoffmaister (1997), North–South R&D spillovers, *Economic Journal*, 107, 134–149.

Collins, S.M., ed. (1998), *Imports, Exports and the American Worker*, Brookings Institution Press, Washington, D.C.

Culem, C. and L. Lundberg (1986), The product pattern of intra-industry trade: stability among countries and over time, *Weltwirtschaftliches Archiv*, 122, 113–130.

David, P. (1985), Clio and the economics of QWERTY, *American Economic Review Proceedings*, 75, 332–337.

Davis, D.R. (1995), Intra-industry trade: a Heckscher–Ohlin–Ricardo approach, *Journal of International Economics*, 39, 201–226.

(1998), The home market, trade and industrial structure, *American Economic Review*, 88, 1264–1277.

Davis, D.R. and D.E. Weinstein (1996), Does economic geography matter for international specialization?, mimeo., Harvard University, Cambridge, Mass.

(1997), Increasing returns and international trade: an empirical confirmation, mimeo., Harvard University, Cambridge, Mass.

(1998a), Market access. Economic geography and comparative advantage: an empirical assessment, Discussion Paper, no. 1850, Harvard Institute of Economic Research.

(1998b), An account of global factor trade, NBER Working Paper, no. 6758, Cambridge, Mass.

(1999), Economic geography and regional production structure: an empirical investigation, *European Economic Review*, 43, 379–407.

Deardorff, A. (1998), Determinants of bilateral trade: does gravity work in a neo-classical world? in J. Frankel (ed.), *Regionalization of the World Economy*, University of Chicago Press and NBER, Chicago, 7–22.

Dewatripont, M., A. Sapir, and K. Sekkat, eds. (1999), *Trade and Jobs in Europe: Much Ado about Nothing?*, Oxford University Press.

Dicken, P. and P.E. Lloyd (1990), *Location in Space*, Harper & Row, New York.

Diewert, W.E. (1981), The economic theory of index numbers: a survey, in A. Deaton (ed.), *Essays in the Theory and Measurement of Consumer Behaviour*, Cambridge University Press.

Dixit, A. and V. Norman (1980), *Theory of International Trade*, Cambridge University Press.

Dixit, A. and J. Stiglitz (1977), Monopolistic competition and optimal product diversity, *American Economic Review*, 67, 297–308.

Dobkins, L.H. and Y.M. Ioannides (1999), Spatial interactions among US cities, Discussion Paper, no. 99–13, Tufts University.

(2000), Dynamic evolution of US city size distributions, in J.-M. Huriot and J.-F. Thisse (eds.), *The Economics of Cities: Theoretical Perspectives*, Cambridge University Press.

Dumais, G., G. Ellison, and E.L. Glaeser (1997), Geographic concentration as a dynamic process, NBER Working Paper, no. 6270, Cambridge, Mass.

Dunning, J.H. (1977), Trade, location of economic activity and MNE: a search for an eclectic approach, in B. Ohlin, P.O. Hesselborn, and P.M. Wijkman (eds.), *The International Allocation of Economic Activity*, Macmillan, London.

(1981a), *The Globalization of Business*, Routledge, London.

(1981b), *International Production and the Multinational Enterprise*, Allen & Unwin, London.

(1992), *Multinational Enterprises and the Global Economy*, Addison-Wesley, London.

Dutch Ministry of Economic Affairs (1998), Ontwikkeling vestigingspatronen Amerikaanse en Japanse Bedrýven in Europa, The Hague.

Eaton, C.B. and R.G. Lipsey (1982), An economic theory of central places, *Economic Journal*, 92, 56–72.

Eaton, J. and Z. Eckstein (1997), Cities and growth: theory and evidence from France and Japan, *Regional Science and Urban Economics*, 27, 443–474.

Eaton, J. and S. Kortum (1996), Trade in ideas: patenting and productivity in the OECD, *Journal of International Economics*, 40, 251–278.

Egger, P. (2000), A note on the proper econometric specification of the gravity equation, *Economics Letters*, 66, 25–31.

Ekholm, K. and R. Forslid (1997), Agglomeration in a core–periphery model with vertically- and horizontally integrated firms, CEPR Discussion Paper, no. 1607, London.

Ellison, G. and E.L. Glaeser (1997), Geographic concentration in US manufacturing industries: a dartboard approach, *Journal of Political Economy*, 105, 889–927.

(1999), The geographic concentration of industry: does natural advantage explain agglomeration?, *American Economic Review*, Papers and Proceedings, 89, 311–316.

Engel, C. and J. Rogers (1996), How wide is the border?, *American Economic Review*, 86, 1112–1125.

Englman, F.C. and U. Walz (1995), Industrial centers and regional growth in the presence of local inputs, *Journal of Regional Science*, 35, 3–27.

Ethier, W.J. (1982), National and international returns to scale in the modern theory of international trade, *American Economic Review*, 72, 389–405.

(1995), *Modern International Economics*, 3rd edn., W.W. Norton, New York.

Ethier, W.J. and H. Horn (1984), A new look at economic integration, in H. Kierzkowski (ed.), *Monopolistic Competition and International Trade*, Clarendon Press, Oxford, 207–229.

Florida, R. and M. Kenney (1994), The globalization of Japanese R&D: the economic geography of Japanese R&D investment in the United States, *Economic Geography*, 70, 344–369.

Forslid, R. and I. Wooton (1998), Economic geography and comparative advantage, paper presented at 1998 ERWIT workshop, CEPR, Rotterdam.

Fujita, M. (1989), *Urban Economic Theory: Land Use and City Size*, Cambridge University Press.

(1996), On the self-organisation and evolution of economic geography, *Japanese Economic Review*, 47, 34–61.

Fujita, M. and P.R. Krugman (1995), When is the economy monocentric? Von Thünen and Chamberlin unified, *Regional Science and Urban Economics*, 25, 505–528.

Fujita, M., P. Krugman, and T. Mori, (1999), On the Evolution of Hierarchial Urban Systems, *European Economic Review*, 43(2), 209–253.

Fujita, M., P.R. Krugman, and A.J. Venables (1999), *The Spatial Economy: Cities, Regions, and International Trade*, MIT Press, Cambridge, Mass.

Fujita, M. and T. Mori (1996), The role of ports in the making of major cities: self-agglomeration and the hub-effect, *Journal of Development Economics*, 49, 93–120.

Fujita, M., H. Ogawa, and J.-F. Thisse (1988), A spatial competition approach to central place theory: some basic principles, *Journal of Regional Science*, 28, 477–494.

Fujita, M. and J.-F. Thisse (1996), Economics of agglomeration, *Journal of the Japanese and International Economies*, 10, 339–378.

(2000), Economics of agglomeration, in J.-M. Huriot and J.-F. Thisse (eds.), *The Economics of Cities: Theoretical Perspectives*, Cambridge University Press (extended version of Fujita and Thisse, 1996).

Fukao, K. and R. Benabou (1993), History versus expectations: a comment, *Quarterly Journal of Economics*, 108, 535–542.

Gabaix, X. (1999a), Zipf's Law and the growth of cities, *American Economic Review*, Papers and Proceedings, 89, 129–132.

(1999b), Zipf's Law for cities: an explanation, *Quarterly Journal of Economics*, 114, 739–766.

Gallup, J.L., J.D. Sachs, and A.D. Mellinger (1998), Geography and economic development, paper presented at Annual Conference on Development, The World Bank, Washington.

Gao, T. (1999), Economic geography and the department of vertical multinational production, *Journal of International Economics*, 48, 301–320.

Gersbach, H. and A. Schmutzler (2000), Declining costs of communication and transportation: what are the effects on agglomeration?, *European Economic Review*, 44, 1745–1763.

Glaeser, E.L. (1998), Are cities dying?, *Journal of Economic Perspectives*, 12, 139–160.

(2000), The new economics of urban and regional growth, in G.L. Clark, M.P. Feldman, and M.S. Gertler (eds.), *The Oxford Handbook of Economic Geography*, Oxford University Press, 83–99.

Glaeser, E.L., H.D. Kallal, J. Scheinkman, and A. Schleifer (1992), Growth in cities, *Journal of Political Economy*, 100, 1126–1152.

Gourevitch, P., R. Bohn, and D. McKendrick (2000), Globalization of production: Insights from the hard disk drive industry, *World Development*, 28, 301–317.

Grossman, G.M. and E. Helpman (1991), *Innovation and Growth in the Global Economy*, MIT Press, Cambridge, Mass.

Grossman, G.M. and K. Rogoff, eds. (1995), *Handbook of International Economics*, vol. III, North-Holland, Amsterdam.

Haag, G. and H. Max (1995), Rank–size distribution of settlement systems, *Papers in Regional Science*, 74, 243–258.

Haaland, J.I., H.J. Kind, K.H. Midelfart-Knarvik, and J. Torstensson (1999), What determines the economic geography of Europe?, CEPR Discussion Paper, no. 2072, London.

Hall, R. E. (1988), The relation between price and marginal cost in US industry, *Journal of Political Economy*, 96, 921–947

Hallet, M. (2000), Regional specialisation and concentration in the EU, *Economic Papers,* 141, European Commission, Brussels.

Hanson, G.H. (1996), Economic integration, intraindustry trade, and frontier regions, *European Economic Review*, 40, 941–949.

   (1997), Increasing returns, trade and the regional structure of wages, *Economic Journal*, 107, 113–133.

   (1998), Market potential, increasing returns, and geographic concentration, NBER Working Paper, no. 6429, Cambridge, Mass.

   (1999), Market potential, increasing returns, and geographic concentration, University of Michigan (revised version of Hanson, 1998).

   (2000), Scale economies and the geographic concentration of industry, NBER Working Paper, no. 8013, Cambridge, Mass.

Harrigan, J. (1994), Scale economies and the volume of trade, *Review of Economics and Statistics*, 76, 321–328.

   (1995), Factor endowments and the international location of production, *Journal of International Economics*, 39, 123–141.

Harris, C. (1954), The market as a factor in the localization of industry in the United States, *Annals of the Association of American Geographers*, 64, 315–348.

Harris, T.F. and Y.M. Ioannides (2000), History versus expectations: an empirical investigation, Discussion Paper, no. 200014, Department of Economics, Tufts University.

Head, K., J. Ries, and D. Swenson (1995), Agglomeration benefits and location choice: evidence from Japanese manufacturing investments in the United States, *Journal of International Economics*, 38, 223–247.

Heijdra, B. (1997), Toch een revolutie?, *Tijdschrift voor Politieke Economie*, 20, 7–33.

Helpman, E. (1984a), A simple theory of international trade with multinational corporations, *Journal of Political Economy*, 92, 451–471.

   (1984b), Increasing returns, imperfect markets and trade theory, in R.W. Jones and P.B. Kenen (eds.), *Handbook of International Economics*, vol. I, North-Holland, Amsterdam.

   (1987), Imperfect competition and international trade: evidence from 14 industrial countries, *Journal of the Japanese and International Economies,* 1, 62–81.

   (1998), The size of regions, in D. Pines, E. Sadka, and I. Zilcha (eds.), *Topics in Public Economics*, Cambridge University Press.

Helpman, E. and P. Krugman (1985), *Market Structure and Foreign Trade*, MIT Press, Cambridge, Mass.

Henderson, V.J. (1974), The sizes and types of cities, *American Economic Review*, 64, 640–656.

   (1977), *Economic Theory and the Cities*, Academic Press, New York.

   (1988), *Urban Development: Theory, Fact and Illusion*, Oxford University Press.

   (1998), Comment on J.L. Gallup, J.D. Sachs, and A.D. Mellinger, geography and economic Development, Annual bank Conference on Development, World Bank, Washington.

(2000), The monopolistic competition model in urban economic geography, paper presented at the seminar *The Monopolistic Competition Revolution after Twenty-Five Years*, University of Groningen, October 30–31.

Henderson, V.J., A. Kuncoro, and M. Turner (1995), Industrial development in cities, *Journal of Political Economy*, 103, 1067–1085.

Henderson, V.J. and A. Mitra (1996), The new urban landscape: developers and edge cities, *Regional Science and Urban Economics*, 26, 613–643.

Henderson, V.J., Z. Shalizi, and A.J. Venables (2000), Geography and development, mimeo., London School of Economics.

Herfindahl, O.C. (1950), Concentration in the steel industry, Ph.D. dissertation, Columbia University.

Hirschman, A. (1958), *Strategy of Economic Development*, Yale University Press, New Haven.

Holmes, T.J. (1999), Scale of local production and city size, *American Economic Review*, Papers and Proceedings, 89, 317–320.

Horstman, I.J. and J.R. Markusen (1986), Up the average cost curve: inefficient entry and the new protectionism, *Journal of International Economics*, 20, 225–248.

Houtum, H. van (1998), The development of cross-border economic relations, Ph.D. thesis, Tilburg University.

Hummels, D. (1999a), Towards a geography of trade costs, mimeo, University of Chicago.

(1999b), Have international transportation costs declined?, mimeo., University of Chicago.

Huriot, J.-M. and J.-F. Thisse, eds. (2000), *Economics of Cities: Theoretical Perspectives*, Cambridge University Press.

IMF (1997), *World Economic Outlook*, Washington, D.C.

Ioannides, Y. and H.G. Overman (2000), Zipf's Law for cities: an empirical investigation, mimeo., Tufts University.

Isard, W. (1956), *Location and Space Economy*, MIT Press, Cambridge, Mass.

(1960), *Methods of Regional Analysis*, MIT Press, Cambridge, Mass.

Jacobs, J. (1969), *The Economy of Cities*, Vintage Books, New York.

Jones, B.J. and B.D. Lewis (1990), The four properties of rank–size hierarchical distributions, their characteristics and interrelationships, *Papers of the Regional Science Association*, 68, 83–95.

Jones, C.I. (1998), *Introduction to Economic Growth*, W.W. Norton, New York.

Kenen, P.B. (1965), Nature, capital, and trade, *Journal of Political Economy*, 73, 437–460.

Kim, S. (1995), Expansion of markets and the geographic distribution of economic activities: the trends in US regional manufacturing structure, 1860–1987, *Quarterly Journal of Economics*, 110, 881–908.

Knaap, T. (2000), Vertical integration in input-output models, mimeo, University of Groningen.

Kooij, P. (1988), Peripheral cities and their regions in the Dutch urban system until 1900, *Journal of Economic History*, 48, 357–371.

Kreps, D.M. (1990), *Game Theory and Economic Modelling*, Oxford University Press.

Krugman, P.R. (1979), Increasing returns, monopolistic competition, and international trade, *Journal of International Economics*, 9, 469–479.

(1980), Scale economies, product differentiation, and the pattern of trade, *American Economic Review*, 70, 950–959.

(1991a), Increasing returns and economic geography, *Journal of Political Economy*, 99, 483–499.

(1991b), *Geography and Trade*, MIT Press, Cambridge, Mass.

(1991c), History versus expectations, *Quarterly Journal of Economics*, 106, 651–667.

(1993a), First nature, second nature and metropolitan location, *Journal of Regional Science*, 33, 129–144.

(1993b), On the number and location of cities, *European Economic Review*, 37, 293–298.

(1993c), Toward a counter-counterrevolution in development theory, *Proceedings of the World Bank Annual Conference on Development Economics 1992*, 15–38.

(1993d), On the relationship between trade theory and location theory, *Review of International Economics*, 1, 102–122.

(1993e), Lessons from Massachussetts for EMU, in F. Torres and F. Giavazzi (eds.), *Adjustment and Growth in the European Monetary Union*, Cambridge University Press, 241–269.

(1995a), *Development, Geography and Economic Theory*, MIT Press, Cambridge, Mass.

(1995b), Increasing returns, imperfect competition, and the positive theory of international trade, in G.M. Grossman and K. Rogoff (eds.), *Handbook of International Economics*, vol. III, North-Holland, Amsterdam, 1243–1277.

(1995c), Growing world trade: causes and consequences, *Brookings Papers on Economic Activity*, 1, 327–362.

(1996a), *The Self-Organizing Economy*, Blackwell, Oxford.

(1996b), Confronting the mystery of urban hierarchy, *Journal of the Japanese and International Economies*, 10, 399–418.

(1998), Space: the final frontier, *Journal of Economic Perspectives*, 12, 161–174.

(1999), Was it all in Ohlin?, mimeo., MIT, Cambridge, Mass. (http://web.mit.edu/krugman/www.ohlin.html).

Krugman, P.R. and M. Obstfeld (1994), *International Economics: Theory and Policy*, 3rd edn., HarperCollins, Reading, Mass.

Krugman, P.R. and R. Livas Elizondo (1996), Trade policy and third world metropolis, *Journal of Development Economics*, 49, 137–150.

Krugman, P.R. and A.J. Venables (1990), Integration and the competitiveness of peripheral industry, in C. Bliss and J. Braga de Macedo (eds.), *Unity with Diversity in the European Economy*, Cambridge University Press, 56–75.

(1995), Globalization and the inequality of nations, *Quarterly Journal of Economics*, 110, 857–880.

Kuiper, F.J., J. H. Kuiper, and J.H.P. Paelinck (1993), Tinbergen–Bos metricised systems: some further results, *Urban Studies*, 30, 1745–1761.

Kuiper, J.H., J.H.P. Paelinck, and K.E. Rosing (1990), Transport flows in Tinbergen–Bos systems, in K. Peschel (ed.), *Infra-structure and the Space Economy*, Springer Verlag, Heidelberg.

Landes, D. (1998), *The Wealth and Poverty of Nations*, Abacus, London.

Launhardt, W. (1885), *Mathematische Begründung der Volkswirtschaftslehre*, Teubner, Leipzig.

Lawrence, R.Z. and M.J. Slaughter (1993), International trade and american wages in the 1980s: giant sucking sound or small hiccup?, *Brookings Paper on Economic Activity 2: Microeconomics*, 161–226.

Leamer, E. and J. Levinsohn (1995), International trade theory: the evidence, in G.M. Grossman and K. Rogoff (eds.), *Handbook of International Economics*, vol. III, North-Holland, Amsterdam, 269–287.

Limao, N. and A.J. Venables (2000), Infrastructure, geographical disadvantage and transport costs, mimeo., World Bank, Washington.

Linneman, H. (1966), *An Econometric Study of International Trade Flows*, North-Holland, Amsterdam.

Lösch, A. (1940), *The Economics of Location* (trans. Fischer), Yale University Press, New Haven.

Lucas, R.E. (1988), On the mechanisms of economic development, *Journal of Monetary Economics*, 22, 3–42.

Ludema, R. and I. Wooton (1998), Economic geography and the fiscal effects of regional integration, CEPR Discussion Paper, no. 1822, London.

Maddison, A. (1992), *Dynamic Forces in Capitalist Development*, Oxford University Press.
  (1995), *Monitoring the World Economy: 1820–1992*, OECD, Paris.
Markusen J.R. (1995), The boundaries of multinational enterprise and the theory of international trade, *Journal of Economic Perspectives*, 9, 183–203.
Markusen J.R. and K.E. Markus (1999), Multinational firms: reconciling theory and evidence, NBER Working Paper, no. 7163, Cambridge, Mass.
Markusen J.R. and A.J. Venables (1998), Multinational firms and the new trade theory, *Journal of International Economics*, 46, 183–203.
Marrewijk, C. van (1999), Capital accumulation, learning and endogenous growth, *Oxford Economic Papers*, 51, 453–475.
  (2000), Factor abundance and geographical economics, mimeo., Erasmus University, Rotterdam.
Marrewijk, C. van, J. Stibora, and J.-M. Viaene (1994), Capital goods and Baumol's Law, Tinbergen Institute, Discussion Paper, no. TI 94–42.
Marrewijk, C. van, and J. Verbeek (1993), Sector-specific capital, "bang-bang" investment and the Filippov solution, *Journal of Economics*, 57, 131–146.
Marshall, A. (1920), *Principles of Economics*, 8th edn., Macmillan, London.
Marsili, M. and Y.-C. Zhang (1998), Interacting individuals leading to Zipf's Law, *Physical Review Letters*, 80, 2741–2744.
Martin, P. and G.I.P. Ottaviano (1999), Growing locations in a model of endogenous growth, *European Economic Review*, 43, 281–302.
Martin, R. (1999), The new "geographical turn" in economics: some critical reflections, *Cambridge Journal of Economics*, 23, 65–91.
  (2001), EMU versus the regions? Regional convergence and divergence in Euroland, *Journal of Economic Geography*, 1, 51–81.
Martin, R. and P. Sunley (1996), Paul Krugman's geographical economics and its implications for regional development theory: a critical assessment, *Economic Geography*, 72, 259–292.
Martin, S. (1994), *Industrial Economics: Economic Analysis and Public Policy*, Macmillan, New York.
McCallum, J. (1995), National borders matter: Canada–US regional trade patterns, *American Economic Review*, 85, 615–623.
Mellinger, A.D., J.D. Sachs, and J.L. Gallup (2000), Climate, coastal proximity and development, in G.L. Clark, M.P. Feldman, and M.S. Gertler (eds.), *The Oxford Handbook of Economic Geography*, Oxford University Press, Oxford 169–195.
Midelfart-Knarvik, K.H., H.G. Overman, S.J. Redding, and A.J. Venables (2000), The location of European industry, *Economic Papers*, Oxford, 142, European Commission, Brussels.
Mills, E.S. (1967), An aggregate model of resource allocation in a metropolitan area, *American Economic Review*, 57, 197–210.
Mills, E.S., ed., (1986), *Handbook of Regional and Urban Economics,* vol. II: *Urban Economics*, North-Holland, Amsterdam.
Molle, W. (1996), The regional economic structure of the EU: and analysis of long-term developments, in K. Peschel (ed.), *Regional Growth and Regional Policy within the Framework of European Integration*, Physica Verlag, Heidelberg, 66–86.
Müller, G. (1999), A smaller productivity gap between German regions when different producer prices are taken into account, IWH Diskussionspapier, 89, Institut für Wirtschaftsforschung (IFW), Halle, Germany.
Mulligan, G.F. (1984), Agglomeration and central place theory: a review of the literature, *International Regional Science Review*, 9, 1–42.
Murphy, K.M., A. Shleifer, and R.W. Vishny (1989), Industrialization and the big push, *Journal of Political Economy*, 97, 1003–1026.

Myrdal, G. (1957), *Economic Theory and Underdeveloped Regions*, Duckworth, London, 66–86.

Neary, J.P. (2001), Of hypes and hyperbolas: introducing the new economic geography, *Journal of Economic Literature,* forthcoming.

Neven, D. and C. Gouyette (1995), Regional convergence in the European Community, *Journal of Common Market Studies*, 33, 47–65.

Nijkamp, P. (2000), Review of Fujita, Kragman, and Venables, *Economic Journal* (forthcoming).

Nijkamp, P., ed. (1986), *Handbook of Regional and Urban Economics*, vol. I: *Regional Economics*, North-Holland, Amsterdam.

Obstfeld, M. and K. Rogoff (1996), *Foundations of International Macroeconomics*, MIT Press, Cambridge, Mass.

OECD (1997), *Employment Outlook*, Paris.

Ohlin, B. (1933), *Interregional and International Trade*, Harvard University Press, Cambridge, Mass.

O'Rourke, K.H. and J.G. Williamson (1999), *Globalisation and History: The Evolution of the 19th Century Atlantic Economy*, MIT Press, Cambridge, Mass.

Ottaviano, G.I.P. (1999), Integration, geography and the burden of history, *Regional Science and Urban Economics*, 29, 245–256.

Ottaviano, G.I.P. and D. Puga (1997), Agglomeration in the global economy: a survey of the "new economic geography", CEPR Discussion Paper, no. 356, London.

Parr, J.B. (1985), A note on the size distribution of cities over time, *Journal of Urban Economics*, 18, 199–212.

Peck, J. (2000), Doing regulation, in G.L. Clark, M.P. Feldman, and M.S. Gertler (eds.), *The Oxford Handbook of Economic Geography*, Oxford University Press, 61–83.

Peeters, J. (2001), Globalisation, location and labour markets, Ph.D. thesis, University of Nijmegen.

Peeters, J. and H. Garretsen (2000), Globalisation, wages and unemployment: an economic geography perspective, CESifo Working Paper, no. 256, Munich.

Peeters, J. and A. de Vaal (2000), Explaining the wage gap: Heckscher–Ohlin, economic geography and services availability, SOM Research Report, no. 00021, Groningen.

Perroux, F. (1995), Note sur la notion de pole de croissance, *Economique Appliquée*, 1–2, 307–322.

Pollins, B.M. (1989), Conflict, cooperation, and commerce: the effects of international political interactions on bilateral trade flows, *American Journal of Political Science*, 33, 737–761.

Porter, M.E. (1985), *Competitive Advantage: Creating and Sustaining Superior Performance*, Free Press, New York.

(1990), *The Competitive Advantage of Nations*, Free Press, New York.

Pöyhönen, P. (1963). A tentative model for the volume of trade between countries, *Weltwirtschaftliches Archiv*, 90, 93–100.

Pred, A. (1966), *The Spatial Dynamics of US Urban-Industrial Growth*, MIT Press, Cambridge, Mass.

Puga, D. (1998), Urbanization patterns: European versus less developed countries, *Journal of Regional Science*, 38, 231–252.

Puga, D. and A.J. Venables (1996), The spread of industry: spatial agglomeration in economic development, CEPR Discussion Paper, no. 279, London.

(1998), Agglomeration and economic development: import substitution vs. trade liberalization, paper presented at 1998 ERWIT workshop, CEPR, Rotterdam.

Quigley, J.M. (1998), Urban diversity and economic growth, *Journal of Economic Perspectives*, 12, 127–138.

Quinzii, M. and J.-F. Thisse (1990), On the optimality of central places, *Econometrica*, 58, 1101–1119.

Radelet, S, and J. Sachs (1998), Shipping costs, manufactured exports, and economic growth, mimeo., Harvard University.

Read, C.B. (1988), Zipf's Law, in S. Kotz, N.L. Johnson, and C.B. Read (eds.), *Encyclopedia of Statistical Sciences*, Wiley, New York.

Redding, S. and A.J. Venables (2000), Economic geography and international inequality, CEPR Discussion Paper, no. 2568, London.

Ricci, L.A. (1996), Exchange rate regimes and location, mimeo., University of Konstanz.

(1997), A Ricardian model of new trade and location theory, *Journal of Economic Integration*, 12, 47–61.

(1999), Economic geography and comparative advantage: agglomeration versus specialization, *European Economic Review*, 43, 357–377.

Rivera-Batiz, L. and P. Romer (1991), Economic integration and endogenous growth, *Quarterly Journal of Economics*, 106, 531–555.

Roehner, B.M. (1995), Evolution of urban systems in the Pareto plane, *Journal of Regional Science*, 35, 277–300.

Romer, D. (1996), *Advanced Macroeconomics*, McGraw-Hill, New York.

Romer, P.M. (1986), Increasing returns and long-run growth, *Journal of Political Economy*, 94, 1002–1037.

(1990), Endogenous technological change, *Journal of Political Economy*, 98, part 2, S71-S101.

(1993), Idea gaps and object gaps in economic development, *Journal of Monetary Economics*, 32, 543–573.

(1994), New goods, old theory and the welfare costs of trade restrictions, *Journal of Development Economics*, 43, 5–38.

Rosen, K.T. and M. Resnick (1980), The size distribution of cities: an examination of the Pareto law and privacy, *Journal of Urban Economics*, 8, 165–186.

Rosenstein-Rodan, P. (1943), Problems of industrialization in eastern and south-eastern Europe, *Economic Journal*, 53, 202–211.

Rothfels, J. and A. Wölfl (1998), Determinanten der Produktivitätslücke in Ostdeutschland: Ergebnisse einer Tagung am IWH, *Wirtschaft im Wandel*, 1, Institut für Wirtschaftsforschung Halle, (IFW), Halle, Germany, 3–11.

Rumley, D. and J.V. Minghi (1991), *The Geography of Border Landscapes*, Routledge, London.

Samuelson, P.A. (1952), The transfer problem and transport costs: the terms of trade when impediments are absent, *Economic Journal*, 62, 278–304.

Schelling, T.C. (1978), *Micromotives and Macrobehavior*, W.W. Norton, New York.

Scitovsky, T. (1954), Two concepts of external economies, *Journal of Political Economy*, 62, 143–151.

Scott, A.J. (2000), Economic geography: the great half-century, in G.L. Clark, M.P. Feldman, and M.S. Gertler (eds.), *The Oxford Handbook of Economic Geography*, Oxford University Press, 18–49.

Seers, D. (1960), A model of comparative rates of growth of the world economy, *Economic Journal*, 72, 45–64.

Shatz, H.J. and A.J. Venables (2000), The geography of international investment, in G.L. Clark, M. Feldman, and M.S. Gertler (eds.), *The Oxford Handbook of Economic Geography*, Oxford University Press, 125–146.

Shone, R. (1997), *Economic Dynamics*, Cambridge University Press.

Simon, H. (1955), On a class of skew distribution functions, *Biometrika*, 42, 425–440.

Sinn, H.-W. (2000), Germany's economic unification: an assessment after ten years, CESifo Working Paper, no. 247, Munich.

Smith, A. (1776), *An Inquiry into the Nature and Causes of the Wealth of Nations*, Liberty Classics edition, Liberty Press, Indianapolis (1981).

Solow, R.M. (1994), Perspectives on growth theory, *Journal of Economic Perspectives*, 8, 45–54.

Stalker, P. (2000), *World Without Frontiers: The Impact of Globalisation on International Migration*, ILO, Geneva.

Spence, A.M. (1976), Product selection, fixed costs and monopolistic competition, *Review of Economic Studies*, 43, 217–235.

Stelder, D. (1998), Central places in the real world: some 2D geographic experiments for Europe with a Krugman agglomeration model, paper presented at the 45th RSAI North American Meetings, Santa Fe, November 10–15.

(2000), Geographical grids in new economic geography models, paper presented at the International Conference on the Occasion of the 150th Anniversary of Johann Heinrich von Thünen's Death, Rostock, September 21–24.

Stewart, J.Q. (1947), Suggested principles of "social physics," *Science*, 106, 179–180.

(1948), Demographic gravitation: evidence and applications, *Sociometry*, 11, 31–58.

Storper, M. (1997), *The Regional World: Territorial Development in a Global Economy*, Guilford Press, New York.

Suh, Seoung H. (1991), The optimal size distribution of cities, *Journal of Urban Economics*, 30, 182–191.

Tabuchi, T. (1998), Urban agglomeration and dispersion: a synthesis of Alonso and Krugman, *Regional Science and Urban Economics*, 44, 333–351.

Thirlwall, T. (1991), *Growth and Development, with Special Reference to Developing Countries*, Macmillan, London.

Thomas, A., Increasing returns, congestion costs and the geographic concentration of firms, mimeo., International Monetary Fund, Washington.

Thünen, J.H. von (1826), *Der Isolierte Staat in Beziehung auf Landwirtschaft und Nationalökonomie*, Perthes, Hamburg.

Tinbergen, J. (1962), *Shaping the World Economy*, The Twentieth Century Fund, New York.

Tirole, J. (1988), *The Theory of Industrial Organization*, MIT Press, Cambridge, Mass.

Trefler, D. and S. Chun Zhu (2000), Beyond the algebra of explanation: HOV for the technology age, *American Economic Review*, 90, 145–149.

UNCTAD (1999), *World Investment Report 1999*, United Nations, New York.

Vaal, A. de, and M. van den Berg (1999), Producer services, economic geography and services tradability, *Journal of Regional Science*, 39, 539–572.

Venables, A.J. (1985), Trade and trade policy with imperfect competition: the case of identical products and free entry, *Journal of International Economics*, 19, 1–20.

(1996), Equilibrium locations of vertically linked industries, *International Economic Review*, 37, 341–359.

(1998), Localization of industry and trade performance, *Oxford Review of Economic Policy*, 12, 52–60.

(1999), Fragmentation and multinational production, *European Economic Review*, 43, 935–945.

Vries, Jan de (1981), Patterns of urbanisation in pre-industrial Europe, 1500–1800, in H. Schmal (ed.), *Patterns of European Urbanisation since 1500*, Croom Helm, London, 79–109.

(1984), *European Urbanisation, 1500–1800*, Methuen, London.

Weber, J.W. (1909), *Ueber den Standort der Industrien*, J.C.B. Mohr, Tübingen.

Weibull, J.W. (1995), *Evolutionary Game Theory*, MIT Press, Cambridge, Mass.

White, Robert W. (1978), The simulation of central place dynamics: two-sector systems and the rank–size distributions, *Geographical Analysis*, 10, 201–208.

Wong, K.Y. (1986), Are international trade and factor mobility substitutes?, *Journal of International Economics*, 20, 25–44.

Wood, A. (1994), *North–South Trade, Employment and Inequality: Changing Fortunes in a Skill-Driven World*, Clarendon Press, Oxford.

(1995), How trade hurt unskilled workers, *Journal of Economic Perspectives*, 9, 57–80.

(1998), Globalisation and the rise in labour market inequalities, *Economic Journal*, 108, 1463–1482.

World Bank (2000), *World Development Report 1999*, Washington.

Young, A. (1991), Learning by doing and the dynamic effects of international trade, *Quarterly Journal of Economics*, 106, 369–405.

Zipf, George K. (1949), *Human Behavior and the Principle of Least Effort*, Addison-Wesley, New York.

Index